THAT BEAST WAS NOT ME

ONE FORENSIC PSYCHOLOGIST

FIVE DECADES OF CONVERSATIONS WITH KILLERS

THAT BEAST WAS NOT ME

ONE FORENSIC PSYCHOLOGIST
FIVE DECADES OF CONVERSATIONS WITH KILLERS

JEFFREY L. SMALLDON

Black Lyon Publishing, LLC

Black Lyon True Crime

Praise for *That Beast Was Not Me*

"I was struck by Smalldon's disarming candor; it's one of the qualities that makes it possible for him to switch back and forth between two very different perspectives: that of an inquisitive but inexperienced undergraduate student, hungry for avenues of direct access to the minds of Manson and his disciples; and that of a board-certified forensic psychologist… Smalldon has produced a sprawling, page-turner of a book that's at once entertaining, instructive, and utterly unique … Take it from someone who knows: Smalldon's a mindhunter—and a crack shot at that."

—**John Douglas**, author (with Mark Olshaker) of *Mindhunter, The Anatomy of Motive, Journey into Darkness, The Killer Across the Table, The Cases that Haunt Us,* and *Obsession*

"In telling the story of the true crime obsessions that propelled him to a career as a leading forensic psychologist, Jeffrey Smalldon has produced an absolute page-turner of a book … gripping, propulsively readable. More than any other book I can think of, it succeeds in bringing near-mythical beings like Manson, Bundy, and Gacy to vivid, chilling life—while conveying the dark charisma that continues to make them objects of extreme fascination."

—**Harold Schechter,** author of *Murderabilia: A History of Crime in 100 Objects; Maniac: The Bath School Disaster and the Birth of the Modern Mass Killer;* and *Depraved: The Shocking True Story of America's First Serial Killer*

"I'll put it bluntly: I spent three years of my life researching and writing a biography of Charles Manson that was both critically acclaimed and a *New York Times* bestseller. After reading Smalldon's book, I have to grudgingly acknowledge that there was a lot I missed. Damn it! Anyway, to sum up: all true crime books promise great things. *That Beast Was Not Me* is the rare example of one delivering exactly that."

—**Jeff Guinn,** author of *Manson: The Life and Times of Charles Manson; Waco: David Koresh, the Branch Davidians, and a Legacy of Rage; Go Down Together: The True, Untold Story of Bonnie and Clyde;* and *The Road to Jonestown: Jim Jones and Peoples Temple*

More Praise for *That Beast Was Not Me*

"... a treasure trove of insights and observations culled from fifty years of personal and professional interest in the ultimate outsiders in American culture: mass and serial killers. Writing as both an aficionado and a forensic psychologist, he (Smalldon) has produced a book that has genuinely new and fascinating things to say about familiar subjects ... essential reading for any fan of true crime."

—**David Schmid**, author of
Natural Born Celebrities:
Serial Killers in American Culture

"Jeff Smalldon is one of the brightest and most interesting people I've ever talked to. After all, how many people can say they've been the consulting psychologist on close to three hundred death penalty cases ... and spent close to 20 hours sparring with Gacy in a death row visiting room? Smalldon is a damn fine writer, and he has an incredible collection of vivid, highly personal stories to tell. In my opinion, *That Beast Was Not Me* stands among the finest, most interesting books in this genre."

—**Donald Ray Pollock,** author of
Knockemstiff;
The Devil All the Time;
and *The Heavenly Table*

"Jeffrey Smalldon follows his curiosity, even when it takes him close to the world's most dangerous—or delusional—people ... Reading this account is like being backstage for the killers' performances; you learn a lot more about them than other correspondents might notice."

—**Dr. Kathryn Ramsland,** author of
The Serial Killer's Apprentice;
Confession of a Serial Killer: The Untold
Story of Dennis Rader, the BTK Killer;
The Forensic Psychology of Criminal Minds; and
Inside the Minds of Serial Killers: Why They Kill

More Praise for *That Beast Was Not Me*

"In this remarkable memoir, forensic psychologist Jeffrey Smalldon turns a clinician's eye onto his five decades of correspondence and conversations with some of history's most notorious killers. Along the way, he meditates on his interactions with these killers and explores the circuitous path that took him, the inquisitive son of an FBI agent, from his job as a hospital administrator to a career analyzing the minds and motivations of hundreds of convicted killers. Fans of true crime will love *That Beast Was Not Me*."

—**Andrew Welsh-Huggins**, author of
No Winners Here Tonight, the definitive
history of the death penalty in Ohio

"Most people would probably decline the offer to converse with a serial killer—but Jeffrey Smalldon has spent the last 50 years seeking out opportunities to do just that. Those of us who understand that delving into the minds of these very dark individuals is a worthy undertaking can be thankful that Smalldon has put his experiences to print. *That Beast Was Not Me* is one of those excellent works that comes along only so often."

—**Kevin M. Sullivan**, author of
The Bundy Murders: A Comprehensive History
and five other books about the Bundy case;
and *Through An Unlocked Door: In Walks Murder*

"What a book! From page one *That Beast Was Not Me* grabbed me by my lapels and refused to let go. Jeffrey Smalldon is an undeniable expert on murders and murderers, but to my pleasant surprise, he's also a first rate storyteller. Come for the fascinating insights into killers and cases you *thought* you knew (Manson, Gacy, Bundy), but stay for the stories you haven't heard—and will never forget."

—**Joe Oestreich**, author of
Hitless Wonder;
Lines of Scrimmage;
and *Partisans: Essays*

More Praise for *That Beast Was Not Me*

"*That Beast Was Not Me* is unique among true crime-related memoirs. Jeffrey Smalldon writes with unusual candor and plenty of hard-earned wisdom about the decades he spent sparring with Charles Manson, Squeaky Fromme, Ted Bundy, John Wayne Gacy, and others of their ilk. If you like true crime, I recommend that you buy a ticket and take the ride on this dark magic bus of a book."

—**Peter Vronsky**, author of
Serial Killers; Female Serial Killers;
America's Serial Killers; and *Sons of Cain*

"*That Beast Was Not Me* is a riveting memoir. The book's most compelling action plays out in the psychological space between the notorious killers Smalldon writes about and the people who comprise the killers' audience. In that space we witness how, over the long haul, Smalldon's intense and troubling encounters with evil irrevocably change him and shape his vocation. With humor, literary flair, and deep psychological insight, Smalldon tells a fascinating tale about the worst people on the planet—and about ourselves."

—**Dr. Dan P. McAdams,** the Henry Wade Rogers Professor
of Psychology and Human Development at Northwestern
University, and the author of *Power, Intimacy, and the Life
Story; Stories We Live By; The Art and Science of
Personality Development;* and *The Redemptive Self*

"Jeffrey Smalldon spent 50 years staring into the abyss and returning with incredible revelations about the minds and motivations of serial killers, mass murderers, and all sorts of other evil men who move and live among us. *That Beast Was Not Me* might make it difficult for you to sleep at night because of its troubling insights, and because you'll be eager to find out what's coming on the next page. Only a skilled psychologist could coax the worst killers to talk so candidly, and then compose such an intriguing memoir about his experiences."

—**Pete Earley,** *New York Times* bestselling author of
The Hot House: Life Inside Leavenworth;
Prophet of Death; and *The Serial Killer Whisperer*

Table of Contents

Photo Gallery

Dedication

For Betsy, of course

Foreword

"That beast was not me."
—Charles Manson in a letter to the author

I'm a native of Scotland. In 1975, I was a Fulbright scholar at Purdue University, working toward my master's degree in English. That fall, Jeff Smalldon, who would become my closest American friend, arrived there and began working toward the same degree. Within a month, Jeff had established a reputation in the English Department as highly intelligent, precocious, genial, and curious about seemingly everything.

He was a captivating storyteller—and he certainly had stories to tell. The Tate-LaBianca murders had occurred just six years prior, and Manson Family member Squeaky Fromme's attempt to assassinate President Gerald Ford occurred just as our fall semester was getting underway.

Jeff and I were close friends during the period when he was exchanging letters with Manson himself, as well as other members of the Manson Family, so I was privy to the details of that saga as it played out in real time. Usually over beers—and always with his trademark enthusiasm—Jeff regaled me with some of the most fascinating stories I'd ever heard.

I have lots of vivid memories of my time in the States—but none more vivid than my friendship with Jeff. In the decades since our years together at Purdue, he's lived a remarkable life. His experiences mark him as something of an outsider himself, like many of the people he's tried so assiduously to understand.

When I learned that he was writing a book about his five decades of encounters with Manson and hundreds of other killers, my first thought was that such a project was long overdue.

As I read *That Beast Was Not Me*, I kept thinking back to the mesmeric lyrics of "Us and Them," the longest song on Pink Floyd's iconic 1973 recording, *The Dark Side of the Moon*. The lyrics tap into wells of myth and identity: "Black and blue/ And who knows which is which/And who is who."

To many members of the song's first audience, the era's zeitgeist had never been so succinctly captured.

"Us and Them" spoke to a catastrophic moral relativism, one in which identities could become perilously unmoored amidst unstable seas. Pink Floyd's lead singer, Roger Waters, once explained, "The song is about all of us in the world, really. It's about how we're divided from one another by the arbitrary boundaries that we create for ourselves. But in the end, we're all the same."

In *That Beast Was Not Me*, Dr. Smalldon provides an extraordinary mélange of memories and observations, detailing how that relativistic ethic came to be subverted in the minds and actions of those infamous few who murdered—sometimes again and again—yet could still assert, in all seriousness, or so it seemed, "I'm just like everybody else."

Indeed, in a letter written to Smalldon, one of the damned, John Wayne Gacy, wrote chillingly, "You're gonna find out I'm a normal person, just like you."

All throughout this important book, Smalldon's disarming candor and open engagement with the problem of discerning the sometimes hard-to-pin-down boundaries separating good and evil, normal and twisted, and innocent and demonic might cause some readers to experience moments of fearful concern.

By Smalldon's own reckoning, he is nothing if not actively involved in all aspects of this troubling, sometimes disorienting investigation. At one point in his narrative, he confides, 'Vaguely, I was aware of being manipulated. Even so, I was young, naive, pleased to have secured Manson's attention, and vulnerable to the appeal of the kinds of messages he was sending. They brought to mind certain of the more appealing planks of the basic hippie platform.'

He continues, "I'd reached out to [Manson] because I wanted to get a sense of what he was like. And because I wanted to figure out if there was a part of him that I might be able to relate to, despite media depictions of him as the embodiment of pure evil."

With such proximities at its center, *That Beast Was Not Me* benefits richly from its involved narrator. Manson's emphatic repudiation of his popular image as a monster—his words provide the book's title—sets the stage for Smalldon's sprawling investigations into some of the darkest corners of murderous minds.

John Gacy's eerie and provocative promise—"You're gonna find out I'm a normal person, just like you"—serves as one of the book's epigraphs and would seem to suggest a point of view very much in keeping with Hannah Arendt's well-known commentary on the banality of evil. In the end, however, Smalldon's book is an exploration of the inhumanity of evil—and of its perpetrators' haughty, stubborn resistance to other people's efforts to define them and explain their reasons for doing what they do.

—Dr. Michael K. Glenday
Author of the books *Norman Mailer; F. Scott Fitzgerald;* and *Saul Bellow and the Decline in Humanism;* and co-editor of *American Mythologies: Essays on American Literature*

Author's Note

"If serial killers appear to be ordinary men,
how can we distinguish between 'apparently' ordinary men
who are 'actually' serial killers and 'really' ordinary men?"
—David Schmid, author of
Natural Born Celebrities: Serial Killers in American Culture

In 2003, not long before my fiftieth birthday, a reporter phoned my mother at her home near Niagara Falls. Only later would I learn that he was prospecting for a quote to help lend context to a story about my career as a forensic psychologist and my longstanding interest in the study of murder. About midway through their conversation, my mom delivered as if on cue.

"Jeff's always been drawn to quirky people," she said.

To my dad, a G-man who came up during the Hoover era, they were "strange agents."

Both my parents knew of my keen interest not just in killers and all sorts of other criminals but in colorful, provocative, norm-defying outliers of every imaginable stripe: carnies, celebrities, professional wrestlers, Beat Generation poets, nudists, illusionists, spiritualists, daredevils, dowsers, witches, freaks, mobsters, snake handlers, gypsies, and the like. The kinds of people whose lives seemed to me to be playing out on stages far removed from my own—which, much to my chagrin, hardly seemed like a stage at all.

Like lots of kids, maybe most, I grew up thinking the world—my world—was way too small. I hungered for a world more strange, risky, and vivid than the one I was stuck with at home. Eagerly, I'd await each new episode of TV shows like *Twilight Zone* and *The Outer Limits*. I was drawn to such shows because they hinted at the possibility that the outermost edges of the world my parents had in mind for me could be pushed back, maybe way back.

Then and later, in front of the television and away from it, I gravitated in the direction of real people and fictional characters whose stories set fire to my imagination because they suggested different values, different angles of vision, different approaches to the calculation of risk, different ways of thinking about relationships, and different choices about how to live.

As a third grader, I visited Ford's Theater with my parents and older sister. At the time, my dad worked at FBI headquarters in Washington. Most kids my age probably would have come away from the experience with a newly activated interest in Abraham Lincoln, or perhaps the Civil War. But I wasn't like most kids. In the aftermath of our visit, I couldn't stop talking about the assassination plot, and about the eight co-conspirators who planned it and carried it out. For days, I poured over the text and photographs in a souvenir pamphlet my parents had purchased for me, called *The Crime at Ford's Theater*. I memorized all the conspirators' names and backgrounds, and before long I could describe in detail the role that each of them had played in the assassination plot. Lodged in my brain were sharp, almost photographic images of each and every one of them. They remain there today, after the passage of more than 60 years.

I was eight years old and already exhibiting signs of the obsessive preoccupation with outsiders and outlaws—all those quirky people, all those strange agents—that would become a hallmark of my adulthood.

For this project, I've adopted a relatively narrow focus. The stories collected in these pages all center around my five decades of encounters with killers and killing. Many of the stories are based on experiences that occurred when I was young and, if I'm being charitable, a highly motivated but still very naive student of murder, with only the most superficial understanding of forensic psychology and the root causes of criminal behavior.

The subject of the book's first chapter is a baffling double homicide that occurred not long after my thirtieth birthday, just off the main hallway at the large hospital where I was then an up-and-coming junior administrator. The Riverside Murders, as they came to be called, became the bridge that linked my college-era attempts to penetrate the thick fog surrounding the Manson case—more on those attempts later—to my eventual decision to pursue a career in the field of forensic psychology.

Perhaps worth mentioning is the fact that I was not yet a psychologist when I spent four days with serial killer John Wayne Gacy on death row in Illinois. More to the point, I'd never before been in the same room with a convicted murderer, let alone a killer of at least 33 boys and young men. I was green. So green, in fact, that my inexperience might have gotten me killed.

In recounting events from the distant past, including some that occurred *nearly 50 years ago*, I did my best to capture the way I was thinking and feeling at that time. I was tempted to hijack some of those early experiences and present them as they appeared years later, when I was able to view them through the filter of an outlook that only became possible for me after I'd completed my graduate studies and begun work as a forensic psychologist. Such an approach would have run contrary to one of my main objectives: to present the stories as they played out in real time.

A few observations about the kind of book I intended, and the kind I didn't. I never had much interest in donning the mantle of expert and promising readers yet another journey inside the mind of the serial killer. That trip's become something of a tourist trap, with too many self-proclaimed expert guides and too few new sights to see.

Instead, my goal was to write a collection of thematically-related chapters, all centering around two subjects: murder and me. I wanted the chapters to be both entertaining and instructive. By entertaining, I mean thought-provoking and *interesting*. The stories are all true. Together, they tell of the unlikely, in some ways even bizarre path I traveled on my way to becoming a board-certified forensic psychologist.

Several publishing industry veterans cautioned me about the potential downside of a writing project that didn't have a clear enough "narrative arc," a strong enough "takeaway," and a beginning-to-end "through line" that would create momentum and carry the reader along. I listened to what they said, and I understood what they were getting at. In the end, however, I stuck with my original plan, and I wrote the book I wanted to write. As I saw it, the entertainment value of my stories *was* the takeaway, at least the main one.

In the chapters that tell of my early correspondences with John Wayne Gacy, Charles Manson, Squeaky Fromme, Sandra Good, and Susan Atkins, I chose to retain nearly all the syntactical irregularities, faulty grammar, and misspellings that appear in the primary documents that served as my source material. I did so because I thought the writers' "voices" could be heard most clearly in letters that were left largely unedited. There were exceptions—but not many. On rare occasions I added a punctuation mark, always because I thought that by doing so, I could render a passage of writing more comprehensible. I did that more with Charles Manson's letters than I did with anyone else's, mainly because Manson almost never used apostrophes.

A note on my handling of dialogue. During my in-person meetings with Gacy, Donald Harvey, Thomas Lee Dillon, Rosie Tate-Polanski, and others, I seldom found it possible— or even desirable—to transcribe verbatim everything that was being said. Instead, I tried, later on, to reconstruct the dialogue as accurately as I possibly could.

In a single instance, I changed several details to mask a minor character's identity. I did so for privacy-related reasons.

Finally, a warning about one section of the book that some

readers might wish to skip. The chapter called "The Clown," which recounts my experiences with John Wayne Gacy, includes graphic descriptions of sexual assault.

A Family Vignette

"[The] bogeyman may be your father,
and hope is a flimsy defense against dread."
—Hilton Als, foreword to Joan Didion's
Let Me Tell You What I Mean

Late on a morning in 2014, my daughter Lacey stands opposite me at the kitchen table in the house where she grew up. She's fully aware that when I retire next year, my retirement will mark the passage of three decades since I left my job as a hospital administrator and took the first steps toward a goal that was brand new to me at the time: becoming a forensic psychologist.

She's aware, too, of the many letters I exchanged with members of the Manson Family a full decade and a half *before* I embarked on my career as a psychologist. She also knows that during the last quarter century, I've provided consultation on close to 300 death penalty cases and evaluated more than 1,000 murderers altogether: serial, mass, spree, all kinds. She's heard more than her share of my work-related stories. Many of them were stories I chose to repeat at home because they allowed me the opportunity to impart lessons that I felt she and her older brother needed to learn.

Always be mindful of where you are, and with whom.

Never accept rides or gifts from strangers, even when they seem kind and helpful.

Always remember that some people can lie but still seem like they're telling the truth.

Don't decide too quickly that people are who they say they are, or who they appear to be.

"Dad," says Lacey from across the table. "I used to wonder, back when I was a kid, what if *you* were a serial killer? How would we know it?"

"That's funny. No need to worry, I'm not a serial killer."

"But that's exactly what you would say if you *were* one."

"I'm not."

"Okay, but I wouldn't expect you to say anything *different*, even if you *were*."

"Have you ever known me to *behave* like someone capable of committing murder?"

"No, but so what? That doesn't mean anything, right?"

And I'm thinking, *That's my girl.*

Prologue

"You're gonna find out I'm a normal person, just like you."
—John Wayne Gacy in a letter to the author

In a perfect world, you'd know the location of the nearest restroom, and you could get there without a serial sex killer's help.

As the noon hour approaches on December 15, 1986, I'm not thinking about a perfect world. I'm seated opposite John Wayne Gacy in a small visiting room on death row at the Menard Correctional Center in Chester, Illinois, fretting over the possibility that I'll wet my pants.

As Jim Morrison used to say, the time to hesitate is through.

"John, I hate to have to ask you this—but is there a restroom back here?"

A little context.

When I arrived at the prison, approximately three hours ago, I signed in at the front desk as Gacy's "friend," just as he'd told me I should. After first securing my wallet and a few other personal belongings in a locker that was located in the small prison lobby, I accompanied a guard-escort through a seemingly endless series of checkpoints, sign-in stations, holding areas, and gates. There was little small talk, in part because I was nervous. Mostly, I just concentrated on doing whatever the guard told me to do.

Prisons, I was learning, aren't like hospitals. There are no color-coded arrows to alert you to your location, and no signs to point you to the nearest exit.

Eventually, after a short outdoor walk, we made our way up a gentle incline until we came to a smallish, older-looking building that seemed somehow set apart from the other buildings that made up the prison complex. This building housed death row—what the guard euphemistically referred to as "the condemned unit."

Walking ahead of him, I entered the building and inhaled its stale, musty odor. Following our participation in a security procedure that the guard called "freezing the gates," we ascended a flight of stairs and arrived at a tall steel gate. On the other side of the gate was the death row visiting area, where I was about to meet Gacy for the very first time.

The guard explained that once he allowed me to pass through this gate, I'd proceed down the hallway until I came to the first visiting room on the right, where I'd find a table and two chairs. Shortly after my arrival, Gacy would join me there. He'd have handcuffs and leg irons on, but he'd be alone, unaccompanied by any of the prison staff. We'd be left to handle our own introductions.

I nodded my understanding.

The guard unlocked the gate using one of the large metal keys that dangled from a chain attached to his utility belt. With his right hand, he gestured in the direction of the room where Gacy and I would be spending the next five hours or so.

Just in case I'd forgotten where I was and whom I had come to the prison to see, he was ready with an assist.

"Remember," he said, just as I was about to pass through the gate, "you're the one who made the decision to come here. I'm sure you know why Mr. Gacy is on our condemned unit. You'll see a video camera mounted on the wall of the visiting room, but there won't be any officers in the room with you. In fact, there won't be any officers on your side of this gate. If Mr. Gacy does anything that places you in danger, or if, God forbid, a hostage situation should develop, there won't be any prison staff back there to assist you. Basically, you'll be on your own. It's against prison policy to negotiate with inmates.

Understand what I'm saying?"

"I do."

What else was I going to say? I'd come to the prison at Gacy's invitation. To get here, I'd driven 450 miles from my home in Columbus, where I was a second-year graduate student at Ohio State. Gacy and I had been corresponding—and occasionally talking on the telephone—since February.

It wasn't as if Gacy had picked me out of a crowd and somehow seduced me into letting my guard down and entering his orbit. I'd been the one to initiate the correspondence, and I was the one who'd chosen to accept Gacy's invitation. I wasn't about to bail out now.

The guard's words knocked me off balance and caused me to lose my concentration. I'd been intending to ask him if there was a restroom in the locked area reserved for death row visits. I forgot. Then, almost before I could even register what was happening, I walked through the gate, heard the loud clanging sound as it slammed shut behind me, glanced back to see the guard disappearing around a corner, and entered the room where I was told I should await Gacy's arrival.

Not more than a minute later, he shuffled in, his movement constrained by a pair of leg shackles that made it impossible for him to move more than a few inches at a time. He didn't smile when he saw me, but he acknowledged me with his eyes. Immediately, I registered the acrid smell of his cologne.

Moving awkwardly but with sure, short steps, he approached the table and leaned forward so that he could transfer onto its surface several items that he'd been clutching to his chest. They appeared to be notebooks, or maybe photograph albums. When he straightened back up, he extended his cuffed hands in my direction. I shook his right hand with mine. I couldn't help but think of that hand's unsavory history.

"Hi John, I'm Jeff. It's good to meet you," I said.

"Jeff, John. Or you can call me JW if you want to. That's what most of the guards call me."

Right away, like it was the thing dominating his thoughts, Gacy started talking about how I was meeting "the man," not the monster I'd been reading about in the popular press. He assured me that I'd soon discover he was "just a normal person," like me, like everyone.

He added that once we'd had an opportunity to "cover [his] case," I'd surely come around to the conclusion that he couldn't possibly have been responsible for the deaths of all the 33 boys and young men he'd been convicted of killing. He emphasized his ironclad commitment to "only the facts," not "the theories and fantasy and speculation" that he insisted had been the foundation of the prosecution's case against him.

Fast forward.

He's now been "motor-mouthing," his term, for the better part of three hours, most of the time talking about how "tunnel vision" prevented the authorities from discovering the truth behind the murders, and about how his attorneys sold him down the river by pressuring him to plead not guilty by reason of insanity, even though he wanted no part of any such plea.

His overriding theme? "I got fucked."

I've been maintaining steady eye contact with him, taking mental notes and occasionally interjecting a question or two — but generally resisting the temptation to challenge his claims, even the most preposterous ones.

But now I'm desperate. So desperate, in fact, that I can hardly even attend to what he's saying. About 45 minutes ago, a moderate urge to pee started becoming something more urgent. I've resisted the urge to speak up because, well, who really wants to have to ask a sadistic sex killer for help locating a restroom?

With each passing minute I've been clinging to the hope that I'll soon hear the reassuring sounds of jangling keys, a slamming gate, and the footsteps of a guard approaching from down the hall. Lunchtime. When the guard appears in the doorway, I'll ask him if he can please direct me to the nearest restroom. A crisis will have been averted.

Wishful thinking.

I'm in a prison, after all, not just a prison but a prison

within a prison within a prison—the locked visiting area on the death row unit at a maximum-security institution. No one here has the slightest interest in adjusting their routines to accommodate me and my need for a restroom or anything else.

It comes down to this one question: How desperate does a man have to be before he decides to ask a serial sex killer—of young men—for help resolving an issue that implicates his genitals? The answer? As desperate as I am now.

So I speak up. "Is there a restroom back here?"

"*Hell* no," says Gacy, like only a fool would ask such a moronic question.

"If you really need a john, you'll have to go out there and yell—and I mean *yell*. The restroom's around the corner from the control desk. Good luck. The fuckin' guards are probably off playing poker somewhere. That's what they do all day. If you expect to get their attention, yell. Maybe they'll respond, maybe they won't."

Taking care not to move any faster than my condition will allow, I push my chair back from the table, get up, and head for the hallway. When I'm sure Gacy can no longer see me, I press my legs together and move with short, measured steps in the direction of the gate where I last saw a guard, almost three hours ago. The small control desk is directly in front of me—but on the other side of the gate. And anyway, no one's there.

"*Excuse me!*" I yell—but not as loudly as I'm capable of yelling. Then again, after a pause of about ten seconds: "*Excuse me!*"

Nothing.

I try once more, a bit louder this time.

Still, no response.

I shuffle back to the visiting room, where Gacy awaits me with a bemused look on his face. He's clearly tickled by my plight. It's an absurd situation. Here I am, alone behind a locked gate with one of the most notorious serial killers in modern American history, and I can't successfully summon a guard to help me get to the nearest restroom. I'm about as vulnerable as a man can be—and a damn fool besides. I know it, and Gacy knows it, too.

"You didn't *lis-ten*," says Gacy, speaking in a sing-song voice like the kind you might use to chide a three-year-old.

"When I say yell, I mean *yell*! Those fuckin' dicks couldn't care less that you're back here. And none of 'em give a shit that you have to pee. All they care about's their goddam poker game. If you're serious, go try it again—but louder this time."

I head back out to the hallway. Once there, I creep toward the gate, my body bent forward in a kind of half-crouch. When I arrive, I place both my hands on the bars.

I'm long past the point of caring how I look or sound.

"*Guarrrdd!*" I yell. This time I hold nothing back.

In the moment, it seems like a miracle when the guard who acted as my morning escort appears from around the corner and saunters in my direction.

"You need something?"

"Yes sir, I do. I need to use the restroom—and I'm pretty desperate."

He smiles. Slowly and deliberately (I swear!), he fingers the keys suspended from his belt before he eventually settles on the one he needs. He uses the key to unlock the gate, then gestures in the direction of the restroom, which turns out to be right around the corner from where we're standing.

The tiny room stinks of shit, piss, body odor, and mildew. When I'm through emptying my full-to-capacity bladder, I flush the toilet and try to scrub my hands clean in the filthy, disgusting-looking sink. The mirror on the wall looks like it hasn't been cleaned in years. I can barely make out my image through the smears and grime.

The guard is waiting for me when I exit the restroom and walk the short distance back to the gate. He seems mildly perturbed, perhaps because I interrupted his card game. As he's about to insert his key into the lock that will open the gate and allow me to resume my visit with Gacy, he pauses for a moment and turns in my direction.

"Everything going alright back there?"

"Yeah, fine."

"No problems with JW?"

"No, no problems."

I don't tell him what I'm really thinking.

What I'm really thinking is that the man on the other side of this gate, the same one who seemed so tickled when he realized I couldn't even get a guard's attention, is going to devote the next several hours to imagining what it would feel like to have me under his complete control—with a chloroform-soaked rag pressed against my face, a pair of handcuffs encircling my wrists, and a garrote slowly tightening around my neck.

1.
A Man on a Mission

Patty Matix was a pixie. Barely five feet tall, she spoke in a soft, high-pitched voice. A lot of the time, she looked like she was trying to suppress a giggle. Known among her co-workers for her quiet, unassuming manner, she had a sweet, friendly disposition. The pastor at the Baptist church she attended would later recall her as "a cheerful, delightful person and a dedicated Christian." On October 4, 1983, she and her husband Bill welcomed their first child, a daughter they named Melissa Lynn.

At Riverside Methodist Hospital in Columbus, then the largest private general hospital in Ohio, she worked in the medical research lab, alongside her close friend Joyce McFadden and four other employees. Joyce was married, too, but she and her husband had no children. Like Patty, she was friendly and easy to relate to—always smiling, always ready with an upbeat greeting. A minister and long-time family friend who knew of her work in the field of medical research would later remark that she dedicated her life to trying to preserve the lives of others.

In December 1983, when Patty and Joyce lost their lives, I was an assistant vice president at Riverside, with administrative responsibility not only for the medical research lab but for the hospital's 138-bed psychiatric and substance abuse unit, as well as a number of other programs and departments. Located just around the corner from the hospital's main corridor, and in close proximity to the radiology department's waiting area, the research lab wasn't much larger than an average living room. A single door served as both entrance and exit.

That month, on the afternoon of the day before I left Columbus to spend Christmas with my parents in western New York, I attended a festive but predictably low-key celebration in the lab. I was there acting as the administration's representative. Everyone seemed in good spirits, there were light refreshments, and we all chatted amiably about our plans for the holidays.

Next thing I knew, Patty and Joyce were both dead, butchered in the place where they worked.

On the afternoon of Friday, December 30, the lab's director, a research scientist named Devi Munjal—who happened to be on vacation that week—found Joyce lying facedown on the floor in a large pool of blood when he stopped by the hospital to collect his mail and check on his phone messages. He ran screaming from the lab, out into the hallway.

A hospital security officer, as well as a physician named Ed Bope, accompanied him on his return to the lab. Dr. Bope checked and found that Joyce had no pulse. Before long, two City of Columbus police officers arrived on the scene. One of them discovered the body of Patty Matix in a small cold room that was used to store tissue samples. Both women's throats had been cut, their hands had been bound with tape, and they'd been stabbed numerous times.

Later, it would be determined that the murders must have occurred sometime between 4:35 and 5:05, which is when Dr. Munjal entered the lab and saw Joyce's body. As it turned out, Patty had phoned her husband at 4:10 that day, to check on their baby and ask whether he needed her to stop at the store for anything on her way home from the hospital. At 4:30, Joyce had spoken to her mother on the telephone. At 4:35, an employee from the hospital's main laboratory, which was located just around the corner from the research lab, had dropped by to inquire about borrowing a piece of equipment. Joyce and Patty were both present, and the employee later told the police that nothing seemed amiss.

At first, no one reported having seen or heard anything unusual during the relevant time frame. Eventually, however, an emergency department clerk whose office shared one wall with the lab informed the police that she might have heard a "thud," maybe even a "scream." In any case, the killer or killers had worked quickly — and then vanished into thin air.

• • •

I still don't know whether I believe in what some people refer to as fate, but I can remember thinking: *It's almost like an invisible hand has reached down to establish a through line in my life, linking events from long ago — when, at the urging of my professor for a course in abnormal psychology, I'd begun exchanging letters with members of the Manson Family — to what was happening now, nearly a decade later and in an entirely different context.*

How else to account for the continuity between two seemingly unrelated chapters of my life? Murder then, murder now.

I arrived at Riverside Methodist Hospital in June 1981. I was about to begin a year-long administrative residency, the final requirement for my master's degree in health services administration at George Washington University (GW). I'd matriculated at GW a year and a half prior, just six months after my return from Ireland, where I'd spent a year learning rudimentary Gaelic and completing a post-graduate diploma program in modern Anglo-Irish literature at Trinity College in Dublin.

On frequent occasions during those early days at Riverside, I'd look around inside the hospital and wonder how in the world I'd ended up in such a place. In the years leading up to 1979, I'd never once considered pursuing any sort of career in the world of business. In fact, any such career would have been about the furthest thing from my mind.

Truth be told, there was little rhyme or reason behind the set of decisions that led me to the field of hospital administration. On a day not long after I'd returned home from Ireland,

I confessed to my mother that I couldn't figure out what to do with the rest of my life. I no longer saw myself as an English professor, which is what I'd aspired to becoming when I graduated from college and began work toward my master's degree in English at Purdue. Once I'd completed that degree, I taught for a year as a member of the English faculty at my alma mater, Valparaiso University. Then I relocated to Ireland, where I lived and studied for a year. Not all at once but gradually, it dawned on me that I probably wouldn't adjust well to the publish-or-perish mentality that seemed to dominate most academic environments at the time.

Briefly, I thought perhaps I'd become an FBI agent like my dad. That plan, which I was never sold on anyway, began to seem suspect when the agent who was in charge of processing applications in the Buffalo field office told me that although I'd performed almost flawlessly on two of the tests that the bureau used for screening-related purposes (there was a spelling test, as well as a second test that was billed as a means of assessing the applicant's "general fund of information"), my results on a personality inventory spelled trouble. A bit ruefully, the agent explained that the results revealed me to be the sort of person who doesn't easily yield to authority.

Cutting me a break, presumably because he was a friend and colleague of my dad's, he said he'd allow me an opportunity to re-take the test. By way of preparation for the re-do, he counseled me to pretend that I was in the military. "Keep in mind," he said, "the importance of being willing to take orders from your superiors." I did my best—but in the end, it didn't matter. My results came back pretty much the same. And so ended my short-lived fantasy of becoming a special agent.

When I told my mom that I still hadn't settled on a path to the future, I'm sure she felt some combination of fear, frustration, and anxiety. Even before the FBI debacle, she'd made no secret of her desire to see me get going—as quickly as possible—toward whatever awaited me down the road. But she was nothing if not practical, and she prided herself on being a creative and resourceful problem-solver—so it came as no surprise that she had something to say when I described to her how lost I was feeling.

She asked whether I'd ever considered the field of hospital administration. I said no, then asked her what hospital administration was.

"I'm not quite sure what it entails," she said. "But there are two nice-looking young men at DeGraff [the local hospital where she worked part time as an RN], and I've heard a lot of people refer to them as the administrators. One of them is Mr. Celmer. I can't think of the other man's name. Anyway, both of them seem friendly whenever I pass them in the hallway. Why don't you arrange a time to talk to one of them? Tell him your mom works at the hospital as a nurse. Who knows? Maybe hospital administration would turn out to be a good fit for you."

It's not like I had a lot else going on. I phoned the hospital, asked the switchboard operator to connect me to administration, and spoke with a man who introduced himself as Mark Celmer. He said sure, he'd be happy to talk with me about his job.

When I met with him a day or two later, he came across as a nice guy: low-key, collegial, and not the least bit pretentious. He couldn't have been more than five years my senior—but I remembered that my mom had referred to him as "Mr. Celmer." I liked it that she seemed to regard him with an attitude of deference.

During our meeting, he spoke highly of George Washington University, where he'd obtained his own master's degree, and he described his job in a way that made it sound both interesting and challenging. As I was getting ready to leave his office, he said, "Here's what I think you should do, Jeff. Why don't you apply to George Washington, get your degree, and then when you're done, come back here and work for me?"

That sounded about as close to a job offer as anything I'd heard in a long time. Whatever it was, it provided an instant boost to my morale. For the moment anyway, that was enough. The very next day, I began the process of obtaining, completing, and submitting my application to George Washington. It was the only school I applied to. My plan was simple and straightforward: *GW or bust.*

Looking back, it's hard to imagine that members of the screening committee would have perceived me as a strong applicant. I'd never completed a single business class, ever. No accounting, no economics, no marketing, no personnel management. In fact, no coursework at all that would have prepared me to assist in the administration of a complex organization like a hospital. I'd never before worked in the healthcare field, and I had zero business experience.

My lack of qualifications wasn't the only obstacle in my way. In addition, I was flat broke after the year I'd just spent in Ireland. Even if I lucked out and got admitted to George Washington, which had one of the top-rated hospital administration programs in the country, I'd only be able to take advantage of the opportunity if the university awarded me something approximating a full scholarship. I had no interest in amassing a lot of student debt. As I saw it, things would either work out in accordance with my dream scenario or I'd be back where I started: stalled at age 26 and at risk of being branded with the dreaded "failure to launch" label.

Without a back-up plan, I just assumed that if things didn't work out for me at George Washington, I'd reassess my situation and somehow come up with a new approach to planning for the rest of my life, one that hadn't yet occurred to me. Presumably, both my parents were praying for a GW miracle.

And then, surprise: I found out I'd been accepted; not just accepted, but offered a full scholarship, too. All I could think to conclude was that the people in charge of screening applicants must have singled me out as a sleeper candidate, different from most of their other applicants, but perhaps worth a gamble. I knew virtually nothing about what I was getting myself into, but that didn't stop me from deciding right then and there that I was going to carve out a career for myself in the field of hospital administration.

It's a strange sequence of events to look back on—especially in light of the fact that my decision to pursue my master's degree at George Washington set the stage for pretty much everything that's happened in my life during the 45 years that have elapsed since.

After I'd completed three semesters of coursework in Washington, including prerequisite classes in both accounting and economics, I was required to serve a one-year administrative residency at a hospital somewhere in the United States. One close friend of mine did hers at a hospital in San Diego; another close friend was assigned to a hospital in Massachusetts. As fate (or something) would have it, I was selected to be an administrative resident at Riverside Methodist Hospital in Columbus. I'd probably passed through Ohio at some point in my life, though if I did, I had no memory of it. I'd certainly never considered it as a place to live. And I didn't know the first thing about its capital city, or about the state's system of health care providers.

As my residency was getting underway in June 1981, I realized that my studies at GW had done little to prepare me for the nuts and bolts aspects of performing as an administrator at a large hospital like Riverside. Fortunately, I knew how to compensate for my shortcomings, at least in the near-term. I learned quickly how to leverage my reasonably good verbal and interpersonal skills to build relationships with many of the hospital's department heads; I convinced my superiors that I was smart, socially adept, and eager to ascend the corporate ladder; and I managed to foster the overall impression that I was a young striver with a bright future in the field of health care administration.

I kept getting promoted. Following the completion of my residency year, I was named an administrative fellow. I expected that position to last for at least a year, but in only a matter of months I was made an assistant vice president, in part, no doubt, so that I'd be perceived as having the requisite gravitas and organizational stature to pull off my next assignment: to serve as the interim administrator at a 50-bed hospital in rural Holmes County—"Amish country"—that Riverside had signed a contract to manage.

During my four months at Joel Pomerene Hospital, I worked hard to develop positive relationships with members of the medical staff and board of trustees; I devoted a lot of after-hours time to conducting community outreach (including to the Amish, who'd traditionally viewed the hospital with suspicion); and I bent over backward in an effort to avoid conveying the impression that I thought I was anyone special just because I'd arrived in town as a representative of the "mother hospital" in the big city.

When my four-month stint as Joel Pomerene's interim administrator came to an end, the trustees who'd worked closely with me sent sparkling reviews back to my boss at Riverside. The next year, I was promoted to vice president.

By then, Patty and Joyce were already dead.

•••

I was home at my parents' when I first learned of the murders. No news could have shocked me more.

When the telephone rang, I answered it because no one else was home. I assumed the caller would be my best friend from high school, probably wanting to go out and do something that night—or perhaps one of my parents' friends. Instead, it was the director of public relations at Riverside, a woman I knew well and considered a friend.

"Jeff, I'm sorry, I have some terrible news."

I didn't know what was coming—but I had an idea. Ever since being assigned administrative responsibility for the hospital's psychiatric and substance abuse units, I made a habit of carrying a pager with me at all times. At night, I kept it on my bedside table.

Some six months prior, the pager had beeped at around two in the morning. When I phoned the hospital to find out why I was being paged, I learned that not long before, a patient on one of the psychiatric units had plunged a Bic pen into his chest and bled to death. Another tragic event had preceded my arrival at the hospital, but not by much. It remained a topic of conversation among many of the employees. Like the Bic pen incident, it had involved a patient from one of the psychiatric floors. The patient, a man in his late-20s, had been granted a temporary pass so that he could accompany his nine-year-old daughter on a walk around the periphery of the hospital campus. During their walk, he killed her.

So, my working assumption was that the public relations director was calling me to report some sort of new crisis that involved a patient on what was then known as the mental health unit.

Turns out, that's not why she was calling at all.

"Patty Matix and Joyce McFadden are dead," she said. "They were murdered in the research lab on Friday afternoon."

"No way."

Those two words were as much as I could muster. For a few moments, I was too stunned to say anything else. Instead, I just listened.

"Devi found Joyce's body when he stopped by the lab to pick up his mail a little after five o'clock. The police found Patty's body in the walk-in cold room when they arrived at the hospital a short time later. As I'm sure you can imagine, everyone here's in shock. No one's been arrested yet, and no witnesses have come forward to report seeing or hearing anything unusual between four and five o'clock, which is when police say the murders must have occurred. Right now, they don't even have a suspect, at least none that we know of. Nobody here has even the slightest idea who could have killed Joyce and Patty, or who would have wanted to."

I heard her words, but they didn't make sense. Patty? Joyce? *Murdered*? Right around the corner from the hospital's main hallway? Just down from the gift shop? Late in the afternoon on a Friday? No witnesses?

I said I'd drive back to Columbus the next day.

• • •

When I arrived back in Columbus, I couldn't bring myself to return to the hospital at first. My knowledge of the killings felt like an invisible barrier, impenetrable. I stayed at my apartment that first night and invited two of my closest friends to join me there. One of them was a senior administrator at the hospital; the other one was a department head. They shared with me what little they knew about the circumstances surrounding the murders. Much of what they knew, they'd gleaned from local television and newspaper coverage.

Reporters were saying that it appeared the women had been killed during a botched robbery. Their wedding rings were missing, and the killer or killers had emptied out the contents of Joyce McFadden's purse.

The last person known to have seen Joyce and Patty alive was the employee from the hospital's main laboratory, the one who'd stopped by at 4:35 to inquire about borrowing a piece of equipment. The women had to have been killed sometime during the next 30 minutes. By now, everyone with an interest in the case knew that Patty had been stabbed 16 times, Joyce 19 times. Their throats had been cut, and their hands had been bound with tape. According to the police, Joyce had been "hogtied."

My mind was already working overtime: How did details like these square with the idea of a botched robbery? Why would the killer have staged the crime scene in the way he did?

The next day, I overcame my resistance and made the short drive to Riverside for the first time since my return to Columbus. Holiday decorations hadn't yet been taken down and put into storage for next year—but everything else at the hospital seemed changed since I left there shortly before Christmas. There was a prickly tension in the air. I felt it immediately, just as soon as I passed through the entranceway that led from the small lot where I parked my car to a corridor that ran alongside the emergency department. Hospital employees whom I encountered as I made my way toward my office all looked haunted and on edge. Many of them were gathered in small clusters, speaking quietly among themselves. I stopped and spoke with several employees whom I knew well. They all said the same thing: they no longer felt safe coming to work each day.

I learned in a matter of minutes that the hospital was

abuzz with rumors. Had Patty and Joyce been killed after uncovering evidence that another lab employee was falsifying research data? Had the murders been committed by one of the non-employee laborers who'd been working on a large construction project that included the area around the research lab? Could Dr. Munjal be the killer? After all, he was the one who reported finding the first of the two bodies. Could the killer be someone else who worked at the hospital? Someone who was continuing to report to work each day, yet betraying no signs whatsoever to suggest he was capable of knifing two women to death on the day just before people all around Columbus would gather together to celebrate the start of a new year? Could the killer be a patient from one of the psychiatric units? Could a rumored relationship between two research lab employees be the key to solving the mystery of who killed the women? There were plenty of questions—but so far no answers.

As I walked the halls of the hospital, I realized that I was looking at people differently, even people whom I thought I knew well. *If I happen upon the killer, will I even know it? Are there signs I should be looking for?*

In the days and weeks that followed, I read everything about the murders that I could get my hands on. I was always on the lookout for new information. Bill Matix, Patty's husband, told a reporter that he'd once heard his wife complain that she felt like "a trapped rat" within the tight confines of the research lab, accessible only through the single door that served as both entrance and exit. I learned that based on all the available evidence the police and the coroner had concluded that neither of the victims offered any resistance to whoever killed her.

The coroner contended that the sheer viciousness of the murders suggested "passion or fear" as the most likely motive—a conclusion that I thought might or might not jibe with the theory of a botched robbery. Did a "panicked thief" commit the murders? The police seemed to think that was a strong possibility.

There were no signs to suggest that either of the women

had been sexually assaulted. It wasn't entirely clear whether Dr. Munjal and the two surviving husbands had agreed to undergo polygraph examinations. According to a newspaper story that appeared a week and a half after the murders, all three men were "very willing" to assist the police—in any way they could. None of the three men were considered suspects, or so the police said.

A representative of the police department revealed that police were in the process of analyzing more than 150 fingerprints taken from the crime scene. I assumed that my prints were among those being analyzed.

One hospital employee reported having seen a "vagrant" on the afternoon of the murders, sleeping in the vicinity of the altar in the hospital's chapel, which was located on the building's second floor. Could he be the killer? There were also reports of an as-yet unidentified "Indian man" who'd been observed walking the corridors of the hospital on the day the murders took place. Could it be him? (I don't recall anyone asking why an Indian man, walking the halls of the hospital, would have been viewed as suspect.)

One of the most intriguing aspects of the case was that police felt certain that whoever killed Patty and Joyce would have been covered in blood. If that was true, how could he (or they) have exited the lab through the only available door—which, again, was located just down the hall from the radiology department's waiting area—and left the hospital complex without anyone so much as noticing? No one seemed to have any idea.

Meanwhile, as verified and unverified information about the murders continued to trickle out in the local newspapers and on television, I continued going to work each day and doing the best I could to stay on top of my responsibilities. It was a difficult time—for me and for everyone else who worked at the hospital.

That period might have been even more difficult for me than it was for most other hospital employees. That's because my job required me to interact, almost every day, with the surviving members of the research lab staff. I arranged to meet with them one at a time. All of them seemed obviously and understandably traumatized. They cried, they spoke of missing Patty and Joyce, they said it frightened them to have to report to work each day, and they expressed absolute bewilderment with respect to the question of who could have committed the murders—and why. Did either Joyce or Patty have an enemy who might have wanted her dead? None of the surviving employees thought so.

It's not something I like to admit, even all these years later, but back then I believed there was a good chance that I'd been staring straight into the eyes of a murderer when I met—not once but multiple times—with the director of the research lab. In the absence of any official theory to explain who killed Joyce and Patty, and why, I considered it possible, even likely, that Dr. Munjal was the killer.

I knew Devi reasonably well. At least I thought I did. We had frequent meetings, and we worked together on a wide variety of operational issues that involved the research lab. Devi was highly intelligent and unapologetically ambitious. On frequent occasions, he spoke with me in terms I could barely understand about the cutting-edge cancer-related research that he and his team members were conducting. He made it clear that he expected to accomplish great things—and he craved the recognition, and the accolades, that would come his way if he did. He wanted to be respected and admired by his colleagues, not only at Riverside but in the larger—he would say worldwide—scientific community.

There were times when we butted heads. More than once, I'd seen him become very angry. He was egotistical, thin-skinned—and volatile. Was he capable of committing murder? Before December 30, I'd have said no. But now I thought the answer might be yes—especially if, as I'd heard through the hospital grapevine, Patty and Joyce discovered falsified research data and threatened to go public with their findings. Not to be forgotten was the fact that Devi saw Joyce McFadden's dead body before anyone else at the hospital even knew she was gone.

In those days, Devi would sit across from me in my office

and weep as we talked about Joyce and Patty, and about the murders. I wanted to feel the same compassion for him that I felt for all the other surviving research lab employees. He seemed just as traumatized as they were, maybe more. After all, he was the first one to observe the carnage. Still, I couldn't shake my suspicions.

I could feel my stress level rising. It didn't help that the authorities seemed no closer to arresting anyone. According to a police department spokesman, the problem, or at least one of them, was that there were too *many* suspects—as opposed to too few. If that was indeed the case, neither I nor any of the people I knew had even the first clue about who the suspects might be.

Was Devi one of them?

My suspicions about Devi grew even stronger about a fortnight after the murders. A headline in one of the local newspapers read, "Lab Chief Quizzed About Hospital Slayings." With the clarity of hindsight, I can see that the headline was misleading and unfair. Readers could easily have jumped to the conclusion that the police had zeroed in on Devi as their primary suspect. They hadn't. All the story did was state the obvious: that since Devi was the first person known to have witnessed the crime scene, the police wanted to obtain as much information from him as they possibly could.

Around this same time, I did something I wouldn't ordinarily do. Now, I can see that it marked a turning point in my way of responding to the murders. I sought help from the hospital chaplain. When we met at his office, I spoke of how stressed-out I'd been feeling, and I told him of my suspicions about Dr. Munjal. I said that I dreaded coming to work each day. As I confided in him, I found that I had to struggle to hold back tears. I almost never cried. He urged me to accept that God was presiding over the criminal investigation, and he assured me that ultimately, everything would play out in accordance with God's will. When I left his office, I knew my days at Riverside were numbered.

•••

On January 4, 1984, just five days after the murders, I attended a memorial service for Joyce and Patty, held in the hospital's large auditorium. It was filled to capacity. As one of the hospital's administrators, I was offered a seat up near the front. Across a narrow aisle from where I was seated were the victims' husbands, Bill Matix and Larry McFadden. Out of the corner of my eye, I watched them as they participated along with everyone else in a call-and-response reading from Scripture, led by a representative from the hospital's pastoral care department: "No evil shall befall you. *No scourge come near your tent.* For he will give his angels charge of you. *To guard you in all your ways.* On their hands they will bear you up. *Lest you dash your foot against a stone.* When he calls to me, I will answer him. *I will be with him in trouble, I will rescue him and honor him.* With long life I will satisfy him. *And show him my salvation.*"

When the service ended, I crossed the aisle so that I could shake hands with the husbands. I told each of them how sorry I was for his loss. They both looked stricken. I thought perhaps they were still in shock. After thanking me, they turned to face a very long line of hospital employees, all waiting for the opportunity to say how sorry they were.

• • •

A couple of weeks after the murders, my parents passed through Ohio on their way to Florida. By the time of their arrival in Columbus, the crime scene had already been thoroughly processed. Access to it was no longer restricted, at least for the small number of hospital employees who had keys to the lab. As the administrator responsible for that department, I was in possession of one of those keys.

I asked my dad, recently retired from the FBI and now working part time for a private security firm, if he had any interest in visiting the site where the murders had occurred. He did.

The two of us went there one evening, at a time when I figured no one would be around to observe us entering the lab and locking the door behind us. The outside company that the hospital had hired to clean up the crime scene hadn't yet begun its work, so the scene looked much the same as it had when the police were done processing it. I'd already visited the lab several times since the murders, so I knew what to expect. Dark fingerprint powder still covered the walls, and dried droplets of blood were still visible on the walls and the floor.

My dad scrutinized the scene without saying a word. After a minute or two of silence, he finally spoke up: "To me, it looks like whoever committed these murders took care to stage the scene. He probably wanted it to look like the women were killed for a reason that's not the real reason. If I had to guess, I'd say it wasn't a botched robbery—but something else."

As we were getting ready to leave the lab, I decided I'd open a couple of drawers, curious about what I might find. I was fairly confident that the police would have removed anything that could potentially have evidentiary value—but I was curious anyway. At first, nothing caught my attention. There were pens, pencils, markers, loose pieces of paper—pretty much what you'd expect to see in any drawer in any office.

Then I noticed one of the ubiquitous pink Riverside Methodist Hospital communication slips, the ones all employees of the hospital used to exchange messages with one another. This particular message slip had been specially formatted for use in the research lab. At the top, next to the word "To," were the names of all the lab employees, organized in a vertical list, with a short horizontal line next to each name. The sender could place a check mark next to the name of the person for whom the message was intended.

On this particular slip, there was a check mark next to "J. McFadden." On the next line, alongside the word "From," Dr. Munjal had written his first name. He'd recorded the date as December 23, 1983, two days before Christmas. On the line just below his name, he'd left Joyce a handwritten message: "See you in 1984. Wish you a happy new year."

• • •

Not long after the murders, a story in one of the local newspapers read, "Detectives ... have said they performed extensive background checks on each of the victims and uncovered nothing that can even remotely be considered a motive for the slayings." Everyone I knew interpreted that statement to mean that family members and close relatives of the victims had been thoroughly checked out, and that no solid leads had emerged as a result of that part of the investigation.

On January 30, 1984, exactly one month after the murders, another newspaper story referred to a man on Ohio State's campus who'd grabbed a woman from behind, put a knife to her throat, and declared, "I killed those women at Riverside." Apparently nothing more came of the incident, at least nothing that linked it in any sort of credible way to the murders at the hospital. The mystery surrounding who killed Joyce and Patty seemed to deepen with each passing day.

In late March, one of the local papers published information that was new to me, a tantalizing lead from law enforcement, and that's putting it mildly.

According to the story, a hospital custodian reported to the police that on the afternoon of the murders—in fact, just minutes before 5:00—he witnessed a former employee, whose job responsibilities had included cleaning the area around the research lab, exiting the lab through the only door that provided access to it. The custodian said that the former employee, known to have been involved in multiple theft-related offenses in the past, was wearing a pair of green hospital scrubs at the time of the sighting.

For reasons unknown to me, this seemingly promising lead apparently led nowhere. I just assumed the police must have had reasons to doubt the witness's reliability.

At least in terms of information that made its way into the public domain, nothing much seemed to change over the course of the next four months. My stress level didn't change much either. I still dreaded having to report to work each day—and I knew I wasn't alone. In one newspaper story about the murders and their aftermath, a pharmacy tech was quoted as saying, "It gives me the creeps to think I might be working with someone who's killing." I felt the same way. And the feeling didn't abate with the passage of time, especially in light of the fact that the police investigation seemed to be going nowhere.

Then, in late August 1984, another newspaper story created a whole new wave of curiosity and dread among employees at the hospital. Were the police about to arrest someone? According to the story, they'd discovered a boot print in the lab. Subsequently, a pair of boots with soles that matched the print in question had been confiscated from a construction worker who was known to have been in the vicinity of the lab on the day of the murders. We were all on edge, waiting to discover whether the lead would pan out, and whether someone would finally be arrested. Days went by, then weeks, and still there was no arrest. As far as any of us could tell, the police were no closer to solving the case than they had been before their discovery of the boot print match.

In the midst of all this uncertainty, I finally decided I'd had enough. I resolved to quit my job, in fact to leave the field of health care administration altogether. I'd never been cut out for a career in business. That much had seemed clear—at least to me—almost from the time I arrived at Riverside. However, the murders, combined with all that had gone on at the hospital in the months since they occurred, made my decision far easier than it would have been otherwise.

I didn't just quit and walk out the door. While I still had the security of a job, I set up interviews with four members of Ohio State's department of psychology, and I began to prepare my graduate school application. I'm pretty sure my parents thought I'd lost my mind. They'd been delighted over the fact that I finally had a job that required me to dress in business attire each day when I went to work. That matched their ideas about what it meant to be successful. They'd been even more delighted by the news of my multiple promotions within a relatively narrow window of time.

When I phoned to tell them of my decision to return to graduate school, my mother expressed her disappointment in two words. "Oh Jeff," she said, sounding a little like Eeyore.

Despite their misgivings, both she and my dad acknowledged that the decision was mine and mine alone.

The following spring, I learned the good news that I'd been accepted at Ohio State; not just accepted, but awarded a coveted University Fellowship. It would cover all my first-year expenses and include a generous cost of living stipend. When I began my studies, in the fall of 1985, nearly two years had elapsed since the murders. Whoever killed Joyce and Patty was still at large.

I had an agenda. It went beyond just traveling down a path that would lead me to a career other than hospital administration. I'd decided that I wanted to become a student of murder, a real one this time. A decade earlier, I'd reached out to Charles Manson and other members of the Manson Family, in part because I was fascinated by some of the more sensational aspects of the Manson case, but also because I wanted to collect the kind of information that I thought might help me to understand what made such people tick—and what, if anything, they had to do with me. Now, I clung to the fragile hope that at some point down the road, I'd be conducting my own assessments of known and suspected murderers. Maybe then, I figured, I could advance a few steps closer to an understanding of the kind of person who might have taken the lives of Patty Matix and Joyce McFadden.

It was a Janus moment. I was looking ahead but looking backward, too. What's past is prologue. In my case, I was feeling more and more like I'd been serving a kind of apprenticeship back in the Manson days, unwittingly laying the groundwork for a career choice that was only now beginning to come into focus.

Call it fate, call it coincidence. As an aspiring health care administrator needing to serve a required one-year residency, I'd landed at Riverside Methodist Hospital in Columbus, Ohio. I could as easily have landed at any one of hundreds of other hospitals located throughout the United States. As it happened, I stayed on at Riverside after the completion of my residency, and two women ended up dead there, murdered in a department for which I'd been assigned administrative responsibility. Their deaths created a link between my past and my present. And they changed my life.

• • •

Now, the second part of this story.

Two years on, the Riverside mystery was still unsolved. There was no good reason to believe the police were any closer to solving the case than they had been in those first feverish weeks after Patty's and Joyce's bodies were discovered in the lab. A January 1986 newspaper headline read, "Two years later, hospital staff uneasy." One employee confided to the reporter who'd written the story, "I feel scared all the time … I never turn my back to an open doorway." The woman refused to let the reporter use her name, ostensibly because employees "had been ordered not to talk about [the murders]."

The Columbus police were "hoping the killer [would] come in and confess to the crime." In other words, they were stumped and stuck.

Then, the bombshell.

On the morning of April 12, 1986, I retrieved the newspaper from my front porch and saw the bold headline, announcing news of "a wild shootout" that had occurred the day prior, just outside Miami. Two FBI agents and two robbery suspects had been killed. Five other FBI agents had been wounded. The shootout was being called the single most devastating firearm-related incident in FBI history. On a residential street, in a little less than five minutes, more than 100 rounds of ammunition had been fired from an assortment of pistols, shotguns, and automatic weapons. According to police, the two suspects who'd been killed in the shootout were "believed responsible for a series of bank and armored car robberies."

The article identified the suspects as Michael Lee Platt and William Matix.

William Matix?

Surely not *that* William Matix, I thought. Couldn't be. But it was.

I was stunned. I and just about everyone I knew at Riverside had been under the impression that Bill and Patty Matix were a conservative, deeply religious couple. That's how the media had portrayed them. Plus, they were the parents of a three-month-old baby daughter, their first child, at the time of Patty's death. I remembered how somber and grief-stricken Bill looked four days after the murders, when I shook his hand at the hospital's memorial service and offered my condolences.

Was it possible that this first-time father, whom the police had described as "religious and devoted to his family," might instead be a stone-cold criminal? A *multiple murderer?*

From that first morning when I read news reports about the gun battle outside Miami, I followed the case as closely as I could. Gradually, an entirely new picture of Bill Matix began to emerge. I found out a lot about him that I hadn't known previously—and I learned the broad outlines of what he'd been up to in the two years and four months that had elapsed since Patty's death.

From a combination of life insurance and worker's compensation payouts, he'd netted approximately $375,000. In addition, he'd filed a $3 million wrongful death lawsuit against the hospital, alleging that Riverside hadn't provided adequate security for the employees in the research lab. (When I read about the wrongful death suit, I thought back to what he'd said shortly after the murders: that his wife had complained to him about sometimes feeling like a "trapped rat" in the tiny lab where a single door served as both entrance and exit.) The suit against Riverside was still pending at the time of his death.

In August 1984, some eight months after the hospital murders, he'd sold his house north of Columbus and relocated to Florida with his infant daughter. As it turned out, he'd hooked up with an old Army buddy of his named Michael Lee Platt. Platt ran his own lawn care business, and he invited Matix to join him.

Not long after his move to Florida, Matix purchased a new, upscale house. He joined a church and signed up to become a member of a church-sponsored singles group. According to a church spokesperson, he was "a little assertive and hasty" in his pursuit of a number of the women whom he met through the church. In fact, he proposed marriage to at least three of them. The only woman who accepted his proposal left him after they'd been married for only about two months. By then, she was pregnant with his child.

In December 1985, almost two years to the day after Patty's death, she gave birth to a boy named Brett. Four months later, just days after Bill's death, a different Florida woman filed a paternity suit, alleging that Bill was the father of her then-unborn child.

Again and again, money popped up as a theme in the Bill Matix story, dating back to the time prior to Patty's death. Matix was said to have had a tough time settling on a career and holding down a job during the period when he and Patty were married. Patty had finally run out of patience—partly because she was so unhappy about the instability of Bill's job situation, she'd moved out of their home for a relatively brief period during mid-1983 when she was pregnant with their daughter. That was a bit of information I hadn't known previously. A former co-worker of Patty's recalled Patty telling her that Bill had "an insatiable appetite for money," and that he often spent it faster than they could earn it.

In the months immediately following Patty's death, people who knew Bill were, as it turns out, alarmed by his spending. He bought a motorcycle, he purchased a new car, and he took on several home improvement projects. After his move to Florida, he continued his pattern of profligate spending. "We tried to counsel him financially," said the pastor at the Columbus-area church he and Patty had attended together. But Matix didn't seem to think he needed any such assistance.

The more I learned about the Matix/Platt crime spree in Florida, the more shocking it seemed. A newspaper article published three days after the shootout indicated that Matix and Platt had been linked to at least two Florida murders, a half dozen bank and armored car robberies, and a couple of other incidents where the duo shot people who ended up surviving.

There was another fact that was of obvious interest. Almost exactly one year after the Riverside murders, Platt's wife died of a shotgun blast to the head. Her death was ruled a suicide. Platt told the police that he'd been in an adjacent room of their house when he heard the shotgun blast that killed her. The police weren't sure they believed his story, but they lacked sufficient evidence to disprove it. (Platt would later suggest to the police that his wife's suicide could have been related to an affair she had—*with Matix.*)

The crimes attributed to Platt and Matix were extraordinarily brazen: broad daylight, lots of witnesses, ski masks and camouflage clothing, and acts of grotesque violence. The authorities investigating the crimes felt certain they were dealing with suspects who had an appetite for extremely high-risk situations.

A woman who rented from Platt described him as "an all-around nice guy [and] an excellent landlord." Platt's brother told a newspaper reporter that Platt was "a smiling, happy guy. No drinking, no drugs, no smoking." Bill Matix's older brother had a different take altogether. To him, Platt had seemed like "a creep." He blamed Platt for dragging Bill into a life of crime.

When the dust finally settled on the Miami-area shootout, there were sharply contrasting depictions of Matix, too. The pastor of the Florida church where he'd been attending prior to his death spoke not just of having recorded Bill's "testimony of his [Christian] belief" but of having heard from members of his congregation that they'd discovered "the light of life" as a result of hearing the story of Bill's faith journey, which included references to his first wife's murder and the emotional challenges he was forced to deal with as a result.

Matix's mother recalled her son as "a shy boy who stuttered." She spoke to a reporter about the "poems of love" he would sometimes compose for his family members. She reported having spent Christmas 1983 with Bill, Patty, and their infant daughter Melissa. According to her, it was a holiday "filled with joy."

Despite these glowing descriptions of Bill the family man, she conceded that she'd been unaware of some pretty important aspects of the life her son led after his move to Florida. For example, she didn't even know that he'd remarried after Patty's murder. Nor did she know—until after his death—that he'd fathered at least one other child besides Melissa, perhaps more than one. The Florida woman who'd given birth to Matix's son described Bill as "a master of deceit and disguise."

To the Florida-based FBI agent who'd pulled up alongside the car Matix was driving on April 11, 1986, Matix appeared to have the look of "an old-time spaghetti-western bad man ... He just looked very, very determined. He wasn't scared. He was a man on a mission."

Matix's stepmother was aghast over the things police were saying about him. "No, no," she insisted, "that could not be" when they informed her of her stepson's involvement in multiple bank and armored car robberies. "He may have gotten killed," she said, "but he wouldn't rob banks. There is something wrong somewhere." She remembered Patty as "a sweet little woman ... [Bill's] world."

•••

So who was Bill Matix? Really?

When I learned that a movie called *In the Line of Duty: The FBI Murders* would be broadcast on television in 1988, I thought that perhaps it would provide a partial answer to that question. Steven Gross, who'd played Alex Keaton's father on the hit TV series, *Family Ties,* was cast as Matix. David Soul was cast as Platt. I was eager to see which version of the killers would be featured in the movie. I was eager, too, to see how explicitly the script would link the murder spree in Florida to Patty's death in Columbus, almost two and a half years earlier.

That said, I knew to expect a Hollywood production. However, I was still hoping that I'd learn some new information about Matix and Platt, the kind that might not have been widely disseminated up to that point. I assumed—rightly, as it turned out—that the people involved in the production of the movie would have had to consult with law enforcement officials, both in Florida and in Ohio.

I probably shouldn't have been surprised, but I was, a little. The movie's Bill Matix bore practically no resemblance at all to the soft-spoken, devout, family-oriented man I'd been led to believe Matix was in the days, weeks, and months after Patty's death. The movie portrayed Matix as callous, abusive, narcissistic, and epically duplicitous.

In one particularly memorable scene, Matix and Platt are shown laughing about a murder they'd committed just minutes before. In a different scene, Matix is depicted at church, offering testimony about his "lovely wife Patty ... so brutally murdered by a robber back in Ohio ... stabbed 16 times. [The robber] slit her throat." He is shown blowing out a candle with a particularly dramatic flourish, then telling his rapt listeners, "You see the way that candle blowed out, leaving me a widower. Small baby girl to look after. Many times I've been tempted by despair, but the Lord wouldn't let me ... I've learned to take the good with the bad. Amen."

Another scene interested me even more than those two did. Months before the Miami shootout, a detective from Ohio shows up at the house Matix is sharing with the woman he'd married not long before. The detective has hopes of perhaps being able to clear up some matters related to the murders at Riverside. When Bill's wife introduces Bill to the detective and explains that the detective is "asking questions about Patty," Matix, sounding cocky and mildly irritated, replies, "Is that so? It's been several years."

When the detective, feigning confusion, asks Matix why he would have taken out several large insurance policies on his former wife, Matix replies, "I wanted security for my daughter." The detective asks why then, if that had been his concern, he wouldn't have taken the policies out on *himself*. Calmly, Matix replies, "I saw things differently."

The detective reminds Matix that he turned down the opportunity to sit for a polygraph examination in Ohio, then adds that the offer remains open if he's willing to accept it. Matix declines. When the detective asks him if he doesn't want to just "put all this behind [him]," Matix explains that he's done that already. What's past is past.

Three of the detective's inquiries pertain to matters that I was hearing about for the first time. He informs Matix of a witness who claims to have seen a letter Matix wrote, discussing how, if Patty were to be killed at work, the killing could be made to look like a robbery. With his new bride seated right alongside him, Matix responds in a voice that sounds at once calm and serene, "As the Lord is my witness, that letter never existed at all."

The detective claims to know for a fact that "immediately" after Patty's death, Matix became involved in an affair with her "best friend." Instead of denying that such an affair took place, Matix insists that during the time that's elapsed since, he's "made [his] peace" with what occurred between him and the other woman.

The detective isn't quite finished. He tells Matix, "She says you raped her." He adds that the woman in question has gone on record claiming that a naked Matix once ambushed her inside her home, then assaulted her. Matix's reply? "She wanted it that way." He goes on to portray himself as the injured party, the one who ended up being taken advantage of: "Her old man wasn't paying much attention to her. She just naturally turned to me. In my grief, I needed love real bad. She saw my weakness."

When Matix is told of a witness who claims that he admitted to killing Patty, or to having someone else do it for him, Matix replies, "I stand before the Lord ... with a clear conscience. And that's good enough for me."

• • •

Patty and Joyce had been dead for the better part of five years when *In the Line of Duty* aired on television. As I'd hoped it would, the movie provided at least partial answers to a few remaining questions I had about Bill Matix. What it didn't do, at least for me, was bring any sort of final resolution to the mystery of what really happened at Riverside. I never felt like I could say, *case closed*. While I was pursuing my PhD and then, later on, when I was practicing as a clinical and forensic psychologist, I kept circling back to the mystery, always certain that there were things about the case I still didn't know.

In 2011, almost 30 years after the murders and 23 years after *In the Line of Duty* aired on television, I decided that I wanted to pursue one last avenue of inquiry. I'd long had a desire to talk to one of the detectives who'd played a major role in investigating the Riverside case. I contacted attorney Mike Miller, a casual friend and professional associate who'd been the Franklin County prosecutor back in 1983, when Patty and Joyce were murdered. Mike put me in touch with homicide detective Dave Morris, who by then had been retired for quite a few years.

It was Morris who took the phone call from the police dispatcher late in the afternoon on Friday, December 30, 1983. The dispatcher told him that a woman's body had been discovered in a pool of blood on the floor of the medical research lab at Riverside Methodist Hospital. (The second body—Joyce's—hadn't yet been discovered.)

Morris also fielded a call on April 11, 1986, from a representative of the Delaware County Sheriff's Department, north of Columbus, informing him of the shootout that had occurred outside Miami. The caller from Delaware County asked him if he knew the name "William Matix." Morris replied, "Yeah, why?" Morris ended up being one of two Columbus police officers who made multiple trips to Miami following the 1986 incident, looking for any evidence that would definitively link Matix and Platt to the murders at Riverside.

To a writer who interviewed Morris before I did, Morris referred to the investigation into the Riverside murders as "the goddamnnest" one of his career. He admitted that the case still haunted him, even after the passage of almost 30 years.

He repeated those same things to me. In fact, he went beyond "haunted" as he sought to convey how the Riverside case had affected him. He admitted that he became "obsessed with" it. For at least seven years after the murders, he returned to the hospital every December 30, "just to walk around and remember those girls." He said he was pretty sure he'd been suffering from "post-traumatic stress" or something similar. When various triggers reminded him of the crime scene he'd witnessed at Riverside, he tended to become agitated and avoidant. He readily conceded that he still sometimes experienced nightmares pertaining to what he'd seen in the medical research lab at the hospital.

He told me some things I'd never heard before.

For example, he said that during the very narrow window of time when the murders must have been committed, there was an off-duty Columbus police officer seated in the radiology department waiting area, just down the hall from the only door that led in and out of the research lab. The officer insisted that he neither saw nor heard anything the least bit unusual during the relevant timeframe.

Morris told me that for a while anyway, he and his fellow officers did, in fact, consider Devi Munjal a suspect. Eventually, however, they were able to rule him out.

He said that senior members of Riverside's administrative team provided little help to the police. According to him, they managed to contaminate the crime scene before the authorities arrived at the hospital. He added that to him anyway, they seemed more concerned with managing the public relations fallout from the murders than with trying to help move the police investigation forward.

One of his disclosures was especially chilling. He said that whoever committed the murders probably killed Patty first, then arranged to have a page sent to Joyce over the hospital intercom system, requesting that she return to the lab from another part of the hospital complex. He thought that in all likelihood, the killer's idea was to use Joyce's murder as a "decoy," that is, a means of making it seem as if the women had been killed together in the course of a botched robbery.

He also said that the police probably would have identified Matix as their prime suspect had budgetary restrictions not prevented them from traveling to Pennsylvania to speak with members of Patty's family. When those interviews finally *were* conducted, in the aftermath of the Miami-area shootout, the family members had little good to say about Bill Matix.

According to Morris, the police heard Michael Platt portrayed very negatively, too. Platt's former sister-in-law spoke disparagingly of him and expressed her belief that he'd almost certainly been responsible for murdering her sister.

Morris told me he'd traveled to Quantico, Virginia and worked with representatives of the FBI's Behavioral Science Unit to help create a "profile" of the Riverside killer. Even after the passage of so many years, he still couldn't figure out how the murderer managed to exit the research lab through the only available door and make his way out of the hospital without calling attention to himself in any way. The regret apparent in his voice, he disclosed that he and the other police officer who traveled to Florida in 1986 never found anything they could use to definitely tie either Matix or Platt to the murders at Riverside.

Morris spent years working the homicide beat in Columbus. He told me that the crime scene at Riverside may have been the bloodiest one he ever saw. Nearly 30 years after seeing it for the first time, he felt certain that either Matix or Platt—he couldn't say which one—was responsible for killing Patty Matix and Joyce McFadden.

• • •

Sometimes, truth really is stranger than fiction.

Years before the Riverside murders, in fact before the thought of becoming a hospital administrator entered my mind, I'd become an obsessive reader of the literature on true crime. One of the books I read—some three years after I'd been introduced to the genre by Ed Sanders' *The Family*, which chronicled the Manson case—was William Allen's *Starkweather: The Story of a Mass Murderer*, published for the first time in 1976.

Allen's book told the story of 19-year-old Charles Starkweather's 1957-58 murder spree, which began in Nebraska and ended in Wyoming. Channeling the look and rebellious attitude made famous by James Dean, Starkweather, accompanied by his 14-year-old girlfriend, Carol Fugate, killed 11 people over a period of two months. It's one of the most notorious spree murder cases in modern American history.

After the December 1983 murders at Riverside, I visited Ohio State's campus, probably sometime during the latter half of 1984, so that I could meet with several faculty members who were affiliated with the Department of Psychology. I was hoping to enlist their support for my tentative plan to be admitted to the university, and to begin work toward my PhD the following year. By the time of my campus visit, I'd made the decision to quit my job at the hospital.

Somehow, I can no longer remember exactly how, I'd become aware that William Allen, author of the book on the Starkweather case, was a faculty member in the Department of English at Ohio State. I figured that since I was on campus anyway, I'd take a stab at trying to meet him. I knew it was a long shot. On the off chance that he'd be in his office that afternoon, I made a special trip to the building that housed the English department.

I located his office without any difficulty. I could scarcely believe my good fortune when I found him there by himself, seated at his desk. A bit sheepishly, I introduced myself, then apologized for showing up at his office without an appointment. I told him how much I'd enjoyed reading his Starkweather book, years before. I didn't have my hardcover copy of the book with me, so I swallowed hard and summoned the nerve to ask him whether he had an extra copy of the paperback version that I could purchase from him and have him sign. He said that he did have an extra copy, then added that sure, he'd be happy to sign it for me.

That's when I realized that I had no cash on me, none whatsoever. Strangely enough, and for reasons I can no longer recall, I *did* have my checkbook. Allen said he'd be fine if I wrote him a check in the amount of $1.75 to cover the cost of the book. That's what I did. On the book's title page, he wrote, "Bill Allen." That was our first and only encounter. It lasted no more than five minutes.

More than 30 years after that meeting, on a day when I

was reviewing my file on the murders at Riverside, I happened upon a reference I'd never seen before. It took me a moment to process it.

In October 1984, ten months after the Riverside murders and about two months before Bill Matix and his daughter left central Ohio and moved to Florida, Matix sold the house north of Columbus that he and Patty had purchased for $59,500 in 1980.

According to the probate court records, the buyer of the house was "Ohio State University professor William Allen."

•••

The Riverside murders are an inflection point in the larger story I mean to tell, about my five decades of encounters with killing and killers. The murders of Patty Matix and Joyce Mc-Fadden revived my interest in events that had occurred years prior. Indirectly, they also created a context that made it possible for me to imagine a future for myself that looked nothing at all like the one I'd been imagining before my co-workers' deaths.

It's strange now to think how things turned out.

Had I not selected hospital administration from the menu of possible career paths that I could have chosen after my return home from Ireland; had I not been selected to serve my residency year at Riverside Methodist Hospital in Columbus; and had I not been assigned administrative responsibility for a small research lab where an unknown assailant killed two of my colleagues, then vanished into thin air, it's highly unlikely I would have become a forensic psychologist.

Probably, I'd have continued to view "the Manson inquiry" as just one among many such chapters in my life, times when I'd directed my attention outward, beyond the boundaries of the world I inherited from my parents, and sent out exploratory probes, hoping that they'd net for me an enhanced understanding of strange, vivid people and the decisions they made about how to live their lives.

In the aftermath of the murders at Riverside, I started

viewing my life through a new lens. My earlier involvement with members of the Manson Family began to look like an apprenticeship of sorts, a precursor to my eventual career in the field of forensic psychology. I was 21 years old when Charles Manson and I exchanged our first letters. That was nearly a half century ago.

Now, for a journey back in time.

2.
The Most Dangerous
Man Alive

In *Cultish*, her 2021 book about the language of fanaticism, Amanda Montell invokes "a nostalgic cool factor" to account for why becoming obsessed with the Manson murder case has acquired a "sort of perversely stylish vintage cache" among members of her generation. "At this point," she writes, "being obsessed with the Manson Family is akin to having an extensive collection of hippie-era vinyl and band tees."

Well, maybe. But it's worth mentioning that Montell wasn't *born* until 1992, more than two decades after the 1969 murder spree that gave rise to Manson's infamy.

To tell my own story, I need to flip the calendar back to 1973. In the words of Lou Reed, those were different times.

In August of that year, about a week after I turned 20, a college buddy and I spent ten days hitchhiking around England and Scotland. We thought of our travels as a kind of prelude to the fall semester of our junior year, which we were planning to spend in Cambridge. On our way south from Scotland, we alighted in England's bucolic Lake District. We reserved part of one day for a stay in quaint and lovely Windermere, just a few miles down the road from Grasmere and Dove Cottage, famous as William Wordsworth's former home. Perhaps no other location is more closely associated with the Romantic movement in English poetry.

I was in the mood for something to read. Inside the Windermere bus depot, on one of those revolving metal book racks, I caught sight of the English paperback edition of Ed Sanders' account of the Manson saga, called *The Family: The Story of Charles Manson's Dune Buggy Attack Battalion*. The book's cover promised "a feast of evil."

At the time, I knew virtually nothing about the notorious crime spree that Manson had set in motion just four years prior. In August 1969, the month of the so-called Tate-LaBianca slayings, I celebrated my sixteenth birthday and began preparations for the fall football season of my junior year in high school. I was oblivious to media coverage of the carnage in Los Angeles. Back then, I never read the newspaper and seldom watched the news on television. For the most part, my world revolved around sports, school, popular music, and my friends. That said, I'd acquired a minor reputation as The Kid Drawn to Strange and Unusual People—roller derby queens, the freaks at the county fair, professional wrestlers, snake handlers, people like that.

Now, four years after the Manson-inspired murders, I found that I couldn't look away from the face on the cover of Sanders' book. Framed by a mane of anarchic black hair, it appeared to be the face of a man with nothing left to lose. The expression was defiant, the eyes dull and baleful. But wait. Was that a tiny *pink flower* on the right lapel of the man's coat?

I bought the book, took it outside, stretched out on the grass, and began reading. In a matter of minutes, I was, as I'd heard the English say, gobsmacked.

What a story!

Almost 50 years later, most people know the basics: Los Angeles, the summer of '69, two nights of murder and mayhem, seven people killed (including pregnant actress Sharon Tate), cryptic messages left behind in the victims' blood, the word "WAR" carved on one victim's abdomen, a band of erstwhile hippies known as "the Manson Family," and a pint-sized, malevolent guru named Charlie.

The tale has been repeated countless times, most famously

in Vincent Bugliosi's and Curt Gentry's *Helter Skelter*, the best-selling true crime book of all time. But to my mind, Sanders' early version remains the grizzliest and most riveting. Sanders, who'd co-founded the experimental rock group The Fugs in 1964, opted for an immersion approach when he accepted an assignment to cover the Manson beat for the *Los Angeles Free Press*. As he himself put it, he sometimes posed as "a satanist, drooling maniac, and dope-tranced psychopath" while in pursuit of his story. It proved a sound strategy. He succeeded where many mainstream journalists failed, unearthing a previously unreported plethora of nightmare-inducing details.

Sanders' narrative offered a portal into a dark, murky world of strange and deeply unsettling occult practices, biker dudes, black market porn, "dumpster diving," homemade snuff films, shady drug deals, apocalyptic warnings, "creepy crawly" home invasions, orgiastic rituals, and acts of almost unimaginable savagery.

I was hooked.

What disturbed me as much as anything was Sanders' casual reference to the fact that more than just a few of the young people who'd fallen under Manson's spell—and who still revered him as a kind of god-like figure—remained free and at large, never having been convicted of a major crime. I'd wrongly assumed, particularly after reading of such epic weirdness and such extreme violence in the pages of Sanders' book, that everyone who'd cast their lot with Manson would surely have ended up in prison.

If that *hadn't* happened, and clearly it hadn't, I asked myself what cues I could rely on to identify Manson Family members if any of them ever decided to cross over from Manson-world into my world. What if no such cues existed? What if the Mansonites would blend in because they looked pretty much the same as everyone else? Of course that possibility was the most terrifying one of all. I couldn't stop thinking about it.

I was an FBI agent's son. And a rule follower, at least most of the time. Oh sure, I'd made my way to the Haight-Ashbury district in San Francisco when my family took our epic road trip to the West Coast in 1967, during the fabled Summer of Love (the evening after our visit to The Haight, my mom recorded this pithy entry in her journal: "frightening and so pathetic to see those weirdos"); and back at home I'd festooned my bedroom with homemade, neon-colored posters, announcing myself as a dedicated follower of musical acts like The Peanut Butter Conspiracy ("It's spreading!"), the Quicksilver Messenger Service, Blue Cheer, and Moby Grape. But I was all of 13 years old. It was tame, pretty bubble-gummy stuff.

Eight years had elapsed since then. But the reality was that I hadn't changed all that much. I was still curious about all kinds of different things—but still pretty much a rule follower. And I was nobody's idea of a real rebel.

For me, Sanders' book had arrived like an urgent dispatch from another world. After reading it, I experienced a vague, as yet unfocused urge to discover an avenue of access—perhaps more than one—to some of the darker corners of the American scene. I wanted to explore that mythical space that cultural commentators were calling "the underground." But I wasn't, and had never been, a damn-the-torpedoes kind of guy. At age 20, I was feeling a familiar tension: between a part of me that craved novelty and adventure, and another part that prioritized personal safety above almost all else. And my default position was to avoid doing things that had the potential to worry or disappoint my parents.

When my semester abroad came to an end, I returned to complete my final three semesters of undergraduate study at Valparaiso University. In 1974, during the fall semester of my senior year, I took a course called Abnormal Psychology. In one of his lectures, my professor mentioned in passing that he'd read *Helter Skelter*, which had been published not long before. I'd read it, too—in a single, caffeine-fueled all-night binge.

After class that day, I stuck around.

My professor and I spent several minutes trading observations about the Manson story and pondering its implications. At one point I remarked that if you were inclined to believe the popular press, you could easily come away thinking that all the young people who comprised Manson's core family of followers had been reduced to one-dimensional robots, virtual automatons who, in thrall to their leader, had all but lost the ability to think and act independently. I asked my professor if he thought the reality might be a bit more complicated than that.

I wasn't expecting what came next.

"Well, you could always write to some of them," he said.

Write to them?

"It might be interesting to learn more about their point of view—and to hear what their voices would sound like on paper," he added.

Never, not once, had the idea of writing letters to members of the Manson Family ever crossed my mind. But later that same day, after I'd returned home to my apartment, I kept circling back to it. Write to them? I decided I'd place the idea on the back burner for a while.

•••

I left it there for several long months—but I found that I couldn't stop thinking about it. At long last, I finally decided that it was time to act on my professor's suggestion. I still wasn't entirely convinced that sending letters to members of a murderous collective like the Manson Family was something that I should be doing. For one thing, I knew that in June 1970, *Rolling Stone* magazine had pronounced Manson "the most dangerous man alive." Hardly a reassuring thought. But every time doubt began to creep into my thinking, I reminded myself that the idea of writing to Manson and his disciples had originated with my professor, the same person who'd taught me the basic concepts of abnormal psychology.

How foolish could it be?

I conducted some research—this was long before the internet—and confirmed that Manson was an inmate at California's notorious Folsom prison, located in the small town of Represa just outside the capital city of Sacramento. In February 1975, I sent him a letter and waited for him to respond. He didn't.

I figured I'd give it one more try. My follow-up letter remains an embarrassment, even though 45 years have elapsed since I wrote it. I'm able to read it not because I kept a copy but because Manson returned the original, with his scrawled response—written in pencil—taking up the lower half of the page, below my typing.

I remember exactly what I was thinking when I sat down to compose that letter. *How can I make Manson want to write me back?* My writing is stilted, my tone excruciatingly earnest. Worse yet, I tried a shamelessly manipulative gambit, hoping it would help me secure Manson's attention.

Like everyone else with even a modicum of knowledge about the background of the Manson case, I knew that Manson was a frustrated musician who'd attempted to ingratiate himself with a number of prominent Los Angeles-area scenesters. People like Dennis Wilson, the drummer for the Beach Boys; Terry Melcher, Doris Day's son and the producer of the Byrds' hit records; and Gregg Jakobson, a songwriter and talent scout who was close friends with the other two. For a period lasting several months, Manson and some of his followers even resided at Wilson's rented house on Sunset Boulevard. Melcher granted Manson multiple auditions. There was a recording session at Brian Wilson's studio.

I thought perhaps I'd be able to coax a response from Manson if I professed an interest in his music and his musical aspirations (as opposed to the grisly details of the murders he'd been sentenced to death for).

Just in case he'd forgotten about my first letter, I reminded him that I'd tried to contact him once before. I addressed him using the familiar "Charlie," then continued, "I wrote to you a few weeks ago and expressed an interest in your songs, particularly your lyrics."

Lying through my teeth, I assured him of my sincerity. In passing, I acknowledged that he might feel some bitterness toward strangers who write to him from outside prison.

I mentioned that I had tried, unsuccessfully, to obtain a copy of the recording of his songs—*Lie: The Love and Terror*

Cult—that his old prison pal Phil Kaufman had produced and released while his murder trial was still in progress.

(Kaufman is a fascinating character in his own right. Then a minor player on the L.A. music scene, he'd acted as the Rolling Stones' chauffeur and assistant during their Beggars Banquet period, which was prior to the Manson murders. Some years later, he would famously incinerate musician Gram Parsons' body in Joshua Tree National Monument and then land a gig as Emmylou Harris's road manager. On August 9, 1969, when news of the Manson-instigated slayings of Sharon Tate and four others first hit the airwaves in L.A., Kaufman was lounging with songwriting wunderkind Jimmy Webb outside Webb's mansion in the San Fernando Valley.)

I told Manson that I'd been trying to get in touch with Squeaky Fromme, one of his earliest and most devoted disciples. That part, at least, was true. Fromme wasn't in custody at the time. (She would achieve her own special brand of infamy about six months down the road.)

"I've attempted to get a letter to Squeaky," I wrote, "figuring that perhaps she'd be able to tell me where I could obtain a copy of [the Kaufman-produced album], but I haven't heard back from her yet." I hoped that maybe he'd be able to tell me how to obtain a copy of the record.

This time, he responded to my letter promptly. And he didn't sound happy.

Apparently, I was one of very few people who'd missed the memo captioned *Don't try to bullshit Charles Manson.* He'd seen right through my manipulative ploy—and he'd seen my guile for what it was.

[As referenced in the Author's Note that appears at the front of my book, here and elsewhere throughout this chapter, I've retained most of Manson's misspellings, syntactical lapses, and grammatical irregularities. They serve my goal of trying to capture Manson's idiosyncratic voice.]

"The album was bullshit," he wrote, "put out to make money. Man I can see you're out of it. Songs and poetry for what?"

Then, the epic dissembler demanded that I come clean and stop lying.

"Be true with me," he wrote. "What do you want from me? I don't know bitterness. I understand truth with no BS. [Here, he drew a line with an arrow from the abbreviation "BS" to the word "bullshit" that he'd spelled out previously—apparently because he considered me a moron.] It's—who are you? What's your trip? & what do you want?"

His scrawled signature appeared at the bottom of the page.

Despite the fact that he'd outed me as a fool and a charlatan, I was encouraged—even excited—by the fact that he'd chosen to respond at all.

I was alert, if dimly, to the troubling implications of my reaction. Briefly, I paused to reflect on the question of why I should care as much as I did that a brutal murderer and remorseless destroyer of countless lives had acknowledged my dishonest, manipulative letter and even responded to it. Self-awareness wasn't my strong suit. In my defense, I was callow and still just 21 years old.

In later years, I would often explain to friends, family members, and professional colleagues that, in truth, I was probably less interested in the psychology of serial and mass murderers than I was in the complicated, in some ways deeply unsettling, dynamics that often play out between killers and members of the majority social audience, many of whom seem to have an insatiable appetite for information about killers' lives and the horrific crimes they commit. Even as far back as 1975, I recognized myself as a member of that latter group. However, I chose not to dwell on the issue or its implications.

For cynical and largely practical reasons—chief among them my belief that if I did what Manson told me to do, there was a greater likelihood of him writing me back—I decided to disclose some personal information, though not much, in my next letter. The first two times I wrote him, I was careful not to tell Manson anything about myself. My thinking? What possible interest would someone like Manson—with his bleak prospects and fifth grade education—have in corresponding with someone preparing to head off to graduate school in the fall? And then, of course, there was this: *Do I want the most dangerous man alive to know even the first thing about me? Especially in light of the fact that he has devoted followers outside prison who can easily track me down if they decide there's a reason to do so?*

In any case, I felt like there had occurred a subtle shift in the dynamics characterizing our relationship, such as it was. Manson had called me out as a phony, demanded to know who I was, and instructed me to tell him the truth about my real reason for writing.

I figured I'd better strike while the iron was hot; I didn't delay responding. In my letter, I explained that I was a senior in college and said I was interested in crime, psychology, and, especially, the way the media had reported on his case. I referenced having read Ed Sanders' book when I was in England in 1973, then added that I'd also read *Helter Skelter*.

I admitted I hadn't been entirely honest when I said I was mainly interested in his song lyrics and music. I told him I was curious about the young people who'd congregated around him and comprised his so-called "family." What intrigued me, I added, was that many of those young people were products of backgrounds not unlike my own. (I realized, if dimly, that I might have been coming across as judgmental—but that didn't deter me.)

Before my letter could have arrived at Folsom prison, Manson wrote to me again. This time, he sent a postcard. Probably, he meant it as a test. Was there some way that I could be useful? Would I follow his instructions?

At the top of the postcard, he wrote the name and address of a woman who lived in Milford, Connecticut. I didn't recognize the woman's name—but I knew I'd heard of Milford. I thought I remembered reading somewhere that former Family member Linda Kasabian had settled in Milford after offering her incredibly damning testimony at Manson's trial. (As it turned out, I was right—and wrong. Kasabian spent much of her childhood in Milford, *New Hampshire,* and it was to New Hampshire, not Connecticut, that she returned following her appearance at the trial.)

Even though Kasabian was present on the night when Sharon Tate and four others were murdered at 10050 Cielo Drive in the Hollywood Hills, she'd been granted immunity in exchange for her willingness to testify against Manson and his co-defendants: Susan Atkins, Patricia Krenwinkle, and Leslie Van Houten.

Directly below the name and address at the top of his postcard, Manson wrote, "It's your job to look into her and why she don't like the family. She wrights judgments & her dog thinks she's got a brain but she keeps comeing to me to git it. And I reached with love & she turned it against me & put it back on us."

My *job*?

I could feel a churning sensation in my stomach. Was Manson really expecting me to conduct an investigation of someone whose name I didn't even recognize? Someone who resided in the eastern part of the United States? Had he and this woman exchanged letters? If so, did that imply the possibility that he could be directing another of his correspondents—someone who wasn't currently in prison—to carry out an investigation of *me*?

If he was, in fact, motivated by a desire to have me investigate this woman from Connecticut, he didn't seem all that concerned about whether I'd do what he was telling me to do. According to him, it was entirely up to me. I could contact her—or not.

"You may see if that's her address or if it's just a front she hides behind & her living in CA," he wrote. "What you see or feel to do with this thought is up to you. But don't sit and ask me what you think I should or should not do. Do you want some more of my troubles & problems or do I stay under it all for you."

● ● ●

The tone and content of Manson's next letter marked a sharp departure. To me, the changes were revelatory. Apparently I'd caught him in a contemplative mood. As I'd come to understand all too well, "contemplative" was hardly Charles Manson's default setting.

He seemed to appreciate the fact that I'd been willing to disclose some personal information about myself. He also seemed to appreciate my honesty about why I'd chosen to write to him in the first place. He still sounded aggrieved, and he still insisted that he'd gotten a raw deal in court. But his words were more measured now—and for the time being anyway, his anger wasn't being directed at me.

He used my first name in the letter's salutation, a slightly jarring note of familiarity. Perhaps because he wanted to make sure he didn't leave me with the mistaken impression that I occupied any sort of special niche in Manson-world, he executed a quick pivot, adding in the letter's first line, "I wright lots of letters and can't keep up with them all."

In my most recent letter, I'd remarked on the sensational media coverage of his case—and at least hinted at my willingness to entertain the possibility that certain aspects of the coverage had painted an inaccurate picture of him and the people who comprised the Family.

"The media is only a cover over the truth as the money sells a picture to the minds of people," he wrote. "Take all you heard of me & think of it as backward. Our side of the family was never told—played over and covered over, shit on & rubbed in—& on & on."

In a long rambling statement that he gave outside the jury's presence at his trial—it was later published as the pamphlet *Your Children*—he'd insisted that the media felt obligated to portray him as a monster because people in America needed a bogeyman to help make them feel better about themselves, and to help them avoid having to face up to the fact that the young people he considered his children were *their* children, too.

"That beast was not me," he continued. "But it's what everyone wants me to be so they make me up to be a reflection of there fears lies & bullshit. I ain't got the time to run it to you on paper with words & they hide me so I can't clean it up."

Clean it up?

That phrase, considered in the context of what I knew, or thought I knew, about Manson and the killings he'd ordered, sounded more than a little ominous. I thought it might be a coded reference to mass murder.

Later, I'd arrive at the realization that what he wrote next was an early version of one of his favorite themes. According to him, the only thing he was "guilty of" was reflecting back at society all the negative thoughts, feelings, and impulses that its citizens were unwilling or unable to acknowledge in themselves.

"I'm the positive holding all the negative reflections of all the sickness madness & evil of your world's confusion," he explained.

Over the course of the next year and a half, he'd make frequent references to his lack of much in the way of formal education. Almost as frequently, he'd write about how difficult it was for him to convey his thoughts and feelings on paper.

"For me to say this with paper words leaves empty words dead in your eyes as you read," he wrote.

Then he returned to the subjects of his image and identity, and to some questions I'd raised about how the media had covered his case.

"You said who are you?" he wrote. (I never asked that question, though he could certainly have inferred my curiosity.)

At this point in his letter, he executed one of his signature maneuvers. He delighted in turning an interviewer's questions back on her, and making it seem like her ostensible effort to learn about him could best be understood as a sign of how reluctant she was to look closely at *herself*. In later years, his jiu-jitsu style of handling interviews would be on extravagant display whenever celebrity questioners—Charlie Rose, Geraldo Rivera, and Diane Sawyer are three who come to mind—tried to coax him into talking about himself and his way of looking at the world.

True to form, he pivoted from the questions I was asking about him to some questions he wanted to ask about *me*.

"Are you what you were told?" he asked. "What about all

that you've not been told?"

He urged me to see the two of us as linked by some sort of special bond.

"You're my kid, my son, my love," he wrote. "You are my reflection stolden and run to the foot of the cross on one end of the world and I'm on the other. They will put you thru all the hell they put me thru & a million heart akes later you wake up in the basement & find the truth is hated hid and kept from the children."

I knew he felt deep contempt for Richard Nixon, who'd famously pronounced him guilty while his trial was still in progress. I knew, too, about his complicated relationships with women, money, and the class structure in American society. His mother was a teenage prostitute and petty criminal; Manson spent most of his formative years living with relatives or in foster homes and juvenile lockups; and during the period in the late-1960s when he was moving in and around the orbit where members of the Hollywood elite lived their privileged lives, he never managed to overcome his sense of being an outsider, one of society's rejects.

"You are Nixson, a reflection of your mom, money," he wrote. "You are everything you see—you are Christ child when left open to be free. Your own self is all—This may sound mad to you—I can't explain on paper. There ain't no one all is one. I'm your eyes your ears & hands."

It seemed like he was trying to pull off a difficult balancing act. On one hand, he encouraged me to feel inextricably bound to him. On the other, he urged me to recognize that I had the freedom to do whatever I wanted to do.

"It's not to know me—To know you is where it's at—You are what's happening—Your world is new—step from your past & be free—all you need is love for you—you—your own center. Sit & be—yourself all—young & free."

Then, sounding a note that I thought seemed vaguely ominous, he added, "Keep my letters to yourself."

While I was reading this most recent letter, I kept thinking to myself, *Where's the wild-eyed killer? And, Maybe this is what a wild-eyed killer really sounds like. Who knows?*

Almost 20 years after Manson wrote me that letter, *Time* magazine's Richard Zoglin offered a provocative assessment after watching a prison interview that Diane Sawyer conducted with Manson for an ABC documentary called *Truth and Lies: The Family Manson.* Referring to the enormous audience for interviews like Sawyer's, Zoglin wrote, "We watch to be reassured these people [like Manson] are monsters, not at all like you and me. And to face the fear that in some basic ways *they are exactly like you and me* [emphasis added]."

I think it's unlikely that Manson ever became a regular reader of *Time* magazine. Still, if he somehow happened upon Zoglin's analysis, I'm certain he experienced a sense of vindication.

Despite the fact that Manson wrote this letter more than four decades before his death in 2017, he reflected, "I'm an old man holding all the bitterness of a million faces. I've learned to be alone—& love my own loneliness & live within my universe & it's all in my soul."

At age 21, I was vulnerable to the appeal of that kind of talk, especially the idea that real freedom is a state of mind, something that can be achieved through mental toughness and a determination not to succumb in the face of physical hardship and bleak prospects.

Not long before, I'd read for the first time *Man's Search for Meaning,* Victor Frankl's account of the mental strategies he'd drawn on to survive the horrors of day-to-day life in Nazi concentration camps. One core element of his message didn't strike me as all that far removed from Manson's claim that he could survive anything, just so long as he remained able to access the "universe" that he contained inside himself.

Even way back then, in 1975, I had enough sense to realize the folly of trying to draw any direct lines of comparison between Charles Manson's thinking and Victor Frankl's. Even so, I found a certain appeal in Manson's steadfast refusal to be defined by his status as a captive.

As I was thinking about what Manson had written, I was reminded of an anecdote that has usually been associated with Manson's old buddy from prison, Phil Kaufman. In Kaufman's telling of the story, a guard at Terminal Island, a federal lock-up near Los Angeles, once taunted Manson by telling him that he was never going to get out. Manson looked up at the guard and asked, "Get out of *where*?"

In the next part of his letter, Manson sounded like he was offering me a pathway to the same kind of stoicism and self-reliance that he said had allowed him to survive the horrific conditions of his own life. I recognized his message as a slightly retooled version of the one he'd used to recruit—and exert power over—the young people who'd become members of the Manson Family.

I remembered that when he first happened upon young Lynette Fromme, who was then seated by herself on a bench or curb near Venice Beach, he told her that people around the Haight-Ashbury district in San Francisco had taken to calling him The Gardener, ostensibly because he "tended the young flowers" that he encountered on the streets there.

"Clean all thoughts of past out of your mind," he told me, "& start a garden wherever you walk. You'll always have food & you don't never need anyone's thoughts but your own. Be reborn as your own mom dad god & all and walk around—and never let nothing enter you as doubts or negative."

I knew from reading *The Family* and *Helter Skelter* that when Manson was in prison with all kinds of time on his hands, he'd been exposed to a wide assortment of personal empowerment-type messages and strategies, derived from the teachings of self-help gurus like L. Ron Hubbard, Eric Berne, and Dale Carnegie.

Now, I felt like he was aiming some of those messages at me. *Step from your past and be free. Start a garden wherever you walk. Be reborn. Embrace the power of your own thoughts. Turn away from anyone who claims to have authority over you. Purge all doubts from your mind.*

Vaguely, I was aware of being manipulated. Even so, I was young, naïve, pleased to have secured Manson's attention, and vulnerable to the appeal of the kinds of messages he was sending. They brought to mind certain of the more appealing planks of the basic hippie platform.

Sounding a little like a parent trying to prepare his child for independent living out in the wide world, Manson closed his letter with a command of sorts, then added a few rhetorical flourishes that, taken together, amounted to a kind of peroration.

"Don't write me until you've done this," he wrote. "And when you have done what I told you there will be no need to wright at all. You are—nothing—& the inbetween are just eyes to experience the existence of being. I can't wright it—I could tell you but them are just words & you are behind all words. You are the new world. Easy. Charles Manson."

I was *nothing*? Yet at the same time, *the new world*? And what was Manson trying to say when he wrote of "the inbetween" as "just eyes to experience the existence of being?" Was it true that I *was behind all words*? And if so, what did that even mean?

I was at a loss—but still, I thought that what Manson had written sounded almost inspirational in a nebulous, non-specific kind of way. To repeat, I wasn't yet 22 years old.

When I first began corresponding with Manson, I was eager to find out whether the voice in his letters would correspond to the voice I associated with the diabolical killer he'd been portrayed as in the popular press. In my naive and startlingly oversimplistic way of looking at things, I reasoned that if it *didn't*, then I'd be forced to grapple with the possibility that Manson was a more complicated, more multi-dimensional person than I'd thought him to be.

This last letter, which of course he'd written only after first denouncing me as a phony, made me wonder if perhaps he was something more than the "beast" he'd been made out to be. When I had no choice except to reckon with the fact that he'd seen right through my own clumsy attempt at deception, my sense that perhaps I'd done something "wrong" had a chastening effect. In any event, Manson's rebuke left me feeling a bit less smug—and a whole lot less virtuous—than I felt when I sent off my first letter to Folsom prison.

• • •

I decided to write Manson back, despite the fact that he'd insisted no further correspondence between us would be necessary, just so long as I did what he instructed me to do.

Perhaps it's a blessing in disguise that I didn't keep copies of my own letters; I'm sure they wouldn't have aged well. The single exception is the second of those letters—and I have the original of that one only because Manson returned it to me, with his scrawled response appearing on the lower part of the page. Back then, almost 50 years ago, the thought never even occurred to me that someday I might want to write about our correspondence. To the best of my recollection, I wrote Manson about 12 times between April 1975 and October of the following year.

The tone of Manson's letters fluctuated wildly, depending on his mood and his ever-changing attitude toward me. Sometimes, he would hit me up—or try—for money and other kinds of material assistance. In one letter that stands out from all the rest, he raged at me, attacked my mother using extravagantly profane language, and signed off with a flourish by demanding that I stop writing to him altogether.

Days later, he wrote me to apologize—sort of. In that letter, he acknowledged that perhaps he'd been wrong to attack me and my family. He also indicated his openness to resuming our correspondence. There were frequent occasions when his letters were so off the wall and disjointed that I found it all but impossible to follow his train of thought, or to determine how he felt about me and our relationship, such as it was.

He had good days and bad days. Given his circumstances, that came as no particular surprise. He was facing a lifetime in prison—not just prison but a dizzying succession of maximum-security lock-ups, located in godforsaken places scattered throughout the state of California. Even though our correspondence lasted for only a year and a half, he mailed his letters from three different institutions: Folsom, San Quentin, and Vacaville Medical Facility. His frequent transfers were due, at least in part, to prison officials' concern that if he became too familiar with the routines and security-related protocols at any one of those institutions, he could conceivably hatch a plan to escape. For obvious reasons, he was considered a high-risk inmate. *The most dangerous man alive.*

In late June 1975, he sent me two postcards, both of them postmarked the 26th. By then, I'd graduated from college and returned home to live with my parents in North Tonawanda, New York. That summer, I got a job as a substitute mail carrier. In the fall, I would begin work toward my master's degree in English at Purdue University.

My parents, especially my dad, who was still with the FBI, were remarkably tolerant. They knew—because I'd told them—that I was corresponding with Manson and a couple of his most devoted disciples. At least they were spared the indignity of ever having to reach into their mailbox and retrieve an envelope bearing the name and return address of one of America's most reviled killers. That's because I always went out of my way to intercept the letters in the morning at the post office, before they could be delivered to our address on Sun Valley Drive.

I remember frequent moments of levity at the post office that summer. I was friendly with the carrier who delivered mail to my parents' address. Soon after I started work that summer, I asked him to be on the lookout for letters addressed to me from the likes of Charles Manson, Squeaky Fromme, Sandy Good—and possibly other members of the Manson Family, too. He rolled his eyes. But otherwise, he appeared to take the news in stride. All that summer, whenever he'd come across an envelope bearing the return address of Manson or some other member of the Manson Family, he yelled loudly, loudly enough so that everyone in the post office could hear him, "*Smalldon!* Get over here! I've got a *hot one* for ya!" It wasn't long before all the carriers and clerks knew my business.

It's not like I was hiding any of this from my parents. I wasn't. Whenever I received a letter from Manson or one of the others, I almost always read it to my mom as soon as I got home from work.

Fortunately, my dad was seldom present for those recitations. He'd usually be away at work until the early evening hours. Looking back, I think his absence probably made it easier for my mom to cope with the situation. I have no doubt whatsoever that the two of them shared the belief that my correspondences with Manson and the others were ill-advised, perhaps even dangerous. Most of the time, I'd wait until later in the evening to update my dad on the latest Manson-related news. To his and my mom's credit (I think), they never once tried to talk me out of doing what I was doing—even though I know they found it unsettling to think that some of my correspondents were writing to me *from outside prison*.

As it turned out, the two postcards that Manson sent to me in late June convinced me to take a course of action that would result Manson flying into a fit of blind rage. I never would have predicted that response. The first of his postcards read:

> *To regain soul just git back all that's been put over it—To regain your will just git it back under what you believe in. Wright just what you want to know from me. What you want from me & what you got & what you will give me. I ask all because I'm not in the spot to tell.* **Send pictures for my photo album** *[emphasis added]—also words of what you're doing for me in the world I love. Out here anyone who cuts trees are in trouble trees and wildlife are in my family & I'm trying to save my family. Be good to you & I'm always there in that.*

I thought that perhaps the second of the two postcards was meant for someone other than me. Another of his correspondents? After all, it's not as if Manson employed an office staff to help manage his affairs. In any case, he began in a way that made it seem like he thought he and I were participants in an ongoing conversation that I had no memory of ever being a part of.

> *On the money thing—Money is only as good as the person dealing it. Some are dealt by money when they should deal money. I don't let it use me. Who backs the money—Why*

*did you want me to fix something. By the way how much do
we have left to work with. Like I put what few dollars I have
in places then I send thoughts to back the dollars I send.
Anyway what's your play on the money—Let me know as
you see to. I don't see that well.*

I had no idea what he was talking about. However, in
these two short passages—and in some things he'd said previously—he was sounding a theme that I knew he viewed as
important. My willingness to provide him with money and
other kinds of material support was going to be an important
consideration going forward. If, that is, we were going to go
forward at all.

In a third postcard, this one postmarked July 10, he again
pressed me for an answer to the question of why I'd chosen to
write him: "What do you want? What do you want from me?
Give, take, what is it?"

As best I could tell, he viewed our relationship in strictly
transactional terms. *What was my agenda, and what was in it for
him? What did I want, and what was I willing to give?*

In truth, I didn't *have* an agenda, at least not one that went
much beyond my interest in trying to figure out some things
about his personality, and about his way of perceiving the
world. When he asked me, "Give, take, what is it?" I thought
to myself, *Well, a little of both. Me sharing my point of view about
some things and you sharing yours.* From my perspective, it was
really that simple. I'd decided to reach out to him because I
wanted to get a sense of what he was like as a person. And
because I wanted to try to figure out if there was a part of him
that I could relate to—despite media depictions of him as the
embodiment of pure evil.

Manson continued, "So you want to teach me something—The blades of grass are worth when you [underlined]
keep a person 30 years in a cage & won't let him look at the
grass as you count your money—your self sits at the bottom of
your ignorances. What more do you want of my blood mag-
got. If you're doing nothing then don't wright this BS."

He seemed fixated on the idea of a loyalty test. He wanted

to see evidence of my willingness to *do something*—for him, for The Family, or at least for the "environment," which he often referred to using the acronym ATWA (air, trees, water, animals). I was feeling increasingly apprehensive, mainly because of how quickly he could pivot from his feelings of generalized aggrievement to his more specific belief that by "doing nothing" to help him, I was making myself complicit in the campaign to "keep [him] down."

Next, he sent me one of his shorter letters. It arrived during the second week in July. Again, he'd written to me using my parents' address. I hadn't revealed to him that I was at home, living with my family, so he had no way of knowing that. All he knew was that I'd moved from Indiana to New York, and that I was spending my summer there. Turns out, he'd moved, too. No longer at Folsom prison, he was now writing from San Quentin.

He began his letter with a gently mocking salutation: "Smalldon Big don."

Students of the Manson case know that Manson was always playing games with other people's names. He assigned nicknames to almost everyone in his orbit. It was one method through which he was able to draw people away from their families of origin and encourage them to adopt new identities. Perhaps equally important, it helped foster an atmosphere of playfulness and fantasy, the kind that made it seem fun for everyone to try on a variety of different roles.

After signing in with the pun on my last name, he quickly dispensed with the lighthearted tone, accused me of deception, and suggested that I was holding out on him.

"I think you're lieing," he wrote. "I think you got money & could give me some for bail for my family."

Bail for his family?

I hadn't told him even the first thing about my financial situation—and of course I hadn't so much as hinted at a willingness to put up bail money for anyone. I had no idea what he was talking about. Once again, the thought occurred to me that perhaps he was confusing me with someone else. (The one thing I *had* offered to do was buy him some postage stamps.

However, he hadn't taken me up on that offer—yet.) In any event, he ended his note with the verbal equivalent of a shrug: "I'm not gona right much cause there ain't that much to say anyway. BE and Easy. CM."

Not much time elapsed before he sent me another postcard. I sensed from reading it that he was becoming increasingly impatient, and increasingly angry. He was still looking for tangible evidence of my commitment to helping him. More specifically, of my willingness to provide him with money and other kinds of material support.

"As you try to slow down & take care of trees & such if you fall asleep on the grave where you hide what you ust to call love—Send me about 50 or 100 stamped envelopes—and *don't write me no words or speak words* [emphasis added] until you know something to wright or say & if you can't come here & I'll bust you in the eye to show you where you hide your earth balance."

I was young, credulous, and ignorant. That said, I knew enough to feel queasy as a result of his reference to me falling asleep "on the grave" where I allegedly hid something I "ust to call love." It didn't help to have him say that he'd like to "bust [me] in the eye," ostensibly to make some sort of obscure point about "earth balance."

He continued, "I got to keep dieing for a world I ain't even permitted to look at. You got no soul dumie. Your last letter was like a 75 year old woman wrote it teaching a mindless fool who is his child's mother. You are a dumie. *Send me pictures* [emphasis added]. I told you that once on this card, do it."

At the bottom of this postcard, he drew the number 8, then added a downward-pointing arrow. I didn't have the slightest clue what either of those things meant.

Unfortunately, I found myself having to reckon with the reality that he'd denounced me as a "dumie," not once but twice. His patience was wearing thin. I had no interest in provoking him further, but I was in no position to comply with his demand that I send him "50 or 100" stamped envelopes. I worried that my failure to comply with his instructions was going to make him even angrier than he already was. Hoping to mollify him, I decided I would focus on the "send me pictures" part of his message. His tone had become increasingly strident. He'd ordered me to "do it."

In one of his earlier postcards, he'd told me to send him pictures for his "photo album." He hadn't been any more specific than that. In the time that had elapsed since, I'd been trying to figure out what kinds of pictures he might enjoy seeing. In retrospect, I can see that what he was after were pictures of *me*. He never said so explicitly, though, and I failed to grasp the essence of his demand. To my way of thinking, he was urging me to send pictures instead of "paper words" because his semi-illiteracy made it difficult for him to communicate in writing.

One day I happened upon a *National Geographic* article about the search for the world's oldest person. Included in the article was a picture that reminded me of Manson's demand. I knew that Manson had long defined himself as an outsider—abandoned by his parents, rejected by mainstream society, and forced to get by on his wits. Of late, his messaging about the importance of the environment and "earth balance" had often been couched in terms of his disdain for the company of other people.

The picture that caught my attention depicted an ancient shepherd from somewhere in South America. The shepherd was shown on a stool, playing a flute made of wood. A dog slumbered on the floor next to him. I thought the picture hinted at a more pastoral alternative to the fast-paced, acquisitive way of life that often passed for normal in America. Manson claimed to loathe the lifestyle to which most Americans aspired, ostensibly because of its oppressive laws, crass materialism, and rank hypocrisy.

I cut the picture out of the magazine, placed it in an envelope, and mailed the envelope to Manson at San Quentin. I put nothing else inside, not even a Post-it note explaining where I'd seen the picture or why I'd elected to send it.

At the time, the thought never crossed my mind that the picture would cause Manson to become apoplectic. Why in the world would it? But it did.

Perhaps it seemed to Manson like I was mocking him. Why hadn't I done what he wanted me to do? Send him a snapshot of myself? He still had no idea what I looked like. Not once but twice, he'd told me he was convinced I was a woman "writing … under a man's name." If that *wasn't* the case, why did I write in such neat cursive? Perhaps he'd been expecting me to send him a picture that would solve the riddle of my identity once and for all. What's clear is that I misread the situation—with results that shocked me.

•••

Less than a week after I mailed Manson the picture of the flute-playing shepherd, he sent what to this day remains the only air mail letter I've ever received from an inmate in a maximum-security prison. *Any* kind of prison. Before I'd even opened the envelope, I noticed the red stamp in the upper right-hand corner. What did it mean? Was it a sign of urgency? Or was its sole significance the fact that it was the only stamp Manson had at his disposal on the day he composed the letter that was inside the envelope? I had no way of knowing the answers to these questions—but regardless, I was eager to see what he had to say.

Apparently, he'd decided that if I was going to send him a picture cut out from a magazine, he was going to respond in kind. The picture he sent me looked like it, too, could have come from the pages of *National Geographic*. It showed a mule, with an enormous burden of cargo piled on top of its back. Using a pencil, Manson had drawn a half-circle extending upward from the cargo. Then, he'd added lines to make the half-circle look like it was part of a globe.

Immediately, I recognized the picture as a graphic representation of one of Manson's most frequently reiterated themes: I'm being forced to bear the burden of your entire world, all the sickness, madness, and evil that you and everyone else in society project onto me because you're afraid to acknowledge its existence inside yourselves.

I glanced at the picture, understood what it signified, and

then shifted my attention to the letter itself. It didn't take me long to identify the writer as Manson at his most unhinged.

"Dear Don," it began. (It was the first time Manson had used that truncated form of my last name as a salutation.) Niceties out of the way, Manson launched into an extended diatribe.

"Forgive me if I made the mistake of thinking you had any man or soul," he began. "I never realy realized how much a fake & phony you are. I thought you were helping me as your self. Ask me what I'm gona do you asshole—What have you done—you leave me under all this madness with it all on my back & then expect me to carry it."

There it was, just in case I'd missed it: the message his doctored picture was intended to convey. From Manson's perspective, *he* was the victim, *he* was the one being forced to bear up under the crushing burden of society's "madness."

I'd known because of some other things he'd written that he was getting angrier and more impatient as a result of my unwillingness to provide him with the material support he'd been demanding (e.g., stamped envelopes, bail money for his associates, and so on). I'd been aware, too, that he was becoming agitated because of my refusal to comply with his demand that I become more actively involved in his campaign to work toward "earth balance" (whatever *that* was).

Now, it seemed, he'd just about had it.

"You sit on your … ass waiting for someone to help you & run your dog shit back on me," he raged.

Of course, I had no idea what "dog shit" he was referring to. And no idea what had caused him to conclude that I was waiting for someone to "help [me]"? *Help me with what?*

"What do you want me to do that you ain't got the guts to do," he thundered. "I can't brake walls down & walk through your machine guns—You gave me no support in court—left me without a voice kept me blind & done nothing but run your mouth with week ass punk shit & what do you expect you done nothing & left your family to die alone. Fuck you."

When did *his* family become *my* family?

Had I written something that made him think I wanted

to become a member of the Manson Family? Not so far as I knew. And what was the "week ass punk shit" I'd allegedly been spewing? No clue.

I was hardly in a position to challenge his claim that I'd given him no support when he was on trial for murder. But I knew for certain I'd never said anything to suggest that I thought he could break down walls or walk through machine guns, mine or anyone else's.

At what point had his feelings of powerlessness become *my* responsibility? As I reflected on Manson's words and tried to figure out what could have triggered them, I kept having to remind myself that all I'd done since my receipt of his anodyne last letter was send him that single picture, the one I'd clipped from an issue of *National Geographic*. I'd thought the picture was something he'd like. I'd misread my audience of one. Manson continued:

> *I'm one little ass hole serving you in places you're to dumb to even know & what the dam hell have you done for your family—nothing—you will stand before it one day & if you can stand with 10% of what I've been carrying for you without falling on your face—or will you run that back on your servent because you got NO love. Drove my chevy to the levey but the levey was dry. The people would give no love.*

There it was again: somehow, his family had become my family. Boundaries were getting blurrier. Maybe that was the point. Especially unnerving was his suggestion that I'd be held accountable someday for my failure to provide him with the kind of assistance he'd been demanding of me.

Was he threatening me with harm? It felt that way. And what was I supposed to make of his choice to include the well-known lyrics from Don McLean's "American Pie"? Surely it hadn't come as a surprise to him when "the people"—all the members of mainstream society—showed him no "love" when he was standing trial for the murders of Sharon Tate and six other people. But for whatever reason, he was downright livid. And he was just getting started.

I hold your nuclear mind & the buttons to all your atom bombs. Thoughts for earth balance and scared fools runing at me—a lot of people want to destroy & other assholes like your self leave it up to someone els to do it for you. 29 years in a cage for your moms BS. BS=Bull Shit. I'm not good enough to fuck, see the sky, walk on grass, or be around my own children or give my sons there soul back. [Here he paused for a brief meditation on the idea of my mother performing oral sex on dogs.] Your mother runs it up my ass because you hold me down with your love for a dollar or your confused minds—I'm a 110 lb asshole who made the mistake of thinking there was some love outside myself— you sit on your dad and let your mom play the one with her ass & you git on a dick your self & she keeps my balls in a baby cribb & you keep it in an old man.

If handwriting could kill, I'd have been dead. By this point he was literally slashing across the paper with his pencil, evidently composing his letter in a white-hot fury. And he still wasn't done.

I remain a fool dieing for you and you are your mom—a 8 year old got more sense & your man can die on the cross for years & years—you sit back & let them put all that lieing BS on us in LA & gave no help at all. I got 17 dollars for defense fund—I've carryed me & family through more madness than your brain could hold & if I ever git out don't come to ride with me cause you showed no faith or love for your own soul dieing for your past mistakes. I didn't like your picture or your letters **don't wright me** *[emphasis added].*

Frankly, I was dumbfounded by the intensity of his rage. Maybe I shouldn't have been, but I was. It caught me off guard and unnerved me. I'd thought I was doing the safe thing by following his directions and sending him a picture instead of more "paper words." I didn't understand what had made him so angry.

Following my receipt of his letter, I could feel my anxiety becoming more and more intense. It didn't help that I'd also been corresponding with Lynette "Squeaky" Fromme and her roommate, fellow Manson devotee Sandra Good. Along with a third woman named Susan Murphy, they were residing in an attic apartment in downtown Sacramento not far from Folsom prison. I knew that Fromme, Good, and Manson were in regular contact. Of late, the women had been demanding that I take specific actions on their behalf, ostensibly to restore "earth balance," and to save the environment from would-be polluters.

As Manson's anger was escalating, theirs seemed to be escalating, too. I knew that if Fromme and Good decided there was a reason, they could always leave California and travel elsewhere in the United States—western New York, for example, where my parents lived, and where I was biding my time until the start of graduate school in the fall. None of the three women—Fromme, Good, and Murphy—had yet been convicted of a serious crime, and it was clear from the letters Squeaky and Sandy had written me that they still regarded Manson as the one person on earth who was strong and powerful and righteous enough to ward off (or effectuate?) the looming apocalypse. For obvious reasons, their fanaticism freaked me out.

Other things were contributing to my anxiety, too. One was Manson's glancing reference to the possibility that he could get released from prison at some point down the road. Another was his menacing declaration that I shouldn't expect to "ride with [him]" in the event of his release (or escape?). Of course I hadn't forgotten his fantasy of someday finding himself in a position where he'd be able to "bust [me] in the eye." Most ominous of all was his insistence that at some unspecified point in the future, I'd be held accountable for my failings.

I decided it was time to end this experiment. Perhaps for too long, I'd been tempting fate at the margins of Manson-world, a place of danger, desperation, and extreme weirdness. Now, Manson had stated his position in clear, unequivocal terms: he didn't like me, he didn't like my letters, he didn't like the picture I sent him, and he didn't want to hear from me ever again. Fine. As far as I was concerned, that was it, the end of our correspondence.

Except it wasn't.

• • •

I had no reason to expect any more letters from Manson. Actually, I was clinging to the hope that he'd forget about me and leave me alone.

That isn't what happened. Three days after he'd launched the [airmail] attack that I'd begun referring to as "the hate letter," he wrote me again. This time, he wasn't reacting to anything I'd said or done. I'd chosen not to write him back. The truth is, I was frightened by his rage.

After he'd composed the hate letter and sent it off to my parents' address, he apparently paused to reflect on some of the things he'd said—and, or so it seemed, to wonder whether perhaps he'd been out of line. Even back then, I recognized this second-guessing on Manson's part as the highly unusual phenomenon it was. Manson was hardly the kind of person prone to episodes of self-doubt. Nor was he the kind to admit that he might have been wrong about something. So I was surprised when I began reading what he'd written.

> *I been thinking about that picture you sent—I don't know if to like it or not—I got some of the family outside that wright me letters saying the other friends are not & everyone keeps playing ping pong with me & I can't see if I'm comeing or going—people ant showed no mursy & I sometimes reflect mean & mad.*

This was a different Manson—or so it seemed. A more pensive, more vulnerable-seeming version. For the moment anyway, he seemed willing to concede that he'd been feeling confused, distrustful, disoriented, and helpless. Maybe he liked my picture, maybe he didn't; maybe his "other friends" were real friends, maybe they weren't; maybe I deserved his scorn, maybe I didn't.

I remember feeling some sort of obscure satisfaction. I suppose it stemmed from my sense that maybe I was being afforded a rare glimpse into Manson's inner world. He was frustrated because it seemed to him as if other people were always "playing ping pong" with his life. He no longer knew whom he could trust. Behind his bravado, he recognized that he was the badly damaged product of a hardscrabble and chaotic personal history. He was willing to admit that sometimes his anger got the better of him. Shockingly, there were even small hints of contrition and regret. He continued:

> *If I reflected wrong at you or on you It's your job to understand that no one's been easy on me & I'm not a easy person to git along with. Everyones useing me for something & it all looks like a play over the play over just to keep me in a cage. 3 years I ant been aloud to walk see the sun grass or anything & I BROKE NO LAW—5 more years on top of 22 for you sorry bastards. I don't mean you personally your hole thing rides on my back so you all can play. Yous only see a little of what I'm under each thought I'm sacrified to & for.*

As Manson saw it, it was my responsibility to acknowledge what a hard life he'd had, and to cut him some slack. He needed me to understand that his beef was with society writ large, not with me personally. Perhaps he'd been wrong to single me out for criticism. Either way, he was no closer to giving up his belief that he'd been treated unfairly. As he often did, he insisted that he himself had broken no laws and should never have been prosecuted for the Tate-LaBianca murders in the first place.

He described his predicament as an artifact of rampant hypocrisy on the parts of people all around the world: "Nixon & ford change seats or goes for a visit to Germany or Russha or the pope shakes hands with Kissinger. Dummies got no minds at all & I got to hold it all up backwards & in reverse." (In just a few short months, Squeaky Fromme would remind everyone of the danger implicit in Manson's tendency to view Nixon and Ford as interchangeable "dummies.")

He believed that most Americans had zero interest in acknowledging his humanity or trying to comprehend all the hardships he'd had to endure. Instead, they seemed determined to make him into something he insisted he wasn't: a monster, a bogeyman, the most dangerous man alive, a repository for all their "fears, lies, and bullshit."

"That beast was not me."

Terrified by what they'd have to confront if they did the hard work of looking closely at themselves, they'd done the easy thing and converted him into a totemic representation — of "mom" if they hated women, and of "dad" if they hated men. He continued:

> *Sad part is its gona hit the working people bad — on one end of this mess I'm one thing & all the blame is put on me for what everyones not sure of & the DAs case & on the other end the other way. I'm mom on one end where everyone hates woman & on the other end I'm dad for everyone who hates man & I'm just here being pushed through dead ilusions & ceral games for everyone [to] justify there lies & BS. It's all with out a brain & it's all been put on me & run through my mind to where there is nothing left — you assholes are cutting my head off one way on a lot of levels & my nuts off in the other way.*

In his own artless way, he seemed to be asking, *Don't people realize that by turning me into a symbol of everything they fear, they're really putting themselves on trial? Don't they understand that when all's said and done, they're revealing themselves to be guilty of the same crimes they're accusing me of? Why do I have to serve as a stand-in for the evil lurking inside everyone else? Can't people see that I'm nothing more than an uneducated bumpkin, a "fool" who never even committed the crimes he was convicted of committing?*

"You dum mother fuckers don't realize it's your own reflections & your own soul your own love trust faith," he groused. "Showing your selves what you realy are & every-ones fighting themselves to keep one little sorry unschooled fool locked up for NOTHING!"

He added a postscript: "P.S. The more I think on your picture the more I like it. I ain't got it straight. Does that mean I'll get out when I'm that old & that everyone plays all the rest of my life for BS?" I assumed it was a rhetorical question.

•••

I dithered, uncertain whether responding to this most recent letter was a good idea or a bad one. The "hate letter" had convinced me that the most prudent (read, "least dangerous") course of action was to stop writing Manson altogether. In fact, Manson himself had demanded that I stop. Now, however, he'd left the door ajar—and invited me to walk through it.

I accepted the invitation, not at all sure I was making the right decision. In the next letter I wrote Manson, I tried to make it seem as if I regarded his fit of rage as no big deal.

He responded with one of the longest letters he ever wrote me. It arrived in August 1975, about a month before I was due to begin my graduate studies at Purdue—and, as it turned out, less than a month before Squeaky Fromme's September 5 attempt to assassinate President Gerald Ford.

Most of his letter was written in blue ink. However, I immediately noticed that he'd used black ink for some of it. The part in black was arranged in a circular pattern around the edge of the letter's first page, giving it the appearance of an add-on, like something Manson might have written after he'd finished composing the rest of the letter.

The black part read, "Your letter has rang a lot of thoughts in my brains phone and since I wrote this I've changed my mind about things I'm beginning to wake up to. I admit I'm a dumie & slow to see the wrightings because I'm so dam mad—at everyone man woman & my own dumb self for gitting in a trap for love that was over to start with. I'll send this anyway but other letters have come to create new thoughts & I'm beginning to see a little."

As I had been when I received Manson's first proper letter, the one in which he'd declared, "That beast was not me," I was struck by his thoughtful, almost contemplative-sounding tone. Typically, he didn't devote much time or energy to the project of considering the validity of his own thoughts and opinions. I wasn't accustomed to him using phrases like "changed my mind about," "beginning to wake up to," and "beginning to see a little."

He seemed open, at least for the moment, to competing points of view—maybe even to the possibility that he'd misjudged some things. I sensed that his thoughts and feelings were in flux. Just a month ago, he was raging at me. Then he offered a half-hearted apology and suggested that perhaps he'd been wrong to make me the target of his rage. Now this. I thought, *Is something unusual going on? Is there a reason why he's questioning himself? Maybe a reason that I know absolutely nothing about?*

"JS." That's how he addressed me in this most recent letter. He'd never before used my initials as a salutation. In the unlikely event that I'd forgotten how little significance he attached to me and our correspondence, he was quick with a reminder: "I've got so much mail & I've been down 6 years & there is no way I could know all the BS games played over me. I know it's all played to keep me here cutting off my balls."

A little farther down on the page, he continued, "I forget what I wrote to you—I only reflected the paper words on paper & the feelings I had on that day—I can't git back involved with the human people emotions & hangup games … All I ever wanted to do is be left alone in my own will to be what ever I wanted without people hanging on me."

Indirectly, he referenced an observation I'd made about the sharp contrast between the tone of his last two letters: "I don't think your fucked up or not fucked up—How in the dam hell could I know what you are or are not—and you say 'at least as far as I'm concerned' & thats the only reality you can know—Man where is your brain and what could I know about you at all. I got no reality in anything at all outside my own self."

In those days, I had only the most superficial understanding of psychology in general and personality disorders in particular—but I knew what the word "narcissism" meant. Manson's insistence that he recognized no reality outside himself struck me as a classic example of the narcissist's point of view. He wanted it understood that he had no interest whatsoever in me as a person, or in the details of my personal life—where I was living, how I spent my time, what I was interested in, whom my friends were, any of that.

> *I'm held in a bullshit illusion of a bunch of empty headed people who pray to death & fear $ mony holds me here—& the powerless people trying to git some over some one els they can't understand—I don't care about you going to NY or your friends. I'm 29 years in a cage so you can wright and tell me about how you live your lives over my grave.*

I detected an undercurrent of desperation. Desperation stemming from his desire to be released; desperation stemming from his recognition that he'd never be afforded the opportunity to start his life over again, with something resembling a clean slate; and desperation stemming from his determination to break free of other people's efforts to define who he was as a person.

> *I want out of prison & left alone—I owe no one nothing—I didn't brake the law—Alive or dead thats gona come out. 29 years in cages for nothing. I'm not gona play goodie games—I'm mean & never pretended to be a good guy ... I don't even remember the picture you sent—If you sorry bastards gona kill me for your fears then do it & thats the end of any chance you got for a git back—if not let me go cause the longer you keep me the worse it's gona git—I'm covered with blood in your karmas balance as it is now. I won't get mad at you cause there is no way you could know but what your leaders tell you & they always git there thoughts from 2-faced snitches anyway—Your letters sound like a woman*

wrighting me under a mans name ... The truth is comeing awake all over the world so best git ust to it.

On one portion of the last page of his letter, he again used black ink instead of blue. It appeared as though he'd done so because he intended the final section of his letter, framed as a postscript, to be read as a continuation of what he'd written around the edges of the letter's first page ("I was doing a P.S. on the front and forgot about this space," he explained).

After first referencing a woman on the outside who'd written to him and seemed "confused," he said he'd been forced to conclude that maybe women as a group were fundamentally incapable of being educated. He added, "I'm begining to see you man." Then, seemingly out of nowhere, he inquired about whether I'd ever been to "Seven Steeples [smiley face]." I had to look it up because I had no idea what Seven Steeples was or where it was located.

Later, I learned that Seven Steeples was a sobriquet given to the women's unit of a large psychiatric hospital that was once located in Indianapolis (a city where Manson spent time when he was around 14 years of age).

He ended his long letter this way: "I didn't mean to be a smart ass. I'm sick & tired of this mess dumped on me—your servant in [on the page he drew a swastika, the same symbol he'd carved into his forehead when he was on trial in Los Angeles] & the family that is on their jobs. If you want me to right send me envelops & so far you as me & we as you in [swastika] in one will."

• • •

Less than a month after my receipt of that letter, Manson's ardent disciple and indefatigable cheerleader, Squeaky Fromme, attempted to assassinate President Ford. All of a sudden, Manson was back in the news, in a big way. Like everyone else, I had all kinds of unanswered questions about how much power he was still able to exert over his followers and sympathizers—especially the ones who weren't in prison. I'd been feeling wary anyway. Now, I was terrified.

I knew from talking to my dad that the FBI in Sacramento had discovered a cache of my letters in Fromme's apartment. Concerned that friends of hers who still weren't in custody might try to get in touch with me, they'd notified the FBI's field office in Buffalo, which is where my dad was assigned at the time. I wasn't sure what to do. I thought seriously about ending the Manson correspondence once and for all.

But that's not what I did. Instead, I waited four months and then wrote to Manson again. In my letter, I acknowledged the attempt on Ford's life by one of his earliest and most devoted followers. (Fromme's loaded .45 caliber pistol had jammed when she pointed it at the president and pulled the trigger. Later, she'd tell anyone who would listen that all she really set out to do was publicize Manson's right to a new trial.)

Manson wrote me back almost immediately. This time, he called me by my first name, something he seldom did. He began his letter as if we'd been rudely interrupted part-way through an ongoing conversation. He never mentioned Squeaky by name. However, "woman"—with a capital W— was very much on his mind (and, at least to hear him tell it, wreaking havoc on other parts of his anatomy).

"I got her on my ass," he began, assuming, I guess, that I'd know what he was talking about. Then he launched into a colorful tirade, its exact target hard to discern. Ostensibly, he was fed up with "the woman balance."

"She took my life in every way & cut my balls off & fed them to dogs & flew her bird up my ass & all I can see in the woman balance is up & down the roads on telephone poles— for every time I've worked to save that lousy bitch she's called for her death & I'm sure tired of the ms. box circle suck game— I could wright for 6 more years & not be as mad."

Say *what*? Was he trying to place the blame on Fromme for somehow worsening his own prospects by targeting the president and then babbling to the authorities about her belief that he deserved a new trial?

He hadn't completely given up on the idea of persuading

me to adopt an advocacy role. "There is no way to do enough unless you can help me," he wrote. "I can see you're on a lot of good thought," he added. Then he continued to rage—but for the moment anyway, not at me.

> *I worked a 3 year old girl up to where I could try to save as many woman as I could & I got my balls thrown in my face & made into be a rabit & a bird I'm not a rabbit & only ran ...to keep from killing fools who need death for proof. Jeff I don't give a fuck what others think I can do my own thinking—The people that dumped ALL that bullshit on me lost there souls but they had none anyway—I'll stop wrighting because I'm so fucking mad it's not a joke no more. It's like the man on earth is womans death thats all they seem to except as real & true.*

It's perhaps a sign of how confused and disoriented I'd become that I saw this letter, the first he'd written since Fromme's assassination attempt, as a step in the right direction. He was frustrated, sure, and of course he was angry; but he was no longer raging at me, not like he had the previous July, two months before the Fromme incident. In fact, when he wrote "I can see you're on a lot of good thought," I thought that was the most positive assessment of me he'd offered to date. I asked myself: *How long can I ignore his pleas for help and still manage to avoid his wrath?*

I wrote him back right away. In my letter, I said no, I'd never been to "Seven Steeples," in fact had never even heard of the place. He returned to the issue in a disjointed, head-scratcher of a note, this one postmarked March 1.

> *Only one knows [swastika] what that is in its will as all is all to be one with itself. Hey JS I got to much mail to answer world [swastika]. Seven Steeples was the state nut house. Yes, man in ego is woman—old thought & face play games over the one of the soul—Ego can be a game & not bad it's only when one gits stuck & forgits It's a game. Ego man or*

woman if not understood is negative—I got envelopes—I'm told they gona move me somewhere else—Jeff I'm always one with you in your faith. Give it to you & I'm there—If I don't wright it's because I'm at work trying to git you out as I'm realy mad & think one day we can be ourselves. Easy.

Much of this sounded to me like complete gobbledygook: "Yes, man in ego is woman—old thought & face play games over the one of the soul?" I hadn't even the first clue what that was supposed to mean. By now, however, I'd grown accustomed to Manson's highly idiosyncratic way of communicating. Even when his writing was barely legible, and even when it lacked sentence breaks and other kinds of grammatical and syntactical conventions, I could usually decipher his words. Figuring out what they meant was a different matter altogether.

I cringed over the swastikas that would occasionally appear in the middle of his letters. I never knew exactly what they were supposed to signify. But his racist ideas were well documented. While his trial was still in progress, he'd carved an "X" into his forehead, ostensibly to signal that he'd chosen to abandon mainstream society altogether. Only later did he tweak the X, converting it to a swastika. In any event, his use of that symbol was hardly a new development.

I wasn't quite sure what to make of the touches of near-familiarity that appeared in his most recent note. Not only did he address me as both "JS" and "Jeff" in the actual text of his postcard, he wrote—once again—as if he saw our fates as somehow intertwined (e.g., "Jeff I'm always one with you in your faith. Give it to you & I'm there"). Then there was his reference to "trying to git [me] out." I was perplexed—and more than a little troubled—by his invocation of a future when both of us would be free to "be ourselves."

Hardly for the first time, I found myself in a quandary. On one hand, statements like those spooked me, for obvious reasons. They seemed to envision a time down the road when the two of us would no longer be separated by thick prison walls and thousands of miles. That was a vision I preferred not to entertain. On the other hand, I was relieved that he no longer seemed to regard me as The Enemy. As far as I could tell, he was on board with the idea of continuing our correspondence. I was on board, too, at least for the time being.

•••

Suddenly, without any prior warning, Dennis Patrick O'Donnell made himself known to me. I'd never even heard his name. Turns out, he was a neighbor and close buddy of Manson's at Folsom prison. O'Donnell's first letter arrived like a bolt out of the blue; I'd had no reason to expect it. Over the course of several months, he sent me eight more letters. They were all written in bold pencil. Most of them were at least six pages long. It quickly became apparent to me that Manson had enlisted him to act as a kind of intermediary.

A hint of what was to come appeared at the top of the first page of O'Donnell's first letter. In large, sprawling print, he introduced himself: "From Dennis Patrick O'Donnell—Descendant of Daniel—one of the one hundred and forty-four thousand—a virgin since birth—and Secretary of Defense for Charles Manson—meaning the Shawl of the Son of Man and the Son of God—Christ ... As my ancestor called Saint Patrick (Jeremiah) drove the 'snakes' from Ireland, so shall I by God's grace—from our land."

In so many words, he admitted that he was coming to me as Manson's agent: "Dear Jeff, Charlie thinks you are a woman writing under a man's name (he lives behind me). Be that as it may, God has made me, like he did Aaron for Moses, Charlie's mouthpiece." He added, as if it was some sort of foregone conclusion, "Charlie is walking in Christ's big footsteps."

A little further on in this same letter, he referenced "the love flowing through Charlie" and emphasized the reputation for selflessness and generosity that Manson had earned for himself among the other inmates at Folsom. O'Donnell portrayed himself and Manson as brother warriors, committed to a higher calling: "Charlie and I are willing to die for the truth," he wrote. "[We] only have time for truth."

He told me a little of his own background. "You've probably never heard of me—but everyone in prison has," he wrote. "I've been in thirteen years, stabbed 6 people in my old life, and was in the Aryan Brotherhood for 7 years."

In a later letter, he explained that he was a "legend" in the California prison system, partly because he'd spent nearly eight years in a medical facility after a legal determination that he was "criminally insane" when he was still in his mid-teens. He said that in prison, most of the other inmates referred to him by one of his two nicknames: Dennis the Menace or The Fighting Irishman.

He wrote me again in late March. I felt a wave of relief wash over me when he began, "I believe you're a man. I received your letter tonight—and I'll send it over to Charlie."

There was a chumminess about his writing, a quality that was largely absent from Manson's letters. "It's obvious you're sincere, Jeff," he wrote. Frequently, he would address me as either "friend" or "brother." "I like you Jeff," he wrote. Then he added, "If Charlie didn't, he wouldn't be writing you."

He announced—something I wasn't expecting—that he and Manson had become brothers in Christ. "I've known Charlie for about two years," he explained. "After I was baptized, God had me baptize Charlie—and ONLY God is good. Charlie or I aren't trying to hang any halos on ourselves. Christ didn't wear one—nor do we, his prophets."

His *prophets*?

Sometimes, he'd end his letters by writing either "Love" or "Your friend and God's." Once, he signed off, "Jeff, stay warm in this 'cool' world."

He encouraged me to continue writing him and Manson, and to keep "mentally fighting for truth." He warned me that much of what he'd say in his letters would be far too advanced—or esoteric—for me to understand. At some point down the road, he said, when God made the decision to grant me the gift of "his ghost," I'd be in a position to grasp the essence of his message. His hope? That he could "bring some light" into my life.

Despite the fact that he'd assured me he was no longer a member of the neo-Nazi, white supremacist prison group known as the Aryan Brotherhood, he promised that when he deemed me ready, he'd provide me with a comprehensive history of that organization, which according to him had roots extending all the way back to Biblical times.

He assured me that he'd avoid trying to overload me with too much information at once. "I can only give you a LITTLE at a time, otherwise it would send you past the bounds of all that's insanity." Since beyond the bounds of "all that's insanity" was nowhere I wanted to go, I agreed that a cautious, incremental approach was the way to go.

In a sense, I felt like I was writing to Manson whenever I wrote to O'Donnell—at least during the period when they were together at Folsom. Frequently, O'Donnell would say things like, "I'm sending your letter over to Charlie" or "I'll pass your letter on to Charlie." I had little doubt that Manson was being made privy to everything I wrote in my letters to O'Donnell.

By May 1976, both O'Donnell and Manson had been moved from Folsom, Manson to the California Medical Facility at Vacaville, O'Donnell to the California Men's Colony at San Luis Obispo (which is where Manson Family killer Charles "Tex" Watson was incarcerated at the time).

In one of my letters, I told O'Donnell that a close friend and I were planning a trip to California that summer. I said I'd made arrangements to take tours of all three of those institutions (which was true). He knew the exact day—because I told him—when I was scheduled to tour the prison at San Luis Obispo. Not long after the day of my tour there, he wrote to say he was sure he'd seen me.

From where I sat, things were starting to feel a bit too familiar and claustrophobic.

"I seen the tour you was in ... when it passed by," he wrote. "The one building you went in was in 'D' Quad—I was standing outside of it, without a shirt on, holding my guitar." He thought divine providence must have been at work that day. "God works in unfathomable ways, Jeff—I seen you—but don't know what you look like—and it's possible you seen me… I have a German Imperial Eagle tattooed on my right side … a leftover from my Aryan Brotherhood days."

In his next letter, he announced plans to write me a customized book, one whose contents would not be for the "squeamish." He cautioned me against showing it to "the wrong people." He was certain I'd find the book both revelatory and inspirational: "You'll 'know' me better [after you read it]—I already know you Jeff! … I dig an intelligent letter—one of the reasons I have high hopes for you … I'm sending you to high places. I'll explain later."

I had no idea what high places he was referring to –and I was pretty sure I didn't want to know.

Right from the start, O'Donnell's startling grandiosity had been on extravagant display. In a letter he wrote me in August, not long after he'd been transferred from the California Men's Colony back to Folsom, he referenced his astonishing artistic gifts and casually compared himself to Michaelangelo, DaVinci, El Greco, and Rubens, whose paintings he said he'd begun to replicate when he was only 12 years old. In a casual aside, he mentioned that he'd begun "sculpting" at age seven. At least to hear him tell it, bigwigs in the publishing world were falling all over themselves in an attempt to secure permission to use his work.

Before much time had elapsed, he sent me another letter. This one was a 16-pager. According to the heading on the first page, he intended it to serve as a "primary History of the Aryan Brotherhood."

The letter was—I'm being kind here—a largely incomprehensible mish-mash. It teemed with wild claims, obscure Biblical references, puns presented as if they were profound truths, highly personalized asides, and admonitions about how important it was that I scrutinize each and every single thing he was saying. Sprinkled throughout the letter's text were references to Babylon, the Garden of Eden, the Levites, the Book of Revelation, the "Aarons or Aryans," the Mongols, the "Jewetts," Thor Heyerdahl, the Aztecs, Billy Graham, the Maccabbees, the Vatican Museum, Red China—and even the famous astrologer, Jean Dixon.

As a means of capturing the letter's overall flavor, perhaps this one representative paragraph will suffice:

"Egypt - ian—is an old Cyparic word—meaning— 'He gypts them'—Who gypts WHO? The Lord the sons of Ham: Ham was given a curse—which was to be carried out, into ALL generations—saying—'He shall be a servant forever'—unto his brothers—Shem (white) and Japath—father of Javan—whom was the Father of the peoples of Japan."

And on and on it went. *For 16 pages!*

In mid-October of 1976, I received one final letter from O'Donnell. He referred back to the reason he'd begun writing me in the first place. "I know what Charlie said about, no one can talk for him. It was Charlie who is having me talk for him—that's to say write for him. Charlie can outtalk a college professor and make a whole lot more sense—but his writing is 4th grade."

Toward the end of this letter, he referred to where he planned to live, and with whom, after his release from prison. That was all I needed to hear. I never wrote him back, and he never wrote me again either.

• • •

So, during most of the time while I was corresponding with O'Donnell, Manson was right there, lurking in the shadows. Soon, he would re-emerge into the light.

But back in March of 1976, *before* he enlisted the services of Dennis the Menace, he'd written me his longest letter yet, six handwritten pages. He was responding to a letter I'd sent him about a week prior.

I was struck by the distinctive handwriting that appeared on the outside of his envelope. By now, he was very familiar with my first name. However, this time he elected to write it as "Seff," not Jeff. My street address at the time was "220 Sheetz Street—Room H," in West Lafayette, Indiana (where I was enrolled at Purdue).

Something about the "Room H" part of the address had

apparently been bothering him. He traced over the letter "H" numerous times, making it dark and very bold. In the body of his letter, he demanded to know, "What's Room H?" (To this day, I have friends from my Purdue days who still take delight in repeating that question whenever we're together.)

For this letter, he'd opted to use a new salutation—one he'd never employed before: my initials, but written upside down. I hoped the upside-down part was intended as a playful gesture and not something more ominous than that. I'd learned not to assume anything where Manson was concerned. At certain junctures in the past, he'd begun on an apparently playful note, only to veer off into a wild burst of vitriol.

I detected a note of insecurity—and perhaps a hint of paranoia?—in the letter's opening lines. He was feeling uncertainty about his ability to wield power and influence from inside prison.

"It's funnie how meaney people are following each one of the people that were once with me," he wrote, "and none will admit it. They seem to have thoughts running on every rommer."

I knew that a number of his former followers had aligned themselves with an individual named Kenneth Como, someone who'd operated on the margins of Manson-world and was said to be a member of the Aryan Brotherhood. I also knew that in the period immediately preceding his arrest, Manson had become wary of the growing influence of handsome and charismatic Family member Bobby Beausoleil, known by the nickname "Cupid." In the recent past, I'd read news reports suggesting that Como had attached Manson in prison. Manson addressed the subject, which I'd mentioned in passing in the last letter I'd written him.

"Your last letter was full of what you think is real & it would take much more than letters to unexplain what you think," he wrote. "Everyone is not after me they just looking to the things & thoughts we're into—The projection of the people who want someone to git me is what you have heard."

In other words, he saw me as someone who was hopelessly out of the loop, *his loop*—and sure to remain there.

He continued," Como didn't 'jump me'—It was a play ack to git some thoughts off me & give me a chance to use 2 faces in a fun off thought—He was christ [smiley face] & Mary [Brunner, who'd been the first woman to join Manson's group, back in 1967] was his woman & I was pharo & Lyn [Squeaky Fromme] was Ka and Blue [Sandy Good] was neps & that was another level of thought."

Don't believe everything you read and hear. That seemed to be Manson's core message. At least to hear him tell it, the alleged attack by Como was nothing more than a staged enactment, orchestrated to advance Manson's interests in some obscure way I couldn't hope to comprehend. It was all part of a "level of thought" to which I could never hope to gain access. Another such level of thought was apparently behind the relationships involving him, Como, Mary Brunner, Squeaky Fromme, and Sandy Good. For the time being anyway, he seemed content to allow me to stew in my own ignorance.

"There are a lot of second chamber thoughts of the world," he explained. "You only think & know about one side—I think & know on both sides the outside in & inside out."

This was typical Manson-speak. Like his pal Dennis O'Donnell, he often made it sound as if he possessed secret, privileged wisdom about things happening at levels of reality that most people couldn't begin to fathom. His claim to possess such wisdom was one facet of his case against mainstream society—whose members, according to him, didn't know the first thing about him, his history, or his way of perceiving the world. Frequently, he'd pose variations of questions like these: "Who are they to judge me?" or "How would they ever know what my motives were?"

"I think backwards & upside down & inside out—Few could understand it even if I explained it" he wrote.

He returned to the subject of Kenneth Como. According to Manson, it didn't matter if Como believed he had managed to lure some of his women away from him. "[It's] alright if he thinks he has all the women in the world," wrote Manson.

He was still stuck on the issue of my identity, and still highly suspicious of my motives. *Was I a cop?* "Why do you want to know the answers to questions you wouldn't understand," he asked. "Are you a woman wrighting like a man—or are you a police?"

He lamented how "sad" it was that I and so many other people were being forced to "live in" the "unreal" thoughts of the prosecutor who'd secured his conviction and sent him to prison. He repeatedly insisted that prosecutor Vincent Bugliosi—co-author of *Helter Skelter*—knew full well that he, Manson, "broke no laws" and should never have been convicted of anything, let alone murder. What it all meant, he said, was that "the money mind destroyed its laws. Same thing happened in rome & bablon."

By the time he reached the fifth page of this lengthy letter, he'd apparently begun to wonder whether I was worth any more of his time and energy. "I can't wright everyone who wants to know what they don't know," he wrote. "I again tell you I can't explain a world in letters to each person that wrights. I can't wright you no more cause I've got to much to do as it is already."

But he still had a little something more that he wanted me to know about Squeaky Fromme and Sandy Good. "The woman like the ones I came with were me—one with me & in my will & love. Squeaky is called Red [Fromme had been decked out in a floor-length, hooded red robe on the day when she tried to assassinate President Ford, six months prior] & is on a thought I put her on balance of the earth trees wild life. Sandy is Blue & on the balance of sky & water & they been trying to fix a mess that no one wants to uncover for fear of what's really there."

Questions about my identity were *still* bothering him. "You haven't told me what you are or what you do & besides most of you earth people ever thing you say is a lie anyway—you lie for jokes or attention."

As he was winding down, now on his sixth page, he amused himself with some extravagant alliteration. "It's of little meaning what others think—they think what TV or money mind movie mind or moma mind tells them anyway." He followed that sentence with a large smiley face drawing.

And again, one last time: "Who are you—what's Rm H? And how did I get started wrighting you?? … Any way. Easy."

•••

That last letter, postmarked March 5, 1976, marked the beginning of the longest gap in Manson's and my correspondence. Even though he didn't write me for nearly six months, during that period when I was exchanging frequent letters with his close neighbor and pal, Dennis Patrick O'Donnell, I always felt confident that my letters to O'Donnell would make their way to Manson.

The return address on the postcard Manson sent me in early September of 1976 indicated that he'd been transferred back to Vacaville Medical Facility

This time around, there would be no beating around the bush. He got straight to the point. He needed money, and he needed it now. He clearly remembered me as the guy who'd first written him a year and a half ago—and expressed interest in his songs and lyrics.

"I need about 5 grand for a friend of mind needs some things," he wrote. "Send now today—It's to much to explain so just send it & I'll send to him & he can use it & if I ever git some you may have it—Don't tell me you don't have it—Git it & you will feel good & I'll send you copys of the music."

The last letter Manson ever wrote me—actually, it was two separate letters rather than just one—arrived in an envelope postmarked October 12, 1976. I was overcome by a sense of weariness as I began reading what he'd written. It was a recycling of the same old grievances: *Society is full of hypocrites. I don't belong in prison. I'm not that "monster" the press wants you to believe I am. I'm tired of having to carry the burden of your sick society on my back.* And so on and so forth.

He relented and told me I could forget about sending the $5,000 he'd demanded from me in his last letter. All he'd wanted, he explained, was to purchase some electronic equipment so his friend and former associate Bobby Beausoleil could record his music in prison. *Didn't I understand that money meant absolutely nothing to him?* "$5,000 to me is like this peace of paper," he wrote.

And didn't I realize that it was irrelevant to him whether I felt one iota of concern about him and what he was going through? "Haha. I've seen [concern] all my life kicking my brains out at the bottom … My children know me. I'm the one who don't treet them like less than people & call them helpless children—you're on a hard wake up call Jeff … The monster you made in Manson you'll live with a long time as if you showed some concern he would of reflected that."

Enclosed in the same envelope was a second letter. This one he labeled "Letter 2." As far as I could tell, he included it because he didn't feel he'd adequately vented his spleen in "Letter 1."

"JS—I just got to thinking about your reaction about that chicken shit money—your brains so tied up in that mony—before your 12 you've lost your soul to it. I believe if it wasn't for money you wouldn't even git up out of bed to walk around in your dead body—moneys your god—you're the monster you try & make me out of."

In previous letters, he'd depicted society as the monster that insisted on fashioning him into its sacrificial "beast." Now, the monster was *me*.

Further on in Letter 2, he lowered the temperature of his rhetoric, at least a little. "I'm not pissed off JS. But I had even forgot I had written you about your god dollar—I don't take anything from anyone who is past redeeming their souls—I was doing you a favor & you mist the chance to sell all you got."

He returned to the media's insistence on portraying him as a "monster," then added, "It was there own reflections of themselves & the people who pay for death wish fear tryps—None of that shit touches my soul it's been free long before you seen my face—none of you know me."

After he'd printed the words "Fuck you" in especially large letters, he apparently felt that he'd said most of what he wanted to say. "I don't know or judge you only the paper words & a lost child trying to play grown up," he said. "7 years in solitary confineing shows what your hideing from your selves. I broke no law and could of proved it. P.S. My children ain't children there people & nothing on earth will stop them—they are life on earth & I serve that."

We'd been down this path before.

I'd sent my first letter to Manson when I was in the second semester of my senior year in college. Now, I was in my third semester of graduate school—taking several courses, working as a research assistant for one of the professors in my department, preparing for general exams, and feeling more than just a little overextended. I no longer had the time or energy—or motivation—to sustain any kind of meaningful engagement with the likes of Charles Manson and Dennis Patrick O'Donnell.

Our correspondence ended just like that. I was tired.

What didn't end was my interest in the issue that had prompted me to write Manson in the first place. Namely, the degree of congruence between the images we fashion of the worst criminals we can imagine and the reality of who those criminals are as people. I remained interested in that issue all throughout my long career as a forensic psychologist.

But the start of that career was still more than a decade away.

For the time being, I was ready to end this chapter of what I'd come to think of as the Manson Inquiry. Two other chapters overlapped with the one involving Manson. The first of those I've already mentioned; it involved Family members Lynette "Squeaky" Fromme and Sandra Good. The second one involved Susan "Sadie" Atkins, a particularly notorious member of the Manson Family who'd been found guilty of multiple counts of murder and sentenced to death.

Even those chapters wouldn't bring closure to the Inquiry.

3.
Squeaky and Sandy

Lynette "Squeaky" Fromme and Sandra Good hadn't killed anyone, at least as far as anyone knew. Still, the two were known to be fervent and outspoken believers in the gospel according to Charles Manson.

I decided to reach out to them at around the same time I decided to reach out to Manson. From the start, I understood that there would be a degree of risk. For one thing, the women weren't in custody. Neither of them had been found guilty of a major crime. I didn't have an address for them, in fact didn't even know where in the country they were living—but I knew they weren't wards of the state of California. And I knew that even if I succeeded in my attempt to locate them, I'd need to provide them with my address, a sobering thought.

Other things concerned me, too. I knew that in December 1969, less than two months after Manson's arrest on suspicion of auto theft, Good's husband at the time, a man named Joel Pugh, had been found dead with his throat slit in a London hotel room. The authorities suspected he'd been murdered, but they couldn't prove it.

In truth, Good gave me the creeps. After she was apprehended by the police during a late-1969 raid on Manson's Death Valley hideout, she was overheard telling another detainee at the Inyo County Jail in Independence, California, "I've finally reached the point where I can kill my parents."

Called as a witness for the defense at the penalty phase of Manson's trial, she told jurors of her belief that Manson had once brought a dead bird back to life by breathing on it. She also declared that "if he so desired," Manson could "shatter [the] building" where the trial was being held.

Both Fromme and Good had been part of a Family vigil outside the L.A. Hall of Justice during nearly the entire time while Manson and his co-defendants—Susan Atkins, Leslie Van Houten, and Patricia Krenwinkle (the trio Truman Capote would later refer to as "those cutthroat young ladies")—were on trial for murder. Mimicking Manson, Fromme and Good had burned "X" marks into the skin on their foreheads, ostensibly to symbolize their wholesale rejection of American society and everything it stood for. In remarks to the press, they'd referred to Manson's ordeal as "the second crucifixion of Christ."

By nearly all accounts, Fromme was Manson's second-in-command. According to prosecutor Vincent Bugliosi, she'd assumed the role as "ex-officio leader of the Family in Manson's absence," and had become Manson's "unofficial spokesman."

I was intrigued by what I knew of the women's back stories. In *Helter Skelter*, Bugliosi reported that Fromme's father was an aeronautics engineer in Santa Monica, Good's an insurance broker in San Diego. Fromme had enrolled in college but dropped out. Good had completed undergraduate studies and begun work toward her master's degree when she encountered Manson and joined the Family.

I recalled Bugliosi's way of portraying the close friends. He wrote of their "little girl" quality—even though Fromme had been 21 and Good 25 when he encountered them for the first time. He also remarked on the fact that both young women were "pretty" in their way.

Recalling the frustration he experienced because of his inability to break through Fromme's and Good's rigid denial of wrongdoing by Manson and other members of the Family, Bugliosi wrote of the two, "All they knew about was love." Whenever he tried to pin them down with respect to specific dates and chronologies, they demurred, insisting, "There is no such thing as time." To Bugliosi, they seemed less like human beings than "Barbie dolls."

When I reviewed footage from the 1973 documentary film, *Manson,* a collaborative effort involving Robert Hendrickson and Laurence Merrick, I could see why Bugliosi had chosen to emphasize the women's doll-like qualities (although I thought he should have compared them to GI Joe instead of Barbie). In the film, Fromme and Good are shown fondling knives and guns, and rhapsodizing about the uses to which such weapons might be put.

Staring directly into the camera, Fromme makes a series of startling statements, among them, "If you find an apple that has a little spot on it, you cut out that spot," "Snitches will be taken care of," "Every girl should have a daddy just like Charlie," "I'm ready to die for Charlie," "It feels good to be ready to face death and love it," and "Yeah, [Charlie] is God. That's why they're hanging him, that's why they're killing him."

Not to be outdone, Good chimes in with some startling statements of her own: "Whatever is necessary, you do it. When somebody needs to be killed, there's no wrong. You do it, and then you move on," "The motive for the murders was love of brother," and "If [the authorities] ever laid a finger on Charlie, they'd have to contend with us. If we were unarmed, we would chew their necks off, anything, claw their eyes out. And they know it—because we haven't hid it, we've made no secret of our feelings."

So yes, I had all kinds of reasons for the feelings of uneasiness I felt once I'd made my decision to forge ahead with my plan to try and get in touch with Fromme and Good.

I felt certain that if I could just get a letter into their hands, they'd answer it—or at least one of them would. They were hard-core zealots. Based on everything I knew about them, I found it hard to imagine them turning away from a new opportunity to proselytize on their leader's behalf.

As it turned out, Fromme actually wrote to me before Manson did, though not by much. She dated her first letter March 17, 1975. That was a little less than six months before her eventual attempt to assassinate the president of the United

States. Her letter and the first note I received from Manson—the one he scrawled across the bottom half of my typewritten letter dated March 16—had to have crossed in the mail. Manson's note landed in my mailbox just a day or two after my receipt of Squeaky's much longer letter.

I'd had no real difficulty figuring out where to send my first letter to Manson. In the epilogue of *Helter Skelter*, Bugliosi had written that in October of 1972, Manson was transferred from San Quentin to the maximum security "adjustment center" at Folsom, which he described as a "prison within a prison," reserved for "problem inmates."

Figuring out how to address a letter to Squeaky and Sandy presented an altogether different challenge. I knew they weren't in prison—but where were they?

It was a long shot, but I decided to seek the answer to that question in the most unlikely of places: the office of the Los Angeles County District Attorney. I remembered from *Helter Skelter* a historical footnote that seemed almost too weird to believe. Steven Kay, one of the deputy district attorneys in that office, had gone on what amounted to a parent-supervised "blind date" with none other than Sandy Good when he was 15 and she was 14—many years before the start of Good's association with the Manson Family. At the time, Kay thought Good seemed like "a stuck-up little snob," the kind of girl likely to "marry some rich guy and live in a big mansion."

I also remembered Bugliosi writing about Charles Melcher, another deputy district attorney in the same office. Melcher had reportedly befriended some of the Manson women when they were sitting vigil outside the Hall of Justice while inside, Manson and his three co-defendants were on trial for murder.

Who could forget the one paragraph in *Helter Skelter* that was devoted to Charles Melcher and his relationships with the Manson Family women? Not only had Melcher's wife baked Christmas cookies for "the Manson girls," Melcher himself—from his position inside the same DA's office that was fighting so assiduously to get Manson and his female co-defendants sentenced to death—came forth as a certain kind of advocate for some of the most reviled people in America. He told the authors of *Helter Skelter* that he hoped to write a book of his own someday. What he actually said was this: "I'd like to write not an exposé of the tragedy and violence, which I do not condone, but a book about the beauty I've seen in that group—their opposition to war, their truthfulness and their generosity."

It occurred to me that Melcher might know where Squeaky and Sandy were living. I wrote the women a letter in which I introduced myself and told them of my interest in their involvement with Manson, I enclosed the letter in a stamped, sealed envelope with my own return address on it, and I placed *that* envelope inside a larger envelope that I addressed to Melcher, c/o the office of the Los Angeles County District Attorney. In the brief cover letter that I wrote to Melcher, I asked him if he'd be willing to complete the address on the envelope containing my letter to the women—if, that is, he knew where they were living—and then place that envelope in the mail.

It may have been a long shot, but it worked. Melcher wrote me back almost immediately. He told me that he did, in fact, know where Fromme and Good were living (of course he didn't actually provide me with their address), and he assured me that he'd sent them my letter.

Just as I'd predicted she would, Squeaky jumped at the opportunity to advocate on Manson's behalf.

Recall that when I initiated these correspondences with members of the Manson Family, I was preoccupied with the idea that if I could create an opportunity for Manson and some of his followers to speak to me directly, maybe they'd force me to conclude that they were more complex, more interesting, perhaps even more sympathetic people than I'd been led to believe they were. With Squeaky and Sandy, my plan was to be alert to any evidence that might make me see them as more than just mindless apologists for the killer who'd been branded the most dangerous man alive.

Now, holding in my hands a letter from Manson's first lieutenant, I was ready to begin my search.

•••

When Squeaky's letter showed up in my mailbox, the envelope containing it was the first thing I noticed. It had a beige flap, with a multi-colored floral design. Not exactly the packaging you'd expect to see from a multiple murderer's most diehard devotee. The addresses on the envelope—my own address and the return address, "Lyn Fromme, 1725 P St., Sacramento, CA 95814"—were written in blue ink, neat cursive with lots of loopy curves. I suppose I should have guessed that she and Good would be living in close proximity to Manson. Represa, the small town that is home to Folsom prison, is located less than 25 miles from Sacramento.

The first page of Fromme's letter had the same coloring and floral design that I'd noted on the envelope's flap. It looked like the kind of stationery a young and ebullient schoolgirl might have chosen. The letter's salutation? "Hello." Next to it was a smiley face that Fromme had drawn.

I remember thinking, *This is the ex-officio leader of the Manson Family?*

I wasn't quite sure what to make of the letter's opening lines. Squeaky's tone seemed friendlier and a lot more moderate than I would have predicted. At the same time, I detected an undercurrent of menace, implied by the words she'd chosen to use.

"We received your letter yesterday, Sandra & I," she began. "I can't quite muster up a commendation for Bugliosi and Sanders but I see that you are coming from no opinion & that is safe. I'm glad you wrote."

I hadn't saved a copy of my own letter, so I had no way of confirming the exact words I'd used to introduce myself. I remembered, however, that I'd told the women of my familiarity with the Bugliosi and Sanders books. I'd also assured them of my openness to the possibility that both authors had some things wrong. Apparently, that latter statement had been enough to convince Fromme and Good that I had "no opinion."

What troubled me, of course, was the thought of how Squeaky might have responded if I *had* expressed an opinion—for example about Manson's guilt and the guilt of the others, or about the legitimacy of the two best-known accounts of the case. Would she still have assured me that my opinion was "safe?"

She continued, sounding a lot like my stereotype of a hippie flower child—but not much at all like my stereotype of the kind of person who would condone the cold-blooded slaughter of at least seven people:

> *The companionship you speak of between us at the [Spahn] ranch was based on an understanding of truth and a thought to raise ourselves by loving. By loving, I mean giving to & for love. We faced the lie, fear, & death. Love is beyond. The positive nature & the number of brains hooked up to this one thought transcended our old thoughts [here she drew a bold cross] which in this world prevail & slowly run us down. [Just above this statement, she printed the words, "They must die."] Outside the negative weights put on our initially clear selves, we are open for new thought of songs for speeches & dances, for motions.*

I struggled to process the contradiction, real or perhaps just apparent. Members of the Manson Family had carried out some of the most savage murders in living memory. I knew for certain that Squeaky possessed detailed knowledge about each and every one of them. I also knew that she was well aware that at one point during his trial, Manson leaped over a table, lunged in the direction of the presiding judge, and declared that someone should cut the judge's head off. She knew these things and many more like them, yet she could still speak, intending no irony whatsoever, of "love" and the "positive nature" of the thoughts that had bound her and other members of the Manson Family together.

As yet, I'd had absolutely no firsthand experiences with either criminals or cults. For that reason, I had no reliable frame of reference for use in trying to make sense of the things she was saying.

What she said next hinted at the kind of improvisational, fantasy-driven lifestyle that she and other members of the

Family had adopted as an alternative to "the straight life," which they decried as a product of parental and societal conditioning. She wrote, "Dances and songs are not to be memorized and sung from memory, but to be sung from the hearts moment to moment in the settings at hand. There is no end to where our imaginations can take us if we, as a people, are willing to give up the cross and the misery thought & recognize that we have died long enough."

I found unsettling her repeated references to death and dying. Such references seemed especially ominous against the backdrop of the brutal murders known to have been committed by members of the Manson Family—in other words, by Squeaky's closest friends.

I didn't realize it at first, but Squeaky was laying the groundwork for a sharp pivot to the subject of Manson himself. "Yes," she wrote, "I am the family as each who wants to raise their love beyond death is the family." There it was again, that word: "death." This time, being used to reference something that Fromme and other members of the Manson Family had ostensibly been able to "transcend."

"Charlie does not have a philosophy," she wrote. "'Love' is a move for a better world. Concern for all concern. Soul."

Then, "Charlie didn't do it, Jeff. He is it. He wants nothing but to be able to walk this earth in peace. He sees that in order to do this the entire earth must be cleaned—& all must be willing servants to her balance."

Her suggestion that Manson's sole objective was to be able to walk the earth in peace seemed to me like gaslighting of a truly epic kind. And why would earth need to be "cleaned" before Manson could achieve his ultimate goal? Cleaned *how*? In my letter, I'd expressed my sincere interest in learning more about her and Sandy. As people, I'd said, not just characters in someone else's story. "I'm glad you're interested in us as people," she wrote [here she inserted a drawing of a smiley face]. That's what we are, not people as people think—We're alikens."

I was finding it difficult to follow her train of thought. Immediately after she made her cryptic reference to "alikens," she turned on a dime and headed off in an entirely new direction.

> *Without the negative garbage that clutters minds we could hook up. Sign language is not but an awareness of what others are thinking by their motions & vibrations—by what we once knew as one mind, our brains—& ESP is just a natural sense. Many on the planet know this but have not been able to put it into activity. Much of this is due to blocks of manipulation—thoughts and desires to use the sense for negative purposes.*

Why, I wondered, had she pivoted so quickly to the subject of extrasensory perception? And what, specifically, were the "blocks of manipulation" she was claiming had prevented the use of ESP to "hook up" people's brains? Even if I wasn't sure how to answer those questions (and I wasn't), there was nothing puzzling or ambiguous about her blanket denunciation of society. To her, the word "society" seemed to stand for parents and every other purveyor of rules, expectations, and authority.

She continued, "Some succeed in using the power of positive thought for evil (or $ 'power' etc.) but will eventually be used by it as much as they have used [it]. It is a cosmic law, goes around/comes around."

I knew how much Manson liked to talk about karma. Whenever he invoked that term, it nearly always served as a thinly veiled reference to something that wrongdoers had "coming to them." Because I knew this, I felt a little queasy when I encountered Squeaky's glancing reference to the "goes around/comes around" theme. *What was she trying to tell me? And did she intend her words as a warning?*

In my letter, I'd alluded, in a way I thought was pretty innocuous, to "charismatic gurus," and to the people who look up to them as leaders. She turned to that subject next. "You're right," she wrote, "there are many charismatic gurus—all with the understanding that people have a basic desire to give—some, like in church—to make up for their guilt (which is church manufactured)."

For her phrase "basic desire to give," I might have substituted "basic desire to belong."

In any case, I knew Manson routinely mocked the concept of "guilt" and denounced it as a meaningless societal construct, having no relevance whatsoever when it came to him and his way of perceiving the world. Was Squeaky consciously parroting his perspective—in effect, making the argument that if someone feels "guilty" about something, it's only because the church or some other source of societal authority has indoctrinated her to believe she should feel that way?

Now, it seemed, she was ready to move on to the centerpiece of her message: Manson's transcendent significance, not only for her and other members of the Family but for the entire planet. "Charles Manson is not of our world thoughts & is only a servant to the balance of his mother, earth," she wrote. "If this is what you wish to be, write back and we shall discuss it further. We are at war with no one—not but a thought which has had us destroying ourselves for years."

Did she mean this as a recruitment pitch? *Was she inviting me to join the Manson Family?* It felt that way. I went back and re-read what she'd written. Basically, she seemed to be saying that if I was willing to commit myself to becoming what she said Manson was, "a servant to the balance of ... earth" (whatever that meant), she'd view me as worthy of her time and attention, and she'd be open to continuing our dialogue.

She knew of the strong possibility that I'd have a tough time understanding what exactly she was talking about because she continued, "Most people don't understand this thought but are blindly running in circles in it, enforcing it, or pushing it for $. Like I say—the thought that is behind it is what is important to look at & change."

She said she didn't want me to feel discouraged just because I might be finding it a struggle to come to terms with the truth of what she was saying.

"This may be new to you," she wrote, "or perhaps you

can see it. Most of us humans have been kept so busy wondering about ourselves, if our breath smells, if we are doing & thinking in accordance with public opinion—that we have not been free of doubt long enough to step outside public opinion to take a good look at ourselves. We will do this yet."

Here as elsewhere, she wrote as if she believed that she and all the other people who'd looked up to Manson and revered his teachings were in the vanguard of a new social and spiritual movement, based on things like universal love, "positive thought," and radical respect for the "earth" as the "mother of us all." I felt like she was asking, *Is this a movement you'd be interested in joining?*

Before ending her letter, she paused to make sure I felt valued and appreciated. "Again thank you for being concerned enough to step outside that mass opinion given by the D.A. and minds of alterior [sic] motive," she wrote. "We got good feelings from your letter, noted your intelligence & your apparent sincerity. Your thought runs very clear and to the point."

Then, "We are in the thought of World Peace—one world of people with concern for people & first for the earth which is a reflection of us all. We have good thoughts & ideas for making this come about. With regard for you, Lyn (Squeak) & Sandy. P.S. How about sending us a picture of yourself? Also tell us about you & what you do."

Accompanying her letter was a black and white copy of a photograph of the wizened face of an ancient-looking Native American man. The caption on the picture read, "Let the rain come down/And wash the dust from the hills/Cleanse the traces of all the years/From the land—From the earth—From the soul."

As I had with the first letter I'd written them, I addressed my reply to Squeaky and Sandy both. At that point, I knew nothing about Susan Murphy, another woman who, as it turned out, was residing with them in their apartment on P Street in downtown Sacramento, just blocks from the capital building. Only later would it come to my attention that Murphy was a newcomer to the Manson circle.

In accordance with Squeaky's request, I enclosed a picture of myself along with my next letter. I can no longer remember exactly which picture I sent. I do, however, remember that I was careful to select an image that bore little resemblance to the way I looked at the time. I wanted Squeaky and Sandy to know that I was happy to hear from them. I also wanted them to perceive me as open to learning more about their thoughts and ideas. I didn't want them to know what I looked like — and how uneasy I felt in the face of Squeaky's effort to seduce me with all the flowery talk of love, unity, world peace, and so on.

And then, of course, there was the elephant in the room: the as-yet unacknowledged subject of … *the murders*.

I wasn't about to broach that subject, at least not yet. I didn't want to provoke or antagonize them. But neither did I want them to view me as a complete rube, ripe for recruitment. It felt like I was balancing on a tightrope, or at least trying to.

On one hand, I was eager to retain their interest. On the other hand, I wanted to make sure they understood that I lived thousands of miles away from where they lived. I hoped they would view me as out of reach. (Here's how clueless I was: I casually alluded to the possibility that a friend and I would be taking a road trip to California, either later that year or sometime the following summer. I don't think it even occurred to me that disclosing such information to the likes of Squeaky Fromme and Sandy Good might not be the best idea.)

• • •

A month went by before I reached into my mailbox and retrieved another envelope with the P Street return address on it. The stamp on the envelope was one that I'd never seen before. It celebrated "Rural America." This time, the letter was from Sandy Good. Her letter had a very distinctive appearance. She wrote in red ink on bright pink stationery.

As it turned out, Good wrote me four letters over a period spanning six weeks. She always used the same pink paper.

Her introductory letter, dated April 29, afforded me my first opportunity to hear how her unfiltered voice sounded.

Like Squeaky, she came across as intelligent and articulate. However, the two women didn't sound the same. Sandy's voice was more direct—and a lot more strident—than Squeaky's.

In the opening paragraph of her letter, she issued a warning which, to me, sounded downright apocalyptic. Considered in retrospect, her tone should have concerned me even more than it did. Back then, my naivete was such that I thought she was just channeling Manson, with all his talk of an impending race war, the collapse of society, and so on. With the clarity of hindsight, I can see that she was hinting at the likelihood of something big that was about to "go down." She began her letter this way:

> *Dear Jeff—Lyn and I received your letter—We have been in Los Angeles doing many things & did not have time to write you back as we have been on the road. I might advise you if you do come to California this summer, you'd be wise to stay out of L.A. as that city's days are numbered and she is set for destruction. The false images that Hollywood has projected to the world for money are no longer holding & all the images people have looked to are being eaten by the angry recipients of the lies. Much Karma there.*

There it was again, the word "karma"—used here to reference a turn of events that would supposedly punish wrongdoers and restore "balance." And that wasn't even the most ominous part.

The entire city of Los Angeles? Set for destruction? I had no idea what she was talking about. What I did know was that Los Angeles was the city where Charles Manson, Susan Atkins, Leslie Van Houten, Patricia Krenwinkle, and Charles "Tex" Watson had all been convicted on multiple counts of first-degree murder and sentenced to death. (Their death sentences were later vacated as a result of a 1972 decision by the Supreme Court of California.)

Did Sandy possess some sort of secret information about catastrophic events that would soon consume the city of Los Angeles? What had she and Squeaky been up to there? I had no way of knowing the answers to these questions. I was, however, aware that Manson had felt excluded and rejected by members of the Hollywood elite—"society" writ large. Were Sandy and Squeaky planning some sort of retributive strike? Sandy continued:

> *You asked what we are doing—many things. Tomorrow we'll see the warden at Folsom about seeing Manson. We haven't been allowed to see him for five years. We would like to build the seed stick. I'm enclosing the basic idea & someone else's plans for making it. Will you make a seed stick for us Jeff—either using the plans we are sending, or one of your own design? When you are finished, bring it to us. You could walk to California with your stick and tell people what you are doing. You are coming to see Manson & are planting seeds for peace.*

I thought this sounded like madness. *A seed stick?* (She enclosed a set detailed instructions for how to make one, about which more in a minute.) I couldn't tell if she was serious when she suggested I should "walk to" California with a seed stick, telling people along the way that I was on a pilgrimage to see Charles Manson. Perhaps she just assumed I'd know better than to take her literally. The reality is that I didn't. I had to consider the possibility that she was some version of nuts.

"This is (the seed stick) only one of Manson's many thoughts for doing for peace," she wrote. "He sees on a world level from the beginning of time & before time—to NOW. He knows & understands world problems—their origins & what will happen if the world is not put in order soon."

What did she mean, *put in order?* Was that phrase somehow related to Squeaky's suggestion that the entire earth would need to be "cleaned" before Manson could hope to travel it in peace? Regardless, how could I not hear an echo of what she'd written in the opening paragraph of her letter—with its ominous-sounding reference to Los Angeles as a city whose days were numbered?

She sounded menacing in a way Squeaky hadn't. That

said, I never forgot the many signs that pointed to the strength of Squeaky's devotion to Manson. Nor was I forgetting about Squeaky's apparent willingness to embrace the inevitability of some sort of karmic reckoning for the society she claimed had turned its back on Manson and failed to support his "earth balance" agenda. Even if their voices sounded markedly different on paper, there was no doubting the fact that Sandy and Squeaky were kindred spirits. Sandy continued:

> *No one knows what they are doing, they're only moving in old destructive thought patterns. For world survival there must be change & a strong love is the strongest power there is. It is no power. There are big things moving in the Middle East now as you may know. Hey if you get a chance—check out Shirley MacLaine's documentary on Red China—It is very interesting & will leave you with smiles on your face [smiley face]. They are unique people—out of the money & greed, death & power thoughts. A people loving & working hard & cooperating rather than competing.*

I thought back to Squeaky's emphasis on the goal of achieving "World Peace." Perhaps it shouldn't have surprised me when Sandy veered off into talking about China and the Middle East. Even so, I was baffled by her suggestion that the Chinese people had turned their backs on things like money, death, and power. That certainly wasn't the same message I'd picked up from the reading I'd done—not much, I confess—about significant milestones in modern Chinese history. I'd never even heard of the MacLaine documentary.

All things considered, though, I was at least intrigued by Sandy's willingness to acknowledge the merits of a project she described as the brainchild of a Hollywood A-lister (even one like MacLaine, with her well-earned reputation as something of a flake).

Like Squeaky, Sandy apparently believed that it was worth her time and energy to try to explain her thoughts and ideas to a complete stranger, not just as they pertained to Manson but as they pertained to global affairs. I couldn't decide how to weigh the contents of her letter. Did she really believe all the things she was saying? Was she genuinely concerned about the well-being of people in China, the Middle East, and other parts of the world?

While I was mulling over such questions, images of blood, brutality, and almost unimaginable cruelty—images, that is, of the Manson Family murders—kept flooding my brain. The effect was more than a little disorienting.

Were the things Sandy was saying meant to reinforce her claims and Squeaky's about Manson's status as a global leader whose wisdom somehow transcended the boundaries of time and history, and whose power had the potential to effect change throughout the entire world? If so, did that mean they were both stark raving mad?

At this juncture in her letter, Sandy switched to a warmer, more intimate tone. "There is nowhere to go," she wrote. "You are home when you know yourself and yourself is not what your mom or dad told you nor is it in books written by tormented poets seeking beauty or their soul through mazes of Christian confusion that they've inherited from their mom and their mom's mom & on down the line."

Clearly, she was channeling Manson. By this time, Manson had already written me the letter in which he'd urged me to "step from [my] past and be free." At the sentencing phase of his trial, in the lengthy remarks that were later published as the pamphlet *Your Children*, Manson had sounded the exact same notes that Sandy was sounding now.

If she was urging me to think about who I was and how I wanted to spend the rest of my life, she was also encouraging me to step back so that I could glimpse a bigger picture, dominated by the figure of Charles Manson.

"Only a mind left out of our world's thoughts can see all thoughts & know the love that is at the bottom of it all," she wrote. "Our soul is in Folsom prison—our life is there. Out here people are running so fast to their death, they are set to take everything with them."

I continued my struggle with the idea that these two intelligent young women had arrived at a point where they'd come to view a career criminal like Charles Manson as their "soul" and their "life." And what was I to make of that last sentence? Was I supposed to check my sense of irony at the door before I entered this claustrophobic space where devoted followers of one of the most notorious killers in modern American history felt comfortable criticizing other people for allegedly "running so fast to their death" that they were "set to take everything with them"? What about the people who already *were* dead? Those who had died because of Manson and the ideas he'd drummed into the brains of his followers?

I knew Sandy had studied literature in college. For that reason, I wasn't all that surprised when she dropped the names of a few famous authors in the course of counseling me about what I should and shouldn't do with my life:

"Anyway," she wrote, "slow down & see yourself in the trees & sunsets & children & not how Wordsworth or Keats or Eliot or any of those Christian fellas see nature because they are projecting their thoughts on nature & it is their Christian mother's thoughts & nature to them tells them things about life—you know, metaphors & similes & all that stuff."

She added, "I majored 5 years in college in English lit [smiley face]—Nature & life just is & a kid has no thoughts only what mom & dad put in his head. So slow down & look at the trees & I'll tell you about our new watches in the next letter [smiley face]."

Their new *watches*? First the seed stick, now watches. Was she serious, or was she toying with me? Either way, I felt sure Manson was calling the shots. He was the one who seemed so eager to break through other people's preconceptions about time, history, and the relative values of human beings and "nature," broadly defined. Sartre may have immortalized the line "Hell is other people"—but the words could as easily have been Charles Manson's.

Ever since Squeaky had introduced the concept of "aliken" in her letter, I'd been curious to know what the word meant. Sandy explained:

Here is what Alikens are. Aliken is kin and like. Not man or

> *woman — just Aliken. People. 100% Man & 100% Woman*
> *in marriage of one & one = one in two parts. That Christian*
> *thing of man, woman, husband, wife, mom, dad, brother,*
> *sister — that's madness and keeps us divided. Alikens are all*
> *that together to each other. No one is under or over each*
> *other. No competition. We Alikens just are. What we are is*
> *no question.*

Could there be any greater irony? I was pretty sure I understood what she meant when she wrote of the need to jettison conventional ideas about families, roles, identities, hierarchies, and so on. That was Manson 101. "All is one." But I also knew that individuals in a position to know had told the police that everyone in the Family competed for Manson's attention and favor. They'd described Manson as the clear, undisputed leader of the group, the one who distributed the acid, orchestrated the orgies, assigned people their nicknames, and meted out punishments, all the while insisting that no one had the right to be "over" anyone else.

No competition? No such thing as status or hierarchies of influence? Sandy was nobody's dummy. For that reason alone, I found it astonishing that she could write such things and fail to appreciate the irony.

She ended her letter on a congenial, almost breezy-sounding note: "Hope you can read my writing Jeff. Sincerely, Sandy."

The plan she'd enclosed for how to construct a seed stick was detailed, obviously the work of someone with advanced design and drafting skills. Accompanying the blueprint was a typed description of the seed stick's symbolism. It was clearly intended as an expression of ideas that had originated with Manson. The typewritten statement even included this familiar-sounding sentence: "Make one [a seedstick] and leave a garden wherever you walk."

It was no longer possible to conclude that Sandy and Squeaky were anything but dead serious about the seed stick. Clearly, they saw it as a tool for use in spreading the message about their concern for the environment. I kept asking myself,

Are these the same women who openly admit to idolizing Charles Manson? The architect of the Tate-LaBianca killings? How was I supposed to reconcile their devotion to someone like Manson with their purported belief in the paramount importance of planting seeds, starting gardens, and promoting the cause of World Peace? A few excerpts from their statement about the seed stick:

> *A seed stick is a walking stick that plants seeds. Make one and leave a garden wherever you walk ... (The man with the thought is locked in prison and will need all our help to make the thought materialize). The walking stick is one of the first tools and extensions of man. The seed stick is both a tool and a symbol for a new beginning of perpetual peace on this planet ... It is the Father's thought to give [the earth] back to herself and the Father is no joke [emphasis added].... When you see seed sticks, remember the thought. We will walk it to the U.N. and ask the whole world to accept us as servants of life—and to help us re-plant.*

The man with the thought. The Father's will. The Father is no joke. Again, I wondered if it would be necessary for me to conclude that the women had taken up permanent residence in la-la land in order for me to accept as sincere their insistence that all Manson really wanted was "a new beginning of perpetual peace" on planet earth.

For obvious reasons, I found it a little difficult to take seriously the image of Squeaky and Sandy traipsing across the country, seed sticks in hand—and appearing at the United Nations to declare themselves "servants of life."

• • •

Sandy wrote to me again on May 11.

As I began reading her letter, I felt uncomfortably close to the women's campaign to gain access to Manson—and to secure his release from prison. "Lyn and I read your last letter while waiting at Folsom for the warden to get out of a meeting," she wrote. "We were later informed that he wasn't there. So we left our message for the warden to 'quit being such a coward, that we wouldn't bite his head off!' We will go to Folsom tomorrow & learn how our message was received. Eventually we'll get in to see Charles."

In the margin she added, "We'll get [Manson] out because we love our earth—we're working on a new trial."

I could sense her growing frustration. Obviously, she and Squeaky believed they were being treated unfairly by the warden at Folsom. And they weren't just feeling frustrated, they were feeling increasingly desperate. No one was taking them seriously. Manson was locked away, and their pleas on his behalf seemed to be falling on deaf ears.

Sandy responded to a question I'd asked her about visitation requests at Folsom, and how they got processed by the prison administration:

> *You asked how they work that—every BS way they can devise—usually ducking a situation they are afraid of. Normally it works—family & friends of the prisoner may visit. We are Charles' family—Lyn is his common law wife. He has not been outside in the sun for 5 years. He has only had a Catholic priest visit him. He is not allowed to have his guitar which he very much wants. We have been working on these matters & much more … We are doing as much as we can for balance of earth & it's getting to where if Manson is not out we have no earth.*

I'd told her in my last letter that I didn't have much interest in politics. She said she didn't either ("It's BS and a waste of time"). Then she launched into a tirade about people and organizations that she believed were playing a role in the destruction of the environment. She sounded genuinely alarmed—about air quality, water pollution, the status of indigenous cultures, fish, trees, and "noise." As she ranted on about these issues, her thinking—and writing—became more and more fragmented and disjointed.

"Jeff, it's not politics," she wrote. "It's $ killing life & it breaks my heart to see one tree cut or little animal lose its home. To put it very brief—Manson must be allowed to speak in the U.N. … Our minds are on many problems."

Then she scrawled, "Many problems to fix: environment, morals, womans lib [she placed a '0' alongside that particular problem], black, Islam & everything, CIA, water, dogs, cats, birds, air, ocean, love, Indians, Mexicans." She drew a bracket around her list and wrote alongside it, "One world garden and PEACE."

At some level, she seemed to appreciate how unhinged she sounded. "Anyway," she added, "this is a crazy letter because I don't have time to write a book or 3 or 7 on what all we have been thinking and doing. We must get Manson out." Above the sentence as she'd originally written it, she added the word "legally," an apparent afterthought.

I couldn't ignore my escalating feelings of anxiety. Compounding them were the clear signs of the women's expectation that I should play an active role in a campaign of terror they wanted to wage against everyone they believed were undermining the cause of "earth balance."

Suddenly, Sandy shifted gears and directed a message straight at me. She wrote, "If you see someone hunting animals—tell them 'Stop, Manson does not like his animals killed.' You may with gentle people gently explain that people don't need meat & there are few animals as it is. If they continue to be sassy & argue, you say 'Look asshole! Don't hurt that animal & don't throw your beer can there, or your refuse in the water, dig a hole & put it there."

She wasn't done instructing me on how to handle encounters with offenders against the environment. She continued:

Use your discretion but keep the earth always in mind wherever you go & do not hesitate to do something wherever you see to do it—and a 'Manson sez' or 'Manson does not like'—animals killed, air polluted, water polluted, etc.—will often cause people to look at their actions. Those who are nice & just ignorant can be told nicely & they may concede to your truth. If they are brutes & crude & insensitive—they need to know 'Manson sez.'

I felt like I was in free fall, tumbling down a dark hole. To me, her writing seemed to reflect her belief that Manson's truth had somehow become my truth, too. Even more concerning, she seemed to assume my willingness to act as a spokesman for Manson's cause. She also seemed to assume my willingness to invoke his name as a tool of intimidation.

Next, she requested that I provide her with information about "environmental groups" and "projects" that were based in the midwestern and eastern regions of the United States. More specifically, she asked me for the names of corporations that environmental advocacy groups were squaring off with in court. Proceed unafraid, she said, urging me not to hold back if I thought that by picking up the telephone, I could help to advance the earth balance agenda, which she assumed was now my agenda, too.

Suddenly, she circled back to the subject of the seed stick. "Your own design is fine!" she exclaimed. She went even further. She suggested that if I was able to come up with my own customized seed stick design, I could spread news of it all throughout the eastern portion of the United States and disseminate copies of the explanatory materials she'd sent to me. "By next summer we should see lots of seed sticks & flowers," she predicted. She added some drawings of a smiley face and a flower.

She wanted me to know about a neighbor of theirs who had offered to lend them a helping hand: "Our neighbor Kathy (she's really pretty!) is doing a garden for us this summer [large drawing of a smiley face]." The image was just too rich. I pictured the two pro-Manson zealots in the yard outside their building, turning over the soil, helping to plant seeds, and chatting amiably with their attractive neighbor. But as I did this, images of the Tate-LaBianca savagery intruded and lent a farcical quality to Sandy's evocation of the idyllic outdoor scene, with one neighbor lending her time and talents to the people who live upstairs, who happen to be Manson followers.

In one of my letters to Squeaky and Sandy, I'd mentioned

that back when I was a kid, I used to look at flowers through a magnifying glass, thinking that if I watched them closely enough, I might be able to see them as they grew. "I liked that how you used to take a magnifying glass & watch the plants grow," Sandy wrote. Then she added a big smiley face, followed by a playful drawing of four flowers, each one taller than the one that preceded it.

At this point, she paused to offer a brief commentary on the letter she was in the process of writing:

If my letter sounds mean today—It's because it's a mean world [demonic-looking face] & I'm just getting the guts to face it. All of us humans must face our worst part & best part—as we are all each other. In each of us is the baddest, rottenest & highest Godself. People don't want to face what we been doing to our earth because they'd have to look at their own unconcern, fear, lies, bullshit, greed, etc.

Then came this head-scratcher: "The reason I can say that is 'cause I done it all [drawing of a smiley face] for 2000 years." In her first letter, she'd implied her belief that Manson was able to operate on a "world level" that transcended boundaries of time and space. Was she now implying that she was able to operate on that same level?

She responded to a question I'd asked her about the son I knew she'd given birth to about five weeks after the Tate-LaBianca murders. I'd been wondering what had become of him. She referred to him as "Cho Cho" and disclosed that he resided in Tennessee, "with other children." According to her, he was happy there, existing in harmony with nature. She added that he'd begun calling himself "Bucky." She said nothing to suggest that she missed him.

The final two pages of her letter included a hodgepodge of references, ideas, and directives. "Just love your earth #1," she urged by way of a summary. She suggested that I might want to consider disengaging from politics altogether. Then she added, a bit ominously, I thought, "Necessity will dictate policy."

She said she'd send me some photographs; she provided the street address of the neighbor who'd been helping them with their garden (as an aside, she volunteered that the neighbor had been visiting Family member Steve "Clem" Grogan in prison; Grogan had been convicted of first-degree murder and sentenced to death); and she offered a final rambling reflection on the paramount importance of "earth balance."

As she was preparing to bring her letter to a close, she was still thinking in terms of how I might be able to assist them. She wrote, "Where are you going to live in New York? Keep in touch. Do you have many friends—What will you do in N.Y.?" Then this: "Do you know of a telephone credit card # you can get for us? Take it easy. Sandy (Blue) and Lyn (Red)."

● ● ●

When her next letter arrived, in early June, my anxiety and gnawing sense of foreboding morphed into something like genuine alarm. There was no mistaking her urgency now, no denying the signs of her escalating desperation. This was the first of two letters I would receive from her in a matter of weeks. She seemed to be careening toward someplace even further beyond the pale, and it worried me that I couldn't tell exactly where she was headed.

She opened her letter with a message I'd hoped never to receive from either her or Squeaky: "Dear Jeff, *We are moving out of the realm of words* [emphasis added]. Words don't do much—look at pictures—look at your world—Don't lament it, look at it & ask yourself what kind of world do you want to live in."

Until now, her infrequent references to the Tate-LaBianca murders had all been oblique. Now, it seemed, she'd lost all interest in euphemisms and subtlety. "Look at the picture that went down in 1969," she wrote. "The warning lights have been up for 5 years. What the family is all about—or the thoughts sent out throughout the world could not be explained in 1,000,000 books. You would have to die 100 times & be reborn to begin to understand."

I knew all about "the picture that went down in 1969." That was, of course, the year of the Tate-LaBianca murders. I cringed at her reference to the "warning lights" that had been flashing for the last six years. What did she mean when she said that I would have to "die 100 times and be reborn" before I could even hope to understand the message she was trying so hard to convey? She'd run out of patience, that much was clear. She wanted a commitment from me, and she was no longer willing to wait for one.

"If you are really concerned about your world," she wrote, "give me your life & quit talking."

She added that if I chose inaction, I could gather all my friends together and just bullshit for hours about how bad things were all throughout the world. Or maybe we could all "get [ourselves] some girlfriends & get married," then let our wives "run [us] around like [our] moms did to [our] dads." Yet another pathetic option would be for all of us to behold "pictures of a dying planet on TV & in *Time* magazine," then lament how "terribly tragic" it was that so many people were so indifferent to the cause of "earth balance."

As she saw it, if I did any of those things I'd be opting for passivity, choosing to remain on the sidelines while warriors like her, Squeaky, and Manson carried out their crusade to save the planet.

Not only was she done talking, she wanted *me* to be done talking, too.

More forcefully now, she again demanded that I supply her with specific information about corporations whose business practices were damaging the environment. Not only that, she ordered me to conduct research at my local library so that I could supply her with "names & phone numbers of chairmen of the boards." I knew she was testing me. "Let me know when you've done that," she wrote.

Then came one of the whiplash-inducing pivots I'd come to expect from her.

"I wrote this before we received your last letter," she said. In the letter she referred to as my last one, I'd made a glancing reference to the four months I spent in England during the fall of 1973. She continued,

> *I saw the scene in England thru your eyes. I've been in England [it might be worth recalling in this context that her former husband died there, with his throat slit, in December 1969] … It is truly beautiful … I know you like the simpler life & it's good. What new time is about is a way to slow down … The rest of the world is going 700 miles an hour — If my letters are mean, I'm reflecting a mean balance—for earth clean up is more than a smile & friendly face & the peace sign held up.*

Then she got down to business. She and Squeaky were done fooling around. No one's words—not theirs, not mine, not anyone else's—were going to change the dire condition of the planet. If "earth clean up" was going to be more than just an empty slogan, it was time to act. They needed me to act, too. She wrote:

> *We are very busy. Earth clean up is more than words — & we have a family in prison & several million children & all the wildlife to take care of … It's come to the point where we are all only moving for one purpose. When our earth comes to peace we can lay down under a blue sky & know we are in one world garden at peace. Until then it's going to get so bad in this U.S. you're going to lose your mind & go mad.*

I was hoping I could hold on to my mind, and if at all possible, I wanted to avoid going mad. My first thought was that her reference to madness might have been a projection, a sign, probably unintended, that she herself was undergoing some sort of mental disintegration. She alluded to all the sacrifices she and other members of the Family had made, ostensibly in the service of "earth balance."

Then she turned her attention to Manson's plight and suggested, once again, that it was inextricably tied to the fate of the entire planet. "Manson has been in the hole for 3 years," she wrote. "His family went to prison for—to the gas chamber. All for the balance of our earth."

For a moment anyway, she sounded like she was done wasting her time on me. Unless, that is, I was ready to stand shoulder to shoulder with her and Squeaky as fellow combatants in a war against people intent on destroying the earth.

"If you wish to do something—Let me know. Okay?" she wrote. Then she added, "Keep loving the love & the stronger your love grows for life—you'll just begin to see us. Sandy & Lyn."

Did she not see the irony implicit in so many of the things she was saying? How could she possibly claim that a "love ... for life" was the bedrock principle behind their efforts—and Manson's! —to save the environment and promote "earth balance"? Did she perceive no contradiction at all between her claim to love all life and the blitzkrieg of violence that Manson had unleashed on the city of Los Angeles just six years prior? She'd enclosed several other things in the envelope that contained her letter. Two of them were photographs. One was of her, crouched down low to the ground and apparently planting something. The second was of Family member Cathy "Cappy" Gilles, standing alongside a mule.

The third enclosure was a four-page typewritten document. Accompanying it was a handwritten note, explaining that the document was from 1970, the year of Manson's trial. She requested that I send it back to them when I was done reading it. (I did as she instructed—but only after I'd made a copy for myself.) Her handwritten note read, in part, "We've thrown away almost all words. Send this back—it is the only copy."

There was nothing the least bit reassuring about the content of the typewritten document. As I began to read it, the voice I heard was unmistakably the voice of Charles Manson. A few excerpts:

The Soul knows all there is to know ... You are tricked away from your godself by words of evil, good, right, wrong, soon. All is good ... Yes, my children, judgment day is due ...

> *I stand alone with my mark [a drawn swastika] as a wit-*
> *ness to the truth ... To me your world is backwards and it*
> *has started to move ... Me—I'm dead, crazy, and never got*
> *a mind to blow ... no mom dad and no school. I am total*
> *fear—all now and growing ... I have given you all I have*
> *and am at peace with no fear, only love for the children who*
> *are misled by the lie your world moves in—calling me to*
> *war with the beast who teaches not to kill when he is the*
> *killer. The only wrong is the wrong he makes up ... Hopeless*
> *world to die—As no tears left in love's eye.*

So here was Manson, five years prior, predicting a day of judgment for anyone unwilling to recognize him as a "witness to the truth," with a swastika carved in the skin on his forehead. The world's "lie" had called him to "war with the beast who teaches not to kill when he is the killer."

When I wrote my response to Sandy's letter, I tried to walk a very fine line. I had no intention of signing on to become one of Charles Manson's eco-warriors. On the other hand, I wanted to avoid saying anything that might cause Squeaky and Sandy to perceive me as their enemy. It was easy enough to throw my support behind the abstract goal of "protecting the environment." But I knew that wouldn't be enough.

I saw clearly now that I was in way over my head. The problem, or at least one of them, was that I hadn't yet come up with an exit strategy. I mailed my letter, uncertain what was going to happen next.

• • •

A day or so after she would have received my letter, Sandy fired off a reply. In bold print at the top of the first page, she recorded the date: June 30.

Never for one single moment had I lost sight of the fact that Sandy and Squeaky were writing to me from outside prison. Along with their friend Susan Murphy (whose existence I still didn't know of at the time), they shared an attic apartment in downtown Sacramento. Of late, I'd been having intrusive thoughts of them showing up unannounced on my parents' doorstep. They knew the address, so it would be easy enough for them to find me.

This last letter from Sandy—that is, the last one she wrote me before she was sentenced to 15 years in federal prison for conspiracy to send threatening letters through the U.S. Mail—scared me in a way none of her other letters had, even the last one. Fourteen handwritten pages long, it read like a terrorist manifesto. It was a desperate call to action—and I was the one being called. Had I done the things Sandy instructed me to do in her letter, I probably would have ended up in federal prison myself.

A woman named Misty Hay who'd begun corresponding with Manson at around this same time was arrested and sentenced to five years in prison for sending threatening letters through the mail. One of her letters was to the president of the Sierra Club, an organization that Sandy wanted me to contact. The language that landed Hay in hot water—e.g., "Do your part to stop them from cutting down trees or else you'll be chopped up yourself"—is eerily similar to the language Sandy urged me to use in the letters she wanted me to write to people she claimed were offending against the environment.

But I'm getting ahead of myself.

Before actually tackling the text of Sandy's letter, I shuffled through the pages and made some mental notes about the letter's *appearance*. As she had for her other letters, she'd chosen bright pink stationery. This time, however, her writing was bold and aggressive-looking, produced with a blue felt-tip Flair instead of an ink pen. For emphasis, she'd underlined whole sections of text; made liberal use of capital letters; scratched out many words and phrases; included bold drawings of angry-looking faces; and arranged large chunks of text in an uneven and haphazard manner.

I was concerned because the letter looked so different from all her other letters. But that concern was nothing compared to the concern I felt when I began to read what she'd actually written.

In my letter, the one she was responding to, I'd described a television segment about a deer-culling operation that was being carried out by a governmental agency somewhere in the area surrounding Buffalo. The story was one I was pretty sure would be of interest to her and Squeaky. I was right. I'd said nothing in my letter to suggest a belief on my part that any kind of intervention was warranted. Now, however, I could see that the women had read my letter in a way I hadn't intended for it to be read. They'd apparently interpreted my choice to inform them about the deer-culling operation as a sign that I was finally ready to join them in their war against those who they believed were harming the air, trees, water, and animals (ATWA).

At the start of her letter, Sandy sounded genial enough: "Dear Jeff, Good to hear from you and that you're moving for clean-up—and not just talking about it [drawing of a smiley face]."

I recognized here an echo of a statement she'd made in her previous letter, about how we were "moving out of the realm of words." In that letter, she'd declared that the time for action was upon us. In fact, she'd stated emphatically that she and Squeaky were done with "paper words" and analysis. Now, she was back and ready to put me to work. First, she assigned me the task of figuring out "who [was] killing deer & what department [was] justifying it."

Then she gave me a specific set of instructions that she wanted me to use to obtain the information she was after:

Jeff—in your meanest most vicious voice [here, in bold print, she drew an angry-looking face] call up the responsible parties most preferably at their homes and tell them to "stop killing those animals or Manson will put YOUR blood on the wall. Try to speak to the ol' wives. If they say Who? tell them MANSON, remember Sharon Tate? Tell the earth & air & water killers to use all their money to clean air etc.—or Manson will send for their heads.

That passage appeared on the first of her letter's 14 pages. There was a lot more she wanted to say. If the warnings about Manson sending for their heads and putting their blood on the wall weren't enough to get their attention, I was to try something else: "Tell them there is a wave of assassins that will sweep through their homes & splash blood from room to room."

Was she serious? Was she really expecting that I would say these things? Acting on her behalf? On *Manson's* behalf?

Without missing a beat, she shifted her focus from deer-killers to lumber companies, whose profits depended on trees being cut down.

"Tell the lumber company executives or their wives that the trees are Charles Manson's cousins & to stop cutting them down or he will chop them down—remember Sharon Tate, etc.?"

Sharon Tate, etc.?

She was very explicit about how she wanted me to deliver these verbal threats: "You may use your imagination but maintain a mean clear voice & FIRM—Don't be nervous or hang up suddenly, check out the reactions & don't hesitate to talk LOUD or even yell."

At this point she pulled back the throttle a little and not for long. She paused for a moment to observe that her heart had been breaking—"to put it mildly"—as a result of "looking at pictures in magazines" and seeing depictions of "endangered species etc."

She referenced a moving letter she'd received from a 16-year-old girl who lived in New York City (she offered to send me the girl's letter the next time she wrote me). The teenager had reportedly expressed how it made her feel "when she [saw] … pictures of poisoned & mutilated animals." Sandy suggested that since I and the teen both lived in New York State, perhaps the two of us could "hook up" as eco-warriors in training.

She directed me to send her "names of environmental control people." After remarking that she had "wonderful" letters she'd like to send them, she drew a menacing face, its features contorted with rage.

She urged me to realize that big changes were on the near horizon. "Tables are turning, Jeff. There is a group or organization called the I.P.C.R., International People's Court of Retribution, & they are an army & they are in truth & the time will be soon when they move to enact justice & it's not pretty for those who have mutilated our earth."

Even though she and Squeaky lived 2,500 miles away from where I lived, her use of the word "army" and her suggestion that members of the army would soon move "to enact justice" had the effect of all but obliterating the distance between us, at least so far as I was concerned.

She had more to say about the strategy she wanted me to adopt when I phoned the homes of the environmental control people. "Might give the heads of those departments (their wives) a call—See, the wives got big fear & control the husbands. The husbands hunt & kill because they are frustrated & don't feel like men. The wives keep them emasculated below the awareness of the man—it's been going on for hundreds of years."

I recognized this as Manson-speak. I knew, for example, that when Manson delivered his lengthy statement during the sentencing phase of his trial, he'd had a lot to say about men and women, and about the power dynamics that he thought defined relationships between the sexes (e.g., "It's the man's fault … [She] blames it on the man … [She] lays around the house and she tells him what he should do … [She] tells him what to wear, when to get up, when to go to work").

Sandy urged me not to get distracted or be deterred by superficial remedies (e.g., fines) that might make it appear as though offenders against the environment were being held accountable for their actions.

"It's a cover up," she wrote. "That's why it must come to MEAN & FEAR—the only thing that will stop them."

She insisted that Manson's was "the only totally positive mind in the world," and that he was the only person alive who could see the totality of "the picture for earth clean up." Everyone else on earth had been "programmed to death." She lamented that words weren't adequate to express the profound "thought" she was trying to convey.

In my last letter, I'd referred to a newspaper article about another inmate who was said to have attacked Manson in prison. She acknowledged that "a jealous fella with much hate" had, in fact, "jumped" Charlie. According to her, instead of fighting back in a way that would have caused "waves throughout the prison & country," Manson adopted a kind of rope-a-dope strategy and just let the incident wash over him.

She reiterated the familiar theme that Manson-the-person was nothing at all like the caricature of him that had dominated coverage of the Family in the popular press. "Subconsciously people follow what they think Manson is," she wrote. "Manson is not a tough guy who fights. He doesn't wish to show competition etc. If he were to fight such a person—it would be final."

In other words, I thought, *he'd kill you before he'd "fight" you.*

She assured me that if I was willing to commit myself to "this earth clean-up project," I could count on the backing of "forces, energy, God—etc., whatever word you want to use."

Then, she interjected this aside: "We are awaiting word on whether we can see [Manson] at Quentin. If we can we'll move to the Bay Area." Next, she segued to a screed against all the people who were living in what she described as "Madison Avenue reality," seemingly oblivious to the importance of earth "clean up."

"Jeff—soon they will go nuts," she predicted.

At this point in her letter, she launched into a fresh tirade focused on a woman named Bonnie Buxton who she said had written a "sick" article in *Cosmopolitan* magazine about what great lovers "Oriental, Hindu, and black men" are supposed to be. She dismissed the article as "women's lib thought" (verboten in Manson-world), provided me with the address of the publishers of *Cosmopolitan*, and suggested that I place a telephone call to Buxton (presumably to tell her how outraged I was because of what she'd written).

Sandy was clearly trying to gauge my willingness to carry out her instructions. She continued, "I have a list I could send you with phone numbers. Let me know when you're ready to get on the telephone." Meanwhile, she wanted me to conduct some independent research. Specifically, she wanted me to locate phone numbers and home addresses of "businessmen and financiers" who might qualify as enemies of the environment.

Apropos of nothing in particular, she paused to observe, "Wish my handwriting was as good as yours [drawing of a large smiley face]. That's my biggest personal problem right now—I gots terrible penmanship. Women's lib would say—penwomanship [another drawing of a large smiley face]."

When I considered it in the overall context of her letter, this playful-seeming aside seemed beyond bizarre.

Her very next sentence? "Duponts are juicy ones to threaten."

She continued, "You yell at them—tell them they been killing our country and other countries too long and either stop now or MANSON'S gonna do 1000 times worse to them [than] what they did to Vietnam babies & the people of this country."

She used my first name, apparently hoping to further personalize her message: "Jeff—those people know in their souls how hideous they are & their guilt is tremendous. They're half dead under the weight of it already & they reflect their death wish on earth."

She promised me that I would experience profound feelings of satisfaction if only I would lend my full support to their earth clean-up project. "You will witness balance in your life time," she wrote. "Stay on your job & balance will be easier on you. You get back what you put out & for the first time in your entire life you got something to do that means something."

She wanted to see tangible evidence that I was, to use her phrase, "on the job." She told me, "Send addresses and phone #'s of those you will call to us."

She was curious about my potential as a networker.

"If you have any friends who are not living in their mommy's fear or girlfriend's mommy's fear & got heart enough to see what needs to be done—they may help you. Don't ask if you have doubts. They will use some goodie goodie 'Oh that's wrong' BS to justify their fear (Mom's fear)," she wrote.

Suddenly, she shifted her attention back to the environmental control outfit that had been carrying out the deer-culling operation in western New York: "#1 call that environmental control group, really get on them. Send me their address (home address preferably of Directors)."

Then this: "Tell them *anyone caught killing deer are going to get their arms chopped off* [emphasis added]. If you know anyone who will hunt hunters—put 'em on their job. They could lay out in the woods—kill a hunter & then leave a note—'There are hunters hunting hunters.'"

After a glancing reference to a few relatively inconsequential practical matters, she added an incongruous-seeming dollop of breezy good humor.

"OK," she wrote. "On the other things—trees, air, water, etc.—get the ph #'s etc.—make a good list, xerox and send to us. We will give you the go ahead to start the phone calls when we hear from you. Got it? Rhight-O (English accent)." Then she added, "Also, if you can get lists of Eastern states fish and game commissions directors & wildlife protection agencies etc. Addresses & phone #'s. Send one to us and keep yourself a copy."

The next page of her letter looked different from all the ones that had come before it. The text was a haphazard-looking array of oversized printing and unevenly spaced cursive writing.

"IDEA. Call the TV station that did the story on deer. Say you were shot at in the woods while hunting. Say you found a note, 'There are hunters hunting hunters.' Make notes—IPCR [International People's Court of Retribution] kills hunters—put on trees in woods. Call the newspaper in that area too."

There was no avoiding the conclusion that she wanted me to supplement my campaign of tele-terrorism with a grab bag of guerilla tactics, all intended to amplify their messages of fear and intimidation.

On the last page of her letter, she proposed a strategy whereby I could charge all my telephone calls to the numbers of the very same people she was asking me to threaten. She seemed delighted by her own cunning and ingenuity: "That's a wonderful idea if I do say so myself!" She ended her letter, "Bye, Sandy & Lyn P.S. Tear this letter up & flush it."

I didn't tear the letter up; nor did I "flush it." Of course I had no intention of doing any of the things she'd ordered me to do. Instead, I began to think in earnest about how I was going to extricate myself from an entanglement that I thought had the potential to get me killed. I wanted out—but with as little drama as possible. And I wanted to avoid a misstep of the kind that could enrage Sandy and Squeaky to the point where they might consider targeting me for retribution.

Accompanying Sandy's letter was a lengthy typewritten document that drew an explicit connection between "earth clean up" and the murders that members of the Manson Family had committed less than six years prior. This document did nothing to quell my fears. Here are some excerpts:

> *I want your complete attention and understanding. Look at your hand, feel your pulse, make a fist. That's life in that hand ... If you have seen the amount of killing that goes on in this country ... you may have great fear as to just how many killers you would need to kill. But we have a solution to that. The Manson Family gave their lives to provide that solution. All killing comes under one law, cause, reason—earth clean up. If you are an animal backed in a corner, you fight with all the strength and cunning you got... The Manson Family already set the stage ... The Tate-LaBianca murders killed thought with the only thing people respect and understand—blood ... 1969 told this story and the reality of Hollywood. Not everyone saw it but they will ... 1969 stabbed a fat grocery story owner [Leno LaBianca] in the stomach and wrote WAR [on his stomach] and stood as a reflection of Nixson's reality and what Nixson does to his children. The Tate-LaBianca murders are Nixson's conspiracy because all*

*of us have been living in the thoughts of others ... Manson
has thoughts that can clean the whole thing but he cannot
save people who don't want saving. He has been pulling us
all uphill as it is and he's tired, and alone, been beat, yelled
at every day, without sunshine, air, exercise and nothing to
do—drugged if he sings too loud! ... And in truth, the word
murder in this country is really synonymous with breakfast ... Manson gave his life to save our lives, his children's
lives, his people's lives, the animals, plants, and this earth...
It wasn't 'too hard,' 'too big' or too crazy for the [Manson
Family] girls to do what their awareness told them. Nobody
can explain those murders but Manson, and the Family. But
those murders stand behind the threats we are making. Soon
the International People's Court of Retribution will move as
a wave of assassins to clean this earth and stop the killing.
I'm going to run down what needs doing. It is your own life
in the balance. All killing under one mind. **Manson is the
balance** [emphasis added].*

Manson. Blood. "All killing under one mind." Murder
and breakfast, neither better nor worse than the other. The lessons of '69. Multiple murder as "the only thing people respect
and understand." A "wave of assassins" that will "clean this
earth and stop the killing." *War.*

I'd heard enough.

It took me a day to come up with an exit strategy that I
thought might work. I wrote Sandy and Squeaky a letter in
which I told them I'd traveled from New York to Wisconsin,
and explained—falsely—that I was planning to spend what
remained of the summer hitchhiking around the country with
a friend.

On the envelope containing my letter to them, I wrote no
return address. I enclosed that envelope in a larger envelope
and mailed the larger one to a close college friend who lived in
Wisconsin, National Public Radio correspondent Jacki Lyden.
I asked Jacki to place the envelope I'd addressed to the Manson
women in a local mailbox so that it would arrive in California
bearing a Wisconsin postmark.

The plan worked. My letter would have arrived in California during the first week in July. The next news I heard from Sacramento came less than two months later, in the form of screaming national headlines: *Squeaky had attempted to kill the president.*

•••

All these years later, I'm still trying to figure out why the FBI never expressed an interest in talking to me, or at least reviewing the letters I'd received from Squeaky and Sandy. In light of Squeaky's attempt on the president's life, it's hard to imagine they wouldn't have had an interest in reading things her roommate and closest friend wrote to me about killing people, chopping people's arms off, and mobilizing a "wave of assassins" to sweep through the homes of people Squeaky and Sandy had targeted and condemned as offenders against the environment. I would have handed over all the materials in my possession had the feds reached out and requested access to them. But they never did.

Federal agents did, on the other hand, notify the FBI's field office in Buffalo that they'd uncovered a batch of my letters in the women's apartment. I was told—by my dad, who was assigned to the Buffalo office at the time—that they'd contacted the Buffalo office because they feared for my safety. (By September 5, when the assassination attempt took place, I'd already relocated from New York to West Lafayette, Indiana, where I'd begun working toward my master's degree in English at Purdue University.)

The next time I heard from Squeaky and Sandy, they were both in federal prison.

There were plenty of people eager to sample Squeaky's thinking in the months following the assassination attempt. I was one of many. I'd sent her a letter after she was tried, convicted, and sentenced to life in prison. She included me as one recipient of a group letter she mailed from the San Diego-area lock-up where she was sent to serve the first part of her sentence.

For reasons unknown, she dated her letter incorrectly. She used the date June 21, 1975, which would have been two and a half months *before* the assassination attempt—and almost two weeks *before* Sandy sent me her last letter, the one I've likened to a "terrorist manifesto." The envelope containing Squeaky's letter is postmarked June 23, 1976, which means that the letter was mailed approximately nine months after her attempt to kill the president.

The voice in the letter was unmistakably Squeaky's: earnest and urgent, with a messianic undercurrent. The letter's opening paragraph ended on a note that brought to mind Sandy's first sentence in the penultimate letter she sent me ("We're moving out of the realm of words"). Now, it was Squeaky's turn: "[The] days grow short that words and thought exchanges extraneous to purpose can be played."

Squeaky made it clear that she was frustrated almost beyond measure—and not just because of her own predicament. She was also frustrated on behalf of all the other Manson Family members who were then behind bars, according to her "for reasons nobody [had] ever bothered to find out." As she saw it, each and every one of them deserved a new trial. The fate of the entire country was at stake. "A new court room could save the U.S.," she wrote.

Just as Sandy had in the letters she wrote me, Squeaky drew an explicit link between the plight of the Manson Family murders and the countless wrongs that were infecting American society. "Lust" and pornography were among the subjects on her mind. "If you have ever or more recently looked through the adult magazines you can see a small part of where reality is going," she wrote. Then she added, in a note that made little sense to me, "It culminates in the Tate House."

She decried the hypocrisy of people who claim to be horrified by murder, yet then turn around and revel in it. "Most... who surrounded the Family during the Tate-LaBianca trials feigned concern," she wrote, "feigned insult or shock and then proceeded to joke and secretly lust for blood ... [We] watched the press people hunger for violence ... on one hand speak of the "grisly' details to an eager audience; and on the other hand, have a party where they all come dressed as the defendants."

As always, Manson was at the forefront of her thinking. Not only did she insist he was innocent of the murders he'd been convicted of, she described him as innocent in the same way a child is innocent. "Manson, himself, had nothing to do with these murders," she wrote, "and yet he has spent 6 and 1/2 years in a hole … He is a child, and is the only child on the face of the earth who has been through as much as long without growing beyond the eyes of a child in the truth."

She added this unassailable observation: "You have never seen anything like him."

Then she continued on in this same vein: "I can see now that there is no one else. He is not in your thoughts and has never been of your thinking. Thus, you cannot know him in words. He is in motions and eyes and the songs that come from the Universe. His awareness spans the skies and the birds … the animals, the trees and for me to write in words what he is never suits me."

To truly understand where she was coming from, she added, "you would have to see and know him."

She returned to the themes of sacrifice and martyrdom, suggesting that the Family members' "willingness to give [their] lives" might ultimately redeem the planet. At the very least, the Family's "circle of truth" had the potential to "save the U.S."

She urged recipients of her letter to do everything in their power to convince the appellate courts in California that "the Family" was entitled to "a new trial." She included herself among those who'd been betrayed by the legal system. Time, she emphasized, was of the essence. "Do it right away," she said. By "it," she meant "press the case for a new trial."

She enclosed a handwritten draft of a letter she said others could use to make the case that her conviction should be overturned. She emphasized that first and foremost, the appellate judge who was overseeing her case needed to receive assurance that she wasn't "a nut." She wanted everyone to recognize that her "sole and whole purpose" on the day she pointed a loaded gun at President Ford was to publicize her "family's sacrifice," and to expose the fact that they "did not get to show themselves and were slandered beyond recognition."

In a postscript to her letter, she urged her readers to point out to the appellate court how absurd it was to suppose that she actually intended to kill the president. "Tell them as you saw it," she wrote. "If you were going to shoot someone, wouldn't you load the chamber, wouldn't you dress inconspicuously [and not in a floor-length hooded red robe], wouldn't you be sure to kill in a small crowd such as that?" [Note: There was, in fact, an empty chamber in her otherwise fully loaded gun. The authorities later found a single bullet on the floor of the bathroom in her apartment.]

In the margin of her letter, she added a handwritten note, intended as a personal reminder to me that sometimes, if there's a particularly important issue at stake, subtle messaging just won't be sufficient to carry the day. "You don't understand or respect your own kids until they make you by beating you over the head" is how she put it.

•••

The last letter I ever received from Sandy Good arrived in an envelope postmarked June 12, 1976. It's a typewritten letter, personally addressed to me. She was responding to a letter I'd sent her after she was shipped off to federal prison.

In December 1975, a little less than six months after my receipt of her unhinged terrorist manifesto, she and Susan Murphy—the third occupant of the P Street apartment—were indicted for "conspiracy to send threatening letters through the mail." The indictment came about as a result of death threats the women had allegedly mailed to 170 corporate executives whose business practices they considered hazardous to the environment. The following March, Sandy was convicted and sentenced to a 15-year prison term.

Clearly, she remembered who I was. However, she incorrectly stated that she sent me her last letter toward the end of August (which, if true, would have meant that she sent it only a week or so before Squeaky's attempt on the president's life). In any case, she signed in by expressing her frustration over the fact that I hadn't been willing to do all the things she instructed me to do.

"Dear Jeff," she began. "I wrote you a lengthy letter in I believe late August or so wherein I gave you a list of meaningful things you [could] do as you seemed in your paper words to have some concern. You did not answer that letter and you are still playing in word confusion and thoughts and opinions of others. You don't know what Lyn did or why or anything." [She was mistaken. I *had* answered her letter. My reply was the letter I'd asked my friend to mail to her from the friend's hometown in Wisconsin.]

She made an ominous-sounding reference to the negative consequences that awaited anyone prepared to "put money over life." Just the year before, she'd written to tell me that such people risked getting their arms and heads chopped off.

She was willing to concede that her unsuccessful crusade to get Manson a new trial and accomplish "earth balance" had taken its toll on her. "I'm not too nice myself any more though I like me a lot," she wrote. "I'm mad at people who know but don't care. Was Christ a selfless do-gooder? Is he angry now?" Repeatedly, she drew a sharp contrast between her own willingness to act and my reliance—overreliance, she said—on education and "paper words." A few excerpts:

Put this in your English books and shove it. The paper comes from dead trees and the forests are disappearing fast….We just shouted these things and you're still in school while we carry your world on our back in prison. And [Manson's] been carrying it all for longer than you know … [Lyn] GAVE HER LIFE (and not in vain) for the balance of our earth … Jeff, I'm writing mean but I see your world—I've been in it—a college robot and a sensitive one at that, and I see how dead and stinking that trip is. Your thoughts are unreal and I don't have time to play word games. You do what you can for what you know needs to be done. If you can't give, and hide in school, don't blame us because you don't understand. I can't give you awareness. Hard times will do that.

In the same way Squeaky had, she portrayed Manson as someone not of this world. "You could NEVER figure where Charlie is coming from," she wrote. "Try to figure out the perfection of the Universe … Manson is coming from all around you in all you know and all you don't know. Manson is not a personality. He comes from a child's mind living in truth and Knowing."

She continued, "In a lot of ways I'm not as nice as [he is]. His love is total—His anger will be total if we all don't get in his will and nothing on earth can stop it. Alive or not, thought has been set. I'm mean and sharp-tongued. Things are not always nicey nice with a smiling face."

She urged me to write California's Second Court of Appeals and demand that Manson, Fromme, and all the other imprisoned Family members be granted new trials.

She closed with one final expression of faith, in Manson and his vision of earth balance:

Try carrying one one thousandth of what [Manson's] been under and you'd go mad in a day. I couldn't carry it. No one could. It's hard communicating with words on paper. Much is said in expression, eyes, motion. We are (Manson women) as good as we are mean and I'm meaner every day and gooder and happier every day in knowing Faith. Have a good day, Sandy (Blue).

She added this postscript: "Lyn and I are Nuns. I wear a blue scarf that looks like a habit every day."

• • •

I never heard another word from Squeaky or Sandy. I never wrote to them again either.

Even though they were in prison, I remained wary of them and uncertain of their reach. Especially after the assassination attempt, I had no way of knowing how far they might be willing to go in pursuit of their objectives.

It didn't help that I remembered something Manson follower Susan Atkins said to a fellow inmate at the Sybil Brand Institute in Los Angeles in late-1969. She said that even though Manson was in police custody, there were other Family members still on the outside who were planning to commit more murders, *many* more. In 1976, I didn't know how many people, in which parts of the country, made up the network of Manson sympathizers.

•••

Now, 45 years on, Sandy and Squeaky are both free. Sandy was paroled in December 1985, after she'd served nearly ten years of her 15-year sentence. In a 2019 interview with a representative of Oxygen Media, she stated, "[Manson and the Family] really saved my health, my brain, my emotional health, my mental health, my physical health. I'm thankful to them all." In 2017, she attended Manson's funeral.

Squeaky left prison on parole in July 2008, some 20 years after she'd escaped from a federal women's prison in West Virginia and spent two days on the lam before being apprehended by the authorities and taken back into custody.

In most respects, she was said to have been a model prisoner. However, at one point during her incarceration she told a newspaper reporter, "The curtain is going to come down on all of us, and if we don't turn everything over to Charlie immediately, it will be too late."

More than a decade after her release from prison, she granted a rare televised interview. Of her relationship with Manson, who'd died two years prior, she had this to say: "Was I in love with Charlie? Yeah … I still am."

4.
Sadie

Susan Atkins: the girl who might start screaming and never stop.

Los Angeles Times reporter David Smith captured the image: "Watching [Atkins'] behavior—bold and actressy in court, cute and mincing when making eye-play with someone, a little haunted when no one pays attention—I get the feeling that one day she might start screaming, and simply never stop."

Prosecutor Vincent Bugliosi had the exact same feeling about Atkins; he said so in the closing pages of *Helter Skelter*. Susan Atkins may have been the Manson Family's second most notorious member (after Manson himself).

I considered writing to her when I began exchanging letters with Charles Manson and Squeaky Fromme, just months before my graduation from college in the spring of 1975. Ultimately, I decided against doing so, in part because David Smith's evocation of the eternal screamer reactivated a childhood memory of mine, one that remained vivid and terrifying despite the passage of so many years, and despite my best efforts to suppress it.

I was about 14 years old when my parents, my older sister, and I visited my paternal grandparents in Massachusetts. Their house was located on the grounds of a state psychiatric hospital. My grandfather, a psychiatrist, was the superintendent in charge there.

One evening after dinner, we all went for a walk around the hospital property. Suddenly, not ten yards from where we were standing, a female patient flung herself onto the ground, emitted a blood-curdling scream, and began demanding that the devil emerge from a small hole that was located about an inch from her face. I froze, then watched in awe and terror as the woman began to claw at the ground.

Was the devil really down there? I wanted to believe the answer was no—but how could I be sure? The woman continued screaming, and she still hadn't stopped by the time my grandfather urged us to move along. My best guess is that only about 30 seconds had elapsed since the nightmarish scenario began to unfold

The more I reflected on what it might be like to correspond with someone like Susan Atkins, the less inclined I was to do it—or to even *try* to do it.

But over the course of the next year, I began to think differently about Atkins and the idea of trying to draw her into a dialogue. By February 1976, I'd concluded that the stubborn memory of the screaming woman who'd been trying to summon the devil from a hole in the ground shouldn't stand in the way of my desire to reach out to Atkins.

Six months had elapsed since Squeaky Fromme's attempt on the president's life; Sandy Good was now in federal custody for sending threatening letters through the U.S. mail; I'd successfully completed my first semester of graduate school; and I already had nearly a year of correspondence with Charles Manson under my belt. I guess I was feeling somewhat emboldened by the success I'd had getting him, Squeaky, and Sandy to respond to my letters—and I was still just as curious as I'd always been to discover whether Atkins was, in reality, the homicidal, unhinged banshee she'd been portrayed as in the popular press.

I had no way of knowing if she'd respond to a letter from a graduate student in the Midwest, someone whose name she'd never even heard before, but I decided to write to her anyway. I was committed to doing my best to keep an open mind. But in truth, it was tough to imagine that even if Atkins defied the odds and answered my letter, I'd learn much about her that I didn't already know. For starters:

• Before even joining the Manson Family, she'd been a sex worker—and also an affiliate of Anton LaVey's notorious First Church of Satan;

• When she testified as a grand jury witness, she acknowledged that there was nothing she wouldn't do for Charles Manson;

• She was an active participant in the July 1969 murder of Manson Family acquaintance Gary Hinman;

• She told Ed Sanders, author of *The Family*, that members of the Manson Family participated in occult rituals that included drinking dogs' blood;

• She was an eager participant in Manson's "creepy crawly" missions, where, to conquer their own fear and instill terror in others, Family members would sneak into people's homes in the dead of night and leave telltale signs meant to telegraph the fact that they'd been there;

• When she was arrested, in October 1969, she said her name was Sadie Mae Glutz;

• During her murder trial, she strolled gaily through the corridors of the Los Angeles Hall of Justice, beaming alongside her co-defendants and singing the words to the Manson-penned refrain, "All is one, all is one, all is one";

• Her fellow inmates at the Sybil Brand Institute knew her by the nickname "Crazy Sadie";

• She told two of those inmates that she performed fellatio on her infant son;

• She told one woman at Sybil Brand that she killed actress Sharon Tate because she "loved her";

• She bragged about licking Tate's blood off her fingers and finding it "warm and sticky and nice";

• She confided to another woman at Sybil Brand that when Tate pleaded for her own life, and for the life of her unborn child, she told the actress, "Listen bitch, I don't care about you. I don't care if you're going to have a baby. You had better be ready. You're going to die, and I don't feel anything about it";

• She claimed that stabbing Tate was "like a sexual release. Especially when you see blood spurting out. It's better than a climax"; and

• Prosecutor Bugliosi referred to her as "ever the animal" and described how she'd defecated on the landing of an apartment complex where Manson left her and two other Manson Family members—expecting them to commit murder—on the same night when other members of the Family slaughtered Leno and Rosemary LaBianca in their house in the Los Feliz area of Los Angeles.

So, a pretty sordid resume—by any barometer. I was curious to discover whether Atkins had changed at all in the five and a half years that had elapsed since she confessed to killing Sharon Tate, then testified in open court that she plunged her knife into Tate's swollen belly because she was "sick of listening to her, pleading and begging, pleading and begging." (She would later retract that part of her confession—would insist, in fact, that even though she was present to witness Tate's murder, she herself did none of the stabbing.)

To many people, the Tate-LaBianca murders probably seemed like old news by 1974. However, everything changed with the publication of *Helter Skelter* that year. The book won the coveted Edgar Award and has since become the best-selling true crime book of all time. It brought renewed attention to the sensational story of the Manson Family and propelled it to a position near the center of the cultural conversation, alongside reporting on the Watergate scandal and news of the approaching end of the war in Vietnam.

During the year that followed the publication of *Helter Skelter*, Squeaky Fromme and Sandy Good took dramatic steps in an effort to make sure the Family wasn't forgotten. Their message to the people of America? *You can lock Manson up, but you'll ignore him at your peril.* In particularly dramatic fashion (Squeaky Fromme's attempt on the president's life took place in September of 1975), they made sure that everyone was aware that Manson still had devoted followers—no one really knew how many—and that his followers would stop at almost nothing in their efforts to bring renewed attention to his plight and win him a new trial.

In early 1976, I was preoccupied with the thought, *What does Susan Atkins make of all this?*

I began to ponder the problem of how to go about arousing her interest. How should I handle my opening gambit? What approach stood the best chance of convincing her that I was someone worth writing to? I had no clear answers to those questions, but I decided on a strategy that was rooted in something I'd read following the release of *Helter Skelter*.

I couldn't remember where, but I knew I'd seen a news release stating that just a few years after the murder spree that initially netted her a death sentence, she'd announced her conversion to Christianity and declared that she'd severed all ties to Manson. I was skeptical—but intrigued nonetheless. Her first book, called *Child of Satan, Child of God*, wouldn't see the light of day until the following year, so when I wrote to her during the early part of 1976, the news of her conversion existed as little more than an unsubstantiated rumor.

In the first letter I sent her, I acknowledged having read somewhere that she'd repudiated her association with Manson and become a born-again Christian. Thinking that perhaps a reference to my own religious upbringing might be the thing that would pique her interest, I disclosed that I'd been raised a Missouri Synod Lutheran but added that I no longer thought of myself as a particularly religious person.

I promised her that I wouldn't question her directly about the crimes she'd been convicted of committing—unless, that is, she gave me permission to do so.

• • •

She must have answered my letter on the very day she received it; otherwise, her reply wouldn't have reached me so quickly.

Just as my expectations were dashed by Squeaky Fromme's floral stationery, hand-drawn smiley faces, and loopy, girlish handwriting in what turned out to be the first letter I received from anyone associated with the Manson Family, I experienced a measure of surprise when I saw what Atkins' letter looked like. I'm not sure exactly what I was expecting. Probably a physical artifact that in some way reflected the disorganized, flagrantly antisocial, and often deranged-seeming behavior that Atkins was infamous for prior to and even after her arrest. (For what it's worth, Bugliosi wrote in *Helter Skelter* that quite aside from the question of whether Atkins met the legal criteria for a finding that she was "insane," she was undoubtedly "crazy.") Her writing, done with a green ink pen, was neat and very carefully organized on the page.

Even before I unsealed the envelope containing what she'd written, I could tell that the envelope contained more than just her letter; it also contained a pamphlet titled *Three Aspects of the Cross*. I learned from reading the back cover of the pamphlet that its content was excerpted from a book called *The Cross and Sanctification*, written by a self-taught Christian apologist named T.A. Hegre.

Atkins opened her letter on a genial-sounding note. "Dear Jeff," she wrote. "Yes, my mail [here at the prison] has opened up. And since it has, it really is a joy to me to receive all the letters sent to me." Of course, I wasn't surprised to learn that other people had written her, too, no doubt for a variety of different reasons.

Most of what she said in that first letter centered around her status as a new believer in Christ. She seemed grateful for my assurances that I wouldn't press her for information related to the crimes she'd been found guilty of committing. "I'm glad you're willing to forego any discussions of my past," she said. "It's relevant only in that it carried me to the present." I remember thinking, *Uh, not exactly.*

"Yes, I've met Jesus Christ," she continued, "and asked Him to please enter my heart, forgive me my sins, and have His way in my life. There is a song which pretty well sums up what He has done with my life. 'Something beautiful, something grand/All my confusion you understand/All I had to offer Him was brokenness and strife/But He made something beautiful of my life.'"

She seemed to be anticipating how I might respond to the news of her conversion. She took great pains to assure me that she hadn't simply shifted gears and exchanged one kind of fanaticism for a different kind. "Ya know what?" she wrote. "I'm not staunch religious either [an obvious reference to what I'd told her about my own attitude toward organized religion]. I just love Jesus and want to be a Child of God. Jesus is a walking relationship—daily living—a way of life; not a religion at all!"

In her next paragraph, I thought I could hear an echo of Manson's dictum, "Step from your past and be free."

On one hand, she said she considered me lucky to have been raised in a Christian household: "How fortunate you are, truly, to [have] been blessed with Christian parents."

On the other hand, she emphasized how important it was for me to recognize that my own faith—such as it was—should never just mirror my parents' faith: "You're … right in not being satisfied with a relationship with God based on your mother's relationship," she said. "There will be NO GRANDSONS in God's Kingdom—only sons and daughters." She added that her wish for me was that I might come to know God in the same way she'd come to know Him: "Jesus wants to know you personally—as Jeff Smalldon."

She sensed, correctly, that I was at a spiritual crossroads in my life.

"SEEK AND YOU WILL FIND!" she exclaimed. "That is a direct promise!" She continued in much this same vein, sounding as if she'd been handed the keys to everlasting life, and as if she wanted me to be able to use those keys, too.

In her formulation, it sounded so simple. All I had to do was invite Jesus into my life; the blinders would then fall from my eyes. "If you are really for real in this—I've no reason to believe you aren't—simply sincerely ask Jesus to reveal himself to you. To allow you to see clearly; and ask Him to come into your heart and be your personal Savior and Lord. He said he would & he doesn't lie."

Her choice to quote a passage from Romans, Chapter 10 seemed more than a little ironic in light of her reputation as a cold-blooded killer. The passage she cited was about how the crucified Christ died and then came back to life. She encouraged me to recognize that if I believed in the Resurrection and was willing to "confess with [my] mouth the Lord Jesus," I was well on my way to eternal life, too. "It's really that simple, Jeff."

Next, she drew a timeline meant to illustrate the path she'd traveled on her way to becoming a Child of God. She used a single word—"sin"—to summarize the first 26.5 years of her life. I knew she was 21 at the time of the Tate-LaBianca murders in 1969. So, her religious conversion had to have been a very recent development. She used the words "Sodom & Gomorrah" to represent the period of her involvement with the Manson Family. At the far right end of the timeline was a description of how she regarded her current situation: "Christ in me. Forever free from sin."

I thought, *Forever free from sin? What does that even mean?* Was she saying not only that she'd been saved, but that she'd been made perfect, no longer even capable of sinning? Or was she simply saying that in her view, she no longer needed to experience her sinful nature as an encumbrance, something that separated her from God? I wasn't sure.

She ended her letter with one more reference to her complete metamorphosis. She urged me to write her back and said that in the meantime, she'd remember me in her prayers.

"Now is daily walking with Jesus," she said, "learning more about Him by prayer & reading God's Word. Truly in [prison] I've much time to devote to my relationship. Thank you for writing. I hope I've helped you some. Thank you truly for being a non-entity. I'll try and answer any more questions you may have. I'll pray for your revelation. Truly in Christian FAITH, HOPE, LOVE, Susan Atkins."

Never before had anyone thanked me for being a "non-entity." I didn't *feel* like a non-entity, and I had no idea why she'd chosen to refer to me as one.

Unfortunately, for me her use of that term triggered an unpleasant association. I remembered that when she testified before the grand jury in advance of the Manson case trials, she used the word "thing" to refer to 18-year-old Steven Parent, the first of the Manson Family's five victims on the night of August 8-9, 1969.

Did she view me with that same level of emotional detachment? I decided I'd give her the benefit of the doubt. Probably, she was trying—if clumsily—to express her appreciation for my willingness to bring a non-judgmental attitude to our correspondence. Or maybe that was wishful thinking on my part.

• • •

I responded to her letter right away. Despite the "non-entity" reference, I was encouraged to learn of her willingness to engage with me, even if she wanted our interaction to take place in accordance with her own terms. What was I to make of the almost unimaginably stark contrast between her reputation as a homicidal maniac and her presentation as a friendly, articulate woman of faith? Would I be a fool to take her at her word? I was 22 years old and completely inexperienced when it came to criminals, long-term incarceration, and the phenomenon of conversions in prison. To be honest, I was puzzled; I didn't know what to think.

Her second letter arrived just two weeks after the first one. My letter had convinced her that I would be open to hearing her spiritual message. She sought to offer me encouragement. She also tried to make me feel like someone special. *One of God's chosen?* She wrote,

Dear Jeff, Hi. Ya know, I receive a lot of mail during the weeks here, and [the letters] all bless me in some way—but let me say honestly—your letter & genuineness in your desire to really know Jesus in your heart—touched me deeply. I want to hug you and let—sort of—as if it really could happen—my experience of Jesus—in me—rub off onto & flow

*into you. Silly me. Your experience will come—I know it
will.*

I wasn't quite sure what to make of the notorious Susan
Atkins saying that she wanted to "hug" me, and to let her experience of Jesus "rub off onto and flow into [me]."

I couldn't help but wonder, *Where in all this is Bugliosi's de-
generate "animal?" Where is the woman who, just six years ago, reveled in the opportunity to describe what it was like to watch Sharon
Tate's blood "spurt" from her body, and who likened the experience
of stabbing her to a kind of super-charged orgasm? And where is the
provocateur who told an acquaintance that the late actress's blood
tasted "warm and sticky and nice" when she licked it off her own
fingers?*

Susan shifted to a tone that seemed even more personal—and playful. "Since I've now grown in dimensions [smiley
face] to you, I'm sending along a flick. It's about a year old. So
take off 10 lbs & add 3 inches to the hair length & put wire rims
round my peepers [here she drew a pair of glasses on a smiling
face] & TA DA—ME!" That last part struck a familiar chord.
It reminded me of the extroverted drama queen who haunted
the pages of *Helter Skelter.*

The picture Susan was referring to was one that depicted
her standing in front of a chain link fence. In the picture, she's
smiling a closed-mouth smile and wearing a long, pretty, rose-
colored dress. Located around her are several pink rose bushes, rising to a height just above her waist.

The woman in the picture was immediately recognizable
as Susan Atkins. In fact, I didn't think she looked all that much
different from how she looked in many of the other pictures
of her that I'd seen, for example those that depicted her smiling broadly, basking in the glow of the media spotlight, and
singing Manson-penned songs on her way to and from court
during the period when she was on trial for murder.

Further on in her letter, she wrote of the millions of people
who were "dying spiritually" because they failed to recognize
Jesus as the only one who could fill the "God-shaped vacuum"
inside themselves. Fortunately, she added, I didn't seem to be

one of those.

"By God's unseen Grace," she said, "you reached out to me. I've given you the cure—Jesus—Love in Him and now it's up to you to take the Pill—the Gos-pill—into you to cure your ills & ease your suffering."

She acknowledged suffering as an inevitable part of living, then posited faith in the risen Christ as the only available antidote that can alleviate such suffering. "Heavy," she added—as if to acknowledge the mystery at the heart of the deceptively simple cure she was proposing.

A little later in her letter, she made an oblique reference to the enormity of her own rebellion against the Commandments set forth by God, then cited her belief in God's willingness to just lump her sins together in a big pile with everyone else's. She said she found it a source of great comfort to know that in the eyes of God, she was no more guilty—and no more lost—than anyone else.

"All that suffering has caused my relationship with God to be rich and wonderful," she said, "and I'm grateful and thankful that I'm forgiven for my sins. I'm so glad Jesus & Our Father in Heaven don't measure sin or weigh it. Sin is sin & the only real sin God counts as sin is denying His Gift of eternal life by rejecting Jesus."

In my last letter, I'd told her that I had read all the major publications pertaining not just to her but to the Manson case in general. I was hoping that by edging closer to the details of her history as a prominent member of the Manson collective, I might succeed in getting her to begin volunteering information about the subjects we'd agreed not to discuss. It didn't work. However, she seemed eager for the opportunity to contrast her own version of her life story with the versions other people had been telling.

"Since you've read all there is to be read on me," she said, "I trust you'll read my book when it comes out. Should be late summer or early fall. I know you'll get blessed by it. In Jesus' love, Susan Atkins." (As it turned her, her book didn't become available until the following year.)

Her letter didn't end with her signature. She went on

to reference having received a "postscript" from me just the night before. I'm not exactly sure what she was referring to. Presumably, I'd written her another, shorter letter after the one she'd been referring to. In any case, in my second letter I must have expressed curiosity about how her former Manson Family friends—Leslie Van Houten, Patricia Krenwinkle, and Mary Brunner, all of whom had been convicted of Family-related crimes and sentenced to terms of incarceration—were faring in prison. I knew that all four women were at the California Institute for Women at Frontera. Susan wrote,

> *P.S. Hi there. Pat [Krenwinkle] and Leslie [Van Houten] are… into writing fiction. I presume they are OK. I've not seen them for some time. They live in other cottages … Same with Mary [Brunner]. Each are [sic] into their own thing doing time. Their state of mind? I wonder too and pray for them continuously that their eyes will SEE [underlined three times in the original] the love Jesus has for them & then that they'll receive it. Had a good day [smiley face] today & I've Faith yours will be good and gooder as the days come to pass! Yours in Jesus, Susan.*

• • •

Her next letter arrived during the third week in March. This time around, she sounded not just upbeat but positively jubilant: "'Tis goin' GREAT cause Jesus has it all under control [astonished-looking smiley face]." She wrote of bedtime in the cottage that served as her prison home. To me, it seemed like she was bent on further collapsing the distance between us. "My mail all arrives late at night, 12 a.m.," she said. "So your letter really delighted my sleepy eyes."

In my last letter, I'd disclosed my rather extensive history of traffic-related citations. In my own ham-fisted way, I was trying to come across as more relatable. I figured that if I succeeded, maybe she'd perceive me as someone to whom she could confide more openly the details of her own history of law-breaking behavior.

That's not what happened. Instead, this infamous woman—who'd been found guilty of multiple counts of murder and sentenced to death—chided me, in a good-natured way, for my own history of lawlessness. "Tsk tsk," she said, referring to my occasional tendency to drive faster than the law permitted me to drive.

She allowed herself to fantasize about what it would be like to have a life outside prison. She knew, because I'd told her, that I spent most of my growing-up years only about ten miles from the Canadian border, midway between Niagara Falls and Buffalo. "Someday I'm gonna see Niagara Falls," she said. "Maybe be corny & when my fiancé & I tie the knot, talk him into takin' [me] to the Falls for the honeymoon [smiley face, drawn with elaborate eyelashes]."

I'd expressed my appreciation for the photograph—"flick"—that she sent me, the one that depicted her wearing a rose-colored dress and standing amid pink rose bushes. "Glad you like the flick," she said. "The roses grew & then the dress came [smiley face]. Now the roses are all gone & the dress hangs unworn in my closet [frowning face]."

At this point in her letter, things began to get a little weird—or so it seemed to me at the time.

To hear her tell it, having me as a correspondent was enriching her life beyond measure. "Oh, Praise the Lord," she said. "You cause Joy to bubble overflowing in my cup of daily living, knowing the Love of Christ can reach out from inked words on paper into another's heart; just knowing how much Jesus loves you really blesses me to no end."

I interpreted those words to mean that it wasn't me as a person who was enriching her life—but, rather, me as a kind of paradigmatic case, illustrating her point that Christ's love can be communicated from one person to another, even through a medium as impersonal as words committed to paper.

Settling on that more impersonal interpretation of her message didn't prevent me from feeling a growing sense of unease. *Was a deepening level of personal intimacy involving Susan and me something that I wanted to encourage?* If the answer was no, then what implications did that have for how I should handle our correspondence going forward?

At this point in her letter, she moved on to the subject of her dreams—more specifically, the dreams that featured me at their center.

"See," she explained, "[Jesus has] caused me to dream of you 3 times, once—the first time—I was battling Satan over your soul. I remember it so well, guess who won [smiley face]: Jesus!"

Faced with this invocation of her dream life and my role in it, I found myself wondering if the guardrails of her Christian belief system always held up while she was, as the saying goes, dead to the world.

I wondered whether in dreams, she might occasionally drift off into the realms of death and debauchery—the places where she was a near-constant presence before she became a lifer in the California prison system. Following her arrest less than seven years before, she'd bragged to one of her fellow inmates at the Sybil Brand Institute in Los Angeles that she'd experienced every sexual thing there was to experience.

So I had this thought: *Did Susan Atkins sometimes dream of having sex with me?*

Some of her disclosures felt uncomfortably intimate—but I was open to the possibility that the problem, to the extent one existed, was mine and mine alone.

Had I been even slightly more psychologically astute back then, I might have framed my discomfort in terms of a nagging concern over the fact that Atkins was a woman with a long history of "boundary" issues. After all, nearly all chroniclers of the Manson case agreed that her personality had basically fused with Charles Manson's—not all that long ago. Once again, I found myself thinking of the testimony she'd given when she appeared as a grand jury witness. *There was nothing she wouldn't do for Charlie.*

In this most recent letter to me, she continued, "The other two [dreams] are vague but I know they were filled with Love. Jeff, honestly I do not dream often, & *never before about someone I've never met* [emphasis added] … so I know these were gifts from God & meant to be shared with you, as signs of love and encouragement."

She couldn't recall exactly what had gone on in the other two dreams that featured me in a starring role. All she knew for certain was that the dreams were filled with "love."

She depicted us as kindred spirits, fellow travelers on the same journey of faith "Truly God has blessed us in an amazing way, Jeff ... I've dreamt of you & Jesus says so powerfully— Love one another even as I loved you."

At least judging from her vague recall of those last two dreams, the ones that she said had been "about [me]," it seemed likely that the dreams hadn't featured acts of fornication including her and me. Regardless, I experienced a sense of relief when she shifted her attention to a new subject.

"I've never read *Helter Skelter*," she said, "so [I] don't know what caused your deep sadness, tho I've heard it wasn't a pretty picture. [In my last letter, I'd remarked on the book's harrowing account of so many lost and ruined lives]. In fact, my life up till a year & 6 months ago was not a pretty picture."

Could she really be that clueless? Was it possible that she didn't know why I'd found Bugliosi's account of murder, mayhem, and madness so harrowing, and so disturbing?

Suddenly, she returned to the subject of her own forthcoming book. "[It's] been in progress since October of '75," she said. "We're believing God for its release SOON, this year." (The book's publication was delayed until 1977.)

She concluded her letter with a kind of benediction: "Shall close for now dear Son of God, a second follower to He who walked the path before us. May his love caress your life—now and forever. In Him, Susan."

Caress? Maybe I was the only one who didn't think of God's love in such sensual terms. In any case I told myself, *Stop making everything about sex.*

• • •

I didn't have a clear sense of which direction I should go with Susan. Her intense religiosity, coupled with her insistence on using it to frame her remarks about pretty much any subject I raised for discussion, made it seem unlikely that I could ever convince her to participate in a detailed back-and-forth about her tenure with the Manson Family—which of course was my primary interest.

At the outset, I'd assured her of my willingness to avoid probing for specific information about her relationship with Manson, or about any crimes she may have committed at his behest. I knew we would only ever get to those things if she decided to let her guard down and go there on her own. And I didn't see that happening. Her unrelenting "God talk" had me thinking that perhaps we'd come to a dead end.

Despite my misgivings, I decided to keep up my end of our correspondence for at least for a little while longer. I wrote her back, and she responded on March 27.

Her letter contained more of what I'd come to expect from her. "May the Peace of God & the state of blessedness continue to abide within you now and forever," she said. And so on and so forth. Again, she portrayed the two of us as fellow pilgrims, traveling on a path toward eternal life. She went even further than that, referring to us as "friends, brother and sister, little children on a journey to the Promised Land."

In my last letter, I'd requested clarification about who her "fiancé" was. Before she'd introduced a casual reference to him in one of her letters, I hadn't even known she was engaged.

She referenced some things I'd told her about my years in western New York, then explained, "Niagara Falls sounds so marvelous. Yes, I'm engaged. Praise the Lord, to a beautiful Man of God named John Daiberl. He lives in Illinois. Only 'close friends' know at this point. We've not made any 'formal announcement'—whatever that is."

She cited her involvement in the creation of a North Carolina-based organization called the New Life Foundation. She explained that its purpose was to serve as "an outreach ministry for destitute, abandoned, neglected, rejected women." She added, "It will be a home & place where really troubled girls can find a purpose for their lives and live happy, useful, and productive lives in Christ." In other words, the foundation's goal was to create a refuge for young women a lot like the young woman *she* had been—when, at age 19, she crossed paths with Charles Manson for the first time.

Also in the last letter I'd written her, I had put out a feeler, hoping to elicit some additional information about her fellow Manson Family members—and fellow convicted killers—Leslie Van Houten and Patricia Krenwinkle. Her response suggested that their prison journeys had diverged somewhat from her own.

"I've a peace now about Pat and Leslie, that a few months ago was a heavy burden [for me]," she said. "They're really into what they've written about [in some short stories]. Too far from God & Jesus from their actions & lifestyles to benefit them. Please pray they'll return or come to Jesus, whichever is the need or case." It was apparent that she no longer felt particularly close to the other women. She ended her letter by writing, "May Jesus carry all your burdens & cares. In Him who is Love, Susan."

•••

Susan sent me two more letters, one dated April 11 and the other dated April 23. After my receipt of the second one, I decided not to write her back. Unlike all of her other letters, these last two were typed.

In the letter dated April 11, she began, "Oh, ya know your letters are such a joy to read, Jeff, not for ... the compliments you so graciously lay upon me [I think I'd remarked on her reliability as a correspondent] but because what you say comes from the heart, every word does indeed touch like a soft hand stroking one's face. It is nice to have such a gentle friend. Truly I can and do thank God for you, Jeff."

Again, she spoke of the man she was planning to marry. She referred to him as "a new Christian" and explained that he'd "met the Lord" through her.

As far as I could tell, she had an utterly fanciful idea of what awaited her down the road. Of plans for a future with her fiancé, she wrote, "We think we are going to wait till I get out of here before we get married, though we could get married in here, though I don't want to. I would crumble if [John] had to walk out of here and not take me with him. I think you could relate to that."

As she so often did, she pointed to her "born again" status and made it sound as if her entire past had been rendered utterly irrelevant the moment she welcomed Christ into her life. "Being a Christian is so exciting," she said. "I had no idea what God had in mind for my life back in September of '74, but I just gave Him the ruined mess I had made of it, and what He has done with it is truly awe-inspiring to me." She predicted that I was going to experience a similar transformation in my own life.

> *Your background sounds so beautiful, Jeff. I know that God has something really great in store for you, and at just the right time He will begin to reveal it to you. He did not give you Christian parents and a Christian background for nothing, all that was preparation for something good to come into your life. Just trust Him and let Him bring you into the fullness of His Spirit. Oh Jeff, I sense a great bath of JOY about to be showered upon you. I pray that you remain open to it, and receive all that God has in store for you.*

She closed by again suggesting that we were brother and sister, inextricably joined by God's love: "Peace my Brother in Christ," she wrote. "Your faithful sister in Jesus, Susan."

I was planning a cross-country camping trip that summer, with an old college buddy of mine. When I last wrote her, I'd floated the idea of perhaps paying her a visit at the California Institute for Women at Frontera. She addressed the issue in a handwritten postscript that began with her sketch of a crying face: "My visits are all limited, sorry [underlined three times]. See why I gots to get out?"

I couldn't imagine she would ever be approved for parole. I was right; she never was. Even her 2009 request for a "compassionate" release was denied. By then, she was bedridden, she was an amputee, and she was expected to die as a result of terminal brain cancer. Our correspondence had ended more than 30 years before her death.

• • •

In the last letter Susan ever wrote me, she sounded much like the person I'd come to know through all of her other letters. She said my most recent letter had "blessed [her] heart." Then she added that she could scarcely even imagine "how much joy [I] was bringing to Jesus." She paused to poke a little fun at herself: "Ya know … sometimes I think [Jesus] must just roll with laughter at me cause I can be such a goose at times, and so silly nilly." There she was again, the playful girl-woman— who just so happened to be a convicted mass murderer.

She still fantasized about being set free some day. "Wow," she said, "most all my mail-type friends are from the east coast… Hmmm, must indicate that I shall be moving east, how else am I ever gonna meet ya'll eh? Smile …"

She expressed absolute confidence that in her fiancé John Daiberl, she'd finally found her one and true partner for life:

> John will be here in 13 days from today, to visit for three whole days, thank you Jesus. Oh yes, Love is patient, and the Lord knows I can wait as long as He would have me wait to marry John. I have never been married before, never felt it was the right person each time I was previously asked, and so put it off, so I guess you could say I waited 28 years to find the right man. I am sure waiting a while longer to tie the knot isn't going to make that much difference. PTL [Praise the Lord].

"A while longer." Since she'd previously said that she had no intention of marrying her fiancé while she was still in prison, she was obviously hoping to be released in the not-too-distant future. A pipedream, I knew.

She was fully aware that her fate was in the hands of the Parole Board and the Governor of California. She spoke of how arbitrary the Board's decisions often were, then said she was content to leave her own situation in God's hands.

The Parole Board here is weird. They could say you're going home tomorrow when ya see them, or they could say we will see you in 6 months, or a year to review your case, or you will go home in 45 days, whatever they decide. Actually, whatever the Lord decides, they will follow through with it, even if they aren't aware of where the decision is really coming from, they can think it's from them, but I know that they too are under His control. Hallelujah for that. My first chance to be paroled is this September, Jeff.

That letter was written in 1976—33 years before she died, still a ward of the California Department of Corrections and Rehabilitation.

She closed her letter by saying, "Keep on looking to Jesus, Know that He is your Source." Then she turned from her typewriter to add this handwritten sign-off: "Love, Susan."

● ● ●

That was it: the end of our correspondence. Perhaps I'd become too jaded. The truth is, I'd become weary of all Susan's talk about Jesus, God, Joy, Love, eternal life, and the nullified past. Plus, I was overextended at school: taking a full load of demanding classes, researching and writing papers, and trying to keep pace with my responsibilities as a teaching associate in Purdue's department of English.

For the record, Susan *didn't* end up marrying John Daiberl, the man she said God had delivered to her as the fulfilment of her dreams. I don't have the faintest idea why.

Instead, about five years after we ended our correspondence she married a wealthy, flamboyant Texas huckster named Donald Lee Laisure. Pictures of them on their wedding day appeared in newspapers all across the country. As it turned out, the marriage lasted for only a few months. To Laisure, it was probably little more than a publicity stunt. According to one news report, Atkins was his *35th* wife.

The far more interesting story concerns Atkins' marriage, six years later, to a man named James L. Whitehouse. At the time of their 1987 wedding, Susan was in her late-30s and Whitehouse was in his mid-20s. They remained married up until the time of Atkins' death in September 2009.

At first glance, they seemed an unlikely couple. In 1985, nearly a decade after Susan and I ended our correspondence, Whitehouse sent her a letter. He'd read her book, the one called *Child of Satan, Child of God*. Inspired by Susan's focus on the transformative power of the Christian message, he thought perhaps there was something she could do to help reverse the downward trajectory of his own life.

Following his high school graduation, Whitehouse had left Ohio, where he was from, and relocated to the San Francisco Bay area. There, he joined a rock band and became immersed in a drug-centered lifestyle. By the time he decided to write Susan, he was spiritually bereft, estranged from most members of his family, and uncertain what to do with his life. Susan offered him friendship, without judgment. The first time he asked her to marry him, she said no. She said no the next time, too, and the time after that. Finally, after his fourth proposal, she agreed to become his wife.

Four years after their wedding, Whitehouse was awarded a scholarship to pursue undergraduate studies at the University of California at Irvine. While enrolled there, he earned two baccalaureate degrees, one, magna cum laude, in chemistry; and a second one, summa cum laude, in the biological sciences. He planned to pursue a career in molecular engineering.

However, as he became increasingly familiar with the difficulties Susan was facing as she tried to position herself for a possible parole from prison, he switched gears and decided to study law. Three years later, he graduated cum laude from Harvard Law School. Following his graduation, he helped represent Susan at a number of parole hearings in the years that preceded her death. Susan was 61 when she died. By all available accounts, she and James remained devoted to one another all throughout a marriage that lasted for more than two decades.

Whitehouse also assisted Susan with the preparation of the manuscript of her second and final book, called *The Myth of Helter Skelter*. True to its title, the book, published three years after Susan's death, contains a great deal of information about the Manson case that runs counter to the "official" narrative proposed in *Helter Skelter*, published some 40 years prior.

According to Atkins' account, Manson, a career criminal, brought tremendous energy and boundless self-confidence to his performative turns as a master con man and brutal narcissist—but was, in the end, nothing at all like the brilliant Svengali that Bugliosi and other chroniclers of the case had made him out to be. Her rendering of the final sequence of events that culminated in the horror of the Tate-LaBianca killings is as cogent and plausible as any I've read. She argues that Manson's apocalyptic babbling about a looming "race war"— "helter skelter"—had very little to do with how things actually played out.

The image of Susan Atkins as a sadistic, frozen-in-time homicidal maniac persists, despite Susan's best efforts, and the efforts of Whitehouse, to expose it as a gross caricature.

In the wake of Susan's death, a writer for the *Houston Press* referred to her as "a stone-cold psychopathic demoness." She appears as an astral-projecting embodiment of pure evil in Kathleen McKenna's 2012 novel, *Family Matters*. At various points throughout that book, Susan is described as "that crazy bitch," "a wild animal," "a living monster," "a psychotic murderous freak of nature," a "hell-born creature," and "one of the [last] century's scariest people." (Whitehouse doesn't fare much better. He's "that nutcase lawyer," "some loser," Susan's "poor fuck of a husband," and "that crazy son of a bitch.")

It hardly seems to matter that a prison counselor who worked with Susan recalled her as a model inmate. The same counselor spoke of the countless hours that Susan devoted to charitable causes throughout her long incarceration.

It wouldn't do to overlook the version of Atkins that appears toward the end of Quentin Tarantino's *Once Upon a Time in Hollywood* (2019).

The Atkins character, named "Sadie" in the movie, is

portrayed as every bit the deranged murderess that emerges from the pages of *Helter Skelter*. In one of the film's final scenes, washed-up actor Rick Dalton, played by Leonardo DiCaprio, straps on an old flamethrower and uses it to incinerate her.

On the day of *Hollywood's* release, I attended a showing of it at a local movie theater. As Sadie's immolation played out on the big screen, the audience members who were seated on either side of me laughed out loud and clapped with apparent glee.

Ding dong, the witch was dead.

5.
The Rover

Would Ted Bundy agree to take me on as a student? I had no way of knowing, but I was eager to find out. Bundy was, after all, a world-renowned expert on the subject of murder. I knew there was plenty he could teach me. If, that is, he viewed me as being worthy of his time and attention.

In the fall of 1984, when I first began to play with the idea of writing to Bundy at his home on death row in Florida, I was still struggling to come to terms with my memories of that period in the mid-seventies when I wrote Charles Manson, Squeaky Fromme, Sandy Good, and Susan Atkins more often than I wrote my own parents. There was no use denying the truth: it had been one of the most stimulating and exciting periods of my entire life. I knew that both my parents were clinging to the hope that I'd moved on. Well, I had and I hadn't.

Something I'd learned from that period of my involvement with members of the Manson Family: imprisoned criminals, even notorious killers like Manson and Atkins, aren't necessarily remote and inaccessible in the way many people assume they are. I'd used the U.S, Postal Service as a means of trying to engage the attention of Manson and the others, never knowing whether my efforts would be successful. As it turned out, they were—beyond even my wildest expectations. During a period that lasted a little over two years, various members of the Manson Family sent me more than 50 letters.

Now, late in 1984, with the holiday season approaching and the one-year anniversary of the Riverside murders looming at year's end, I began to wonder if perhaps I could persuade Bundy to enter into a dialogue with me. My reasons for wanting to pick his brain were personal in a way my reasons for wanting to pick the brains of Manson, Fromme, Good, and Atkins never were.

•••

That November, when I finally decided to pull the trigger and send a letter to Bundy, my mind was, for better or worse, teeming with thoughts and images of murder. Patty Matix and Joyce McFadden had been dead for almost a year. At least so far as I knew, no one, including the police, had any idea who killed them or why. (News of the shootout in Miami, and subsequent revelations about the double life William Matix had been living, were still a year and a half down the road, as yet unimaginable to those of us in Columbus who were struggling to come to terms with what had happened at Riverside.)

The police investigation seemed to be going nowhere, nowhere fast anyway. Everyone I knew was stumped. *What sort of person would have committed two such brutal, seemingly senseless murders? Late in the afternoon no less, right around the corner from the main hallway in the largest private general hospital in Ohio?* I thought that if anyone could shed light on the matter, maybe Bundy could.

For some time, Bundy had been insisting that he was victimized by a flawed legal system and maligned in the court of public opinion. His campaign of aggrievement notwithstanding, it still didn't seem like much of a stretch to think that he knew a thing or two about murder. He'd been sentenced to death, first in 1979 for the murders of Margaret Bowman and Lisa Levy at the Chi Omega sorority house on the campus of Florida State University in Tallahassee; then again the following year, for the murder of 12-year-old Kimberly Leach in Lake City, about 90 miles farther south.

Despite his claims of innocence, the authorities felt certain that Bundy was responsible for many more murders than just the three in Florida, perhaps as many as 100 altogether. In addition to the murders of Bowman, Levy, and Leach, the police believed Bundy had murdered women in Washington State, Oregon, Utah, and Colorado.

Bundy was known for his extraordinary mobility. In FBI parlance, he was a "rover." Something else he was known for: creating the illusion that certain of his victims simply vanished into thin air. In the immediate aftermath of some of the murders he was thought to have committed, *he* vanished into thin air, too—or so it seemed. In her memoir, his former girlfriend referred to him as a "phantom"

In my fantasy of, in effect, seducing Bundy, that is, convincing him to participate with me in a dialogue centering around the subject of murder, Bundy would light up in response to my curiosity and flattery, then lead me, over time, to an enhanced understanding of how someone could have savagely attacked my two co-workers and then just disappeared from the hospital without a single witness seeing him leave. In retrospect, my fantasy seems naïve. But back then, I was hopeful.

I reasoned that by writing my letter in longhand instead of typing it, I might stand a better chance of connecting with Bundy at a personal level. My first priority was to activate his interest. It was the same first priority I'd had when I reached out to Charles Manson almost a decade earlier.

Despite the passage of so many years since 1975, I hadn't really changed that much. I was still curious, still almost painfully earnest, still lacking much in the way of practical or relevant experience (I hadn't yet met anyone who I knew to be a killer), and still open to engaging in frankly manipulative behavior if I thought it would help to advance my agenda in some way. As I sat down to compose my letter to Bundy, my hope was that his arrogance would make it difficult for him to resist an apparent bumpkin's desire to inventory the contents of his mind.

I didn't try to disguise my intentions. "Dear Ted," I wrote.

"I'm not sure what a letter from a stranger in Columbus might contain that would [make it stand out] from other letters and prompt you to want to respond." The sub-text? I see you as someone important, someone whose thoughts are very much in demand—and I hope you'll decide to honor me with a return letter.

I went on to explain that I had no intention of trying to act as either his apologist or his advocate. Instead, I was interested in hearing more about his background and learning more about his perspective on a variety of different subjects: the crimes he was alleged to have committed, some things about his case that the authorities might have gotten wrong, and his opinion of the "system" that had found him guilty and sentenced him to die. I figured that if I could entice him to participate with me in a dialogue about these and some related issues, the subject of the Riverside murders could wait; I'd broach that subject later on, in one of my subsequent letters.

I bent over backward in an effort to convince him of my sincere interest in having him share his thoughts about his predicament: "I'm trying to see behind the images of you that I've received through the media, and to come to terms with the fact that in a place totally unfamiliar to me, in Florida, in a prison cell on death row, there exists a person who's alone with himself," I wrote. "Either genuinely outraged by the real injustices [he's had to endure], or else aware at some level that he is—or part of him is—the person who [the prosecutors] described him as being in court."

I told him I was curious about "that part of [him] no one understands (the genuinely good part?)," and about the relationship of that part to the many people in society who regard him as a one-dimensional monster. By referencing different "parts" of him, I was trying to suggest a strategy he could draw on to admit-but-not-admit to certain of the things he'd been accused of doing.

I included a blunt admission of my own: "My only motive in writing you is selfish," I said. I explained that even after reading a number of books about his case, I still regarded him as "an enigma." I wasn't out to "save" him; neither did I "admire" him. Mainly, I said, I was struggling to understand how he could have done all the things the two Florida courts had concluded he had done.

Cynically, I paused to inject a dollop of flattery. I said I had little doubt that he'd present in person as "bright, witty, [and] articulate." That's how he'd been portrayed by nearly every chronicler of his case. I invoked an image of the two of us having a conversation, then added, "I'm sure I would puzzle over the seeming incongruity: that [there could exist right in front of me] an outwardly 'normal' person [who had been] driven ... to commit violent crimes ... yet who, at the same time, possessed enough self-control to fool me and lots of other people, too."

I wrote as if I believed the question of his guilt or innocence might still be in play. In reality, I didn't—and it wasn't. But I knew how invested he was in a narrative that featured himself as the persecuted victim. My cynical calculation went something like this: If Bundy thinks he can sway me in the direction of his preferred narrative, maybe he'll be less likely to toss my letter in the wastebasket. In a fit of pique, Charles Manson had once denounced me as a complete phony. Now, almost a decade later, here I was still trying to identify an angle, any angle, that I could leverage to persuade a repeat killer that I was someone worthy of his time and attention.

I commented that if he really did commit all the crimes the authorities suspected him of committing, the question of motive was of obvious interest to me. If, on the other hand, he wasn't responsible for all those crimes, I wondered how it must feel to be confined in a prison cell, with a death sentence hanging over his head. I added that I could scarcely even imagine what it must feel like to be confined inside "a cage."

For Bundy's consideration, I floated a few other possibilities. Maybe he was guilty—but maybe he'd somehow convinced himself that the authorities shouldn't hold him "accountable for" whatever crimes he committed. Or perhaps he was "psychologically incapable of" owning up to his guilt— even if it was true that he'd committed all the crimes the authorities said he'd committed.

Setting aside for the moment all that I'd learned about psychopaths from my obsessive reading of true crime narratives, I told him it was hard for me to imagine all the "psychological energy" he'd have to spend if each and every day he had to carry around "the knowledge and images of" all those alleged victims and all those alleged crimes—which included dismemberment and necrophilia in addition to rape and murder.

I added—this part at least was true—that what interested me most of all was his own thinking about his identity, his actions, his public image, and the assorted narratives that had been proposed to account for his career as a serial killer. "Who are you to you?" I asked. "If you're not who you've said you are, then … you're left as the only one who's in a position to reconcile all the apparent contradictions," including the most glaring contradiction of all, the one between "your public image" and "your private self."

Toward the end of my letter, I made a glancing reference to the possibility that I'd be leaving my job as a hospital administrator and re-enrolling in graduate school to pursue my PhD in psychology. I admitted to a certain degree of "clinical curiosity" about his psychological makeup. I said nothing at all about the murders at Riverside, and of course nothing about my hope that at some point down the road, he might be willing to offer some observations about the kind of person who could have committed them. For the time being, all I wanted was for him to write me back. The rest could wait.

I signed off with a little more flattery, accompanied by my acknowledgment that he was the one in control of whatever happened next. "You'll choose whether or not to respond to my questions," I said. "I hope you'll feel that I might be a worthwhile correspondent."

Bundy didn't reply. As far as I was concerned, that was the end of it. When I made the decision to write him, I told myself that I wouldn't write him again unless he responded to my first letter. I had no interest in him perceiving me as a pest. So that was that. Except it wasn't, not quite.

Despite the fact that Bundy hadn't taken the bait, I continued to read about him, and to learn more and more about the many murders he was thought to have committed. By any barometer, his was among the most fascinating serial murder cases in modern American history.

One of the most intriguing aspects of the case was Bundy's carefully curated and well-maintained public persona. He was handsome and photogenic; he was capable of great charm when he perceived the need to be charming; he was well-spoken; he was intelligent; he'd often spoken of wanting to pursue a career in either law or politics; and he was, insisted a former friend of his, "one of us," a person like most other people— or so it had seemed to many of the people who thought they knew him reasonably well.

Further adding to his mystique, if it can be called that, he was a chameleon who often looked different from one photograph to the next; he was remarkably savvy and elusive, almost phantom-like, in the way he carried out many of his crimes and then seemingly disappeared into thin air; he was a suspect in murders that had been committed in five different states; and not once but twice, he'd escaped from custody, both times in Colorado.

● ● ●

More than a year went by. I'd long ago given up hope of ever hearing back from Ted Bundy. Then one day, I pulled an envelope out of my mailbox and saw the name "T Bundy" written in cursive in the envelope's upper left-hand corner. Inside the envelope was a greeting card, produced by "Chaplain Ray" and his International Prison Ministry.

I was familiar with Chaplain Ray. Years before, in a letter sent to me by Manson Family killer Charles "Tex" Watson, Watson had cited Ray as the person most responsible for his spiritual growth in prison.

On the front of the card was an image of abundance: a photograph of a burlap sack, overflowing with colorful apples. Inside, Bundy had written the date, December 18, 1985, along with this message: "Dear Jeffrey, I send my best wishes that you will have your best Christmas ever and that your new year will be filled with love and … peace. ted." The card's generic message appeared in bold print: "May this be the greatest year of our lives."

Also inside the envelope was a short letter, written on the front and back of a single sheet of paper. The handwriting was unlike any handwriting I'd ever seen. The first word of every line began with a dramatic, right-leaning thrust of the writer's pen. I found the effect mildly unsettling.

During the years while I was in practice, I gave many talks on the subject of serial murder. Whenever I gave such talks, I typically included stories about some of the infamous killers with whom I'd corresponded. I also included stories about some of the hundreds of killers with whom I interacted in my professional role as a forensic psychologist. The Bundy letter, short as it is, nearly always gave rise to some of the most spirited and interesting discussions. Usually, I'd introduce the letter by saying a few words about its provenance.

It bears repeating that Bundy was awaiting execution when he composed this letter. The way things played out, he ended up being executed just a little more than three years later. By the time he finally wrote to me, he'd been in possession of my letter for more than a year. I'd heard nothing from him that entire time. So far as I knew, he was continuing to proclaim his innocence, and still telling anyone who would listen that he'd fallen victim to an epic case of bad luck and a preposterous set of coincidences (involving, for example, a trail of gas receipts that placed him in the vicinity of many of the murders the police suspected him of committing). To hear him tell it, the authorities were hellbent on leveraging such coincidences to frame him for all kinds of things he never did.

To writer Stephen Michaud, who'd conducted more than 100 hours of interviews with Bundy in 1980 and then co-authored the true crime classic, *The Only Living Witness* (1983), Bundy had, in essence, agreed to act as an expert on the psychology and behavior of someone who might have committed the crimes he kept insisting he himself had not committed. Michaud knew how to bait the hook—with an offer that allowed the ever-arrogant Bundy to share a lot of what he knew without directly implicating or incriminating himself. In the end, Michaud's was an offer that Bundy could not—or chose not to—refuse.

When I received Bundy's letter, five years had elapsed since Michaud's interviews, and two since *The Only Living Witness* had landed in bookstores nationwide. So when Bundy wrote to me, he knew I knew that in conversation with Michaud, he'd agreed to posture as an authority on "the Bundy case," all the while continuing to maintain his innocence. He also knew that when all was said and done, Michaud hadn't accepted his innocence claims. And he was well aware that he was fast running out of legal challenges that stood any chance at all of delaying his execution.

Here's how he began his letter: "Dear Jeffrey, You wrote me over a year ago. I've kept your letter all this time. I just came across it amongst my papers." *Amongst his papers?* I thought, *Who talks that way?*

Still sounding more like a snooty professor than a serial killer awaiting his date with the executioner, he added, "Please excuse me for taking such an inordinately long time to answer it." He offered up an explanation for the long delay. "It was just about the time you wrote that I withdrew into a cocoon of sorts and ceased writing to practically everyone. I'm only now getting back in touch."

Not surprisingly, Bundy's letter to me was hardly the first instance of him adopting a vainglorious posture and employing stilted, pretentious-sounding rhetoric in an effort to convince someone else to take him as seriously as he took himself.

As part of a statement that he composed for investigators when he was in custody in the mid-1970s, he wrote, "I suppose some will turn to a plethora of clandestine hypothesis [sic] which lack only one thing: evidence to substantiate them." He continued, describing himself as "perplexed at the imaginative insinuations" of people prepared to see the "miscellania" discovered in his car at the time of his arrest as evidence of criminal wrongdoing.

In a 1976 letter that he wrote from Utah State Prison to

his old friend and later biographer, the true crime writer Ann Rule, he included some of his poetry. One poem that he wrote as a paean to the attorney who was representing him at the time ends with these words: "This man's a creation/A master of oration/Concerned by a client's perturbation/An immaculate legal mutation."

There are plenty of other examples I could cite, all pointing to Bundy's extraordinary grandiosity and air of self-importance.

The year preceding Bundy's decision to answer my letter hadn't gone well for him. In June 1984, about five months before my letter to him would have arrived at the prison in Starke, the Florida Supreme Court decisively rejected his request to be granted a new trial in the case involving the Chi Omega murders. That same summer, prison officials discovered a hacksaw hidden in his cell. No one is entirely certain how it got there. What is certain is that Bundy had used it to saw through the top and bottom of one of his cell bars, apparently because he was planning to attempt a third daring escape from custody. After the authorities thwarted his most recent plot, they moved him to a different cell and subjected him to a far more intense level of scrutiny.

In May 1985, seven months before he wrote his response to my letter, he experienced yet another legal setback. This time, the setback came in the form of a unanimous decision by the Florida Supreme Court, rejecting his bid for a new trial in the case involving the murder of Kimberly Leach. He hadn't yet been assigned an execution date, but he knew to expect one soon. Florida governor Bob Graham signed a death warrant for him in February 1986, less than two months after Bundy sent the letter that I'd received in December of the preceding year.

The warrant indicated that Bundy was to die the very next month, in March. As it turned out, he still had three more years left to live. But in any case, it would have been crystal clear to him that his time on earth was fast running out.

Despite Bundy's claim that he'd withdrawn into a "cocoon of sorts," in part, perhaps, as a result of all the legal setbacks that occurred in 1984 and 1985, according to his biographer Ann Rule he never stopped posturing as a pundit on the subject of serial murder. He failed to grasp the irony implicit in his choice to pontificate on a subject about which he insisted he had no firsthand knowledge. Rule wrote that to a small coterie of "judiciously selected criminologists," Bundy "expounded for hours on his opinions, theories, [and] feelings. He [considered] himself an expert on the mind of the serial killer."

In his letter, Bundy thanked me for writing him, then patronized me with a smidgen of feel-good feedback. "Anyway, thanks for your letter," he wrote. "I thought it was especially searching and thoughtful." To me anyway, it sounded as if he considered it entirely reasonable for someone like me to want to see the world as it looked through the eyes of someone like him.

I was startled by his next sentence. In retrospect, I probably shouldn't have been. He wrote, "As for your questions, all I can say is that I've never felt better in my life, spiritually, mentally, physically." He added, "I hope the same can be said for you."

The reason I probably shouldn't have been surprised by Bundy's counter-intuitive self-assessment is that he had a history of claiming that he could somehow rise above even the most dire sets of circumstances.

In one of the several books that Kevin Sullivan would later write about the Bundy case, Sullivan referenced the fact that Bundy seemed always to be "at peace," even when nothing at all seemed to be going his way. When Stephen Michaud interviewed Bundy in 1980 and asked him how he felt in the aftermath of the Chi Omega and Kimberly Leach murders, Bundy replied, "I was super confident and [was] feeling really happy about the way things were."

Utah State Prison psychologist Al Carlisle spoke to Bundy on the telephone shortly after he was recaptured by the authorities following his escape from the Aspen, Colorado courthouse. Despite the fact that the police would later describe Bundy as having seemed desperate and completely exhausted by the time he was taken back into custody, Bundy told Carlisle, "I'm doing quite well, frankly." To a reporter who spoke with Bundy while he was awaiting trial in Colorado for the murder of Caryn Campbell, Bundy said, "I'm doing well. I feel good." He even went so far as to tell Stephen Michaud that he thought being in prison "[had] done good things for [him]."

So, it's not as if Bundy was adopting a new messaging style when he wrote me from his cell on death row that he was in tip-top condition and feeling better than he'd felt at any other time in his life.

The most tantalizing, teasing, and provocative part of Bundy's letter to me came at the very end. "Take care," he wrote. "Watch yourself. Travel light." Then, "peace, Ted."

Bundy's cryptic, ominous-sounding sign-off exemplifies the malign "playfulness" for which serial killers are well known. It has it all: the teasing tone, the passive-aggressive subtext, the hint of menace, the reliance on innuendo.

Bundy's terse, end-of-letter directives can be read in two sharply contrasting ways. On one hand, they work well as a succinct recipe for how to commit murder and avoid detection: *Be careful. Know your surroundings. Prioritize your own needs over all else. Stay "light," unencumbered, and mobile—so you can disappear at a moment's notice.*

On the other hand, they work equally well as a cautionary set of instructions, a blueprint for how to avoid falling victim to a predator like Bundy: *Be vigilant. Know where you are at all times. Be aware of who you're with. And be prepared to flee at a moment's notice.*

I have no doubt that Bundy knew exactly what he was doing when he opted to end his letter in the way he did. His vaguely menacing message—"watch yourself" and so on—stands as a perfect expression of the delight he took in playing games with people, especially in situations where he perceived some sort of power differential between himself and the person he was interacting with. In the updated 1989 version of her classic book, *The Stranger Beside Me*, Ann Rule portrayed Bundy as the consummate conman/trickster. She wrote that as an inmate on death row, he "played the games … all prisoners play"—but with a joy and panache all his own.

In his book focusing on "the social construction" of the serial killer, Richard Tithecott presented Bundy as the very prototype of the killer who delights in "teasing" anyone who might try to "read" his apparently random crimes and solve the riddle of his identity. According to Tithecott, part of what motivates a criminal like Bundy is the desire to act in the role of gatekeeper, able to control others' access to that rarefied place: "the mind of the serial killer."

John Henry Browne is an attorney who, for a while during the mid-1970s, served as Bundy's legal representative. In a memoir that he wrote years later, Browne provided yet another example of the sort of game Bundy delighted in playing. By means that still aren't entirely clear, Bundy managed to father a child while he was serving time on death row in Florida. He named his daughter Rosebud (he called her "Rosa" for short)—just a minor variation on Roseland, the name he used in 1974 when he impersonated a police officer to lure one of his victims (Carol DeRonch) into his car outside a shopping mall near Salt Lake City.

Take care?

It's something Bundy himself nearly always did—to an extreme degree. In his "comprehensive history" of the Bundy case, Kevin Sullivan wrote, "Bundy paid the greatest attention to what was around him at all times, even down to the tiniest detail, for all the wrong reasons."

Travel light?

Bundy was among the most mobile of all serial killers. Steven Winn, another chronicler of the case, stated in a 2020 Amazon Prime documentary that Bundy acted "like an animal migrating somewhere ... in search of prey" when he escaped from custody a second time and headed cross country, eventually landing in Florida, his final destination.

During one of Bundy's 1980 conversations with Stephen Michaud, Bundy himself suggested that whoever was responsible for "the Bundy murders," as they'd come to be known, was the sort of person "whose modus operandi" included "using large amounts of distance" between his crimes as a way of thwarting efforts by the police to identify and apprehend him.

In the early-1980s, criminologist Steven Egger coined the phrase "linkage blindness" and used Bundy as his prototype to explain why highly mobile killers present such unique challenges for law enforcement officials who don't always communicate well across jurisdictional lines.

The first of Kevin Sullivan's Bundy books teems with references to Bundy's relentless travel: "He had traveled far to strike this time (some 250 miles)"; "Bundy believed (quite rightly) that while they searched for him in one place, he could kill in another"; "Never satisfied with hunting victims in one locale … Bundy would travel"; and "[Bundy] was driving hundreds of miles … seeking victims." And those are just a few examples.

So, what game was Bundy playing when he composed his letter to me? He was no doubt chuckling to himself when he wrote the words "Watch yourself" just above the words "Travel light." He knew—and he knew that I knew—he was the roaming, cross-country killer that he kept telling everyone he wasn't. As he wrote me from his cell on death row, he opted for some cleverness, and for a little tongue-in-cheek humor.

I was flattered, a little. Bundy saw me as someone he could count on to get the joke.

I never wrote him back, and I never heard from him again. I'd initiated the correspondence on the outside chance that an exchange of letters between Bundy and me might progress to a point where I'd find myself in a position to tap Bundy for some useful observations about the mysterious circumstances surrounding the murders at Riverside. That didn't happen. What did happen, though, helped to shape my perspective on serial killers and how they think.

Years later, I would draw on the lessons of the Bundy correspondence, for example when I was conducting my evaluation of serial sniper Thomas Lee Dillon: another malevolent trickster who knew a thing or two about how to hide in plain sight and get away with murder.

6.
The Clown

"Hey Jeff, how 'bout a cigar?"

"Sure, I'll take one, but I think I'll save it, maybe for when I get back to Columbus."

"Aw, c'mon! Smoke it here, buddy, the fucking guards don't care. *I'm* gonna smoke one."

"No, I think I'll wait."

"Whatever. You do what you want."

With that, John Wayne Gacy shrugs, smiles a thin smile as he looks me straight in the eye, extends his cuffed hands across the table in the small room where we're seated, and places a cellophane-wrapped cigar in my right palm.

It's early in the afternoon on December 16, 1986, the second day of the first of my two visits to the Menard Correctional Center in southwest Illinois, where Gacy is on death row.

That was almost 38 years ago.

I still have the cigar, and it's still wrapped in the original cellophane.

I know, I know: there are times when a cigar is just a cigar. This isn't one of those times. Gacy is the homosexuality-denying murderer of at least 33 boys and young men. Psychiatrist Helen Morrison, who consulted on his case at trial, calls him "America's most notorious serial killer."

The cigar Gacy hands me isn't just a cigar. I know it, and he knows it, too. His smile gives him away.

In the late Michelle McNamara's book about her obsessive search for the Golden State Killer (later revealed to be a former cop named Joseph James DeAngelo, Jr.), McNamara conjured the image of the crafty killer, toying with his interrogator and basking in his sense of superiority. The killer is "the string puller with the haunting smirk."

That's Gacy. As he hands me the cigar, a faint smirk on his face, he understands that he's setting in motion a chain of associations that includes—has to—cocks, blow jobs, torture, and murder.

Of course he does.

Remember Harvey Schlossberg? The Freudian psychoanalyst and former NYPD member who famously suggested that for the Son of Sam killer, a .44-caliber pistol was actually a substitute penis? Presumably Schlossberg would have a thing or two to say about Gacy's choice to gift me a cigar—and to want to watch me while I sucked it.

In letters Gacy and I have exchanged over the past ten months, and in our several phone conversations, too, Gacy has described himself as a "non-judgmental, outspoken liberal" and casually acknowledged the many times in his life when he's engaged in oral sex with boys and young men. According to him, he participated in those acts just to "get off," never because he was gay. (*Hey Jeff! A mouth's a mouth!*) He knows I know that in 1967, in Waterloo, Iowa, he had oral sex with a teenage boy—more than one, actually—and was sentenced to ten years in the state pen. (A model inmate, he earned early release after only 14 months of confinement, then relocated to his hometown of Chicago to serve out his parole.)

For a few seconds right now, I consider saying something to Gacy about the cigar's pretty obvious phallic implications. It doesn't take Freud. But before any words come out of my mouth, I recall an incident from a few months back.

The incident now seems like it was a kind of dress rehearsal for a moment just such as this one. When it occurred, Gacy and I were separated by about 450 miles. Here's what happened.

Gacy had mailed me a single sheet of white paper, divided up into a lot of small squares. He referred to the little brain-teaser of a game as the Polish College Entrance Exam. Each square contained a pictorial puzzle. My job was to try and solve as many of the puzzles as I could. The challenge was to come up with the word or phrase that each of the puzzles "stood for." Working at home, with an occasional assist from my wife, I managed to solve all but just a few of them. In letters that we sent back and forth, Gacy and I agreed that we'd go over my answers the next time we talked on the telephone.

Not long after we reached that agreement, Gacy called me collect on a Saturday morning.

At some point during our conversation that morning, Gacy suggested that we turn our attention to "the Entrance Exam." Everything was hunky dory until we came to an item where the visual puzzle needing to be "solved" consisted of the word "ground" positioned above a horizontal line. Just below the line there were six footprints all arranged in a row. I'd had no difficulty at all coming up with the correct solution: "six feet underground." When I said those three words out loud, Gacy emitted a snort-chuckle and then quipped, "That's a cute one."

I thought, *a cute one?* This coming from the same man who'd buried 26 bodies in the crawlspace beneath his house, and several others elsewhere on his suburban property? (He also tossed at least four bodies into the Des Plaines River—after he'd run out of space on the home front.) I chose not to say anything. However, I knew Gacy could sense my unease, even over the telephone. For the remainder of our call, there was an undercurrent of tension. Neither of us acknowledged it.

It bubbled to the surface in some letters that we exchanged not long afterward. For better or worse, I'd decided that I was going to comment on the "six feet underground" puzzle. More specifically, I was going to tell Gacy that his dismissive manner of responding to it made me uncomfortable, especially given the facts of his case. I knew there was a distinct possibility that he'd get angry with me—but I was determined to have my say.

"I enjoyed going over the Polish College Entrance Exam," I wrote, "but to be honest, I wasn't quite sure how to respond when you said 'That's a cute one' after I gave the 'six feet underground' answer. I didn't say anything at the time, but I think we were both aware of the irony, given the crimes you were convicted of committing. Did you mean that particular puzzle, and what you said about it, as a joke? Were you just meaning to acknowledge the irony? I couldn't tell."

Gacy said he couldn't believe my nerve. In fact, he proposed that we end our correspondence right then and there. In his next letter, he wrote,

> *I have come to the conclusion that I don't think you're looking at me as a pen pal or friendship, but rather a project or assignment. You seem to want to find fault in everything I say. I feel the best thing to do is discontinue writing you. You wanted to add something to me putting in the Polish joke 'six feet underground.' You question what I was thinking when I did it, as if to say in some way it was connected to my case. Hey, at the time I wrote it up I was not thinking of the crawlspace, nor the crime, nor what was found [29 corpses!] at one of my houses. I get the feeling you wanted it to be some link to the past or the crime. There was no irony to it, no thought of the crime.*

As far as Gacy was concerned, my comments were just the latest example of the "theories" and "fantasy" and "suppositions" that people were always wanting to substitute for the "facts" of his case. In his view, I was way out of line to suggest any link whatsoever between the phrase "six feet underground" and the 29 corpses that were found on his property.

Who did I think I was? And, *Did I have any idea at all what it was like for him to have to spend his days on death row?*

He wrote in his letter of sitting in his tiny cell 22 hours each day, completely secure in the knowledge that he "did not commit the crime(s)" he was convicted of committing (notwithstanding the fact that he confessed to them in detail, not once but several times).

As he was preparing to end his letter, he adopted a slightly more conciliatory tone. He said he'd let *me* decide whether we should continue our correspondence. I wrote him back and said I hadn't intended to upset or offend him.

"It's in the past," he wrote in his next letter. "Let's just forget about it."

For me, though, it was a lesson learned.

Now, seated across from him in a death row visiting room and faced with the choice of either keeping my thoughts to myself or remarking on the cigar's obvious—to me—phallic implications, I decide to keep my mouth shut.

Gacy doesn't seem angry that I've declined to smoke the cigar in his presence. But I can tell that he's disappointed. He was hoping for the opportunity to observe me closely as I sucked the end of the cigar and moved it around in my mouth. For him, it would have been a nice association—and a trigger for a pleasant journey down memory lane.

•••

During a three-year period, from February of 1986 until February of 1989, Gacy sent me more than 50 letters. Often, his letters ran to four and five and six typewritten pages. From time to time, we also talked on the telephone.

Twice during that three-year period, first in December of 1986 and then again the following September, I drove the 900-mile round trip between my home in Columbus, Ohio and Chester, Illinois, where Gacy was at Menard awaiting execution. On each of those trips, I spent two consecutive days with Gacy in a small room in a locked visiting area in a building that was located on a knoll above the Mississippi River. In all, we spent close to 20 hours in that room. *Alone.*

In August of 1985, I'd begun work toward my PhD in psychology at Ohio State. That fall, it occurred to me for the first time that perhaps I could come up with some way of making serial murder the primary focus of my doctoral dissertation. It was a subject I'd been interested in for a long time. At that early juncture in my studies, I had no idea what such a project would look like—but at least I was beginning to think about it.

As the 1985 Christmas holidays were approaching, something unexpected happened. From his cell on Florida's death row, serial killer Ted Bundy finally got around to responding to a letter I'd sent him a year prior. That letter certainly hadn't been the first one I sent to a notorious killer. Nearly a decade before, I'd begun corresponding with Charles Manson and some of his closest associates. But the belated response from Bundy once again reactivated my interest in the possibility of using letters as a means of establishing avenues of access to the minds of repeat killers.

In early 1986, during my second semester at Ohio State, I settled on the idea of trying to initiate an exchange of letters with yet another killer who'd claimed many victims. Then as before, I thought that perhaps by corresponding with killers, I could achieve a more complete understanding of how their minds worked than I could ever hope to achieve simply by reading books that chronicled their crimes.

This time, I chose Gacy.

Less than a year and a half after his December 1978 arrest, Gacy was found guilty of killing more people than anyone else in American history up to that point. He had 33 known victims. Many law enforcement officials who worked on or studied his case felt certain there were more.

By the time Gacy and I began corresponding, I'd already read three books about his case. *The Man Who Killed Boys*, by Clifford Lindecker, appeared in 1980, the same year as Gacy's trial. *Killer Clown*, which prosecutor Terry Sullivan co-wrote with Peter Maiken, appeared three years later. (Gacy was known—had by now become infamous—for the charity work he did as Pogo the Clown.) *Buried Dreams*, which Tim Cahill wrote based on Russ Ewing's investigative reporting, came out only about a month before Gacy and I exchanged our first letters.

In the letter that I intended as my introductory overture, I explained to Gacy that I was a graduate student at Ohio State, working toward an advanced degree in psychology. I emphasized that I had no interest in wasting his time or becoming a nuisance. I disclosed that I'd already read several books about him and his trial. Now, I said, I was hoping to hear his point of view, not just about his legal case but about other aspects of his life as well.

He responded almost immediately. According to him, the books I'd cited were, for the most part, nothing more than just "fantasy." He said I was wrong if I thought I'd learned even the first thing about him from reading them. He stated his position in blunt terms: "I am sorry to have to tell you, you don't know nothing about me." He complained that 80 percent of what the mass media had reported about him and his case was "not factual."

With respect to my interest in hearing his point of view about other aspects of his life story, he told me he'd have "no comment." I'd just have to await the release of his autobiography, which he said he expected to be "on the market" before the end of the calendar year. He explained that in his cell on death row, he painted and wrote letters, mostly just "to pass the time away."

Despite his mildly testy tone, he seemed open to the idea of correspondence. He ended his letter, "Look forward to hearing from you, have a nice day."

• • •

When I made the decision to try writing Gacy, I had no idea that we'd maintain contact with one another for as long as we did. As it turned out, we exchanged letters, on average every couple of weeks, for a period of almost exactly three years.

Many of the first lessons I learned about Gacy, I learned as a result of reading his letters. We'd been corresponding for about ten months by the time of our first in-person meeting.

It didn't take long—at all—before I found myself bumping up against the evidence of Gacy's startling egocentricity. As he saw it, pretty much everything had to be about him: his point of view, his opinions, his persecution, his prospects. He displayed precious little interest in me as a person (though I've no doubt he would have skewered that as a complete mischaracterization).

Some years after our relationship, such as it was, had run

its course, journalist Alec Wilkinson learned through a friend of his that Gacy was willing to participate in a multi-part interview in the months just prior to his execution, which was slated to take place in May 1994. Wilkinson spent hours with him, then wrote in the *New Yorker*, "What personality [Gacy] may once have had collapsed long ago and has been replaced by a catalogue of gestures and attitudes and portrayals of sanity … He seems to have no capacity for intimacy or friendship. Another person makes no impression on him at all." That's the Gacy I came to know.

Of Gacy's particular brand of guile, which of course Gacy employed with lethal efficiency to ensnare his victims, Wilkinson wrote, "Visiting Gacy is like spending time with a person who is pretending to like you to separate you, violently, if necessary, from something you possess." Like, for example, your life.

In his letters, Gacy was often prickly, irascible, and defensive. The slightest thing—and it was hard to predict which—could provoke a temper tantrum. Frequently, he complained that I was "twisting [his] words," trying to make it seem like he'd said something he never meant to say. Sometimes, he groused about me assuming things he said I had no right to assume. He bristled whenever he thought I was trying to second-guess him. On occasion, he even took issue with the words I chose to use.

Time and again, he accused me of falling back on "theory" and "supposition" to support my opinions. According to him, he and he alone knew what was "fact" and what wasn't, about his legal case and all kinds of other things, too.

I realized almost from the get-go that he was going to be a high-maintenance pen pal. As I've said, he threatened to pull the plug on our correspondence—very shortly after it began—if I wouldn't agree to "stop challenging [him] on everything." From that point on, I made a concerted effort to be reasonably tactful and accommodating. Sometimes I succeeded, sometimes I didn't.

After one of our phone conversations, he wrote to say how much he'd enjoyed talking to me. When I responded to that letter, I mentioned that I was glad he'd found it a "pleasant" conversation. "Who said I thought it was a 'pleasant' conversation?" he demanded to know. "That's your word, not mine." And so it went. From his end, a continuous hum of aggrievement.

But there were other times when Gacy could seem downright chummy. In a letter he wrote to me in April of 1987, four months after the first of my two visits to Menard, he signed off, "Always your buddy, John." At around that same time, when I informed him that my wife and I were planning a trip to the British Isles that summer, he wrote, "I expect postcards."

In the early part of 1989, at right around the time when our correspondence was finally running out of steam, he ended one of his letters, "Later, gator." Often, he began his letters with the jaunty, "Hi Ho Jeff." When my wife and I relocated to Connecticut in August of 1988, so that I could begin my one-year pre-doctoral internship at a state psychiatric hospital there, he wrote, "Don't forget to send me your new address ... so we can keep writing."

Despite such friendly-seeming overtures from Gacy, I often felt like we were constantly in the process of negotiating and re-negotiating our terms of engagement. One minute he'd be offering me his assurances that he was an open book, willing to respond to any questions I wanted to ask him just so long as they pertained to subjects his attorneys had given him the go-ahead to discuss; and the next minute, he'd be threatening to bail out altogether if he thought I was trying to turn our correspondence into "a question and answer forum."

In one letter, he'd request my opinion about something; in his next letter, he'd take me to task for expressing it.

In a 2021 television documentary called *John Wayne Gacy: Devil in Disguise* (Peacock), law enforcement officers who'd worked his case characterized Gacy as a "braggart" and a "blowhard." One officer said he was "full of hubris and arrogance." Another called him a relentless "BS-er." I found him to be all those things.

He held forth on an astonishing range of subjects, always with the kind of grandiosity and bloated sense of self-regard that I associate with bar stools and excessive drinking.

We wrote back and forth about politics, painting, his various "pen pals," baseball, the books that had been written about his case, psychopathy, sex, NFL football, marriage, parenting, the media, psychology, psychiatry, B.F. Skinner, business, music, animal behavior, art, religion—and of course serial murder. (He seemed only dimly aware that presenting himself as an authority on the psychology of the serial killer might strike a discordant note, given his insistence that he wasn't one and never had been.)

•••

As our correspondence took off and proceeded in accordance with a fairly predictable rhythm, I often tried to steer Gacy in the direction of subjects that were of interest to me, and about which I thought maybe he'd have something interesting to say. Psychopathy, for example.

For a class I was taking at Ohio State on the psychology of delinquency, I wrote a paper that examined the question of whether the term "psychopathy" stood for a distinct clinical condition or an abstract concept—perhaps better understood as representing a continuum that could include many people who don't adopt an explicitly criminal lifestyle.

In the same paper, I posed the related question of whether it might be reasonable to assume that many members of a given population—including some people who are high-functioning contributors to society—are more or less "psychopathic."

My professor for this particular class—a well-known expert on the subject of "moral reasoning"—rubbed me the wrong way. In class, he came across as politically very conservative and, to me anyway, unnecessarily judgmental. I hoped he was going to read my paper in the way I intended it to be read: as a challenge to some of his rigidly held views about psychopathy and criminality. He did. In fact, he wrote "Rubbish" across one entire paragraph, even though he gave me an A for the assignment.

I decided it might be interesting to hear Gacy weigh in on

the subject of psychopathy. I sent him a copy of my paper and invited him to respond to it if he was so inclined.

He *was* so inclined. Predictably, he was very sympathetic to the idea that certain people who would come across as "normal" in most ways could still be seen as more or less "psychopathic" because of how they live their lives and treat other people. He went even further, writing, "I believe at one time or another you could consider anyone to be [psychopathic], it's so general."

As usual, and as I'd hoped, he was quick to place himself at the center of the discussion. He asked me if I was aware that testifying experts at his trial had referred to him as both "antisocial" and "a psychopath." I was. He also asked me if I was aware that some of those experts had used those two terms interchangeably, as though they referred to exactly the same thing when they didn't. I was. Ever cynical about mental health professionals and the role they play in our legal system, he added, "Just shows you how they like to make something more than it is, and confuse the jury."

In my paper, I'd referred to one theorist who cited impulsivity and an apparent absence of guilt or remorse as hallmarks of the psychopathic personality. That reference piqued Gacy's curiosity.

Clearly referring to himself, he wrote, "Now, how can you have guilt or remorse if you didn't do whatever they're saying [you did]? Sure, there'd be absence of guilt and remorse if you didn't do it. You notice how they never address that part of it? They go along with the theory you're guilty just because you were charged, which to me is bullshit."

In another part of my paper, I'd discussed the example of Beat Generation legend Neal Cassady. Some commentators see Cassady as a classic "psychopath"; others portray him as a misunderstood spiritual seeker. In an essay about Cassady from which I'd extracted a passage for my paper, an acquaintance of his wrote that during his relatively short life, Cassady "accomplished personally and for others far more than most men" accomplish in their longer lives. To Gacy, that particular reference was like catnip to a cat:

I have done that, too, and I can't see how anyone could consider that a problem. Some people are go-getters, and can get more done. I know if someone said something couldn't be done in a certain amount of time, I was always out to disprove them. And if I was successful at doing it, then I was considered a manipulator. Well, tell me how else do you … get ahead if you aren't aggressive and [what some people might] perceive as manipulative? How would you get it done?

He was quick to ally himself with my own underlying cynicism about the tradition of drawing such a close link between psychopathy and criminality. Gacy thought the label "psychopath" could apply to "anyone." He was full of resentment toward the kinds of mental health professionals who would label someone a psychopath, then smugly believe that they'd said everything that needed to be said about that person.

Gacy had strong opinions about practically everything, and he reveled in the opportunity to express them. In fact, he prided himself on being "not tackful [sic]."

There are plenty of examples I could use to make the point. I'll cite just a few: According to Gacy, the media had no choice except to portray him as a "monster" because the image of the criminal-as-monster is "what sells." Courtrooms, he insisted, are all about "perception," never "truth." He rejected "normal" as an utterly useless concept. According to him, psychologists and psychiatrists base all their conclusions on "theory" instead of "fact." He claimed that the "so-called science of psychology" is nothing more than just "a witch hunt." And on and on it went.

Gacy tended to perseverate on a relatively narrow range of subjects. One such subject was his strong resistance to being saddled with a label, or to being placed into any sort of general "category." He was fond of quoting psychiatrist Lawrence Freedman, who was a testifying expert at his trial. Freedman called him "one of the most complex" individuals he'd ever encountered. Gacy loved that quote and repeated it often (though when he repeated it, he always substituted "complexed" for "complex").

In one of his letters to me, he referred to himself as a "maverick" among men, the kind of person who needs and deserves his own category. In another, he wrote, "These doctors feel their success or failure depends on whether or not they can examine a person and fit him into some group ... Isn't it possible a person doesn't fit at all?" He objected to the whole idea of "labeling people, trying to make them fit."

He even went so far as to suggest that he and I were alike in this way, both of us too "complexed [sic]" to be contained within an arbitrary category of any kind. "How can they come up with simple answers to fit us?" he asked. "They seem to think that everything has an answer, and that you can fit into whatever group they want to fit you in. I don't agree with that ... What ever happened to individualism?"

Then he sneered, "Labels, I just love them, people who don't know what they are talking about always want to put a label on you. Doesn't matter if it fits or not."

Gacy was also highly preoccupied with truth standards, and with the issue of who should and shouldn't be allowed to police them. If you weren't present to actually observe something, he'd ask again and again, how could you possibly know what really happened? As he saw it, direct experience was the only reliable way of knowing what was true and what wasn't. Not surprisingly, he leveraged that position to claim that people who insisted he was responsible for the deaths of all those 33 boys had no idea what they were talking about. *Were they there?* Or were they just relying on "supposition" and "theory?"

In one letter, he wrote to me, "I think it's crazy that people can make opinions of a person they have never met." In another letter, he wrote, "In any given incident, if you're not the one involved, many stories can come out of it."

He refused to submit to other people's efforts to define him. One thing he was particularly adamant about: he didn't want to be perceived as mentally ill. He thought being saddled with a psychiatric diagnosis would diminish him as a person—and he didn't want to be diminished, in any way, *ever*.

More than once, he told me that he'd vigorously opposed his attorneys' decision to pursue an insanity defense at his trial. At least by the time he and I began corresponding, he was insisting that people needed to view him as a man in complete control of his faculties.

Not only that, he was a tireless promoter of the image of himself as a highly motivated, highly competent go-getter, someone who had set goals at every stage of his adult life and nearly always managed to attain them. He declared himself a practitioner of "positive mental attitude" or "PMA." To hear him tell it, it was his embrace of PMA that had made it possible for him to achieve so much "success" in life. (He seemed to have an incomplete grasp of the irony implicit in his portrayal of his as a great success story when he was writing about it from a vantage point on death row.)

He rejected the media's depiction of him as a "monster," but he went even further. To me, he insisted that he was nobody unusual, "just an average guy." Often, usually in the course of claiming that he was no more "abnormal" than anyone else, he'd encourage me—in the same way Charles Manson had before him—to reflect on the behavior of other people, including people who had played an active role in creating "the media monster," which according to him was a brazen fabrication.

If I'm such a monster, he seemed to be saying, then why do so many people, including many law enforcement officers who helped send me to prison, write me letters requesting signed paintings and pictures? Why are my paintings becoming more and more valuable with each passing year? And, come to think of it, why are supposedly "normal" people so fascinated by killing and killers in the first place?

He was familiar with *The Only Living Witness*, the landmark account of the Ted Bundy case, so he was aware that toward the end of that book, its authors, Stephen Michaud and Hugh Aynesworth, had paused in the middle of their analysis to pose this tantalizing question: "Who is crazy, and who isn't?"

That issue was of interest to me, too. Whenever friends and family members would ask me about my apparent fascination with serial killers, I'd usually respond by telling them that in reality, I was less interested in the killers themselves than I was in the complicated relationship between killers and members of the majority social audience, many of whom would say that even though they condemn killers and what they do, they still find killers' behavior endlessly fascinating, even entertaining.

There were times when I felt like Gacy and I were bonding over our shared interest in this subject. In any case, I never had to work very hard to draw Gacy into a discussion of it. Ever the narcissist, he invariably placed himself at the center of such discussions. He asked many variations of the same basic question: *Why would anyone perceive me as abnormal?*

We'd been corresponding for only about two months when Gacy wrote, "I guess [people who come to visit me] are expecting to meet this monster image that has been projected of me, and they find someone *no different from them* [emphasis added]." Two weeks later, he returned to the same subject. "[The media] made the monster image, not based on meeting the man but based on what they were fed by the state. Do you actually think the public wanted to hear I was a nice guy?"

About a year further on down the road, he wrote, "Jeff, I am just as human as you." He was frustrated over the fact that a number of publishers had declined to publish his own account of his case—which he'd originally called *The 34th Victim,* referring to himself. He was pretty sure that their lack of interest stemmed from his firm refusal to dwell on "sex and gore."

"They are actually wanting the monster, not the man," he groused.

• • •

Despite Gacy's claim to be normal, just like everyone else, he kept pressing the case for his uniqueness, and for his special standing in the world. Sometimes his grandiosity was down-right shocking.

More than once, he wrote to me of his hope that he'd be able to "enlighten" me about something or other. Even though he said he didn't consider himself to be a true artist, he thought nothing of mentioning himself in the same breath with DaVinci and Michaelangelo, who he cited as his primary influences. In the same vein, he remarked casually on the paintings of his that he felt certain were destined to become "classics." In one letter, he tossed off this line: "Picasso had his style, I guess I have mine."

Repeatedly, he urged me to get out ahead of the burgeoning demand for his work and acquire some of his paintings while I still could. He explained, "The 'Hi Ho' series is probably going to be my most famous. That one and the clown series, of course."

Consider that in the preface to his limited-release memoir, where he alternated between using the first and third person pronouns, he included the following sentence: "A Pulitzer Prize winner would not find it an easy task to describe this man [himself] unless he wished to wax creative to appease the expectations of a reading public which has come to believe him to be a man of monstrous dyssymmetry." And no, he wasn't joking.

• • •

On many occasions, I was left feeling astonished by Gacy's apparent inability to register irony. His brain didn't seem wired for it.

Despite the fact that he'd had no contact with his two biological children for many years, he thought nothing of crowing to me about the child-rearing advice he would sometimes dispense to correspondents of his who had young children.

Shortly after the disappearance of his final victim, 15-year-old Rob Piest, the authorities leaned hard on Gacy to appear at the police station and go on record with an official statement. Gacy seemed astounded by their callousness. *Were they not aware that his uncle Harold had passed away just the day before?* Outraged because of the pressure they were putting on him, Gacy registered one of his more famous protests, "Don't you guys have any respect for the dead?" He made that particular complaint when the police were at his house on W. Summerdale. At the time, 29 corpses were rotting on the property.

In his memoir, Sam Amirante, Gacy's lead trial attorney, recounted an anecdote that speaks about as clearly as anything could to Gacy's impoverished capacity for recognizing and appreciating irony.

Shortly after Gacy's arrest, Amirante planned to spend a quiet Christmas Eve at his parents' house. By that time, Amirante had been publicly identified as Gacy's legal representative. Not long after the announcement of Amirante's role, an anonymous vandal used a screwdriver to write on the side of his father's car, "Your son must be a fag. No one but a fag would represent a fag like Gacy."

Gacy, who was in custody at the time, learned about the incident from a story he read in one of the local newspapers. On Christmas Eve, he phoned Amirante and asked if he'd put his father on the line. When Amirante reluctantly complied, Gacy said to his father, "I'm sorry, Mr. Amirante, that some jerks vandalized your car just because your son is my lawyer, but … ya know, there are a lot of nuts out there."

According to Amirante, Gacy seemed utterly oblivious to the irony. Just days before, he'd confessed to killing more than 30 people.

Another example: After his arrest, Gacy thought nothing of requesting a pen from one of the police officers who was assigned to his case, then using the pen, along with the rosary he said he always kept on his person, to demonstrate how he fashioned the homemade garrote that he used to strangle most of his victims.

There are scientists who have tentatively identified several regions of the brain that they believe are implicated in what's been called "irony apprehension." If it's eventually demonstrated that the brains of serial killers show lower-than-normal levels of activation in these regions, few students of serial murder will be surprised.

Chroniclers of the misdeeds of serial killers like Ted Bundy, Dennis Rader (the "BTK" killer), Gary Ridgway (the "Green River Killer"), Arthur Shawcross (the "Genesee River Killer"), and Keith Jesperson (the "Happy Face Killer") have all commented on their subjects' apparent inability to appreciate the ironic implications of the things they said and did.

Following Gacy's execution, psychiatrist Helen Morrison took possession of his brain and held onto it until she finally handed it over to one of Gacy's final attorneys, Karen Conti. Although it wasn't easy, Morrison had found a pathologist who, after first being given a promise of anonymity, agreed to cut slices from the brain and examine them under a microscope. He told Morrison that as far as he could tell, Gacy's brain was normal.

•••

Now, it's December 15, 1986. Today, I'm slated to meet Gacy face to face for the very first time, on the death row unit at the Menard Correctional Center in Chester, Illinois. From the many letters he's written me during the past ten months, I've become reasonably familiar with Gacy's personality style—at least as it's been expressed through his letters. What I don't know is what it'll be like to be alone in the same room with him.

I'm about to find out.

This I know: Gacy has a history of scaring the hell out of people, even seasoned professionals.

Dr. Morrison, who evaluated him and testified at his trial, found him to be a "scary guy." She said she "immediately ... felt threatened" by him. In her memoir, she recalled the lasting impact of his "leering and arrogant" smile. To her, it seemed like the smile could "grow feral" at any moment, and that Gacy could "sprout fangs." In the end, she concluded that he was "far worse than a psychopath." At his trial, Morrison famously testified to her belief that he would have killed Rob Piest, his last victim, even if there had been a uniformed police officer present at the scene. In other words, she saw him as an out-of-control killing machine.

In Gacy's own memoir, he recalled another psychiatrist who was "manifestly terrified" of being left alone with him.

I knew of a highly unusual passage that had appeared toward the end of the prosecution's April 1980 charging document, submitted to the court while Gacy was awaiting trial.

Addressing the judge who'd been assigned to preside over Gacy's case, the prosecutors wrote, "You are dealing with a man capable of the cruelest sexual sadism imaginable and who now truly has nothing to lose. He is a con-man, a malingerer, a manipulator, a skilled torturer, and an equally skilled killer. Accept his word at your peril. Allow him contact with other inmates at your peril."

As I'm preparing myself to face Gacy, I'm trying to stay focused and in the moment. I'm not terrified—but I'm undeniably nervous.

In the future, once I've completed my graduate studies, I'll conduct psychological evaluations of thousands of criminals, many of them with histories of extreme violence. But as of right now, I've never before interviewed a convicted murderer, let alone a serial killer. In fact, I've never before been in the same room with someone known to have killed even a single person.

Let that sink in.

Over the years leading up to this point in my life, I've delivered television sets; I've spent four summers as a substitute mail carrier; I've worked at a paper mill; I've manned the front desk at a municipal swimming pool; I've completed three years of graduate study in English and modern Anglo-Irish literature; I've studied Gaelic on the smallest of the Aran islands; I've spent several years as a hospital administrator; and I've begun work toward my PhD in psychology. Full stop.

Fortunately, I don't have much time to dwell on my lack of experience.

Because here comes Gacy, all by himself, no escort.

As Gacy shuffles into the room where I'm awaiting his

arrival—the place where we'll spend the next six hours to-gether—he looks directly at me but doesn't smile. My nose registers the overpowering scent of his cheap cologne. He's wearing shackles around his ankles, and as a result his move-ments are slow and clumsy. With his handcuffed hands and thick forearms, he's clutching several items to his chest. They look to be books or albums of some kind. His grey hair is cut short, in a burr. He has a salt-and-pepper beard, bushy at the chin and shorter and more wispy on the sides.

Gacy seems a little tentative but not at all nervous or self-conscious. He takes a few short steps, then leans forward to transfer the things he's carrying onto the table where we'll be sitting. Now unencumbered, he extends his handcuffed hands in my direction. I shake his right hand with mine.

He has long, narrow fingers. I'm surprised by how limp his grip is, and by his soft skin. If he has any calluses on his right hand, I can't feel them—not exactly what I expect a con-struction worker's hand to feel like. Prior to his arrest, Gacy ran his own business, called PDM Contractors (Painting, Dec-orating, and Maintenance). But I know the history: he hired teenage boys to perform most of the manual labor.

I can tell Gacy's sizing me up. His eyes are moving up and down, over my entire body. A few awkward seconds of silence follow our handshake and introductions. When he finally be-gins to speak, I'm surprised at how high-pitched and nasal his voice sounds, even though we've spoken by telephone sever-al times since February. I note a barely perceptible lisp. And when he talks, he *whines*. His inflections are a sure sign of the deep well of aggrievement with which I'm all too familiar by now.

Even before we have time to settle into any kind of con-versation, he seems mildly perturbed by the thought that he's going to have to push back against all my "presuppositions" about who he is and how he's likely to come across during the time we spend together.

"Not what you expected me to be like, huh?" is how he signs in. "You probably came here looking for the monster. That's the media creation. Well, now you're meeting *the man*.

The man's nothing like what you've read about in those books. Those are fantasy."

He pauses for a moment to let his message sink in.

"I haven't granted any interviews since my trial," he says. "You know why? I don't need to correct the errors in the media. Fuck 'em. You're gonna find out I'm a normal person, just like you. And you'll find I'm an easy person to talk to. Oh, by the way, when did you get in last night?"

"I guess it was around 8:30. I stopped and got dinner in Carbondale, or I would have arrived here sooner."

"You staying at the Royal Motor Lodge? That place I recommended?"

"Yeah. I have to say, though, it's a pretty seedy joint."

"Well, welcome to Chester. You have any trouble getting processed out front?"

"Not really. I got here before eight. Seemed like the guy at the front desk was expecting me. He knew my name, had it written down. When he checked me in, he asked me if I was a reporter. I told him no, just like you said. Told him I was a friend. No real problems, but it seemed like it took me forever to get to this building. Lots of gates, a bunch of security checkpoints, and a pretty long wait in a room that had a bunch of vending machines in it."

"Hey, you're in prison, Jeff. Best get used to it. Nothing happens quickly around here, and everything's inefficient as hell. Anyway, have a seat. I've been looking forward to your visit."

• • •

Gacy is shorter than I expect him to be. He's shorter than me, and I usually tell people I'm 5' 8". He's wearing prison-issue clothing: snug-fitting navy-blue pants and a light blue short-sleeved shirt, with a white T-shirt underneath. He has a watch on his left wrist. As he takes his seat opposite me at the table, I notice that he's wearing black nylon socks and black leather loafers, with tassels.

He's relatively slender around the hips, but he has a

bulging gut and a barrel chest. His droopy jowls and pallid complexion mark him as a creature of the indoors. (Later, I'll recall his appearance when I come across writer Christopher Berry-Dee's description of him as a "potato-faced … doughy monster.") It's been more than six years since his last period of extended time outside these walls. He lives in a windowless cell.

Once we're seated, he immediately launches into a description of the various items he was clutching to his chest when he entered the room.

"This here's my logbook," he volunteers, pointing to a thick notebook that's in front of him on the table. "I take it with me everywhere I go. Document every meal I eat, every piece of mail I receive, every letter I write, every painting I sell, and every visit I have."

He opens the logbook to a random page, apparently wanting me to appreciate the scrupulousness of his documentation. It occurs to me that there's a larger issue at stake here: his credibility.

If I'm this careful about documenting my meals, my mail, my sales, and my visits, doesn't it stand to reason that I must be telling the truth when I say I kept detailed records before my arrest? The kinds of records that, if the State hadn't destroyed them, would have helped me to demonstrate that the prosecution's case against me was bullshit? Like I've told you in my letters?

"And over here's my photo album," he says, pointing to his left. "We'll get to that later. And this here is your file." He points to a manila file that he's placed on the table to his right. It has my name written across the tab. Next to my name is my date of birth. Next to that are the words, "Wife, Betsy."

Gacy's manner is faux-folksy. I find it easy to imagine being seated next to him at a bar. He'd look pretty much like any another patron, and in all likelihood he'd come across as a normal, blue collar-type guy, friendly and accommodating. Probably, he'd strike up a conversation. I'd find him pleasant enough company, at least for a while.

Right now, his top priority is putting me at ease, making me feel comfortable. Or so it seems. He starts out with some small talk. About the day's overcast weather. About the Mississippi River that runs past the prison, just down the hill from the building where we're seated. About the tight security precautions that were in place when he arrived here five years ago. (*Hell, it was like a fuckin' presidential escort!*) About the "dumb fuck … hick" guards who work at the prison, the local "morons" who the State of Illinois hires to manage the inmate population. And about the "freezing the doors" protocol that's deployed for safety-related reasons whenever a visitor comes to see someone who's on death row.

I'm eager to plunge into a discussion of his legal case—but not as eager as he is. Once he gets going, it's hard to get him to stop talking. (Years later, Dr. Morrison will write of his "logorrhea," a technical term for speech that is excessive and sometimes incoherent.) He wants to remind me, first of all, that he's here on death row only because he got railroaded at trial. (I'm familiar with this claim; his letters overflow with it.)

Sam Amirante, who'd just opened his private practice when he was appointed to serve as Gacy's legal representative, was, says Gacy, "in way over his head." Gacy himself lobbied for the involvement of celebrity attorney F. Lee Bailey (who was eager to sign on to the Gacy cause). However, Amirante wanted no part of Bailey.

"Sam felt threatened, Jeff, he didn't even want Bailey involved. Okay, you're the one who's studying psychology, *think about it.* Imagine they put you on the witness stand and want you to talk about Charles Manson's mind. You'd be out of your league, am I right? I'm not putting you down, it's just the way it is. Same thing with Amirante. I still like the guy personally, just sent him a Christmas card. But like I say, he was in way over his head."

He reiterates something he's emphasized in his letters, that he never wanted to plead not guilty by reason of insanity. At least according to him, Amirante and his co-counsel convinced him that he really had no choice. Gacy claims he was "naive," so naive, in fact, that he didn't grasp the fact that jury members would probably view an insanity plea as a tacit admission of guilt.

"But you did admit to the murders, right?" I say. "Didn't you confess to all 33 of them?"

"Well, now there you go with the bullshit," he says. "You're getting into all the fantasy. The thing of it is, show me the tape recording of the supposed confession. There isn't one! That's because I never confessed! The State knowingly knew that. All they had were the made-up notes written by the Des Plaines police. And how self-serving were those? They said I confessed. On the same token, they were under so much pressure to solve the case, they just wrote down whatever they felt they needed to. There *was* no confession! It was hearsay, plain and simple."

"But wait, I thought you even confessed to your attorneys?"

"Again, the thing of it is, Jeff, there's no record I did any such thing! And I was so drunk and high on Valium that night at Amirante's office, who knows what I might have said? It's bullshit! I'm tellin' ya, the State's entire case was based on theory and hearsay, conjecture. They got tunnel vision, and they never even investigated anyone else. Hell, at least 12 other people had keys to that house. But they assumed *I* was the one who had to have buried all those bodies in the crawlspace!"

He can't wait to talk to me about two of his former employees, teens named David Cram and Michael Rossi. They've come up before, in some of his letters. I'm aware that both Cram and Rossi resided at Gacy's house on W. Summerdale for extended periods of time in the years prior to Gacy's arrest.

"Why weren't Cram and Rossi viewed as suspects?" he asks, sounding outraged. "*They* had keys to the house! *They* were in and out all the time! And hell, both of *them* were dealing drugs. I had sex with 'em, sure, and both of 'em did favors for me. It was a good arrangement for everybody. I let 'em use the company truck whenever they wanted to. They had free run of the place. But why didn't the police look at *them*?"

"Well, I know the police interviewed them, and they both testified at your trial. Apparently they were ruled out as suspects. No?"

"There's the bullshit again! Jeff, don't you see, that's the thing of it, it's all just supposition. You're smarter than that! You're just going with the fantasy and the theories from all those books you read. Hell, I've heard Rossi's been arrested twice just since my trial! Kidnapped some people! Tied 'em up! But his uncle's a judge in Chicago so they let him off with a slap on the wrist."

He tells me that Rossi once confessed to him that he and Cram took a drug client of theirs out into the woods, stole all his money, and beat the crap out of him.

"Hell, there were times when I returned home to the Summerdale house after a business trip and found a strange coat or sweater lying around. If I asked Rossi who it belonged to, he'd say, 'Don't worry, I'll take care of it.' Then it'd be gone, I'd never see it again. You tell me? Does that sound like suspicious behavior to you?"

He keeps yammering on about Cram and Rossi. After a while, I start to think that if I can't manage to steer the conversation to a different subject, he'll continue talking about them until it's time for me to leave. *They were punks, they were shitheads, they took advantage of me, they were druggies, they were liars.* And on it goes.

"I have no idea who did all the killings, any more than you do."

As for me, I'm in need a restroom break, and I need it badly. Finally, I get one—but not before I have to scream at the top of my lungs to get the attention of a guard who was whiling away the hours somewhere out of sight, on the other side of the gate that separates Gacy and me from the rest of the world. When I return after emptying my full-to-bursting bladder, Gacy, who's clearly found it entertaining to watch me bump up against the reality of our isolation back here in the death row visiting area, still wants to talk about his two former employees.

Finally, I've heard enough about Cram and Rossi.

"*John*! I get it! I get it that you think Cram and Rossi should have been looked at for some of the murders. But can we talk about something else? How 'bout your sexuality? Everyone who's written about your case seems to make a big deal out of it."

"Yeah, sure, I don't mind talking about it," he says. "See, like I've told you in my letters, I'm open-minded, but I'm no homosexual. That was the police theory, but they didn't know jack shit about me. I'm liberal about sex. I used to say I was bisexual—but I should say I'm asexual."

"Asexual? I'm not even sure I know what that means."

"Well, you're the psychologist." (In truth, I was a second-year graduate student.) "You tell me!"

"Well, if you say someone's amoral, it usually means the person doesn't operate according to *any* moral code. But I don't think you're using asexual that way, are you?"

"What I'm sayin' is this. When you say 'bi' you're sayin' two. That's what 'bi' means, right? When I say I'm asexual, I just mean *I like sex*! Doesn't matter to me if it's with a male, a female, or both. If I wanna get off, I don't really care who it's with. Like I say, a mouth's a mouth."

He offers to tell me about his first consenting sexual encounter with a male partner. He was 17 at the time. After a night of heavy drinking with a male friend, John passed out. When he came to, the friend was "going down on" him.

"I suppose I could have stopped it at that point," he says with a shrug. "But what the hell, it felt good!"

He explains that from that point on, he figured he could double his chances of "getting off" if he was open to having male and female partners. As he saw it, the sex was strictly transactional. "You get what you want, I get what I want, no big deal," he says.

With another shrug, and speaking in the same matter-of-fact tone of voice he might use to describe the way he likes to move back and forth between boxes of Thin Mints and Do-Si-Dos, he tells me of his policy of never turning anyone away, male or female, who is willing to satisfy his sexual cravings.

"Look," he says, "some guy tells me he likes to have it crammed up his ass, I'll cram it up his ass."

He wants me to know that he always preferred the role of "pitcher" over the role of "catcher." I'm pretty sure I know what that means, but I ask him to explain himself anyway.

"You're really gonna get an education here!" he declares with a broad smile and a barely perceptible wink. "A pitcher's the one who gets his rocks off in the other person, either by a blow job or by giving it to him up the ass. The catcher's the passive partner. I never wanted to be that guy."

He's determined to make the sharpest possible distinction between his own bisexuality—or "asexuality," the term he prefers—and homosexuality. "I've never been a homosexual," he insists. "In fact, I've always hated faggots. My old man used to say I was one. Faggot, sissy, fruit picker, all that shit. But I never was one. Sex is sex. That's how I see it. So I say I'm bisexual or asexual."

"But what about the fact that all the people you were found guilty of killing were boys and young men?"

"The thing of it is, Jeff, and here you're going back into the supposition and the police theories of the case, I wasn't responsible for the deaths of those kids. I have no idea who did all the killings, any more than you do. Where's the motive? I was family-oriented. And hell, I worked 12- to 14-hour days. The prosecution knowingly knew I was out of the state when 16 of those kids went missing. I couldn't have killed them! But the police destroyed my business records, so I couldn't use them to prove it."

My sexuality is a subject that is of obvious interest to him. He's referenced it in his letters, too. His approach is to bring up the subject, then point out that he could ask me all sorts of questions about it but won't.

"You have all these questions about my sexuality," he says. "And the police want everybody to believe I was a faggot out killing boys because of something having to do with sex. It's bullshit! All theory. And it's self-serving."

"I could jump to a conclusion about you and *your* sexuality," he continues. "You didn't marry 'til you were over 30. Most people get married when they're about 21. So either you were dating other women or jacking off, right? Hell, no! Maybe you just had other things goin' on in your life! But I could jump to the conclusion there was something wrong with you! See how it happens? See how it could develop? People get a theory and then they try to make everything fit into it."

He'll raise the same issue—that I waited to get married until I was in my 30s—three or four more times during this first two-day visit. Right now, I'm hoping to redirect the conversation back to him, and to the crimes he was found guilty of committing.

"Just so I'm clear," I say, "are you telling me you don't know anything about any of the bodies that were found in your crawlspace?"

"Listen, Jeff, I'll tell you this much, and I probably shouldn't be sayin' it. I know something about five of 'em. The kid I brought home from the Greyhound bus station. I never knew his name but that was way back in, what was it, '71? '72? The four others I know something about are Butkovich, Godzik, Szyc—and then I know a little about Piest, the last one. That's really all I can say. You know how it is, I gotta listen to my attorneys, it's part of the appeal. Maybe later, like if you come back for another visit, I'll be able to tell you a little more. Like I say, I know something about five of 'em, that's it."

●●●

A guard arrives with our lunches. Gacy has already informed me that he arranged to have an extra lunch delivered for me ("That way, you can see what they feed us in here").

The guard places two Styrofoam boxes on the table, each containing a mound of sloppy joe mix, some canned green beans, a lumpy pile of mashed potatoes, two pieces of white bread, a scoop of coleslaw, a small carton of orange juice, and two cookies. Gacy says I'm welcome to his lunch, too, he doesn't want it.

None of the cooked food looks even mildly appetizing, but I'm concerned not to appear ungrateful. Eventually, I eat a few green beans, a little coleslaw, half a slice of bread, and both the cookies from my own Styrofoam box. Gacy's lunch goes untouched. As I'm finishing the second of my cookies, Gacy reminds me that tomorrow morning, I can purchase up to ten dollars' worth of vending machine food as I'm being processed into the prison.

I ask him what he'd like me to purchase. He says he'd love it if I brought him some microwave popcorn, a box of Good and Plenty candy, a couple of candy bars, and a sandwich of some kind. I say no problem, I'll do it.

Then he starts talking about his weight.

"I know I shouldn't eat so much junk food," he says. "But I don't eat most of the food they give us, and I only get stuff from the vending machines if I have a visitor. My weight's up to around 240. At one point I was down to 170. I don't get much exercise. Wait, let me show you a picture. That way, you'll know I'm not bullshittin' ya when I say I used to weigh 170."

He reaches for his photograph album and flips through the pages until he comes to a picture of himself looking down-right svelte compared to how he looks now.

"See? See what I mean?" he says. "See how much thinner I am in that picture?" He volunteers that he weighed between 220 and 230 at the time of his arrest eight years ago. "You can tell how bloated I was when you look at that mug shot they keep puttin' in the papers," he says with a rueful chuckle.

I think it'll be interesting if I can get him to talk with me about the members of his family. He's made some glancing references to them in his letters, but I want to hear him talk about them in person. That way, I'll have a shot at gauging his emotional reactions. I opt for an indirect approach.

"How did your mother deal with all the negative public-ity after your arrest?" I ask. "And how did she hold up during your trial? By the way, just tell me if I'm getting too personal."

"My mom, God bless her, she's the strong one in the fam-ily. She always supported me and my younger sister, that's Karen. See, my dad took it out on us when our older sister dropped out of nursing school to get married. After that, he wouldn't give me or Karen a cent for anything. But Mom helped us whenever she could. She lives with Karen now. They're out in Arkansas."

He almost looks like he could become emotional as he's talking about his mother's loyalty and unwavering support.

"Do you still talk to your mom?" I ask.

"Yeah, but her memory's getting really bad. We'll be talking, and she'll ask me if I'm coming to visit over the summer. Recently, she asked me if I was coming for Christmas. I just said, 'No, Mom, I don't think I'll be able to make it this year.'" He says that after their conversations, Karen will sometimes ask his mother who she was just talking to. She'll say she can't remember.

"What about your dad?"

Gacy had said things—to me and others—suggesting that his father was a physically and emotionally abusive tyrant who would drink in the basement of their home, then emerge to terrorize him and the other members of his family.

"My dad was drunk a lot," he says, "and when he drank he used to hit Mom and us kids. He never went out to drink, he'd always just go down to the basement. When he got drunk, all anybody had to do was look at him sideways and he'd hit 'em."

His relationship with his father worsened around the time he hit puberty. That was also when John started sticking up for his mother.

"I can remember telling Dad, 'Hit us if we do something wrong, but don't always be hitting Mom!'"

He tells me he himself has never hit a woman and never would. He adds that he can hardly even imagine a situation where violence against a woman would be justified.

"I don't believe in it, never have," he says, sounding about as emphatic as he has sounded about anything. "Never once hit either of my wives. If I got mad about something, I'd go somewhere and cool off for a while. Then I'd come back later, once I'd gotten control of myself."

He can remember times during his childhood when he'd ask his mother why she didn't just leave his father. She'd say, "I have nowhere else to go." He'd tell her, "Go *anywhere!* Just don't stay here and keep lettin' him do that to you!"

He explains that as far as his father was concerned, he could do no right.

"It didn't matter what I did. To Dad, I was always dumb

and stupid, dumb and stupid. He'd tell me I was a faggot, a fruit picker, I'd never amount to anything. I guess that's where my drive came from. I wanted to prove he was wrong. That's what I brought to my work, too, whether it was selling shoes, working as a chef, running my own business, whatever."

"Well," I say, "that's something else I wanted to ask you about. You've written in your letters about positive mental attitude. You call it PMA. Sometimes you sound like Norman Vincent Peale! Even in prison, it seems like you're busy all the time. Always setting goals, always trying hard to achieve them, always looking ahead."

"You're right, Jeff. And that goes back to my childhood. Like I say, my dad always said I was stupid and not worth anything. I remember one time I tried to help him paint a house and I got some paint on the windowpanes. Big fuckin' deal, right? All you had to do was scrape it off with a razor. But for him, every mistake I made had to be some huge fuckin' deal! I worked my ass off when I left home. I guess I wanted to show him I could be a success. He never thought I could be."

• • •

Since we've been told we need to wrap things up by 2:00 today and it's now 1:30, Gacy decides it's time to turn our attention to his photo album. He invites me over to his side of the table. I'm uneasy about accepting his invitation, but I'm determined not to appear nervous. It occurs to me how easy it would be for him to lift his cuffed hands, place his thick forearms on either side of my head or neck, and start squeezing. Just as easily, he could strangle me using the length of chain that runs between his handcuffs.

I make a split-second decision. I move my chair to his side of the table and place it alongside his—but I'm mindful of the need to be extra vigilant. I place both my feet flat on the floor and position myself so that I can push away from the table and move quickly to my left if I perceive the need to. It's tough to relax. In truth, I don't want to.

The first picture he shows me is a full-page photograph of

himself, dressed up in his Pogo the Clown costume.

"See, the thing of it is, Jeff, I loved clowning. At nursing homes, children's hospitals—sometimes even at private parties. I just liked making people laugh, liked making 'em feel good. That's the kind of person I was. But see, that's another example of how people can twist things around and make 'em sound bad so they'll fit with their theories."

I can't resist this opening, so I jump on it.

"Did you really make the statement, 'Clowns can get away with murder'?"

"Well yeah, I'm sure I said something like that. But big fuckin' deal! They try to make it sound like it has something to do with my case, like it was something *bad*. It wasn't like that."

"Well, what did you mean?"

"I just meant, like, if you're dressed up as a clown and you're marching in a parade or something, nobody expects you to stay in formation like everybody else. On the same token, you can run up on people's lawns, take a drink of their beer, give a lady a feel, whatever. And no one knows who you are. I just say you can get away with murder when you're dressed up in a clown costume. No big deal. See what I mean? It's just an expression. But people try to make it sound like I'm talking about murder. And that's fuckin' bullshit!"

He seems annoyed when I mention that some people have said the "pointy" paint around Pogo's mouth could easily scare children and isn't really in keeping with widely-accepted standards for how clown make-up should be applied.

"Ok now, first of all those aren't points!" he says, gesturing toward the picture. "The thing of it is, the face paint around the mouth is actually *rounded*. It's just that when I'm dressed as Pogo and I smile, it looks like there are points around my mouth. People want to make it seem like Pogo's an evil clown or something, and nothing could be further from the truth. All I wanted to do was bring happiness to people."

Now he's getting antsy, edgy. I can tell. He seems distracted, and he keeps glancing toward the doorway. I assume it's because he's anticipating the arrival of the guard who will tell us our time's up.

A minute or two later, I hear the iron gate opening and closing, then the sound of the guard's approaching footsteps. When he appears in the doorway of the visiting room, I realize that he's observing me seated on the same side of the table as Gacy. I wonder if that's against prison rules. Apparently, it's not. He says nothing to suggest that there's anything wrong or the least bit unusual about the arrangement that has me sitting right alongside the serial killer.

"Okay, JW," he says with a smile. "Two o'clock. Time's up."

Gacy and I get up from our chairs, turn toward each other, and shake hands.

"See," says Gacy, "it's like I told you, the time goes by fast. I really enjoyed the visit. Be sure you get here before 8:00 in the morning. That way, we'll get our full time in. And don't forget the vending machines."

"I won't forget. See you tomorrow."

Just like that, day one of my visit is over.

I'm glad.

• • •

When I return to the prison the next morning, I use my time in the vending machine room to purchase everything I promised Gacy I'd purchase, plus a few extras. I also fork out $5.00 for the privilege of having a guard take two pictures of Gacy and me at some point later in the day. I'll keep one, the other one will stay with Gacy.

Unfortunately, it occurs to me as I'm paying that Gacy will almost certainly use his picture of me for masturbatory purposes. What's to be done? It's not like I can say, "Here, John. This one is yours to keep—but only if you promise not to look at it when you jerk off." After all, I've chosen to come here, chosen to spend time in the company of a sadistic sex criminal who happens to be attracted to boys and young men.

This morning's set-up differs a little from the set-up yesterday. When I get to the visiting room on death row, Gacy's there already, awaiting my arrival. Someone out front must have sent word that I'd arrived at the prison and was making my way to the condemned unit.

"Hey, Jeff, good to see ya," says Gacy, rising to his feet as soon as I enter the room. He sounds chipper, eager to get underway. "How was your night back at the motel?"

"It was okay," I say. "But like I said, it's a little shabby. If I come back for another visit, I'll probably stay somewhere else."

"Well, at least you'll know your way around next time. And I hope you *do* come back."

He's already sitting down. He gestures toward my chair, on the opposite side of the table. "Make yourself right at home," he says with a cockeyed smile. "I saved your seat for you."

I'm relieved that he's not expecting me to sit on his side of the table, at least not now. That's where I was when we ended our visit yesterday. I'll be surprised if he doesn't invite me back over there before it's time for me to leave this afternoon. I notice that he has brought along his now familiar set of props: the logbook, his photo album, and the manila file with my name written on the tab.

But today he's brought something else, too. It's a brightly colored painting of the Seven Dwarfs from the Disney movie, *Snow White*. The painting is to Gacy's right, propped up against the wall.

"I brought out a painting for you to see," he says. "I'm not trying to be heavy-handed, it's not like I'm saying you have to buy it. But remember, selling my paintings is how I pay for postage, envelopes, and stationery. This one's part of my Hi Ho series. It might be my most famous one. Along with the clown series, of course. If I were you, I'd get one. I try to keep my prices down, but you know the paintings are just going to go up in value."

"Let me think about it," I say. "Don't forget, I'm a poor graduate student, but I do want to get another one at some point."

I already own a Gacy painting. It's "one of a kind" — that's how Gacy billed it. He "customized" it for me a few months back. It cost me $30. Actually, it's a knock-off of Picasso's famous mid-20th century ink drawing of Don Quixote seated astride his steed Rocinante and accompanied by his loyal squire, Sancho Panza, who is shown seated on his donkey, Dapple. Gacy titled his painting "Quest" and put my initials—"JS"—on Don Quixote's shield, symbolizing, he said, my "crusade to find the truth."

Today, there's none of the awkwardness that I felt during the first minutes of yesterday's visit. The morning begins on an upbeat note. I hand over to Gacy the food I purchased for him from the vending machines. From his reaction, you'd think I had just announced arrangements for us to enjoy a catered ten-course dinner together.

"Oh man, I love Good and Plenty, haven't had that in a long time," he says. "And thanks for the popcorn and candy bars! What kind of sandwich is it? Ham and cheese? Good, it'll taste a lot better than that shit bologna they give us all the time."

With the opening vibe so positive, I decide to jump-start the day's conversation.

"I was hoping maybe we could talk today about some of the other people you write to," I say. "And about how the media's handled your case. I know you said yesterday that you haven't done any formal interviews since your trial."

"That's right," he says. "I've been contacted by *60 Minutes, 20/20, The Phil Donahue Show*, all of 'em. Now Oprah Winfrey says she wants me. But I won't talk to any of 'em. Why the hell should I? The media created the monster, now let 'em live with it. And you know what else? I don't like the publicity about my case because it's not for something I *did*. If my renown was for social work, or for some civic thing I did, I'd say good, I like it. But the way it is now, it's all just a bitch."

On top of these remarks, he piggybacks a sneering reference to the hypocritical law enforcement officials who he says treated him like a monster, then turned around and asked him if they could purchase one of his paintings! He claims he's sold 75 paintings to officials who investigated him and participated in the events that led to his conviction, including prosecutor

Terry Sullivan, who co-wrote the book *Killer Clown*. He references guards at the Cook County Jail who used to snatch up his cigar butts and take them home to save as souvenirs.

"You tell me who's crazy!" he says. "Hell, when the police tore down my house on Summerdale back in '79, people came from all over to get bricks and pieces of sod. And those are the same people who want to say there's something wrong with *me*!"

He speaks derisively of a New York-based black repertory company that staged a play called *The House on Summerdale*. "Can you believe that shit?" he says. "Not even any black victims, no black nothing, but the n----rs still want to get involved with it!"

"Tell me more about some of the people you write to."

"I write to lots of people, all over the U.S. Other countries, too. There's a 25-year-old woman from Maine says she wants to marry me! Second one since my trial!"

He reaches for his photo album and turns to a picture of the woman from Maine. There is a handwritten inscription on the picture. It begins, "You're such a sweet man." He speaks of her with evident disdain, adding, though, that they got along reasonably well when she traveled from Maine to visit him.

"She's real religious," he says, "claims she wants to start a campaign of writing letters to newspapers, saying how I got such a bum deal at my trial and shit." He hunches his shoulders, extends his arms toward me, and turns him palms upward. It's a set of gestures meant to convey utter astonishment. "Can you believe that shit?" he says. "Just what I need. Some broad going to the papers and talking about how Jesus loves John Gacy. I told her no fucking way!"

He flips to a picture of another of his correspondents, a boy who looks like he might be 14 or 15 years old.

"That kid sort of looks like Donny Osmond," I say.

"He's a fuckin' goody-two-shoes."

In one of the letters he wrote to me, Gacy mocked one of his pen pals for being so ignorant and naive that he'd written asking whether inmates at the prison got to select their meals from a menu.

"Is he the one you told me about?" I say. "The one who asked you whether there were menus in prison?"

"Nah, he's not *that* stupid," says Gacy. "But this dumb fuck writes and tells me his girlfriend is whacking him off and there's blood in his semen! Wants me to tell him what he should do! Can you believe that shit? What am I supposed to say? *Go to the fucking doctor, shithead!*"

Among his other correspondents are a journalist named Harlan Mendenhall, who Gacy says plans to write his authorized "biography" someday; a minister's wife who says she wants to save him; a journalist from out west who claims to be a former classmate of novelist Louis L'Amour's; an 83-year-old man who says he's lonely and in need of company; and a member of a California-based punk rock band who says he's written a song based on Gacy's case.

"Y'know," says Gacy, sounding almost wistful. "There are some people I've gotten real close to, people that if I got out of here I wouldn't mind at all spending time with, having as my friends. And you're one of 'em."

●●●

I hear a guard approaching from down the hall. He has our lunches. They're in Styrofoam containers, just like yesterday. This time, the meal consists of bologna sandwiches, accompanied by chips, cooked carrots, an orphan slice of white bread, a carton of milk, and two sugar cookies. There's nothing the least bit appetizing about the smell of the bologna and carrots. It reminds me of the stale stench in the cafeterias where I and hundreds of other Boy Scouts used to convene to eat our meals—and then scrape the leftovers off our plates into large garbage cans—during the Jamboree campouts of my youth.

I decide I'll stick to the chips and cookies—but I'm not ready for them just yet. Like Gacy, I move quickly to close the lid on my Styrofoam container once I've seen and smelled its contents.

I'm eager to hear Gacy talk some more about murder. At

one point yesterday, he made a passing reference to "the elite ten" serial killers in modern American history.

"John, when you referred to the elite ten serial killers yesterday, which ones were you talking about?"

"Well," he says, "you got Wayne Williams down in Georgia, you got Bundy in Florida, you got Berkowitz in New York, you got Manson out in California ..."

"Hold on," I say. "What about Richard Speck, right here in Illinois? I know that technically he wouldn't be classified as a serial killer, more a mass killer or spree killer. But what about him?"

"He's not even that big anymore," says Gacy with a shrug. He could as easily be talking about Billy Idol.

Apropos of nothing in particular, he starts grousing about people who seem incapable of appreciating his sense of humor.

"See, like I say, Jeff. I don't like being serious all the time. I like making people laugh, it's just the kind of person I am."

"Okay, but ..."

"Don't forget. I was a clown! Kids, old people, the whole nine yards. Hell, it's like that time with you, remember? That fuckin' bullshit about 'six feet underground'? I didn't mean that to be about my case! But you took it the wrong way. Acted like ... what was it you said? Like, I was trying to be ironic or some shit? It was a fuckin' *joke*! I said lighten up!"

"Whatever, we dealt with that and said we'd move on."

"Yeah I know, but I'm just sayin', you're not the only one who took something I said as a joke and tried to make something serious of it. Y'know Jeff, there were lots of Gacy jokes told during my trial. You heard any of those? Like, 'Do you know what John Gacy does for Christmas? Digs up the Vienna Boys Choir.' Or, 'Did you hear about the Gacy house? It's in a nice neighborhood, it's been remodeled, and it sleeps 29.'"

He seems to think such jokes would be a hoot to anyone who didn't take themselves too seriously.

He pauses to offer me a cigar. I accept but say I'm going to wait to smoke it until I get back to Columbus. He's clearly disappointed; he wants me to smoke it now. He lights one himself and starts puffing away. (I choose not to ask why he's permitted to have a lighter on death row.)

Finally, not long after we're both done picking at the food in our Styrofoam containers, the thing I expected would happen finally happens. He invites me over to his side of the table, ostensibly so that we can continue browsing through his album of photographs. I accept his invitation, but today I'm no more comfortable with the arrangement than I was yesterday.

After about 15 minutes, I'm relieved to hear the sound of a guard opening and closing the steel gate and approaching our room from down the hall. As it turns out, he's come to take the pictures I paid for this morning. He's holding a Polaroid camera, the kind that can process and print pictures almost instantaneously.

He asks Gacy and me where we want to pose. Without saying anything, Gacy gets up from the table and turns to face him. I stand and position myself to Gacy's left. As the guard looks at us through the lens of his camera and prepares to snap the first picture, he jokes that "JW" — that's how he addresses Gacy — is taking up a lot more space in the picture frame than I am. I grin, involuntarily. Gacy, with his cuffed hands dangling in front of his bulging belly, does not.

When the guard hands me the pictures, Gacy glances at them and tells me I can keep whichever one I want. To me, they look pretty much the same. I place one on the far side of the table, where I began the day, and I hand the other one to him.

"Well, they could be worse," he says. "You look good, I just look fat."

After the guard leaves, we return to our seats and continue our perusal of the photo album. He shows me pictures of his mother, his father, his two sisters, and his two former wives. There are also pictures of some of his paintings.

Then we come to a series of pictures depicting a model of the house on W. Summerdale. Gacy explains that he constructed the model out of popsicle sticks, at his attorneys' request. Proudly, he assures me that he did it "to scale."

These pictures interest me primarily because I think they might help me convince Gacy to resume talking about what his living situation and lifestyle were like prior to his arrest.

"Tell me what things were like back when you were at the Summerdale house and running your business," I say.

"Well, like I've said in my letters," he says, "the Summerdale house wasn't what most people think of when they think of a home. You know, kids playing, TV on, mother working all day, that kinda shit. It was basically a business property. Hell, most nights I didn't even sleep there!"

He's certain that if people understood those things, they'd have a much easier time believing his claim that he has no idea how all those bodies ended up down in the crawlspace.

While we're looking at the pictures of the popsicle stick model, he produces a rough sketch of the W. Summerdale Ave. property. It's on a pad of paper that he brought along with him to our meeting. He uses the sketch to argue that a young man who claims to have endured a protracted session of sexual torture at the Summerdale address couldn't possibly have been there. The man's name is Jeffrey Rignall.

"Listen Jeff, Rignall's a jerk-off!" he says. "He broke down crying at my trial. Hell, he even puked on the fuckin' witness stand! He's a punk! Even the cops knew it. He claimed he leaned on a railing in front of my house and there wasn't even a railing there! He said there was a doorbell, and there wasn't a doorbell! He claimed he was hung from the ceiling in the bar area, and he says I stuck a fire poker up his ass! That's bullshit! For one thing, that ceiling would never support the weight of someone who weighed what Rignall weighed. And for another, I didn't even have a fireplace! What the fuck would I be doing with a fire poker?"

He stops talking, looks distracted for a few moments. I wonder what he's thinking. When he starts up again, it's with a startling reference to the 33 boys and young men he was found guilty of killing.

"Y'know, the thing of it is Jeff, back in my cell I've got pictures of every single one of those kids they say I killed." He holds up his cuffed hands and positions his fingers like he's holding a fanned-out deck of playing cards. "I shuffle through those pictures, I look at each one of those faces, and those kids are no more real to me than … "

He pauses for a moment, apparently unsure how to finish his sentence. Suddenly, his attention shifts to the brightly colored painting of the Seven Dwarfs that is propped up against the wall.

"… than the cartoon characters in that painting."

I think, *That might be the first indisputably true thing he's said all day.*

In an interview conducted six years later with FBI behavioral science analyst Robert Ressler, Gacy will volunteer that the boys and young men he was convicted of killing were nothing more to him than just "names and faces."

Still thinking about the outrageousness of the State's case against him, he segues into a diatribe about the pornography the police claimed to have found inside his house.

"Hell, it wasn't even pornography!" he protests. "Those were schoolbooks about sex. Oh, and then in the bar area there was some joke stuff, y'know what I mean? People never knew what to get me for my birthday. Hell, I had everything I wanted, it's not like I wasn't making a shitload of money! Like, there was one book, a hundred different ways to screw. Big fuckin' deal! And there was a knitted dildo with balls, that kinda shit, y'know?"

He then launches into a diatribe—another one—about how police and members of the media latched on to things he said and did, then "took them out of context" and tried to make them seem more sinister than they were.

He repeats the anecdote about how the police came to his house not long after Rob Piest's disappearance and demanded that he give them a formal statement. They didn't seem the least bit sensitive to the fact that his uncle had passed away just the day prior. He recalls getting annoyed and asking them, "Don't you guys have any respect for the dead?"

"People want to make a big fuckin' deal out of that!" he says. "All I meant was that I thought they were disrespecting my uncle and my family!"

He makes several other comments that I find equally startling, mainly because of what they imply about his rigid and excessively literal thinking, and because of what they reveal about his obsessive preoccupation with details, even ones that are largely irrelevant.

"Hell," he says, "we were at the Summerdale house when I made that statement about the cops not having any respect for the dead. And they want to make it sound like it was me disrespecting the dead! Jeff, the thing of it is, it was bullshit! *The bodies in the crawlspace at Summerdale weren't even under where we were standing at the time!* We were in the *back* of the house. The bodies were under the floor in the *front!*"

Just like yesterday, he's showing signs of becoming agitated as the two o'clock witching hour approaches. He knows that's when a guard will appear and tell us we need to break for the day. In the morning, I'll begin the drive back to Columbus. Gacy starts flipping rapidly through the pages of his photo album, in search of a few remaining things he wants to show me.

One is a picture of a street sign from the neighborhood in Chicago where he grew up. It reads "Menard." "Now there's something ironic," he says. "You wanna talk about *ironic*! Can you *believe* that shit? And here I am, at Menard Correctional Center. Weird!"

He shows me a picture of a teenage girl who he identifies as his goddaughter. He explains that a motorcyclist hit and killed her last year. "The bastard came around the corner and just hit her," he says. Then he flips through a few more pages.

He displays a picture of Manson Family killer Charles "Tex" Watson, shown alongside Watson's wife Patrice and their infant child (conceived during a conjugal visit at the California prison where Watson was serving his sentence). Gacy explains that "Charles" and Patrice are both deeply religious. They've written him letters, hoping to convert him to their brand of evangelical Christianity.

He also shows me a picture of two investigators — "Lindy and some guy" — who he says were part of the defense team at his trial. The picture captures them in a room where there's a clown lamp that Gacy says they salvaged from his house on Summerdale. On the wall behind them is one of Gacy's clown paintings, as well as a framed page from the Chicago Tribune, with the headline "Gacy Guilty!" Gacy chuckles softly as he reads the inscription that one of the investigators wrote on the photograph: "To our most notorious client."

He then flips to pages that display letters he received from Oprah Winfrey and Truman Capote. The letter from Winfrey, dated September 23, 1985, consists of two pages and is written in longhand. It begins, "Dear Mr. Gacy."

In the body of the letter, Winfrey explains who she is — the host of "the most popular talk show in all of Chicago" — and tells him of her interest in being afforded access to his "thoughts and feelings" in the aftermath of his trial and conviction. She urges him to please call her collect. She understands, she says, that he can't possibly accept the offer of every single media representative who wants to talk to him — but she hopes he'll "allow" her the opportunity to interview him. With a dismissive shrug, Gacy says he has no intention of talking to her.

The letter from Truman Capote is shorter and more to the point. Capote asks if Gacy will consider authorizing him to write his life story.

Gacy is obviously pleased for the opportunity to show me these letters, one from a writer who was already famous (Capote), the other from an up-and-coming media star in his hometown of Chicago (Winfrey). I sense that what he appreciates most about the letters is their tone of respect-bordering-on-deference. Winfrey's tone is downright fawning.

A guard shouts from down the hall that we need to wrap up our visit in five minutes. We're only about three-quarters of the way through the album of photographs. Gacy is annoyed. He gets up from the table, shuffles over to the doorway, and yells down the hall, "It's only ten minutes to two! We have at least ten minutes left!" The guard says fine, just be sure to wrap things up by 2:00.

Gacy sits back down at the table and takes aim at the prison staff.

"As soon as shift change rolls around, the guards have gotta start playing their fuckin' power games," he says. "I'm tellin' ya, these fuckin' hicks are stupid as shit!"

He takes out a newspaper clipping from between the pages of his photo album. It's a story about the recent arrests of three guards from the prison, one for sexual assault, the second for drug dealing, and the third for slashing tires on cars parked outside a Christmas party where the attendees were prison employees.

"That's the kind of fuckin' morons you have working in this place!" he says.

Finally, our time is up. The guard appears in the doorway, waiting to escort me out. We get up from our seats as I prepare to leave. Gacy extends his handcuffed hands in my direction, a familiar gesture by now. I shake his right hand and tell him I've enjoyed our two days of visiting.

"I really hope you'll come back," he says. "I find you an interesting person to talk to. Time flies when you're talking to someone who has something to say, and that's how I see you. By the way, you look younger than I thought you'd look."

"Well, I guess I'll take that as a compliment," I say. "It's been good seeing you, John. I'll send you a letter when I get back to Columbus."

"Okay. Good seeing you, too. Tell Betsy I said hi."

• • •

Fast forward to September 1987. I'm back at Menard, gearing up for another two-day visit with Gacy. We've been corresponding for a year and a half now.

Most things at the prison are as I remember them from last December. The sign-in procedure is the same; I pass through all the same security checkpoints; I encounter the same bank of vending machines as I make my way to the condemned unit; and the guard who escorts me directs me to the same room where Gacy and I met nine months ago.

One thing is not the same. This time, the guard who accompanies me doesn't pause to tell me that if anything goes awry while I'm with Gacy, I shouldn't expect the prison staff to bail me out. It's just as well. I vividly recall last year's warning and, besides, I don't really need reminding that if Gacy decides to kill me, he probably can and will.

When I enter the visiting room, Gacy is there already, awaiting my arrival. He stands up, shakes my hand, and greets me like an old friend.

"Hey, buddy! Good seein' ya! How was the drive?"

I tell him I had a good trip, then add that this time I've elected to stay at a Holiday Inn in Carbondale, some 30 miles east of the prison.

"Probably not a bad idea," he says. "I know you weren't wild about that place you stayed at when you were here in December. Only thing is, when you come here for your shorter visit tomorrow, you're gonna have to retrace your steps all the way back to Carbondale when you head east for Columbus."

In December, I stayed three nights at the motel in Menard. He knows that this time, my plan is to head home immediately after our second day's visit.

"Yeah, I thought about that, but it's not like Carbondale's all that far from here. It'll be a long haul back to Columbus, but that's okay."

Gacy looks different than he looked nine months ago. Gone is the beard, and his hair's longer. It's slicked back now, and I can smell whatever product he uses to hold it in place. Without the beard to partially cover his chin and cheeks, his face has a more rounded look than it did before. His overall appearance is softer somehow, a little less severe. He looks like your pudgy uncle. His skin is even more pallid than I remember it.

As I take my seat opposite him at the table, I'm conducting a mental inventory of the subjects I hope we'll be able to touch on today. I remember Gacy saying that if I returned for a second visit, he might be willing to share some additional details about the five murders he admits to knowing something about.

My plan is to broach that subject once we've had time to settle in and get comfortable. That is, as comfortable as the setting and situation will allow.

After some preliminary small talk about my drive from Columbus, my graduate studies at Ohio State, the trip my wife and I took to England and Ireland over the summer, the upcoming slate of professional football games, and the NFL betting pool Gacy is in charge of overseeing on death row, I decide to find out if he meant what he said in December.

"Hey John, remember when I was here last year, you said that if I came back, you might be willing to tell me a little more about five of the victims in your case?"

"Yeah, I remember saying that. I gotta be careful, though. My attorneys are always on my back, telling me not to talk about that shit because it's part of our appeal."

"I get that. And I promise you I won't push it. You mentioned the first one, a kid you said you brought back to your house from the Greyhound bus station. And then you mentioned John Butkovich, Gregory Godzik, John Szyc, and the last one, Rob Piest. What about the first one, the one from the bus station?"

"Well, that kid and I partied a little at the house, had sex, and I let him stay the night in my spare bedroom. I woke up in the morning, I was still in my bed, and I saw him coming at me with a knife in his hand. I guess it was a knife from the kitchen. Anyway, I tried to defend myself, and he ended up getting stabbed. That's about all I can say. The thing of it is, I was acting in self-defense."

"Did he end up in your crawlspace?"

"Well, that's where they found him, yeah. But that's really all I can say about that."

"What about John Butkovich?"

"Butkovich worked for me. My former wife used to call him Little John. I was Big John. Anyway, his dad kicked him out of his apartment after a beer party, and he came to my house with three of his Indian friends. Later that same night, he got hit over the head with a cue stick at a bar. His Indian friends could have testified to that, but they never even got called as witnesses at my trial!"

"But wasn't Butkovich's body found buried on your property, like, under the floor of your garage or something? How did that happen?"

"I can't get into that."

"How about Gregory Godzik?"

"Godzik had only been working for me a couple weeks when he went missing. He stopped showing up for some of his shifts. I talked to his mother and asked her what the hell was goin' on. She said her son was missing, and she told me how much he loved working for me. She begged me to give him another chance. Wanted me to help get him off drugs and shit."

"But wasn't *his* body found in your crawlspace, too?"

"I told ya, I can't get into all that."

"How about Szyc?"

"Same thing, I really can't go into it. Hardly knew the kid. We drank some beer, I know that much. There was an argument about his car. That's about all I remember. I think Michael Rossi might have been there that night, too."

I'm especially keen to draw him out on the disappearance and murder of 15-year-old Rob Piest, his final victim. I know they crossed paths at Nisson's Pharmacy in Des Plaines, where Piest was employed. Gacy had stopped at the pharmacy to discuss a remodeling job with the owner. Supposedly, Gacy told Piest he could offer him a job making more money than he was making at the pharmacy. Piest told his mother, who was in the parking lot waiting to take him home, that he'd be right back, he was going to talk to someone about the possibility of a new, better paying job. No one saw or heard from him ever again.

"What about Rob Piest?" I say.

"I'll tell you this much, Jeff, the search warrants the police used to search my property were bullshit. Way too general. Any lawyer would tell you that. Hell, you say you're lookin' for tan pants, a medium size T-shirt, and a blue parka, no size specified. Then you go searching a house where only males live. Is it surprising you'd find that kind of shit?"

"Well, how 'bout we forget about whatever might have been wrong with the search warrants. I assume your attorneys are working on that part. Didn't the police conclude that the articles of clothing they found in your house *did* belong to Piest?"

"Well, now you're gettin' into theory. They *could have* been his. They *looked like* his. That's what his parents were saying."

I'm eager to ask him about a photo receipt that the police found in a trash container in his house. According to another pharmacy employee who'd borrowed Piest's windbreaker from him on the same day as his disappearance, she placed the receipt in the pocket of the jacket and neglected to remove it when she returned the jacket to Piest.

"Wasn't a photo receipt from the pharmacy found at Summerdale?" I ask. "And wasn't that considered a key piece of evidence connecting Piest to your house?"

"Yeah, they found a photo receipt there, big fuckin' deal. *Whose* receipt? Remember, I was at Nisson's, it could have been *my* receipt. Hey, I'll tell ya somethin', Jeff. I think it *was* Piest's, or at least I think it came from his jacket. I'm not sayin' he wasn't at the house. Rossi had been with me at that job site the first time I went there, maybe other times, too. Maybe he knew Piest. Hell, *I* don't know. But everybody concludes that since Piest was at Nisson's and I was at Nisson's, I must have taken Piest to Summerdale and killed him. That's just bullshit, it's all the prosecution's theory."

I decide to use this opportunity to ask him something else I've been wanting to ask. I read somewhere that during closing arguments at his trial, one of the prosecutors made a dramatic show of tossing pictures of 26 of his victims through the door leading to a model of his crawlspace that had been constructed for use at the trial.

"What did you think of it when the prosecutor threw all those pictures of the victims into the model of the crawlspace during his closing argument? Sounds like it was some major courtroom theater."

"Oh shit, Jeff, you shoulda *seen* it! Drama, that's all it was. Hell, the prosecutors wanted to bring the fuckin' heads of those kids into the courtroom! In jars of fuckin' formaldehyde! Well I'll tell ya what, we put a stop to *that* shit."

It's lunch time. The lunches the guard delivers to the visiting room look a lot like the lunches Gacy and I were served the last time I was here. A couple slices of bread, two slices of bologna this time, a medium-size pile of canned green beans, a small container of pudding, a carton of juice, and two chocolate chip cookies. I eat a little of my pudding and both my cookies, nothing else.

Gacy devours his bologna sandwich, even as he's complaining, "They serve us the same shit pretty much every day. How'd you like to live here and have to eat like this all the time?"

We spend the better part of an hour talking about Gacy's history of involvement in the food service industry. He's proud of it. He explains that in 1966, his first wife's father gave him three Kentucky Fried Chicken franchises to run in Waterloo, Iowa. A number of the employees at his restaurants called him "The Colonel." He claims to have trimmed costs and boosted productivity at all three locations.

In 1968, because a "young punk kid" told "a bunch of lies" on him, he ended up being sentenced to ten years in prison for sodomy. Before long, he was running the kitchen at the Iowa State Reformatory at Anamosa, where he was sent to serve his time. When he was awarded early release after only about 14 months, he returned to his hometown of Chicago, moved in with his mother, and secured a job at a restaurant called Bruno's.

"While I was at Bruno's, I used to prepare meals for guys on the Chicago Blackhawks!" he boasts. "All kinds of cops and politicians came in there, too. I knew all of 'em! And they all knew what I could do in the kitchen. And I'm sure you've heard about the backyard parties I used to host at Summerdale. Barbecue, you name it. Hundreds of people would show up, and I'll tell ya what, nobody left hungry!"

His history of employment as a "chef" affords him a lofty peak—his view—from which to comment on the fare we've been served for lunch.

"I'm sure you can imagine what it's like for me to have to eat this shit," he says. "Hell, on the outside I was a gourmet fuckin' *chef*!"

He reaches for the vending machine bounty that I purchased for him on my way into the prison this morning.

"I'll eat this stuff any day of the fuckin' week!" he says. "It's a helluva lot better than the shit they feed us, I'll tell ya that much!"

After he downs two candy bars, he grabs a container of microwave popcorn, shuffles out into the hall, and calls loudly to get the attention of the guards, who I gather are nowhere to be seen. After a minute or so, I hear Gacy addressing one of them.

"Hey, Donny," he says. "Do me a favor, will ya? Can we get this popcorn popped in the microwave? Thanks, buddy. I'll wait here for ya to bring it back."

After about five minutes, Gacy returns to the room where I'm waiting, the container of popped popcorn in his right hand.

"You'd think I was asking the fucker for his left nut," he says. "If there's anything those fuckers hate, it's having their poker game interrupted."

He seems to regard the microwave popcorn as an enormous treat. He rips open the bag. For the next half hour or so, we both pick at the contents, one or two kernels at a time. It's like we're savoring some sort of rare delicacy.

I decide to shift our focus to a new topic of conversation. "I've been wanting to ask you about your business," I say. "Before your arrest, what were your goals? Did you have dreams for the future? Were you planning to expand? Just keep doing what you were doing? Or what?"

"Well, the first thing is, I wanted to get more diversified," he says. "Like, I wanted to renovate condemned properties, that sort of thing. Hell, you'd *have* to make money doin' that shit! The truth is, I had more work than I knew what to do with."

"Why do you think you were as successful as you were? Everyone says you were a hard worker, and you've talked about positive mental attitude. But what else helped you succeed?"

"Well, my word was my bond, I've told you that. My customers all knew they could trust me. Plus, you gotta realize, Jeff, I was always trying to come in under deadlines, and I tried to keep my prices competitive. I was a perfectionist, too. I wanted everything done the right way—and if it wasn't done the way I wanted it done, I'd order it done over. Anyone who hired me knew they were getting someone who was conscientious, maybe to a fault. But like I said, I made sure everything got done just the way I wanted it done."

We only have about a half hour left. During the time remaining, we banter back and forth about a wide range of different subjects.

Gacy brings up the Iran-Contra arms scandal, which has been dominating the news lately. Not surprisingly, he has strong feelings on the subject. "Reagan's insulting the intelligence of the American people," he says. "Everybody knows he knew what was goin' on."

For some reason, I guess because we'd been talking about the current Republican president, he shifts the focus and begins talking about former President Nixon. "I'm a liberal Democrat," he says, "always have been. But ya know what? I ended up admiring Nixon. Not at the beginning but at the end. Guy says, 'Okay, ya got me. Now I'm gettin' the hell outta Dodge.'"

The subject of gun violence comes up, prompted by something Gacy saw on television the other night. He says he's in favor of gun control legislation. He recalls how things played out when his former mother-in-law moved into the Summerdale house in the early '70s, joining him and his former wife there, along with his former wife's two children.

"Listen, Jeff, I don't even believe in guns! Never have! And I don't believe in killing animals either. When my former mother-in-law moved in with Carole and me and the two kids, I found out she brought a fuckin' gun with her! I said no fuckin' way! No guns around the kids!"

Our day ends with a brief exchange about the contrast between his pre-arrest reputation as a genial, successful businessman and the police portrayal of him as a calculating, deadly predator. "Well, there's the monster thing again," he says, shaking his head back and forth. "It's just the media myth. But

I'll tell ya somethin', Jeff. Hell, with all the Valium I was taking I'm not even saying I couldn't have killed somebody! But why would it have happened? See, that's what I'm sayin'. It woulda been so out of character! Where's the fuckin' motive?"

"Gotta hit the road, John. I'll be back in the morning."

"Okay, I'll see ya then. Be sure to get here early. I know you've got the long drive home. We don't wanna miss out on any of our time."

•••

The following morning, again Gacy is there in the visiting room, waiting for me when I arrive. We both know that today's visit can't exceed three hours; I'm hoping to get home before nightfall. We shake hands and exchange pleasantries as I join him in the visiting room. Gacy is visibly relieved to see the pile of junk food that I'm cradling in my arms. I dump it onto the table.

For reasons unknown to me, he gets up and starts dragging his chair around the end of the table. I watch him but don't say anything.

"I'm glad you got here early," he says, still in motion and appearing somewhat distracted. "How 'bout you sit on the other side of the table today?"

"Sure," I say. "I don't care which side I sit on."

He doesn't explain why he's doing what he's doing, and I don't ask. Even though he's decided he wants to reverse our positions at the table, he's keen on keeping the same chair for himself. He moves it to where my chair was; then he moves my chair over to where his was.

"What time did you turn in last night?" I say when he's through rearranging things.

"Well," he says. "Let me look in the logbook." You'd think he was about to research something that happened five years ago. "By looking in here, I'll be able to tell you *exactly* what time."

He opens the logbook, runs his index finger along a line of cramped handwriting, and says, "One-thirty, it's right here.

How 'bout you?"

"Well, let's just say I beat you to bed by about four hours." Suddenly, I'm struck by the weird intimacy—and awkwardness—of this exchange. I'm talking to John Wayne Gacy about my bedtime, like it's a perfectly natural thing to do. It's a thought I choose not to dwell on.

The truth is, little of much consequence happens during these last hours of my final trip to Menard. That's how I planned it. I've decided to keep things light. I want to avoid saying anything that might make Gacy irritable or defensive.

With all the vending machine food spread out on the table in front of him, Gacy looks content, like someone who thinks his day has gotten off to just the right kind of start. I want to maintain the mood. The atmosphere this morning feels easy and relaxed. We've become accustomed to each other's company. We're not friends, not by a long shot—but still, little effort is required as we commence the kind of improvisational, meandering conversation that two people reasonably familiar with one another might have over a cup of coffee, or a beer. We flit lightly among a variety of subjects, none of them weighty.

For example, we spend time shooting the breeze about several players from our favorite NFL teams (for me the Buffalo Bills, for him the Chicago Bears); we trade observations about presidential politics, in particular the chances that a Democrat might prevail in next year's election; I gripe a little about how difficult it is for psychologists-in-training to land good pre-doctoral internships; Gacy offers some remarks about his "technique" as a painter; and, at around eleven o'clock, we start making preparations for my departure.

There's little doubt that Gacy has enjoyed having me as a visitor. Why wouldn't he? When he doesn't have a visitor, he's locked inside his small, windowless cell for 22 hours a day. Plus, he doesn't have access to the junk food that visitors can bring him from the vending machines.

When our three hours are almost up, we push our chairs back from the table, approach one another just inside the door that leads to the hallway, and shake hands one last time. I notice that Gacy grips my hand more tightly than he ever has previously. We both say how much we've enjoyed our time together. I'm certain as I turn to leave that I'll never come back to this place, but I don't tell Gacy that. Instead, I tell him that since I'm now familiar with the prison and its routines, things will be even smoother if I come back a third time.

"I hope you will come again," he says. "I really like talking to you, and time flies when the company's good."

"Okay. Bye John," I say. "I'll write when I can."

"Drive safe," he says.

As it turns out, Gacy writes me a letter before I'm able to find the time to write one to him:

> It's not even been 24 hours since you left and I'm still thinking about some of the things we never got to. But it sure was great to see you again and I thank you for coming. I enjoyed the time we had and I hope you came away even more enlightened than before. I don't know if you noticed but I hated to see you leave. I'm glad you're not as serious as you come across in your letters ... You were looking good, and I could see you were more relaxed than on the first visit ... Thanks again for coming as I enjoyed it a lot. Some things I couldn't explain to you but you'll understand them more clearly when my appeal comes down. In any case, you're far ahead of anyone else who seems to want to talk about me with no knowledge at all.

● ● ●

Gacy and I continued exchanging letters for 18 more months, up until February of 1989. That's when I finally decided I'd had enough. We'd been corresponding for three years, trading letters, on average, about once every two or three weeks. The correspondence ended not with a bang but a whimper.

I wrote Gacy one final time on February 7, 1989. In my letter, I mentioned several books I'd been reading, all on the subject of serial murder. I invited him to comment on Ted Bundy's execution, which had taken place just two weeks prior.

In a letter I'd received from Gacy not long before, he'd

signed off, "Later, gator" — so at the end of my letter, I wrote teasingly, "I'll look forward to hearing from you. Later, gator? Ok. Jeff."

Gacy wrote his final letter to me later that same month. He was happy to have acquired a new typewriter.

On the subject of Bundy's execution, he wrote, "Hell, I don't know [Bundy] so why make a judgment call on him? I have seen what [people in the media] have done to me and I won't lower myself to their level. I only know that all that was printed on him is not fact, it's much easier to print sensationalism. His statement about porno being the root of his behavior was taken out of context ... so says an FBI agent who was present.

"I think his execution was a sad day for this country. What it shows is what the real American people are like ... sick bloodthirsty humans bent on revenge. The man was paying for his crimes, why turn it into a circus? All it did was disgrace the American people to the world. What's your opinion? And by the way it has no effect on my case as I am not a Ted Bundy, nor from Florida."

He ended his letter this way: "I hope you're well and things are going good for you. How much longer are you staying out east [in Connecticut]? And you never say much about your place or the area there. Get with it. Later, bird? John."

I didn't write him back, and I never heard from him again.

• • •

Finally, Gacy ran out of appeals. He died by lethal injection on May 10, 1994. For his last meal, he ordered a bucket of KFC, a dozen fried shrimp, french fries, fresh strawberries, and a Diet Coke. He prayed with a Catholic priest. Then he was escorted to the execution chamber.

By all accounts, it was a tough execution. The process dragged on for close to 20 minutes. A delay occurred when the chemicals being used to kill him got clogged up in Gacy's IV line, necessitating the line's replacement.

There was no eleventh-hour confession. Nor were there any expressions of regret or remorse.

Shortly before his death, Gacy said to a guard who'd been assigned to accompany him to the death chamber, "Kiss my ass."

Those may or may not have been his final words. Accounts differ.

•••

Almost 30 years after his execution, Gacy remains one of America's most prolific and notorious serial killers. In his 2012 update to *Killer Clown*, the book he co-authored shortly after Gacy's conviction, prosecutor Terry Sullivan noted the case's enduring fascination and even suggested that it brought about significant changes in the way parents raised their children, not just in the United States but all around the world. Gacy has been the subject of countless books, articles, movies, and documentaries. I check out as many of them as I can, always hoping for a new perspective on Gacy from someone who knew him well.

Joseph Kozenczak, who was the Chief of Police in Des Plaines, Illinois at the time of the investigation that led to Gacy's arrest, co-wrote a book that came out when Gacy had only two years left to live. Kozenczak was present all throughout the trial, and he sat through days of expert testimony about Gacy's psychological makeup. For him, the Gacy enigma endured. He wrote, "[Gacy] was as much of a mystery to me at the end of the trial as he had been at the beginning."

Barry Boscelli, a childhood friend of Gacy's, published a memoir called *Johnny and Me*. He hoped to help his readers glimpse "the other side of the coin" when it came to Gacy's life and character. What he wanted most of all was to portray his old buddy just as he knew him back in the day. He recalled "the many wonderful ideas" Gacy used to come up with when they were kids, as well as "the normal childhood games" the two of them played together. According to Boscelli, he and Johnny were children "no different from anyone else," both aspiring to "whatever God wanted" in their lives. Before Gacy morphed into "the most terrible serial killer in history," he was, wrote Boscelli, an "extraordinary person."

In his letters to me, Gacy often wrote of a man named Harlan Mendenhall. He described Mendenhall, a retired journalism professor who'd once been named Teacher of the Year at Southern Illinois University, as someone he'd come to regard as a close friend and confidant. In December 1986, the same month as my first trip to Menard, Gacy wrote to Mendenhall's daughter and said that he'd come to view Harlan as part of his "adopted family."

Gacy led me to believe that Mendenhall perceived him in much the same way he perceived himself—as a grossly misunderstood and persecuted man: "the 34th victim" in his case. He assured me that at some point, Harlan was going to write the authorized, definitive version of his life story. He added that when that version finally appeared, it would become clear to everyone that the previous books about him had been little more than just "fantasy."

In 1996, two years after Gacy's death, Mendenhall did, in fact, publish a book. He called it *Fall of the House of Gacy.* For his subtitle he chose, *The Only Authorized Biography of John Wayne Gacy, Serial Killer.* Mendenhall claimed to have based his account on 550 hours of conversations with Gacy, spanning a period of years. The book's final sentence? "[Gacy] publicly claimed his innocence until the end." Mendenhall knew better.

I had to wait until 2011 for a book I'd been hoping to see for years, a memoir by Sam Amirante, Gacy's lead trial attorney. By the time of the memoir's publication, Amirante was a retired Cook County Circuit Court Judge. A hint of the story he intended to tell appeared in the book's subtitle: *Defending a Monster.* Amirante's own words made it clear that he viewed his infamous client with a mixture of awe and revulsion.

He recalled how "absolutely fucking surreal" it was to hear Gacy confess to "at least 30" murders on the night just prior to his arrest. Referring to himself and a second attorney who was present to hear the confession, he wrote, "We were listening to a killer, a true killer."

He called Gacy "a psychiatrist's wet dream" and emphasized how "crazy" and "fucked in the head" Gacy was. As he was casting about for an explanation that he thought could perhaps help to account for Gacy's behavior, he entertained the possibility that Gacy was someone who came into the world irreparably damaged, a "profoundly broken" man whose brain was "mis-wired at the factory, so to speak." He described Gacy as "frumpy," "fleshy," "sweaty," and a "sickly blubbery cream puff of a man." He called him "a death merchant."

Elsewhere in this chapter, I referenced a portrait of Gacy that journalist Alec Wilkinson published in the *New Yorker* less than a month before Gacy's execution. In early 1994, Wilkinson visited Menard six times. The Gacy he portrayed in his lengthy article is unmistakably the same Gacy I came to know.

The opening sentence of his article? "John Wayne Gacy is obsessively fond of defending his innocence, which is imaginary." Indeed.

Wilkinson experienced the same feelings of monotony and boredom that I sometimes experienced when I was listening to Gacy prattle on about his alleged persecution. "Occasionally," wrote Wilkinson, "[Gacy's] company was so dreary that I would take off my watch, so I couldn't see how slowly the time was passing."

Just as I did, Wilkinson struggled with the conundrum presented by a man who didn't seem obviously deranged, yet who persisted in saying the most preposterous things: "I never had the feeling that [Gacy] heard voices or saw things I didn't, but he was delusional in that he believed himself to be someone else: an innocent person."

As I read Wilkinson's account, I was transported back to that moment when Gacy told me of times, alone in his cell, when he'd shuffle through pictures of his supposed victims and realize that to him, all those boys and young men were no more real than the Seven Dwarfs depicted in the painting he'd propped up against the wall in the visiting room that day.

Gacy told Wilkinson, "For a while, I would tape newspaper pictures of the victims to the wall beside my bed and go to sleep seeing if I would dream about them, or if I could recall if I ever met them. I would look at them and say, 'Who the hell are you, and how did you die?' I don't have fantasy-type dreams, and I don't ever have nightmares."

During another of their visits, Gacy said something that came close to blowing Wilkinson's mind. Here's how Wilkinson recalled it: "[Gacy] had been talking about how he couldn't have murdered anyone, because he was nonviolent, a coward, someone who would walk away from a fight. Furthermore, he said, he had all the sex he needed, so there was no reason for him to have sex with the boys he was said to have killed. 'Why would I want to kill these boys, anyway?' he asked. 'I'm not their father.'"

Wilkinson thought, *their father?*

The next day, when Wilkinson reminded Gacy what he'd said and asked for some clarification, Gacy insisted he'd never spoken the words Wilkinson heard him speak.

Wilkinson found him to be just as prickly and contrary as I did. "I didn't mean to argue with Gacy," he wrote, "but I didn't seem able not to."

Toward the end of his article, Wilkinson speculated about what it must have felt like to be John Wayne Gacy. "Gacy is an outcast," he wrote, "a lonely and isolated man who has had experiences unlike those of a civilized person. He has failed again and again to restrain homicidal impulses that might occur to other people but that they manage to stifle or defuse. He has caused profound suffering and sadness. He lives with the knowledge of having done something horrible by refusing to live with it. He is like someone who inhabits a parallel world, which is unreality."

● ● ●

Something I know now but didn't know back in 1986 and 1987: I was in real danger during the entire time I spent with Gacy. I didn't see it. That's how naive I was, and how ignorant. Sure, I felt somewhat uneasy when I first realized I was going to be left alone with him, in an untended visiting room. And of course I experienced feelings of discomfort on the occasions when Gacy invited me to sit right alongside him. But I never really believed I was in danger. About that and plenty of other things, I was as wrong as wrong could be.

A book called *The Last Victim*, published five years after Gacy's execution, forced me to revisit my encounters with Gacy, and to consider them in a new light. My working assumption is that the book's author, a young man named Jason Moss, told the truth about his own experiences with Gacy.

Moss's mentor and former professor, well-known and widely-respected psychologist and researcher Jeffrey Kottler, wrote the Prologue to Moss's book and contributed his imprimatur. More than 15 years after Gacy's death, in 2010, Kottler published a book of his own, called *The Lust for Blood*, in which he wrote at some length about the history of his relationship with Moss—and never once questioned the accuracy of what Moss wrote about his interactions with Gacy.

It's not like I completely ignored the words of the guard who warned me that I'd be on my own if something went awry while I was alone with Gacy, in the death row visiting room. But I worked hard to compartmentalize his warning. I think I made a conscious decision not to reflect too deeply on its implications. I wanted to be able to relax while Gacy and I were together. Foolishly, I considered relaxation a goal worth striving for. It was not.

I know now that Gacy could have assaulted or even killed me in that room. I'm fortunate that he didn't.

Moss was a teenager and a freshman in college when he decided to initiate a correspondence with Gacy in November of 1993, about four and a half years *after* Gacy and I stopped exchanging letters. When Moss began writing to Gacy, he viewed himself as a budding scholar, with murder his specialty subject. He had a thesis to write for an honors seminar he was taking at the University of Nevada at Las Vegas. He thought that if he postured as Gacy's "ideal victim," Gacy might take the bait, with the result that Moss would be able to use their correspondence, along with letters he hoped to coax from a number of other incarcerated murderers, as the basis for an illuminating inquiry into the psychology of the serial killer.

Gacy took the bait—hook, line, and sinker. Over a period of several months, Moss managed to convince Gacy that he was the sexually confused product of a dysfunctional family. He and Gacy exchanged pornographic fantasies. Responding to Gacy's explicit urging, Moss even assured Gacy that he was willing to initiate a sexual relationship with his younger brother.

After they'd been corresponding for several months, Gacy invited Moss to visit him at Menard. Their plan was that the visit would take place over a three-day period. This was in early 1994. As it turned out, a terrified and traumatized Moss beat a retreat after two days.

There is one crucial distinction between Moss's experiences with Gacy and my own. During the period when I was corresponding and visiting with him, Gacy was still clinging to the hope, no matter how slight, that his conviction, or at least his death sentence, would be overturned on appeal. He brought the subject up regularly. He knew he needed to avoid engaging in any behavior that had the potential to undermine his attorneys' attempts to secure relief for him through the courts.

By the time Moss entered the picture, and certainly by the time he visited Gacy at Menard, it would have been clear to Gacy that the end was near.

Like I was when I visited Menard for the first time, Moss was startled to discover that he was going to be left all alone with Gacy, and that no guards would be present in the death row visiting area where their meetings were going to take place. Prior to Moss's visit, Gacy had offered him assurances that there would be tight security at the prison. There wasn't.

When Moss first encountered Gacy, he thought Gacy "seemed ordinary in every sense." He looked like "a harmless man who wouldn't hurt a fly." However, when they shook hands, Moss felt Gacy's index finger gently caressing the inside of his wrist.

At that point, it crossed his mind for the first time that Gacy might have bribed the guards to give the two of them some private time together.

He'd been with Gacy for only about an hour or so when Gacy started to become verbally abusive. He attacked Moss for being weak and helpless. Then, while fingering his own crotch, he told Moss, "Just remember who I am." For the next two hours, he subjected Moss to an angry, withering interrogation.

After Moss had managed to coax Gacy into disclosing that he "dumped" his first victim, "the Greyhound bus station boy," into the crawlspace beneath his house and subsequently "buried" him there, Moss tried to change the subject by asking Gacy when he thought they could expect the arrival of one of the prison guards, someone who could take the pictures that Moss had paid for that morning.

Gacy's response? "The guards are on the other side of the bars. Do you know how long it would take them to get in here if you screamed? Probably two minutes. I could kill you right now if I wanted. You know that, don't you? I could take this pen and stick it right there in your neck."

According to Moss, Gacy was standing behind him when he said these things. Moss, who was muscular and trained in the martial arts, moved quickly and assumed a defensive stance. Gacy continued his rant. "You'd bleed to death all over the floor by the time you got any help," he said. Then he reached into his sock and pulled out a small packet of baby oil. He pointed to a chair across the hall and told Moss, "That's where I'd do you. They wouldn't find your body until all your blood ran on the floor."

It got worse.

Hoping to create a diversion, Moss grabbed hold of Gacy's logbook and began to leaf through it. Somehow, Gacy was able to maneuver behind him again. This time, he placed his hands around Moss's neck and made as if to kiss him.

When Moss pulled away, Gacy yanked his penis out of his pants and started to masturbate. He said to Moss, "Look at my cock!" Then he demanded that Moss "get on it!"

When Moss refused, Gacy became livid. "Do you know how many little shits died for this cock!" he said. "Do you want to die for this cock? I should have you bend over. Then I can tear the shit out of your tight little ass. You'd like that, wouldn't you? You want me to beat you, don't you?"

Gacy continued to stroke his penis and bark out commands.

"Open your mouth so I can piss down your throat," he said. "You should like piss. You're just a pile of shit yourself… Come on, Jason, get over the chair there. You'll be a little bloody, but that's nothing. A real man can take pain, especially from another man."

Moss started to cry. Gacy was disgusted by his tears and demanded that he leave the visiting room. Then, within a matter of moments, he reversed course and "turned the charm back on."

As Moss was getting ready to leave the prison that first day, Gacy handed him a pair of bikini briefs—he'd had them stashed in his own underwear—and instructed him to wear them for the next day's visit. He also gave Moss a silver bracelet that he retrieved from one of his socks.

That was day one of Moss's visit.

Moss considered not returning to the prison, but he worried that he'd feel like a failure if he aborted his plans after spending only one day with Gacy.

His second day was at least as harrowing as the first one. When he arrived at the prison, he wasn't wearing the briefs that Gacy had given him. However, he led Gacy to believe he was. He had the silver bracelet on his wrist.

At an early juncture during the visit, Gacy produced the autopsy reports for each of his victims. As he and Moss were perusing them, Gacy said of the victims, "They all deserved to die. If you led the kinds of lives they did, something was bound to happen."

As he had the day before, Gacy pulled his penis out from his pants and started to masturbate. He resumed the prior day's torrent of verbal abuse.

"You're going to choke on this cock … until you beg me to stop," he told Moss.

When Moss tried to change the subject, Gacy refused to follow his lead. According to Moss, Gacy said, "Last night I lay in my bed thinking about what I'm going to do to you today. I thought long and hard about how I'm going to rape you. It doesn't matter if you want it or not, you're going to get it. After I'm done with you, you're going to lie on the bloody floor so I can piss all over your face."

He was continuing to masturbate as he said these things.

Just when Moss was beginning to think he'd have no choice except to fight Gacy, they heard a guard, accompanied by a civilian friend of Gacy's and another death row inmate, approaching the visiting room from down the hall. Fumbling quickly, Gacy put his penis back in his pants.

So ended day two of Moss's visit to Menard. He didn't return for the third day.

These events took place three months before Gacy's execution.

Five years later, Moss published *The Last Victim*. Three years after that, he completed his law degree at the University of Michigan. Then he opened a private practice, focusing on criminal defense. He also married his wife, a woman named Charlotte.

On the sixth day of the sixth month in the year 2006, he shot himself in the head.

•••

Thinking it would do me more harm than good, I put off opening a Facebook account for as long as I could. Finally, in the fall of 2020, I opened an account so that I could use it as a means of getting in touch with someone I'd been having trouble locating through other channels.

I quickly became aware of the many online groups I could join if I chose to. Most of the groups I joined were music-related. However, I also joined a few that I could tell functioned as on-line marketplaces for the advertisement and sale of "murderabilia," artifacts associated with infamous killers.

I did this for two reasons.

One, the amateur cultural anthropologist in me wanted to gain some familiarity with murderabilia culture, which I'd read about in other places. I wondered, *What kinds of people join such groups, and how do they manage their communications with each other?*

Two, I wanted to get a sense of how much money people were willing to pay for serial killer artifacts. I owned plenty of them. I wasn't looking to sell my three Gacy paintings. Nor was I looking to unload my extensive Gacy correspondence, or my letters from notorious criminals like Ted Bundy, Charles Manson, Susan Atkins, Squeaky Fromme, Thomas Lee Dillon, Diane Downs, and Arthur Shawcross. At the same time, I was curious about their market value. I thought that maybe I'd decide to sell them at some point down the road—and even if I didn't, my descendants almost certainly would.

About six months into my Facebook experiment, I decided to send out a feeler. Of the three Gacy paintings my wife and I owned, one was a gift from Gacy to my wife (even though they never met or exchanged letters); the other two I'd purchased from Gacy for $30 each.

I posted pictures of the paintings on one of the murderabilia sites and asked if anyone might be interested in purchasing them. The response was immediate. In fact, borderline ecstatic.

In a matter of hours, I had multiple offers. Had I decided to sell the three paintings, I could have turned a neat profit of about $7,000. *That day.*

Gacy wasn't wrong when he urged me to recognize his paintings as red-hot assets, sure to appreciate with the passage of time.

I was reminded of the moment at Menard when Gacy sneered at the hypocrisy of people who portrayed him as a monster yet thought nothing of purchasing his artwork, asking him for signed photographs, saving his cigar butts as souvenirs, and showing up in droves at the house on W. Summerdale Ave. to scavenge for bricks and pieces of sod when the house was being demolished the year after his arrest.

"You tell *me* who's crazy!" he'd demanded. I was stumped. After I put out my feeler, to get a sense of how much people were willing to pay for the Gacy paintings I owned, I noticed that another site participant was conducting some market research of her own.

Her product? Baggies of "authentic Gacy crawlspace dirt."

Buyers could acquire a baggy for just $200. For the really cost-conscious, there was another option. They could obtain one of the baggies for the bargain price of $160. "But only with PayPal."

7.
The Sniper

In late 1991, authorities in Ohio had reason to suspect something strange and alarming was happening in the southeastern part of their state. By the following spring, they knew they'd been right. There was a serial killer on the loose.

His preferred targets were hunters and fishermen. However, his first known victim was neither of those things. When Donald Welling, a jogger, was shot at point-blank range on April 1, 1989, along the side of the road in a rural section of Tuscarawas County, it was a tragic local story. No one knew what to make of it. There were no witnesses, the killer left no evidence at the scene, and there were no suspects.

A year and a half later, in November of 1990, a second shooting incident left the police and public feeling similarly baffled. It was another murder, this time in Belmont County, about 100 miles to the south. Jamie Paxton, a 21-year-old deer hunter, died as a result of three bullets fired at him from a distance of about 100 feet. Again, there were no witnesses, and the killer left no spent shell casings at the scene. Investigators had no reason to believe Paxton's killer had even approached his body.

Just 18 days after the Paxton killing, a 30-year-old hunter named Kevin Loring died in Muskingum County—south of Tuscarawas County and west of Belmont County—as a result of a single bullet that struck him between the eyes. Police estimated that the bullet had to have traveled a distance of about 75 feet. Again, no spent shell casings, nothing.

Then, a lull.

The police caught an enormous break the following November, in 1991. The editor of a Belmont County newspaper received a lengthy letter that began, "I am the murderer of Jamie Paxton."

Whoever chose to make that announcement had written in response to a series of letters that Paxton's mother had had published in the newspaper. Suspecting, correctly as it turned out, that her son's killer would be tracking local publicity about the case, she'd addressed him personally in her letters, reminding him that he had her son's blood on his hands and urging him to think about all the anguish he'd caused her and the members of her family.

Her most recent letter had appeared in October, just a month before the arrival of the killer's response. In the October letter, Jean Paxton had written, "It's been nearly a year since you killed my son. Has your life changed in the past 11 months? Our family hasn't lived since last November 10 [the date of Jamie's death]. We are surviving one day at a time."

As it turned out, the killer's letter provided police with a goldmine of useful information. For one thing, it included certain details that only Paxton's killer could have known, for example the color and orientation of Paxton's car on the morning of his death; the type of weapon that had been used (a .308 bolt action rifle); and the precise steps the killer had taken to avoid leaving ballistic evidence at the scene.

But there was much more. The killer identified himself as a stranger who'd never set eyes on Paxton before he shot him. He said there was no motive for the murder except "the murder itself." He admitted he'd murdered at least three people—which he thought meant that "technically," he "[met] the definition of a serial killer."

He described himself as "an average looking person with a family, job, and home." He gloated about his lack of remorse, insisted, in fact, that he "thought no more of shooting [Paxton] than shooting a bottle at the dump," this despite the fact that he claimed Paxton was the only one of his victims for whom he felt any "pity." He drew comparisons between himself and infamous serial killers like Ted Bundy, Jeffrey Dahmer, and Henry Lee Lucas. He said he'd returned to the scene of Paxton's murder and even visited the cemetery where he was buried.

The killer's letter included a couple of sentences that were of particular interest to the authorities. The killer wrote things that most people would never have thought to write: "So there you have the details [of Paxton's murder]. The where, with what, and why have all been revealed. The 'who' can never be discovered unless I choose to turn myself in. This would serve no purpose at this time."

The investigators were left wondering, *What kind of killer thinks in such literal terms? About the who, where, why, and how of his crime/s?* They'd have their answer soon enough.

Just in case anyone was wondering, the killer volunteered, toward the end of his letter, "I knew the difference between right and wrong ... and was sane." He said he had a drinking problem and claimed that when he was sober, he didn't think about committing murder. "Let's all hope that this will be the end of the killing but at this point I don't know," he wrote. "I mailed this letter only because I felt the Paxton family should know the details of what happened. I don't believe they should live the rest of their lives without knowing. This is the only correspondence you will ever receive from me." The letter was signed, "The murderer of Jamie Paxton."

The law enforcement officials who read the letter were quick to note its teasing, here-I-am, catch-me-if-you-can quality. It was the same quality police would detect in the taunting notes sent to them nearly a decade later by the Wichita-based serial killer who branded himself BTK (bind, torture, kill).

The authorities now believed there was little doubt they were on the trail of a serial killer. In part because they were hesitant to do anything that had the potential to compromise the integrity of their investigation, they chose to keep much of what they knew under wraps. Meanwhile, the killer was content to bide his time—but not for long.

Two more suspicious murders occurred the following spring. The victim in the first one was a fisherman named Claude Hawkins. In mid-March, he was shot on federal land in Coshocton County, which was located northwest of Belmont County, where the Paxton killing had taken place. At that point, the FBI joined the investigation. Law enforcement officials from Tuscarawas, Muskingham, Belmont, and Cochocton counties compared notes and recognized the striking similarities among the unsolved homicides in their respective jurisdictions.

In early April, a gunman killed fisherman Gary Bradley in Noble County, which was located southeast of Coshocton County and adjacent to Belmont County. The authorities were especially alarmed because these two most recent homicides occurred less than a month apart.

In May, a newly-convened task force came together so that everyone could compare notes and exchange information. The FBI participated, along with representatives of the five counties where the murders had been committed. At this point, the serial murder investigation began to pick up steam. Even so, members of the public remained in the dark. They still had no idea that the authorities were increasingly confident that a single person was responsible for the deaths of Donald Welling, Jamie Paxton, Kevin Loring, Claude Hawkins, and Gary Bradley

In August, that changed. By then, the police were convinced that the killer they were looking for had meant it when he said he had no intention of sending out any more letters. Investigators chose to issue a press release, informing the public that they suspected a serial killer had been targeting outdoorsmen in a number of counties in the eastern part of Ohio.

Predictably, their announcement set in motion a feeding frenzy among members of the media. That feeding frenzy continued up through the time of Thomas Lee Dillon's arrest outside a Tuscarawas County convenience store on November 27, 1992. It didn't let up until after July 11, 1993, which is when Dillon pled guilty to five counts of aggravated murder and was sentenced to five consecutive life terms.

It warrants mention that when the police arrested Dillon, they didn't charge him with any of the murders. Instead, they charged him with violating probationary terms he had agreed to in August of 1992, when he'd pled guilty to a federal charge of possessing an illegal silencer. As part of the plea, he'd agreed not to possess any firearms.

The authorities knew for a fact that he'd violated that part of the agreement. They'd had him under surveillance. Not only did they have evidence that he'd purchased two firearms not long before his arrest, they'd observed him using a gun to shoot at a sign and some other inanimate objects.

●●●

Several developments that occurred following the August press release had made it possible for the authorities to zero in on Dillon as their primary—though not yet publicly identified—suspect in the five murders they were in the process of investigating.

The first development involved an old high school friend of Dillon's named Richard Fry. Fry and Dillon were gun enthusiasts and hunting buddies. Over time, Dillon's behavior had begun to concern Fry. He'd been mildly put off by how much Dillon seemed to relish the opportunity to shoot at rats, other rodents, and even "wild" dogs—but his concern rose to an entirely new level when he witnessed Dillon shooting animals that he was sure belonged to someone.

One day when he and Dillon were out driving, Dillon remarked on how easy it would be to get away with shooting someone in an isolated rural area. How could the police identify the killer if there were no witnesses, no evidence left behind, and no discernible motive? On a different day, when the friends were en route to a gun show, they'd been discussing the Ted Bundy serial murder case when Dillon suddenly asked Fry if Fry thought he'd ever killed anyone. Fry said no, he didn't think so. Dillon's response? "Then you don't know me very well."

Although not without some difficulty, Fry managed to get in touch with the police during the last week in August. He suggested that they investigate his friend as a possible suspect in the five murders he'd read about in the recent press release. He provided them a wealth of information about Dillon's background. That background information provided the investigators with a partial roadmap. With the roadmap as their guide, they began gathering additional information about Dillon from a variety of other sources.

The more they found out about him, the more they thought he resembled the "unknown offender profile" that Special Agent Larry Ankrom of the FBI's Behavioral Sciences Unit had drawn up after the formation of the multi-jurisdictional task force earlier that year.

According to Ankrom's profile, the killer was probably a white male, a loner, over 30 years of age, of above-average intelligence, an outdoorsman, a weapons enthusiast, non-confrontational—even "cowardly"—in his approach to handling interpersonal conflict, and inclined to commit his crimes within an area he considered his "comfort zone." The profile also noted that if the killer was married, he "probably had the ability to be independent with time, especially on weekends."

In mid-October, the task force members had begun tracking Dillon by ground and by air. They watched as he occasionally drove more than 100 miles on his weekend rambles around rural areas of eastern Ohio. Sometimes, they observed him purchasing beer as early as 7:30 in the morning, before he set off on his long, meandering drives. Once, they saw him get out of his truck and point a gun at a stop sign. They knew he owned a crossbow. On one occasion, they found two cows that had been killed by arrows shot from a crossbow in an area in Belmont County where they knew he'd been on the day in question.

Later, Richard Fry helped them match the arrows found in the dead cows to arrows owned by Dillon. Fry also helped them link a Dillon-owned gun to a bullet they'd recovered from a dog that someone had shot that September, in Tuscarawas County.

Despite all this tantalizing information, they still had no direct evidence linking Dillon to any of the five homicides. Feeling skittish about the onset of Ohio's deer hunting season on November 30, they decided to take a chance and nab Dillon for violating the terms of his probation on the federal firearms case. As noted previously, they arrested him on November 27. At his arraignment in federal court in Akron, the authorities argued in favor of keeping him in custody. To strengthen their case, they identified him as their primary suspect in the killings of five men between April 1989 and April 1992.

In the wake of the arraignment and the massive wave of publicity that followed, they finally got the break they'd been hoping for. A man who had been monitoring media coverage of the case came forward and told them he'd purchased a Swedish Mauser bolt-action rifle from Dillon on the same day as Gary Bradley's murder the preceding April. Ballistic tests proved it was the same gun that had been used to kill Bradley and, the month before, Claude Hawkins.

The authorities now felt secure in the knowledge that they had their man. For Dillon, it was time to begin reckoning with a new reality. His deadly game of cat and mouse had finally come to an end.

While these developments were being exhaustively chronicled in my local newspaper, I permitted myself the fantasy that Dillon's attorneys would retain me as their psychological consultant.

In death penalty cases, and the Dillon case was certain to be one of those, it was standard practice for defense attorneys—there were always two—to hire a psychologist. For one thing, they needed a mental health expert to advise them on matters pertaining to their client's competency to stand trial and mental state at the time of the alleged offense/s ("sanity"). For another, they needed to plan with an eye toward the [strong] possibility that their client would be found guilty of one or more death penalty-eligible offenses. Under that scenario, there would be a separate sentencing hearing where the jury would have to weigh statutorily-defined "mitigating factors" (e.g., the defendant's age, background, and mental condition) against "aggravating circumstances" that the prosecutor would use to argue in favor of death. Psychological testimony had the potential to steer the jury away from death and toward a sentence of life in prison.

By this time, I'd already consulted on several death penalty cases, including one that involved a massive amount of pre-trial publicity. However, I was still only four years out of graduate school. As it turned out, a presentation I'd given to a state-wide group of mitigation specialists helped to convince Dillon's attorneys that I was the psychologist they should retain as their consultant.

Mitigation specialists work closely with attorneys and their experts in the preparation of "mitigation" for use at the sentencing phase of death penalty trials. As part of my presentation, I'd shared my experiences with several notorious mass and serial murderers, for example Charles Manson, Ted Bundy, and John Wayne Gacy. I'd paid special attention to some things I'd learned as a result of my in-person interactions with Gacy, which had taken place across four days in 1986 and 1987.

A mitigation specialist who'd been present for my presentation reached out to Dillon's attorneys and recommended that they bring me on board as their expert. In early April, they contacted me and asked me to evaluate their client.

I hadn't yet even met Dillon when an article in my local newspaper gave my fledgling career a tremendous boost. The article stated that in their motion requesting funds for my consultation, Dillon's attorneys had stated to the presiding judge that I was "uniquely qualified" to assist them and came "very highly recommended." They went a step further, arguing that my involvement as an expert would be "essential" to their efforts to defend their client. The judge approved their motion— and in just a matter of days, I was brought on board.

•••

On May 3, I was slated to meet with Dillon for the first time. One of his attorneys accompanied me on my trip to the Lake County Jail, located in the northeastern part of the state. The attorney, David Doughten, Esq., was there to make introductions, and to assure Dillon that I was now a part of the defense team. When we entered the room where our meeting was to take place, Dillon was there already, seated at a small table. He looked up at us, winced slightly, and said simply, "You're late."

Over time, I became accustomed to Dillon's high control needs and abiding preoccupation with punctuality. He began each of our meetings by requesting an estimate of how long we'd be together, and by asking about the day's agenda.

A mildly humorous—and telling—exchange occurred toward the end of one of our last meetings. Dillon and I both knew that things were winding down for the day, so we began to shoot the breeze, talking back and forth about sports and a variety of other things that had nothing whatsoever to do with any matters pertaining to Dillon's case. One of the jail deputies who was stationed just outside the room where we were meeting opened the door, stuck his head in, and informed us that time was up. Dillon immediately shot back, "We need four more minutes!"

The deputy shrugged, said fine, and closed the door. For the moment, Dillon seemed satisfied. Of course we didn't need four more minutes, or even one more. The point was, Dillon opposed on principle the idea that someone else was going to decide exactly when our conversation should come to an end.

I was reminded of these and other such episodes years later, when I read the accounts by Claudia Rowe and M. William Phelps of their own encounters, respectively, with serial killers Kendall Francois and Keith Jesperson.

According to Rowe, Francois calculated that she was exactly five minutes late when she arrived for their scheduled meeting at Attica Correctional Facility. Phelps wrote that when he arrived to see Jesperson at the Oregon State Penitentiary, Jesperson signed in by asking him to explain why he was late for their appointment.

In the span of about seven weeks, I met with Dillon five times. During a multi-part interview that lasted somewhere between 20 and 30 hours, we talked about Dillon's childhood, his education, his work history, his interests, his hobbies, his fantasies, his roles as husband and father, and his long history of antisocial behavior, much of it not then known to the authorities (in early July, not long before his plea hearing, he would spend five and a half hours giving a detailed confession to the police and the FBI's case agent).

We also talked about all five of the murders he would eventually be charged with committing. On that subject, he was not the least bit reticent.

To supplement the interview, I administered an extensive battery of psychological and neuropsychological tests. I also traveled to Magnolia, a small rural community just south of Canton, so that I could interview his wife, Cathy. While I was there, seated with Cathy in the living room of their nicely maintained ranch home, their young son arrived home from school. After Cathy introduced us ("This is Dr. Smalldon, from Columbus"), their son snuggled up next to his mom and placed his head on her lap.

In early July, I summarized my findings and impressions in a 50-page, single-space typewritten report. Much to his attorneys' chagrin, Dillon promptly released a copy of the report to a Columbus-based journalist who'd been covering the case. As a result, the report's contents were leaked to the public before the plea hearing could even take place.

• • •

From the lengthy interview, I was able to gather a lot of detailed information about Dillon's formative years and young adulthood. His father died of Hodgkin's disease when Tom wasn't yet two. Tom had no memory of his mother ever even referencing his father's name in the years after his death.

According to Tom, his mother was an emotionally remote parent who seldom if ever hugged him, never told him she loved him, did little to enforce rules around their house, and seemed largely indifferent to his academic performance. He couldn't remember ever being praised or criticized for his grades or much of anything else.

Despite the fact that he and his mother had such a distant relationship all throughout his childhood and adolescence, he visited her regularly after she suffered a stroke in her late-sixties or early-seventies and had to be placed in a nursing home. I expressed mild surprise to learn that he'd been so attentive to her during the final years of her life. "She needed me," he said with a shrug. Then he added, in a soft voice, "She was all I had."

He recounted a telling anecdote, dating back to his elementary school years. On the day in question, his teacher went around the room, asking each student for his or her parents' names so that the names could be added to an emergency contacts list. When she came to Tom, he gave his mother's first name and was then mortified to realize that he didn't even know what his father's first name was. His classmates howled with laughter. Realizing how much the incident had upset Tom, his teacher phoned his mother and told her what had happened.

Tom was the youngest of three boys in his family. His oldest brother, 14 years his senior, was effectively gone from the home by the time Tom entered elementary school. Although his other brother was nearer to him in age, the two of them were never close. In fact, Tom told me they "hated each other" during their years growing up

The same man—Tom—who a journalist would later describe as having "a steel-trap memory" insisted to me that he could remember very little about his childhood. During one of our discussions, Tom told me that his first 18 years seemed to him like "a big blank." He denied any history of physical or sexual abuse.

What he remembered most clearly were the long hours he'd spend sitting alone in front of the television set, glued to shows like *Combat, Rat Patrol, 12 O'Clock High,* and *The Gallant Men.* During those childhood years of boredom and inactivity, he lived mostly inside his own head. Often, he would fantasize about combat and the Wild West. Looking back, he could see that even then, fictional tales of adventure, excitement, challenge, action, power, and glory dominated his imagination.

He'd always felt at something of a remove from most of the people around him. It was almost as if "there was a wall separating [him] from everyone else." This sense of isolation produced feelings of alienation. But at the same time, it contributed to his sense of being special, a case apart.

Years later, when he was a middle-aged adult man, he would scrutinize the caption on the indictment charging him with a federal firearms violation — "The United States of America vs. Thomas Lee Dillon" — and see it as a kind of symbolic validation of the profound sense of "apartness" he'd felt ever since childhood.

He was a chronic academic underachiever. School hardly interested him at all. When he wanted to acquire knowledge about something, he'd seek it out on his own. He speculated that most of his former classmates would probably remember him as "the guy who just sat there." He didn't much care about the actual world he was living in, so he "made up [his] own [world]." It existed inside his head. In that world, other people looked up to him and recognized him as someone deserving of special status.

By the time he entered middle school, he was nervous, shy, self-conscious, and withdrawn. He developed a stammer. In part because of the stammer, he dreaded the prospect of ever having to get up in front of his classmates to give a presentation. To cope with his anxiety, he'd refuse to attend school on days when he was slated to present — an avoidant, non-confrontational response style that would, in later years, remain his preferred approach to handling interpersonal conflict.

Little changed when he entered high school. He participated in no extracurricular activities and went on only one date, to a dance. The date ended badly when the girl who'd accompanied him to the dance left in the company of another boy. When I asked him if it bothered him that he didn't have any other dates during his high school years, he shrugged and said, "Nah, I didn't care. I had my TV." He felt "adrift," like he was living in "[his] own little world."

In the fall of 1968, he matriculated at The Ohio State University. He started out as a chemical engineering major but eventually switched to journalism (which of course helps to explain his focus on questions of who, where, why, and how in his response to Jean Paxton's letters). During college, he emerged from his shell, sort of. His summary description of his four years at Ohio State? "A lot of girls, a lot of beer, a lot of grass." In addition, he experimented with LSD, barbiturates, and amphetamines. He also did some shoplifting.

In 1975, he met Catherine ("Cathy") Elsass on a blind date. They married several years later. Cathy gave birth to their son on Christmas Eve, 1980.

•••

In July of 1980, about midway through his wife's pregnancy, Dillon shot at a human being, according to him for the very first time. Years before, probably when he was 12 or 13 years old, he'd begun to fantasize about committing acts of violence against other human beings. As I've said, he loved watching television programs about war, crime, and the Old West.

He'd also begun to enjoy books that featured the same narrow set of subjects and themes. For him, the books and TV shows provided an escape from reality. They were also a way to relieve stress. He was stimulated by the vicarious thrills he derived from the stories he read about and watched. Increasingly, his fantasies featured him in a variety of roles that were linked by themes of power, control, and grandiosity.

He told me that he first fantasized about killing a specific person when he was a senior in high school. His history teacher tried to pressure him into standing in front of the class and giving an oral report. Tom refused. In his fantasy, he shot the teacher to death, with his classmates all witnessing the spectacle.

Some other significant developments preceded the July 1980 shooting incident. When Tom was about 24, he began setting fires. In subsequent years, he became a serial arsonist. By the age of 14, he'd already begun killing animals. At first, he targeted birds, just as many of his agemates did. Then he started shooting at stray or "wild" dogs. By the late-1970s, he'd begun going out for the express purpose of "just killing something alive. It didn't make any difference what it was, they were all the same."

During one of our meetings, he told me he'd killed all kinds of animals: birds, groundhogs, squirrels, deer, dogs, cats, cows, and horses. He was quick to point out, however, that he'd never been cruel to animals when he was a child. He added that on at least three occasions during his marriage to Cathy, he brought home stray animals to keep as pets, mainly because he "felt sorry for them."

I asked him what criteria he used when he was deciding whether to kill a particular animal or turn it into a household pet. His response? "Well, if I wanted a pet at the time, I'd take the animal home. If I didn't want a pet, I'd just open fire on it." Once, when he was describing his decision to kill a cow, he remarked on the fact that the animal he was about to kill seemed to him "just like a baby."

Thinking that perhaps he was trying to communicate to me that he'd felt some degree of ambivalence about killing such a helpless creature, I inquired about whether there was any special significance in his perception of the cow as infant-like.

"Nah," he said, shrugging. "I don't feel remorse about any of the animals I killed." When he told me of his eventual decision to start shooting horses, he said he remembered thinking to himself, "You've killed every other animal in Ohio, you might as well try a horse."

At multiple points during the interview, he drew an explicit connection between killing animals and killing people. In fact, he even went so far as to say, "They're all the same— shoot a squirrel, shoot a man. They're both living organisms."

To that provocative statement he added a couple of rhetorical questions that were typical of many other such questions that he posed during our conversations. "Wouldn't it *feel* different if there was any difference between killing a squirrel and killing a man?" he asked. "Wouldn't I *feel* some remorse about killing a man if there was a difference?"

Often, such questions seemed to serve the dual function of highlighting his struggle for self-definition and buttressing the case for his uniqueness. He also enjoyed being provocative—though I'm pretty sure he would have denied that.

This exchange concerning the difference—or rather the lack thereof—between animals and humans caused me to think about England's infamous serial child-killer, Ian Brady, who'd once explained to Myra Hindley, his partner in crime, that yes, he'd tortured and killed animals when he was younger, but he'd now arrived at the point where he was ready to inflict pain on humans—since humans existed on "a higher plane."

Dillon didn't see it that way.

Tom and his wife Cathy had been married for just over two years when, late on a July evening in 1980, after a few hours spent hunting groundhogs, Tom stopped his vehicle in a sparsely populated area and—on impulse, he said—shot a man who was seated inside his picture window. Tom referred vaguely to a voice in his head that told him to "go back and shoot that guy." He explained, "It was just like that, y'know? Maybe he was just such an attractive target, I couldn't resist shooting him."

He said he experienced a sense of depersonalization at the moment when his gun went off. It was almost as if he was watching someone else pull the trigger. At least to hear him tell it, he drove home after the shooting and went about his business as though nothing unusual had happened. A day or two later, he read a short newspaper account of the incident. To him, it seemed "like somebody else must have done it." Fortunately, his victim survived. No one back then ever connected Tom to the shooting.

This seemingly strange phenomenon of a predator shooting someone and then returning to "normal" life almost as if the event had never even occurred turns out not to be all that uncommon, at least among serial killers. In his book about

Dennis Rader, the BTK killer, former FBI behavioral sciences expert John Douglas wrote that Rader would just go "back to everyday life" in the aftermath of a murder. In a letter Rader wrote to a Wichita media source, he himself said that he'd kill someone, then "just resume [his] normal life."

In one of his books about Ted Bundy, Kevin Sullivan referred to Bundy as "the master of compartmentalization." He wrote of how Bundy would commit a murder, maybe even more than one, then go to sleep and "awaken to a world new again, where he could, at least for a few hours, or days, or weeks, be normal ... again."

Bundy's former girlfriend, Liz Kendall, reported to the police that on a day when, as it turned out, Bundy had kidnapped, sexually assaulted, and killed two women, he told her he'd "eaten two hamburgers [after the murders] and enjoyed every bite." He remembered exactly what he'd done—but as far as he was concerned, the episodes of sexual assault and murder were "over" as soon as he knew the women were dead.

As far as anyone knows, nine years elapsed between the night Dillon shot the man through his picture window and the next time he shot at another human being. That's hardly a typical pattern among serial killers. When I pressed Dillon on the matter and pointed out that most repeat killers don't wait anywhere near that long to shoot a second person once they've shot the first one, he shrugged and suggested that the birth of his son may have slowed his progress on the path toward becoming a serial killer.

●●●

Even if it's true that Dillon wasn't shooting at people between 1980 and 1989, he was causing all kinds of other damage. For one thing, he brought an attitude of casual, thoughtless cruelty to his relationship with his son (who he described to me as the single most important person in his life). Tom reported, for example, that when his son was younger, he'd sometimes taunt the boy by telling him that there was a monster lurking under his bed. On one occasion, Tom teased him by saying that he and his mom had purchased him from someone for less than two dollars. On still another occasion, he tried to convince his son that he'd been adopted.

One day, Tom killed a chipmunk in their backyard and chased after his son, holding the dead chipmunk in his hand. When he caught up to his son, he pressed the dead animal into the boy's face. Much later, after Tom's arrest but before his plea hearing, Tom once jokingly suggested to his son that perhaps he should attend the hearing and tell the judge that *he* was the one responsible for the five murders, not his father.

It was never entirely clear to me how Tom felt about these aspects of his behavior. He repeatedly spoke of how much he loved his son. If dimly, he seemed to recognize how ironic it was that he'd treated him so poorly. Once, when he was describing his pattern of cruel teasing, he narrowed his eyes, shrugged, and asked me, "Why would somebody *do* that?" He relished the opportunity to present himself as inscrutable, an enigma for others to try to solve. Despite his obvious intelligence, he seemed to have little if any insight into how his actions may have affected his son.

He could be cruel and abusive to his wife, too. Although he'd later claim that Cathy provoked him each and every time he responded to her with any kind of violence, he admitted to multiple incidents of physical abuse. He also admitted that on one occasion, he mocked her for a short haircut she'd gotten, telling her it made her "look like a boy." On at least one other occasion, he told her she was "ugly." Despite these incidents of physical and emotional abuse, he placed a high premium on Cathy's loyalty. And whenever he discussed her with me, he always highlighted her many positive attributes.

During one of our meetings, when we were discussing the rumor that a well-known author was planning to write a book about his case, I asked him what he thought the book's central theme would be. He shrugged, winced a little, and said, "Bad man, good woman ... How could she be married to this maniac? (laughing) Nurse, church-going woman, nice kid—and this guy's going out blowing people away!"

It turns out that during the decade of the 1980s, Tom was responsible for millions of dollars of property damage. He set fire to abandoned buildings; once, he spent hours breaking every stained-glass window in a church building that was located in an isolated rural area; and to entertain himself, he would often open fire on electric meters, signs, transformers, and a wide variety of other inanimate objects.

In response to my repeated questions about the kind of satisfaction he derived from setting fires, he always offered some version of the same answer: "I don't know, just did it." He'd ask me, "Do you think that's odd?" Then he'd chortle to himself, at least hinting at his own realization that of course it's "odd."

He speculated that he'd probably killed somewhere in the vicinity of a thousand animals, all kinds. "Target shooting" he called it. To him, the act of killing was no big deal.

• • •

He seemed to derive special pleasure from fielding my questions about his richly elaborated fantasy life. The roots of that fantasy life extended all the way back to his boyhood, in particular the many hours he spent watching television and reading books, always with an eye toward cranking up the level of excitement in his life—and relieving the day-to-day tedium.

When I urged him to talk with me about his fantasies, his mood brightened and he became noticeably more animated. At one point during his long recitation of his invariably narcissistic fantasies, he paused, shook his head from side to side, and said, in an almost wistful-sounding tone of voice, "I got a lot of pleasure out of those fantasies." He added that when he was out by himself, driving around in his beloved red pick-up truck, he "could be anybody" and experience "everything at once."

One day he talked for almost an hour about the various roles he envisioned for himself during times when he was immersed in his own private fantasy world. Those roles invariably featured him being powerful, influential, and famous, able to exert control in a way that inspired other people's awe and envy.

Here's just a small sample of some of the roles he envisioned himself playing.

He liked imagining himself as a major league baseball pitcher who throws an Opening Day no-hitter for the Cleveland Indians; as a Cleveland Browns quarterback who leads his team to Superbowl wins, first when he's a young man and again, years later, when he's "brought back out of retirement"; as a literary artist who wins the Pulitzer Prize—at age 15—for writing the famously abstruse Thomas Pynchon novel, *Gravity's Rainbow*; as a pilot who gains fame for making a solo flight on the Voyager space probe ("I went all by myself, I didn't need anyone else"); as an explorer on an expedition to the North Pole; as a climber scaling Mt. Everest; as the recipient of 20 gold medals at the Olympic games (this fantasy had a particularly interesting wrinkle in that it featured him winning a race, against all odds, even after officials insisted that he perform without using an artificial leg that he had acquired as a result of a war injury); as a Beverly Hills mogul; as the charismatic preacher in the movie *Elmer Gantry*; as the composer, two years running, of the Academy Award-winning movie soundtrack; as the manager of the Beatles; as the lead singer of the Doors; as the discoverer of a cure for AIDS; and as a recording artist whose songs comprise 25 percent of *Billboard's* top hits over a period spanning a quarter century.

Just after he'd finished describing these and numerous other thematically linked fantasies, nearly all of them featuring him in one or another kind of socially-approved role, he asked me an interesting question. He asked if I thought the content of his preferred fantasies meant that deep down, what he'd really been after was the approval of the same people from whom he'd felt alienated all throughout his life.

Lending some credence to that idea was an observation he made about another of his fantasies. In that particular fantasy, which took place back when he was still a student in high school, he performed a series of deeds that earned the admiration of his classmates. He wondered if, in his subconscious, the fantasy might have "made up for [him being] a nobody" when he was a "real life" high school student. He explicitly identified "a lot of public gratitude" as the pay-off for the things he was able to accomplish in his fantasies.

He didn't shy away from talking about the darker dimensions of his imaginative life. In one of his fantasies, he played an active role during the notorious 1968 massacre at My Lai. He also fantasized about killing prostitutes, and about causing mass casualties by blowing up a bridge or derailing a train.

Former FBI special agent John Douglas, who's written extensively about the role of fantasy in the lives of serial murderers, has cited as representative the case of Dennis Rader, Wichita's infamous BTK killer. Rader "lived for the fantasy." According to Douglas, Rader's imaginative life was far more vivid and stimulating than his "normal" life ever was. In Rader's own words, he spent much of his time inhabiting "an immense fantasy world," teeming with images of "violence, bondage, and sadism."

During one of our conversations, Dillon and I discovered that we both had a longstanding interest in the literature of true crime, especially the sub-genre having to do with serial murder. Tom was slow to open up about the extent of his own interest. At first, he said things to suggest that his interest was casual, nothing at all serious. However, before long it became clear to me that he'd been sandbagging.

Not only was he well-informed about famous cases like those involving Ted Bundy, David Berkowitz, Jack the Ripper, Peter Kurten, Edmund Kemper, Jeffrey Dahmer, and the "Hillside Strangler/s," he had more than just a passing familiarity with the criminal careers of people like Leopold and Loeb, John Dillinger, Pretty Boy Floyd, Caryl Chessman, Carl Panzram, and Bonnie and Clyde.

Several of the comments he interjected are of more than just passing interest. Often, he'd remark on a particular crime's news value. For example, just after he'd referenced Marc Lepine's 1989 mass murder of female students in Montreal, he added with a barely perceptible wince, "It wasn't a real big story in the paper." We'd both read Darcy O'Brien's *Murder in Little Egypt,* the story of a physician who was convicted of murdering both his sons. Shrugging, Dillon volunteered, "I didn't think [the story] warranted a whole book. Guy kills his two sons, big deal; that happens all the time."

There was a similarly detached quality to the things he said about some other multiple murder cases. We'd been discussing England's notorious "Moors Murders" case, in which Ian Brady and Myra Hindley collaborated in the abduction and murder of young children. Dillon quipped, "Why'd they do it? Kicks, huh? At least we're not the only country where that stuff happens." Of Jack the Ripper he said, shaking his head and wincing slightly, "That guy really did the job."

Sometimes he'd lapse into self-referential asides. For example, when he was talking about the attempt by Nathan Leopold and Richard Loeb to commit "the perfect crime" during the 1920s, he remarked, "They created the perfect crime but left behind the eyeglasses! That's as bad as selling a Swedish Mauser!" Still on the subject of Leopold and Loeb, he commented, "It was a mental exercise for them ... I can see where they were coming from." He claimed to have little interest in the case of John Wayne Gacy, mostly, he said, because Gacy's victims were "just homos."

• • •

During our conversations about published accounts of famous and lesser-known murders, but at other times as well, he often seemed intent on making the case for himself as a killer unlike any who'd come before him. At one point he remarked, "This is very unique, [my] crimes. How many people in Ohio ever committed crimes like these? *No motive.* Maybe one in a thousand?" Later, he asked, "This is not your typical case, right? Maybe one in ten thousand?" He effected an attitude of curiosity and bewilderment when he was posing these and related questions about the crimes that he'd committed.

Often, he seemed to be casting about in search of a niche for himself among serial murderers. Recall that in the letter he sent to the *Times-Leader* in Belmont County, responding to letters Jamie Paxton's mother had published in the paper, he made a surprisingly pedantic-sounding reference to the fact that "technically," he met "the definition of a serial killer (three or more victims with a cooling off period in between)."

Despite his willingness to concede similarities between himself and certain other members of the serial killer category, he was eager to have people acknowledge the unique aspects of the crimes he himself had committed. More than once during our discussions, he spoke of how "perplexing" his acts were. If, he seemed to be saying, *I* can't understand what motivated me to do the things I did, then how could *you* ever hope to? On multiple occasions, he asked me if I'd ever heard of someone else doing the kinds of things he did. Was he the most complicated and confounding person I'd ever interviewed? He wanted to know.

Each time I met with Dillon, he was alert, lucid, engaging, and loquacious. He never came across as even mildly threatening—even though a deputy at the county jail where we had our first meeting felt it necessary to remind me how easy it would be for Dillon to stab me to death with one of the disposable pencils I let him use during my administration of a psychological test battery.

There was a certain "gaminess" about Dillon's manner of fielding many of my questions. Probably, it had to do with his high control-related needs. He'd often parcel out information in tiny increments, then wait to see if I'd come up with just the right question to elicit the rest—or part of the rest—of what he knew about the subject we were discussing. Sometimes, I had the feeling that he was deliberately withholding information until he could figure out exactly what I already knew about the topic under discussion.

Dillon's signature gesture was the dismissive shrug. He'd pose a rhetorical question related to his own behavior, something along the lines of, "Why would anyone do something like that?" Then he'd shrug his shoulders, lower his eyes, and shake his head from side to side. *Figure that one out*, he seemed to be saying. He was subject to frequent mood changes. In a matter of minutes or even just seconds, he could shift from seeming aloof and sullen to seeming animated and jocular.

His mordant, at times downright corrosive sense of humor surfaced at regular intervals. It was everywhere apparent in *Akron Beacon-Journal* reporter Jolene Limbacher's seven-part series, describing her five months of near-daily telephone contacts with Tom in the months leading up to his plea agreement. No matter how outrageous, many of the things Dillon said were undeniably funny—as Limbacher was the first to acknowledge. Tom poked fun at everything and everyone, including—especially—himself. The headlines of the first two installments of Limbacher's series point to the central paradox she was struggling to understand: "A disarming nature in a dangerous man" and "No trouble sleeping and an appetite for death."

Many of the letters Dillon wrote following his arrest included crudely drawn cartoons. Often, they were macabre and darkly hilarious. He used the cartoons to lampoon his attorneys for charging too much money; to characterize himself as a crazed, gun-happy killer; to depict his young son, armed with a rifle and declaring "I want to be just like my dad!"; to mock members of the media because of their seemingly insatiable appetite for gossip and gaudy headlines; to portray himself as a criminal whose over-the-top celebrity status might require the use of tanks for security; to make fun of other criminals, who he shows yelling things in his direction like "Castrate him!" and "Hang him!"; to show himself committing mass murder at a K-Mart and, as a result, "missing [out on] the blue plate special"; to portray his victims' family members as heavily armed and prepared to gun him down at the first opportunity; to depict his wife and son as destitute without him, forced to survive on a diet of "fried cats"; and to joke about lawmen having sex with his wife while he's locked away in prison.

Many of the cartoons are over-the-top outrageous. Of course that was the whole point. Dillon delighted in his ability to induce shock in other people. He loved pushing boundaries, and he delighted in violating other people's expectations of how he should behave. If anyone would have protested to him that his cartoons were offensive and in bad taste, I have no doubt that he would have responded with a shrug and his signature smirk. *So what?*

The testing I did revealed Dillon's "very superior" intellect. He was well aware of his intelligence, but he postured as if the confirming test results were of no interest to him whatsoever. Some of the other test data suggested his high level of cognitive rigidity. He found it difficult to switch from one way of looking at something to a different way, even when the second way offered obvious benefits. That particular finding dovetailed with my clinical impression of his obsessive-compulsive-type thinking style.

His personality test results pointed to a profoundly narcissistic individual, someone whose veneer of arrogance almost certainly obscured deeply-rooted feelings of inadequacy. The results also pointed to his largely unacknowledged feelings of rage.

I was struck by the startling discrepancy between a claim he made during one of our meetings—"I don't get angry"—and his longstanding pattern of extremely aggressive behavior, including arson, vandalism, and lethal violence, directed at both animals and humans. Uncomfortable with his negative feelings, he tended to avoid confrontations with people, preferring indirect ways of discharging his hostility.

Hardly surprising in light of his narcissism and antisocial behavior, he exhibited an attitude of disdain toward societal rules and expectations. Putting something over on people, especially people in positions of authority, fueled his feelings of grandiosity and entitlement. When he succeeded, it felt to him like affirmation. He really *was* special. He could operate outside the lines that most other people accept as the parameters within which they have to live their lives.

●●●

While Dillon was in jail awaiting the resolution of his case, by his own admission he developed an infatuation with a Steubenville-area television reporter named Lisa Kick. During a phone conversation with Kick, he confessed his crimes even before he'd confessed them to the police. (What better way to thumb his nose at the authorities!) A day or two after his plea hearing, the Noble County Sheriff permitted Kick to visit him at the local jail, and to make a video recording of their conversation.

Kick's interview includes any number of remarkable exchanges with Dillon. The ones highlighted below speak not only to Dillon's egocentricity and lack of empathy, but to his often astonishing tone-deafness.

Referring to the first of his five murders, the one involving roadside jogger Donald Welling, Dillon says to Kick, "I just kept going [after the murder], like normal behavior. Nothing out of the ordinary. And I forgot about it in a few weeks."

Of the murder of Jamie Paxton, which occurred about a year and a half later, he says, "It just happened. I went home, forgot about it. Didn't occur to me something happened, I don't know." He speaks of the other murders with a similar level of detachment. He seems to be bending over backward in an attempt to convey the impression that he's just as perplexed as everyone else over why he would have done the things he did.

Kick invites him to reflect on the five lives he chose to end. She asks him if he thinks of Jamie Paxton on a "nightly basis." Shrugging, Dillon responds, "No. I think about them as a group, not as individuals."

It's a startling admission. This tendency to objectify and devalue victims—to, in effect, "lump them all together"—is hardly unusual among people who commit serial murder.

In Martha Elliott's book about serial killer Michael Ross, she comments that Ross's individual victims "didn't seem real to him." During an August 2005 interview on NBC News, Dennis Rader, the BTK killer, referred to his victims as "objects" and explained what he meant by that: "I don't think it was actually the person I was after. I think it was the dream … They were just an object. That's all they were."

In her book about serial killer Kendall Francois, Claudia Rowe describes an exchange that occurred when Francois was being interviewed by the lead prosecutor on his case, who happened to be a woman. The prosecutor was trying to determine the likely state of decomposition of the various corpses Francois had placed in the attic of the house where he'd been living at the time of the murders. When she inquired about one of them, Francois replied, "I don't know. They're all mixed together."

And then there's this: psychologist Paul Dawson's description of an exchange he had with Ted Bundy during the period when Bundy was awaiting execution on Florida's Death Row. Dawson had encouraged Bundy to reflect on the process he used for selecting his victims. Bundy's response? "[The] girls I killed were just symbols, images and objects. I was looking for an idealized, abstract woman—avoiding any personal connection. Reasonable facsimiles of women as a class in the mythological sense—using them as objects."

At one point during her conversation with Dillon, Kick asks Tom if he feels remorse for having taken five lives. Sounding almost offended at being asked such a question, he says, "Sure! I have a lot of remorse!" Then, apparently confusing "remorse" with regret over all the trouble he'd created for himself, he executes a sharp pivot: "*I* don't wanna be here!" he says. "You think I wanna be here? It didn't need to happen. It just did, though." Then, the dismissive shrug.

Kick asks him what he thinks would happen if the authorities decided to set him free. "Three hundred and sixty-four days out of the year, I'd be fine out in society," he says. "But that one day ... I could kill someone. That one day out of the year, I'd probably lose control and it would be over." Kick encourages him to clarify what he means. "Probably kill somebody," he says. "It would happen [shrugging]. It would *have to* happen."

Just as he did when talking with me, Dillon goes out of his way to highlight the strangeness of his behavior and the uniqueness of his case: "None of these [victims] antagonized me or did anything ... I didn't know 'em, didn't rob 'em, didn't sexually molest 'em, didn't do anything. I didn't know 'em!"

Kick pushes a little harder: "Everybody wants to know why." Sounding puzzled himself, Dillon replies, "I don't *know* why. That's the big mystery here ... They just think it naturally progressed, to where it didn't make any difference to me whether it was a dog or a groundhog or a deer or a man, I don't know."

He pauses for a moment and thinks back on what his life was like before his arrest. To hear him tell it, he seldom if ever took time to reflect on the implications of his behavior, or to wonder what in the world might be wrong with him: "Go home, go to work, I was able to function, y'know? I can't be that much out of whack here ... Sometimes I'd think to myself, not everyone in Ohio's doing this today." He recalls driving around in his truck on weekends, drinking a beer and thinking to himself, "You're unique."

At a later juncture in the interview, he circles back to this same theme: "If I shot my wife, there'd be no interest in that, happens all the time ... But five strangers I didn't even know. That's why [people are] fearful. That could've been them. They don't understand, and they never will."

He declares that he'd be happy for the opportunity to meet "one at a time" with the family members of each of his victims. He sounds as if he views their situation and his own predicament as basically equivalent. If he had the opportunity, he'd explain to them, "I was so out of control, I didn't realize it."

Still referring to his victims' loved ones, he adds, "They're gonna have to live with it just like I'm gonna have to live with it, I guess." A little further on, commenting on the plea deal that netted him five consecutive life sentences, he states, his tone matter of fact, "[The authorities] get their five cases, I can keep contact with my family, everybody's happy."

When Kick asks him if he considers himself a "serial killer," he replies, "Technically, yes." Then, "But I don't feel like I *did* anything, really."

●●●

After the plea hearing, it bothered Dillon when he learned that his youngest victim's mother was telling reporters that she considered him a "pathetic coward." The next evening, he phoned Jean Paxton from the county jail where he was being held. She'd been wanting to speak to him for some time. They talked for nearly an hour.

According to news coverage of their call, Dillon told Mrs. Paxton that he "wished he could change things." However, she detected no signs in his voice of any real remorse. She later told reporters that she expressed no "anger" or "hatred" toward him. Instead, she tried to get him to acknowledge the trauma he'd inflicted on her and her family.

She came away with the sense that he didn't really see himself as blameworthy at all. "It's like he felt he wasn't responsible for all of these deaths," she told a reporter. She said she'd upbraided him for his "cocky attitude" and threatened to hang up on him if he persisted with it. She spoke to him of the importance of love, family, and God—and urged him to read the Bible before it was too late.

•••

After Dillon was sent off to prison, he and I remained in touch, if sporadically, for the better part of a decade. It's not like either of us regarded the other as a "friend." But Tom knew that my interest in him and his case didn't end with the finalization of his plea agreement. I was always glad when I received one of his letters.

At first, he was focused primarily on his goal of being assigned to a prison not far from where his wife and son lived. He dreaded the prospect of being sent to the maximum-security prison at Lucasville (where a much-publicized, 11-day riot had occurred not long before). He knew that Jamie Paxton's mother and Gary Bradley's widow had spearheaded a petition drive aimed at thwarting his wishes and seeing that he did, in fact, get assigned to Lucasville. By December of 1993, that's where he was.

In his letters, he'd sometimes dwell on the mundane aspects of prison life. For the most part, it seemed, he was content if people just left him alone with his television and his books. He hated noise and dismissed many of his fellow prisoners as "really worthless" loudmouths.

His dark humor was still very much in evidence. "I wish I could check out my Swedish Mauser [rifle] and fifty pounds of ammo and put it to use down here!" he wrote. I wasn't surprised to hear him say that much of the time, he "amused [himself] with elaborate daydreams." He speculated on the likelihood that day-to-day life at his old house near Canton was humming along nicely, even without him there to participate in it. "I guess I was just an impediment to progress there," he wrote. "The world is getting along very well without me."

In January of 1994, less than a month after his arrival at Lucasville, he expressed concern about the likely negative impact of any further publicity about his case. Then he added, "The first day here, I got kicked in the nose and punched and slapped by the guards. They are pissed off because I killed deer hunters and [they] hate me. There are some real rednecks down here."

In July of that year, he invited me to visit him and said a few things that captured my attention. "I never told you [or the FBI] a lot of things that happened or things I did," he wrote. "I didn't feel that any more cases or media hype could be handled by myself or my family … I maybe someday will go into greater detail about the Early Years." I was interested in his choice to use capital letters to reference a chapter in his life that he apparently regarded as an important part of his story.

In that same letter, he lamented that his attorneys hadn't made greater use of my report at his plea hearing. He thought they'd failed miserably in "the Public Relations Department." Without even a trace of irony, he remarked on his belief that they should have made him "more appealing to the general public."

In a May 1995 letter, he wrote that the events of 1993—when he entered his guilty pleas—were "just starting to sink in." He likened what he was experiencing to "a post-traumatic stress syndrome, delayed reaction." He could see, looking back, that he'd "started going downhill" in the late 1980s. He continued, "By late '92 I was a zombie. I had no interest in my job, family, or myself. I needed counseling badly but failed to get it. I guess that is my own fault. The alcoholism took away any reasoning power I had left. I was powerless to stop myself."

In one respect, I was sorry that the Dillon case had resolved in a plea agreement as quickly as it did. Had I had more time, I would have tried gathering information from a number of other sources. For starters, I'd have tried to interview Dillon's two brothers, his old hunting buddy and friend Richard Fry, some of his work associates and neighbors, and some of his former classmates and teachers. Also, I would have interviewed his wife at least one more time. As it was, my investigation effectively ended when Tom agreed to plead guilty to the five murders.

In the years since 1993, I've answered a lot of questions pertaining to Dillon.

Do I think he wanted to get caught? No.

Do I think he was remorseful? No.

Do I think he spent most of his waking hours between 1989 and 1993 thinking about killing? Yes.

Do I think he committed more than just the five murders? Probably.

Do I think he derived satisfaction from the "hiding in plain sight" aspect of his criminal career? Yes.

Do I think he considered himself smarter than the police? Yes. (Dillon insisted that the police never would have caught him had he not bungled and basically solved the case for them.)

Do I think boredom played a role in his decision to become a serial killer? Yes.

Do I think he considered sniper-killing a "mental game?" Yes.

Do I think his "killing years" were the most exciting years of his life? Yes.

Do I think he'd have killed more people if the police hadn't arrested him? Of course.

• • •

By the mid-1990s, I thought that for all intents and purposes, I was done with the Dillon case. I wasn't.

Almost a decade after Dillon's plea hearing, a series of events would catapult the case—and me, for a minute—into the national spotlight.

I mentioned that once Dillon got settled in at Lucasville, he reached out and said he'd like to meet with me. I made tentative plans to visit him. One of his trial attorneys, who was still on record as his legal representative, suggested an arrangement whereby he would pay me a nominal fee to act as his consultant and in that way create a framework that would allow me to conduct confidential interviews with Dillon in the prison setting.

I regret it now, but I never followed through on my plan to visit Tom. I was over-extended at work, and I never seemed able to carve out the full day that I knew the trip to Lucasville would require.

I did, however, have a brief, serendipitous encounter with Tom during one of my frequent trips to the prison, which is where Ohio's death row was located at the time. On the day in question, I was there to evaluate a death row inmate.

When I was done conducting my evaluation, I left the professional meeting room that had been allocated for my use and walked out into the general population visiting area. There, seated at one of the small metal tables, were Tom and his wife, Cathy. Tom beckoned me over, but before I could advance more than a few steps in their direction, the corrections officer whose job it was to oversee the room ordered me to stop. He explained that inmates were only permitted to interact with their officially sanctioned visitors.

"I'll write you!" Tom hollered as I turned and headed toward the exit.

That was the last time I ever saw him.

In the ensuing years, I'd still hear from him occasionally, and I responded every time he wrote me a letter. However, I didn't give him much thought, in part because I had my hands full with numerous other capital cases, and with a wide variety of other criminal and civil case referrals.

Then came October 2002. That's when the so-called Beltway Sniper was at large, terrorizing the public in southern Maryland and northern Virginia. A reporter from *Time* magazine contacted me for a story she was writing about the Beltway case. She'd discovered that almost a decade prior, I'd been the defense-retained psychological consultant on a rare serial sniper case here in Ohio—the Dillon case.

By the time her article was published, the unknown Beltway Sniper had already shot and killed eight people in the area surrounding the nation's capital. She informed her readers, "One of the more instructive analogies [to the Beltway case] ... may be the case of Thomas Lee Dillon." She described my role in the Dillon case and quoted me several times in her article. The statements I made to her all pertained to Dillon and not the Beltway Sniper, about whom I knew no more than anyone else at that point.

Her mention of my name in relation to the Dillon case triggered a tsunami of interest on the part of the national media.

In the week following publication of her article, I made appearances on *Larry King Live, Good Morning America, 60 Minutes II, 48 Hours, Connie Chung Tonight*, and several other nationally syndicated television programs. I also participated in interviews with journalists from a number of other countries.

Now, it all strikes me as a bit unseemly. In retrospect, I wish I'd have maintained a lower profile. Even though I was careful to point out to everyone who interviewed me that I could only contribute observations based on things I'd learned firsthand as a result of working on the Dillon case, some of the interviewers tried hard to coax me to venture beyond my comfort zone, and to act as one of those pontificating "talking heads" who so often got under my own skin when I watched television stories that focused on true crime cases and other headline-grabbing stories. It clearly frustrated them when I rebuffed their attempts to get me to "profile" the Beltway Sniper. Some of them urged me to venture out on a limb and draw all sorts of conclusions I was in no position to draw.

I have especially vivid memories of my experience with Scott Pelley and *60 Minutes II*. Pelley was already a well-known and highly-regarded broadcast journalist. Just the month prior, for another segment that aired on *60 Minutes II*, he'd conducted an exclusive interview with President George W. Bush on the occasion of the first anniversary of the attack on the World Trade Center. I'd watched that interview when it aired on television. Now, Pelley wanted to travel to Columbus to interview me. His production crew spent an entire weekend converting a large suite at a local Marriott hotel into a make-shift studio for us to use on Monday morning.

I admit that I was a little starstruck. I remember feeling mildly apprehensive as I watched Pelley emerge from the limousine that had brought him from the airport to the hotel. The segment's producer, who was waiting with me in the hotel lobby, introduced me to Pelley, who seemed relaxed and down to earth. The three of us chatted amiably as we rode the elevator to the floor where my interview was to take place.

It was October 21. As I've said, a Monday. Perhaps sensing that I was still a little nervous, Pelley tried to be reassuring. "Just relax and have a conversation with me," he said. "Don't worry about making mistakes, the editors will clean things up later."

There's a reason why I'm telling this story.

About 15 minutes into the interview, a member of the production crew interrupted us and signaled that we had to take a break. He announced that he'd just been alerted to some important breaking news. I overheard part of his and Pelley's whispered conversation. The authorities had arrested two men near Richmond, Virginia. They thought that perhaps the men were responsible for the sniper shootings that had begun almost three weeks prior. Pelley took his cellphone with him and moved out into the hallway. I couldn't make out what he was saying, but I noticed that he was making a deliberate effort to speak softly.

Suddenly, everyone involved with the production of my

segment seemed nervous, edgy, and awkward. There was a lot of whispering. No one seemed sure what to say. If the sniper or snipers were indeed in police custody, that would be great news. Right? A possible end to the Beltway Sniper's reign of terror.

Yes, but …

What about this segment we were in the middle of filming?

If it turned out to be true that the people responsible for the sniper attacks were now in custody, this segment about the Dillon case would get quashed before it could air. The current plan was for it to air in two days on Wednesday evening. The whole idea was that I and several other people who'd worked on the Dillon case might be able to offer insights that would advance the public's understanding—and perhaps even the authorities' understanding—of the sort of person (or persons) who would be capable of carrying out a lethal campaign of "remote" terror against complete strangers.

I felt conflicted—and uneasy over the fact that I did. I generally thought of myself as a fundamentally decent person, and as an upstanding citizen. If both those things were true, I should have been rejoicing over a turn of events that could signal the end of a tragic killing spree. And yet …

I couldn't deny that I was eagerly anticipating my appearance on *60 Minutes II*. I'd been watching the original *60 Minutes* since I was a kid. For the few moments I allowed myself to think such thoughts, I wondered if my real but hard-to-acknowledge hope that the men currently in custody weren't the ones responsible for the sniper attacks meant that I wasn't all that different from some of the remorseless killers I evaluated and offered expert opinions about. *Was I secretly wishing for an outcome that could very well set the stage for the loss of more lives?*

Just then, Pelley returned from the hallway. He announced that we were going to continue with the interview. According to him, the authorities were still uncertain whether the men they'd taken into custody were responsible for the sniper attacks. We resumed our positions under the studio spotlights and picked up where we'd left off. If the men in custody *weren't* the snipers, our segment would air on Wednesday evening, as planned. For the remaining part of the interview, I had a hard time maintaining my concentration. I kept thinking that this entire production might be a waste of everyone's time.

As it turned out, the suspects who'd been taken into custody that day weren't responsible for the Beltway killings. Instead, they were undocumented immigrants who ended up being turned over to the Immigration and Naturalization Service.

Part of me felt relief, knowing that the Dillon segment would, in all probability, air as planned. The hard truth was that I welcomed the news that the Beltway Sniper was still at large. I was left to grapple with the troubling implications. *What did it say about me that I wasn't more bothered by the fact that the sniper was still out there, still in a position to claim more victims?* I tried not to dwell on the question, but it was a hard one to avoid. It bothered me then, and it still does.

I was sure I wasn't alone. There were others involved in the production of the Dillon segment who clearly shared my hope that the sniper-related drama would play out for at least a few more days. I thought to myself, *Is that just a necessary part of what it means to work in the news-gathering business? Is it just assumed that you'll spend much of your time with your fingers crossed, hoping that real-world situations, including very negative ones, won't resolve before a story you're working on can reach its intended audience?* I wondered if I could work under such conditions—and whether I'd feel morally compromised if I chose to.

Tragically, the tenth murder attributed to the Beltway Sniper occurred on the very next day after I was interviewed for the Dillon segment. The segment did, in fact, end up being televised that Wednesday evening—and John Allen Muhammad and Lee Boyd Malvo, the two people responsible for the three-week campaign of terror, were arrested the next day.

Sadly, I can remember thinking: *Good, I'm glad it's finally over—but I'm also kind of glad that the killers eluded the police dragnet long enough so that the Dillon segment could air as planned.* It's a tough thing to have to admit.

Dillon died of natural causes more than a decade ago. Even so, his case remains a source of fascination for true crime afficionados. Three weeks ago, a reporter interviewed me for an upcoming cable TV documentary about Dillon's life and crimes. A private investigator phoned me just yesterday. She explained that she was putting together a podcast about Dillon and actively exploring the possibility that he was responsible for more than just the five murders.

●●●

Things I read and hear about often remind me of the Dillon case.

In 2013, cultural critic Chuck Klosterman published one of his provocative, wildly imaginative books. This one was called *I Wear the Black Hat: Grappling with Villains (Real and Imagined)*. The book was billed as a look at "the culture of deliberate malevolence," and at society's struggle to come to terms with it. One passage in particular pried open the Dillon file that I still carry around in my head.

> *The presidency is not a job for an honest man. It's way too complex. If honesty drove the electoral process, Jimmy Carter would have served two terms and the 2008 presidential race would have been a dead heat between Ron Paul and Dennis Kucinich. Expressing outrage over a president's lack of honesty is like getting upset over a sniper's lack of empathy: It's an integral component of the vocation.*

All in a day's work, right? And did I think to mention? A favorite pastime of Dillon's was imagining himself as Donald Trump.

8.
A Contented Killer

In 1988, Thomas Lee Dillon was still a year away from committing his first known murder. His arrest and eventual indictment on charges that would make him eligible for Ohio's death penalty were still four years down the road.

For me, 1988 was a year of transition. Patty Matix and Joyce McFadden had been dead for nearly five years. Two years had elapsed since the shootout in Miami. No one I knew applied the word closure to the Riverside case, but even if details were hard to come by, few people doubted that William Matix and his buddy Michael Platt were the ones responsible for the murders.

In 1985, the year before the Miami shootout, I'd gotten married, abandoned my career in hospital administration, and begun work toward my PhD in psychology. Now, three years in and with my coursework behind me, I was getting ready to leave Columbus for Middletown, Connecticut, where, in August, I would begin my required one-year pre-doctoral internship at a state psychiatric hospital. The internship and my dissertation were the last remaining hurdles standing between me and my degree.

Three years had elapsed since Ted Bundy advised me to take care, watch myself, and travel light. I was still corresponding with John Wayne Gacy—and still trying to wrap my mind around the idea that Bill Matix, the soft-spoken and seemingly bereft widower whose hand I shook at the memorial service for his slain wife and her co-worker, was, in fact, a remorseless killer.

In every way I could think to, I was continuing to gather the kind of information that I thought might help me when I wrapped up my studies at Ohio State and began work toward establishing my practice as a forensic psychologist.

In August of 1987, when I was still completing my course-work at Ohio State's main campus in Columbus, a slight, handsome, almost cherubic-looking former nursing assistant named Donald Harvey pled guilty to killing 37 patients and admitted to the police that he'd killed many more. According to his confession, he'd committed the vast majority of his murders during periods of employment at two Cincinnati-area hospitals.

For me, the Harvey story was irresistible. For easy enough to understand reasons, the story had generated massive amounts of media attention, not just in Ohio but nationwide. As I looked ahead to a career that I hoped would provide me with opportunities to evaluate serial killers and other violent criminals, I wondered if perhaps I could learn a thing or two from Harvey, whose killing grounds were just down I-71, the main north-south artery that connects Cleveland, Columbus, and Cincinnati.

In his book *The Killer Across the Table* (2019), legendary FBI profiler John Douglas referred to Harvey as "maybe the most prolific serial killer in American history" (this was pre-Samuel Little). Harvey began his killing career in Kentucky, when he was still in his teens. More than a decade would elapse before his final arrest, in April of 1987.

When the police first tried to interview him, Harvey attempted to cast himself as an altruistic, misunderstood "angel of death." (Other medical serial killers—people like Charles Cullen, Beverly Allitt, Orville Majors, Kristen Gilbert, and Reta Mays—would later adopt a page from the same playbook.) As part of his plea agreement, Harvey received three life sentences, to be served consecutively, as well as a variety of other sentences that were to be served concurrent with the first three.

By pleading guilty and thus obviating the need for a trial, he escaped a near-certain death sentence.

At the time of my decision to reach out to Harvey—it was during the year just prior to the start of my internship in Connecticut—he was incarcerated at the Southern Ohio Correctional Facility in Lucasville, a maximum-security prison located just north of Ohio's border with Kentucky. My hope? That I could coax him into responding to a number of questions, just as I was about to immerse myself in the process of writing my doctoral dissertation.

Basically, I intended my dissertation as an investigation into how members of various knowledge communities—lay and professional alike—respond to the challenge of having to formulate the sense in acts of so-called "motiveless murder." That is, murders that don't fit neatly into the taxonomy of motives that's traditionally been used to explain why people kill one another: greed, lust, revenge, jealousy, power, and so on.

I wondered if Harvey would be open to answering some of my questions—and, in a more general sense, to engaging with me in a dialogue about his career as a killer. I also wondered if perhaps he would even contribute an observation or two that I could somehow incorporate into my dissertation.

In the letter I sent him, I identified myself as a graduate student in psychology. I told him of my interest in the kinds of murders that commentators sometimes describe as "motiveless" or "senseless," usually because observers seem unable to account for them by invoking any of the motives that are typically used to explain crimes of lethal violence.

I knew that initially Harvey had claimed he dispatched many of his victims for altruistic reasons.

I told him of my belief that many people probably viewed that claim as implausible. If they rejected the altruism explanation, then they were faced with the challenge of having to come up with some different way of accounting for him and his behavior. If he wasn't a merciful "angel of death," who *was* he? The alternative way of accounting for him and his actions had to be one that, all things considered, people thought made sense—or at least *more* sense. I asked him if he'd be willing to participate with me in a dialogue about these issues and some related ones, either by letter or in person.

He never responded to my letter.

I was disappointed but not deterred. I'd failed in my first attempt to draw Harvey into a conversation, but I thought that perhaps I'd get another opportunity, at some point further on down the road.

In the meantime, my wife and I moved from Columbus to Connecticut; I wrote my dissertation and completed my pre-doctoral internship; and in August 1989, I graduated from Ohio State with my PhD in psychology.

Fast forward six years.

By 1995, I'd already consulted on ten death penalty cases in a number of jurisdictions in and around Ohio. One of them was the case involving Thomas Lee Dillon. Fresh off my work on the Dillon case, I decided to have another go at Harvey.

I remained convinced that there were things he could teach me, if only I could get him to talk openly with me about the many murders he committed over a period of years. My hope was that he would agree to an in-person meeting. If he did, I wouldn't have to travel far to get to him. I knew he was still incarcerated at one of the state prisons that were located in the southern part of Ohio.

Between the years 1988 and 1995, I'd come to understand the importance of always working through a prison inmate's legal representative—if, that is, he had one. In Donald Harvey's case, I knew that the place to find an answer to that question was the office of his trial attorney, William Whalen, who was based in Cincinnati.

When Whalen was appointed to serve as Harvey's legal representative, no one in the local legal community, least of all Whalen, had even the slightest idea that Harvey might be a serial killer. I knew from reading press coverage of the case that Whalen had continued as Harvey's attorney right up through the time of the plea agreement that brought closure to the criminal proceedings and probably saved Harvey's life.

When I phoned Whalen's office, I was pleased but mildly

surprised to learn that he was present and willing to take my call. He confirmed that he was, in fact, still Harvey's attorney of record. I explained to him that I was a Columbus-based forensic psychologist with a longstanding interest in serial murder. He was familiar with my name, in part because I'd consulted on a couple of very high-profile death penalty cases that were tried in Cincinnati.

I asked him if he'd be willing to grant me permission to interview his client. He said he'd have no objection to such an interview, just so long as he could be present when it took place. I told him I'd be fine with such an arrangement. He promised to discuss the matter with Harvey, then get back to me with an answer.

True to his word, he sent me a letter about two weeks later. He said he'd discussed my request with Harvey, who'd agreed to the interview. It would have to take place at Warren Correctional Institution, near Lebanon, Ohio, where Harvey was housed on the Protective Custody Unit, reserved for high-profile inmates and others who the prison administration assessed as too vulnerable to be placed in the general population. Whalen gave me several dates that would work for him, then invited me to choose one, inform him of the one I'd chosen, and proceed with making whatever arrangements needed to be made through the warden's office at the prison.

I phoned the warden and requested his help. I assured him I had already been in touch with Harvey's attorney, Bill Whalen, and added that the plan was for Whalen to be present on the day of the interview. The warden said he'd be glad to help facilitate the meeting. We settled on Friday, September 22, as the day when the interview would take place.

The warden agreed to allot a total of three hours, to begin at noon on the 22nd. He stipulated that the interview would take place in one of the private rooms adjacent to the visiting area reserved for inmates who were in the general population.

I passed all this information along to Whalen. After agreeing that he'd meet me in the prison lobby at around 11:30 on the 22nd, he assured me that even though he planned to be present in the room with Donald and me, his plan was to sit off to the side and say nothing. That way, Donald and I could do all the talking.

• • •

After driving south from Columbus, I arrive at the prison just before 11:30 on the 22nd. I find Whalen waiting for me in the prison lobby. A soft-spoken man with a genial, welcoming manner, he explains, just after we shake hands, that in the years since the plea agreement that brought closure to Harvey's case, Donald has come to view him as far more than just an attorney. In fact, the two of them have become fast friends. He tells me that he tries to visit the prison as often as he possibly can, adding that my request for an interview with Donald came along at just the right time. He'd been looking for an excuse to check in on Donald and see how he was doing.

After securing our belongings in lockers located just off the lobby and then navigating our way through a series of security checkpoints, we arrive at a sliding gate that opens on to the general population visiting room. Visible through the window of a door leading to one of the private visiting rooms is the smiling face of Donald Harvey.

Immediately, I know it's him. He looks pretty much the same as he looked in the many pictures of him that I've seen in newspapers and on television. He's slight and not very tall. He has brown hair and a rounded, strikingly handsome face. He's neat, clean-shaven, and well-groomed.

When Whalen and I enter the private room where Harvey's been awaiting our arrival, I'm relieved to see that Donald's movements aren't constrained by either handcuffs or leg manacles. My goal is for him to feel as comfortable as possible. He greets Whalen with a light hug, then turns to face me. I introduce myself ("I'm Jeff Smalldon, good to meet you, Donald"), we shake hands, and I tell him I appreciate it that he's agreed to my interview request.

"My *pleasure*," he says, smiling and sounding like he means it. He's so friendly and boyish-looking, it would be very easy to forget that he's a remorseless killer, responsible for at least 37 deaths—in all likelihood many more than that.

I'm glad to have Whalen with me. His presence affords me instant credibility, or so it seems. I want Donald to view me as someone with whom he can talk freely and openly.

Even at this relatively early juncture in my career, I've had plenty of experience conducting inmate interviews at county jails and state prisons all throughout Ohio. I'm proud of the fact that I've been able to get along well with every inmate I've been asked to evaluate so far, even those whose attorneys have described them as obstreperous and difficult to deal with. Sometimes, however, it takes time to build the kind of rapport that I'm always striving for.

With Harvey, it takes no time at all. Right off the bat, he's polite, affable, and engaging. His demeanor borders on buoyant, and it stays that way during nearly the entire time while we're together, even when we're talking about murder. He never gets defensive. Right at the outset, he offers me his assurances that he'll do his best to answer any questions I want to ask him.

(Something worth noting: Neither of us makes any reference to the letter I wrote him some seven years ago. Perhaps he's forgotten all about it. I haven't—but it's his memory that matters most.)

Whalen sits quietly, off to one side. He seldom looks up from the paperwork he's brought along with him. Just as he promised, he never once interrupts the flow of our conversation.

As part of my preparation for meeting with Harvey, I went back and reviewed the partial transcript of an interview that Columbus-based reporter Michael Berens conducted with him in 1991. At the time of Berens' interview, Donald was more than willing to opine on the mind of the serial killer.

"All serial killers follow a pattern," he explained, "whether they know it or not. Serial killers want to watch their victims die. I wanted to make sure [my own victims] didn't come back and tell on me."

Harvey told Berens of his ongoing interest in the case of Ted Bundy, who had been executed two years prior. He also disclosed that he'd been paying close attention to news stories about a number of prostitutes whose bodies had been found alongside major highways in Ohio and three neighboring states. Like most serial killers, his interest in murder extended far beyond the boundaries of his own case.

Berens wrote that Harvey appeared to revel in his status as a notorious killer. Prosecutors had accused him of hyperbole and portrayed him as a braggart, bound and determined to win for himself a place in the *Guinness Book of World Records.* To Berens, Harvey spoke of the "historical" nature of his killing career.

Berens pointed to the paradoxical nature of Harvey's presentation: "His boyish face, infectious smile, and effeminate voice mask a stone-cold killer instinct." Harvey spoke openly with Berens of his assiduous effort to maintain a facade of normality, right up until the point when authorities closed in on him and forced him to reckon with the fact that he would never be a free man again. Not once did he express an iota of remorse. In fact, according to Berens he took pride in having earned his reputation as the most prolific serial killer in Ohio history.

Berens asked Harvey why he'd killed. "Well, people controlled me for 18 years, and then I controlled my own destiny," Harvey explained. "I controlled other people's lives, whether they lived or died. I had that power ... I appointed myself judge, prosecutor, and jury. So I played God."

He admitted that he'd killed a number of patients in Kentucky when he was still in his teens. Subsequently, he enlisted in the Air Force, hoping to resolve some lingering questions about his sexuality. It didn't take him long to conclude once and for all that he was gay. Less than a year after his enlistment, he triggered his own discharge from the military by downing a bottle of cough medicine, either because he coveted attention or because he'd decided life was no longer worth living. When he returned to Ohio, he resumed his career as a killer.

To Berens, Harvey claimed 87 victims in all. He scoffed at authorities who accused him of exaggerating. As he saw it, they were unwilling to face "the truth."

• • •

I decided in advance that I wasn't going to take notes while Donald and I were talking. I wanted to avoid doing anything that might cause Donald to feel self-conscious. Equally important, I didn't want to have to interrupt the flow of our conversation. Since I wasn't conducting the interview for any kind of official purpose, I saw no need to keep a contemporaneous written record of every word that was spoken. I'd record notes later, from memory.

The day just prior to the interview, I prepared a short outline of topics I hoped Donald and I could cover. Included on the outline: Donald's family background; his abuse history; his medical history; his work history; the circumstances surrounding his first deliberate killing; the methods he used to kill; the feelings he experienced when he took another person's life; and the approach he used for selecting his victims.

As Donald and I begin conversing, it's clear almost immediately that he delights in finding himself the center of attention, even with an audience consisting of only two people. He beams throughout nearly our entire meeting, appearing relaxed and exuding an air of self-satisfaction. Even when I pose questions that call for him to disclose explicit details about some of the particularly grotesque murders he's already confessed to committing, he never flinches. In fact, he seems to relish the opportunity to regale me with stories about his murderous exploits.

He describes a hardscrabble childhood, replete with poverty, neglect, instability, and abuse. However, he doesn't sound sad when he's describing it. Never once does he shed a tear. Equally striking, he never expresses any overt feelings of anger toward the various adults who mistreated him during his years growing up.

"It's just how things were," he explains, shrugging and extending his arms outward in a what-ya-gonna-do kind of gesture.

"My mom had a tough time of it herself," he adds. "She was raped young, and she was only 15 when she married my father. He was a lot older, like, 16 years. A few years after their wedding, I came along." He says he can't remember his father being around much during his childhood. In any case, the two of them never bonded. On the other hand, his mother doted on him. "But she was just a child herself!"

"I was good at school," he crows. "But I wasn't there long." He dropped out during his ninth-grade year, in part because his family didn't have the money needed to pay a fine he owed because of a mistake he'd made in a shop class he was taking. Later, he went on to obtain his GED.

He describes a dizzying succession of abusers. An uncle began sexually abusing him when he was just four years old. He admits to harboring ambivalent feelings toward his earliest abuser, who he says showered him with attention and made him feel loved and needed. The abuse continued for years, according to Donald up through the time of his young adulthood. An older male neighbor started abusing him when he was five. Like the abuse he suffered at the hands of his uncle, the neighbor's abuse continued for years.

There were other abusers, too. Sounding matter of fact, almost bored, Donald identifies several of them by name. Striking to me is his reluctance to use the word "abuse" to describe the things that happened to him. Looking back from his current vantage point, he's inclined to view himself as at least partially responsible for a lot of what went on. He readily admits that he craved his abusers' attention and relished the special role that he played in their lives.

"It made me feel important to them," he says. "They got pleasure *because of me*."

He tells me that he sustained a head injury when he was around five years of age. While he was standing on the running board of his father's truck, he tumbled off and hit his head on the ground. To the best of his recollection, he never completely lost consciousness. However, he can remember being told that his eyes "rolled together." In any case, he ended up with a mean gash on the back of his head.

"I don't really know what effect it had," he says, alluding to the head injury. "Maybe none, maybe a lot."

"I want to switch to a different subject," I say. "Can you tell me about the first time you killed someone on purpose?"

According to Donald, it occurred when he was 18 years old. At the time, he was employed as an orderly at Marymount Hospital in northern Kentucky. He'd been assigned to help provide care for an elderly, incontinent man who also happened to be a curmudgeonly alcoholic. At one point, the man reached out and smeared feces on Donald's clothing.

"Now *that* really pissed me off," says Donald. He remembers flying into a rage. He grabbed a blue plastic cloth and a pillow, then used them to suffocate the old man. Everyone expected the patient to die anyway, so no one suspected foul play.

"How did you feel when you realized you'd killed him?"

"Relieved, I guess," says Donald, shrugging.

I know I won't have nearly enough time to ask him about all the murders he's confessed to committing. Even so, one thing seems certain: he'd be delighted to revisit each and every one of them, and to tell me everything he's able to remember. He isn't at all shy or reticent when it comes to providing the specifics. In fact, he's startlingly nonchalant in his manner of discussing the methods he used to dispatch his victims.

He explains that during his young adulthood, while he was employed at Marymount, he never killed using poison. Instead, he manipulated his patients' oxygen supply.

There were times when he used a different approach, one that he thought might be "safer."

"I knew I could kill some of them just by positioning their bodies in certain ways," he says. "Like, I could move them so it was impossible for them to breathe."

Sounding almost giddy, he launches into an account of one especially gruesome murder.

"I hated having to take care of this one guy," he says. "He didn't like me, and I didn't like him. I'm not sure if he got mad at me or what. Maybe he was just confused or something. But he grabbed a portable urinal and hit me with it. So hard that it knocked me out. When I came to, my clothes were soaked with pee."

The next day, still fuming and now bent on exacting revenge, Donald deliberately fitted the man with an oversize catheter. Then he straightened out a coat hanger and inserted it into the catheter, puncturing the man's bladder and causing peritonitis. The patient went into shock. Within a couple of days, he was dead.

Still smiling as he processes that memory, Donald shifts gears and begins describing another chapter of his life story. It's one he seems eager to revisit.

Once, when the police were questioning him about a burglary that occurred at Marymount during the period of his employment there, he confessed to having caused the deaths of 15 patients. The police, convinced his confession was nothing more than a blowhard's frantic bid for attention, released him soon afterward.

"Ha!" exclaims Donald. "If only they'd known ..."

Shortly after his nineteenth birthday, he enlisted in the Air Force.

"I wanted to get away from Kentucky," he explains. "Plus, I wanted to find out once and for all if I was really gay." It didn't take him long to figure out the answer. He was.

He can remember struggling with questions pertaining to who he was, and who he wanted to be. During a relatively narrow window of time when he was stationed in Texas, he sought out an affiliation with the Church of Jesus Christ of Latter-day Saints. Turns out, that was a short-lived experiment.

His discharge from the Air Force, which occurred following his aborted suicide gesture, became official less than a year after his enlistment.

He says it was around that same time when he started developing an interest in various occult-related practices. He doesn't elaborate, and for time-related reasons I opt not to pursue that particular subject any further. (Years later, I'll learn more about it as a result of reading Bill Whelan's memoir.)

"I even thought about becoming one of those lay brothers in the Catholic church!" he exclaims, sounding delighted for the opportunity to resurrect that particular memory in the context of our conversation about his career as a killer.

A few years later, he signed up to become a member of the National Socialist Party, a white supremacist organization that was headquartered in nearby Mason, Ohio. "I was never really a white supremacist," he explains. "I think I was just curious or something."

He was adrift, searching for some sense of belonging.

"I was doing a lot of drinking, too," he says.

Despite wanting direction and stability, he had no idea how to go about achieving those things. When he returned to the Midwest, he secured jobs—usually as an orderly or ward clerk—at three different health care facilities in Kentucky. None of them lasted for very long.

• • •

In September of 1975, he took a job as a nursing assistant at the Veterans Administration hospital in Cincinnati. While there, he also did some custodial work. The hospital's background check failed to uncover anything concerning about his employment history in Kentucky.

He casually admits responsibility for causing multiple deaths during his employment at the VA hospital. He explains that he continued his practice of manipulating patients' oxygen supply, often with lethal consequences.

"I did other stuff there, too," he says with a shrug. "At least once, I took a hypodermic needle and used it to inject air into a guy's veins. And I'm pretty sure—I can't swear to it— that I used a pillow to smother another guy when I was there. I know for sure that I killed one guy by giving him an overdose of heparin."

Toward the end of the 1970s, he became involved in a relationship with a man named Carl Hoeweler. They'd met at a bar. Donald moved in with Carl in August 1980. It irked him when he learned that Carl was seeing other men on the side, for one-off sexual trysts. To exact revenge, he began putting small quantities of arsenic in Carl's food. Not enough to kill him, just enough to make him ill and unable to report for work. Carl conferred with multiple physicians, hoping to discover the cause of his symptoms. None of the trained professionals diagnosed arsenic poisoning.

Donald's ego swelled.

"It made me feel like I'd put one over on [the doctors]," he says.

He and Carl had a mutual friend named Diane. She and Carl worked at the same hair salon. Donald took steps to poison her, too, in part because he was jealous of her friendship with Carl. Fortunately, the poison she ingested wasn't strong enough to kill her.

A woman who lived in the apartment upstairs wasn't so lucky. Donald feared the possibility that she would come between him and Carl. Even though he considered her a friend, he poisoned her by adding arsenic to some of her leftover food. She died as a result.

"I don't know for sure if the arsenic actually caused her death," he says. "But I'm pretty sure it moved things along." He's smiling broadly as he says this.

"I even acted as a pallbearer at her funeral!" he exclaims. No one suspected him of having caused her death.

When Carl disclosed to him that his father was seriously ill and thinking of ending his life, Donald decided there was a role for him to play. Once again, he employed arsenic. In a week's time, Carl's father was dead.

"Kidney failure and stroke. Those were listed as the causes of death," says Donald.

He was starting to feel invincible.

In mid-1985, he lost his job at the Veterans Administration hospital. Acting on a tip, a member of the hospital's security staff stopped him and found a loaded gun in a gym bag he was carrying. It was a violation of hospital policy for any employee to have a loaded firearm on the premises. As a result of the incident, Donald got fired. However, because the hospital staff bungled aspects of their investigation, the circumstances surrounding his termination never became part of Donald's permanent employment record.

● ● ●

In December of that same year, Donald applied for and was offered a job as a nursing assistant at Drake Hospital in Cincinnati. He began work there in February of 1986. Drake would be his final place of employment before his arrest, which occurred just over a year later.

"How many people did you kill at Drake?"

"Well, there were at least 24," he says, pursing his lips. "Probably more."

When he begins talking about the period of his employment at Drake, I find it hard to keep up with him. At times, he appears to be struggling to recall certain details. Even so, in most respects his memory seems uncanny. Sometimes, for example, he'll preface a description of how he killed someone by referencing that victim's exact room number. He chats amiably about murder in a tone not unlike the tone most other people would employ to chat about the quotidian aspects of their day-to-day lives. He never sounds sad or even the least bit angry. He maintains his steady, affable demeanor as he relates the story of one of the most extravagant killing sprees in modern American history.

By the time he landed at Drake, he'd settled on arsenic and cyanide as his preferred killing agents. But they weren't the only methods he used. To hear him tell it, he "felt sorry for" many of the patients he was assigned to care for on the skilled nursing unit where he worked. He smothered some of them. To put them out of their misery, he says. He experimented with different means of introducing poison into their systems.

Sometimes, he'd mix the poison with their food. Other times, he'd dissolve it in a glass of orange juice or water. There were also times when he'd inject it into their IV tube. While he's telling me of these activities, the thought occurs to me that he could just as well be talking about how to trick a cat into taking a pill prescribed by the vet.

"Most of those patients wanted to die anyway," he observes. "In my mind, I was just helping them do what they couldn't do themselves."

I'm curious to hear more about what his personal life was like during this final, almost frantic chapter of his killing career.

"Well, my relationship with Carl was going to shit for one thing," he says. "By August of that year [1986], I'd had about enough. I was *done*." He moved out of Carl's place and into a mobile home that he'd acquired for himself.

Naturally, I'm wondering why in the world no one at the hospital suspected him in the deaths of so many of his patients. As it turns out, a large number of his co-workers *were* suspicious. But Donald had no idea that was the case.

Most patients who died on his watch never underwent autopsies. In the relatively small subset of cases where an autopsy was performed, the pathologist typically attributed the patient's death to some life-threatening medical condition that was present at the time of death. Pneumonia, for example, or cardiac arrhythmia, or a stroke.

While we're having this conversation, I'm thinking of psychologist Paul Ekman's well-known 1985 book, called *Telling Lies*. In that book, Ekman introduced the phrase "duping delight" to describe the intense pleasure that habitual liars tend to experience when they're able to tell a lie and get away with it. The phrase comes to mind as I'm listening to Donald talk animatedly about how satisfying it was for him to be able to pull the wool over the eyes of physicians and other medical professionals at the hospital, people whose education far exceeded his.

He resented the fact that during his time at Drake, he was often expected to handle duties that he thought should have been *theirs* to handle, especially on weekends. Sometimes he'd find himself stuck at the hospital while the doctors were out playing golf and doing other "fun things."

Killing, lying, and escaping detection fed Donald's ego and allowed him to feel superior, at least for a while. As he saw it, he was "getting back at" people who didn't seem to value him in the way he thought he deserved to be valued.

Years later, I'll think back to my conversation with Donald while viewing the Netflix limited series called *Murder Among the Mormons*, about the extraordinary exploits of Mark Hofmann, who was not only a master forger and skillful liar but a murderer to boot. When the police finally uncover Hofmann's illegal activities, an interviewer invites Hofman to describe the feelings he experienced when he learned that even renowned documents experts hadn't been able to detect his forgeries. After a brief hesitation, Hofmann replies, "Fooling people gave me a sense of power and superiority." It could have been Donald Harvey talking.

What finally brought Harvey's killing spree to an end was the March 1987 death of a patient named John Powell. Harvey killed him using cyanide. Because Powell, a man in his forties, had suffered a traumatic brain injury the year before, Ohio law required that an autopsy be performed. The physician who performed Powell's autopsy was familiar with the "bitter almonds" smell that is associated with cyanide. He realized that in order for cyanide to be present in a human body, someone had to have introduced it through unnatural means.

The physician filed a report with the police. It was the beginning of the end for Donald Harvey. During the first week in April, Harvey was formally charged with first-degree murder. Bill Whalen's appointment as his legal representative occurred by sheer happenstance. Whalen's name, along with many others, was on a list maintained by the local public defender's office of attorneys who were willing to accept felony cases. At the time, no one had even the slightest idea that Harvey would soon be revealed as one of the most prolific serial killers in American history.

"I guess when you were charged, you knew that was the end," I say.

"Yeah, everything went downhill from there," says Donald.

Unlike a lot of other serial killers, who often express haughty disdain for law enforcement officials and blame themselves for whatever missteps led to their detection and capture, Donald maintains the same upbeat demeanor that he's maintained all throughout the interview as he recounts the series of events that led to prison becoming his permanent home: the coroner's discovery of the cyanide, his own refusal to sit for a polygraph examination, his decision to confess to having injected cyanide into Mr. Powell's G-tube, Bill Whalen's appointment as his attorney, his admission to Whalen that he'd killed many more people than the police knew about, and Whalen's successful negotiation of the plea agreement that probably saved him from a death sentence.

By now, Donald and I have utilized nearly all our allotted time. We need to wrap things up. After once again thanking Donald for his willingness to meet with me, I say it's been good talking to him.

"No problem, no problem *at all*!" he says. "I've enjoyed it! Is it just me or did those three hours really fly by?"

"It feels that way to me, too," I say.

I thank Bill Whalen for arranging the interview, and for driving up from Cincinnati to be present for it.

"You're very welcome," he says. "It was time for me to come visit Donald anyway. Right, Donald?"

"Yeah," says Donald. "You know how much I always look forward to seeing you."

A friend later asked me if I was able to come up with a diagnosis for Harvey. I told him no. I explained that even though I spent three hours interviewing Donald, I didn't evaluate him in any formal sense and didn't do many of the things I would have had to do in order to formulate a diagnostic impression (even if that had been my goal, which it wasn't). Still, I said that I left the prison with a set of preliminary ideas about Harvey's psychological makeup.

When Scott Pelley of *60 Minutes* conducted his own interview of Harvey, Pelley offered Donald an opportunity to say whether he had any regrets. Harvey's response? "I regret getting caught."

During my meeting with him, Harvey never expressed remorse for any of his actions. In fact, he seemed pleased to talk with me about all the people he killed. And he loved being the center of attention.

After listening to him recount his life story, I came away thinking that he was an insecure but pathologically self-involved person. In the years leading up to his arrest, he lurched from one experience to another without ever formulating a coherent plan for what he wanted to achieve in life. Or where he wanted his journey to take him. Not just at work but in other domains of his life as well, he was consistently manipulative and deceitful in his manner of interacting with others.

On the surface, he could seem charming, polite, intelligent, and engaging. That's one reason why he was able to escape detection for as long as he did. Below the surface, he was often angry, depressed, resentful of others' successes, and desperate for the recognition he felt certain he deserved. When another interviewer used the term "serial killer" to describe him, Donald bridled at the limits implied by such a well-worn phrase. "I'm Donald Harvey," he insisted. One of a kind, unique. Or so he thought.

There were other dimensions to his personality as well. He attempted suicide—or something like it—on any number of occasions. Probably, these were attention-seeking gambits rather than actual attempts to end his life.

Even though he was often bitter toward other people, he typically took great care to conceal his resentment, and to avoid confrontations. If someone made him angry, and plenty of people did, he would typically strike back through indirect, passive-aggressive means.

Across the various domains of his life, he exhibited an abiding preoccupation with control.

Nearly any mental health professional would probably feel comfortable saying that Harvey had a severe personality disorder, one that included prominent antisocial, narcissistic, passive-aggressive, and "borderline" features.

When used in this context, the word borderline implies a chronic pattern of highly unstable and chaotic interpersonal relationships, as well as some combination of the following: a history of serious mood-related instability, an unstable sense of personal identity, an intense preoccupation with the possibility of abandonment, a highly impulsive decision-making style, a history of maladaptive attention-seeking, chronic feelings of emptiness, the absence of a coherent life plan, and recurring thoughts of suicide.

•••

Almost exactly a decade after he attended my meeting with Harvey, Bill Whalen published a memoir that detailed his role as Donald's legal representative. The book contained plenty of information that was new to me.

For example, I hadn't known the full extent of Donald's involvement in matters related to the occult. Neither had I been aware that he told Whalen of an occult spirit guide named Duncan who allegedly helped him to select some of his victims.

From reading Whalen's account, I also acquired more detailed information about Harvey's history of sexual abuse; about the important role that television newsman Pat Minarcin played in exploding the story of Harvey's killing career; and about the delicate plea negotiations that brought closure to the criminal case against Harvey.

Of particular interest to me were Whalen's disclosures about the nature of his and Harvey's relationship. They helped to explain Whalen's insistence on being present for my interview. They also helped to account for the warmth and familiarity I observed when he and Harvey were greeting one another.

According to Whalen, Harvey considered him not just "the best lawyer in the USA and the world" but his "adopted brother," "best friend," and the closest thing to a father he ever had.

In her April 11, 2022 *New Yorker* article about the self-described serial killer "expert" named Stéphane Bourgoin (who turned out to be something of a fabulist), journalist Lauren Collins quoted a member of Whalen's family as saying that Whalen remained "very proud of" his role as Harvey's defense attorney, right up until the end of his life.

In 2012, Whalen died of suicide.

• • •

On March 28, 2017, five years after Whalen's suicide, Donald Harvey was discovered severely beaten in his cell at the Toledo Correctional Institution. Two days later, he died.

In 2019, an inmate named James Elliott was charged with aggravated murder and a number of other crimes related to Harvey's death.

According to Elliott's confession, he did what he did because he wanted to call attention to the prison's lousy food—and because he grew up in Kentucky, not far from some of the relatives of Harvey's victims.

In a letter to *The Toledo Blade,* he described exactly how he killed Harvey.

"I initially attacked Harvey with facial punches," he said. "After the third or fourth punch, he was knocked unconscious. After which, I stomped his head off the floor seven or eight times with my foot."

He wanted it known that all that pummeling and stomping wasn't done solely for the purpose of ending Harvey's life. He explained that he had another goal: bringing "peace of mind" to the families of Harvey's victims.

9.
The Sole Survivors

It's October 2000, late afternoon on a drab day. Just minutes ago, I arrived in Lancaster, Ohio, best known as the birthplace of William Tecumseh Sherman. The small city in rural Fairfield County is about 30 miles south of Columbus, where I live and maintain my private practice.

Earlier today, I spent five hours in a cramped room at a county jail in the southeastern part of the state, interviewing and doing some preliminary testing of a young man who's charged with aggravated murder. For me, pretty routine stuff.

As I turn left off Rt. 33 and steer my car toward the parking lot of a Lone Star steakhouse, I complete the mental work necessary to make the transition from my role as a forensic psychologist to a different, albeit still very familiar role: Manson case obsessive.

Here, the rabbit hole awaits me.

I've never met Rosie Tate-Polanski—but that has to be her, the diminutive woman I see crossing the parking lot in the direction of the restaurant entrance. She has short, shag-style hair, dyed to a whitish-blond. There are bangs covering her forehead and an up-do dominating the top of her head. She has on a short, form-fitting black dress and matching black shoes. Around her neck is a black choker, about two inches in diameter.

On a weekday afternoon in Lancaster, it's a look bound to turn heads.

As I step from my car and begin my slow walk toward the restaurant door, I fiddle with the clasp on my briefcase and keep my gaze pointed downward, affecting a look of nonchalance. Surely Rosie can see me out of the corner of her one eye, but she doesn't turn her head to look in my direction. *Has* to be him. Who *else* could it be?

I'm in casual business attire: a navy-blue blazer, a white button-down dress shirt, open at the collar, charcoal grey dress slacks, and black shoes.

When the woman's path and mine finally converge, I glance up from my briefcase and our eyes meet for the first time.

"Rosie?"

"*Right!*" she says gaily. "And you must be Jeff!"

I reach out, grab her extended hand, and squeeze it lightly. I notice that she doesn't squeeze back.

A week ago, I had reason to believe today's meeting might never take place. With little advance notice and no real explanation, Rosie backed out of an agreed-to plan to meet me at my office in Columbus. I was relieved when she agreed to reschedule the meeting at some as-yet-unspecified public place closer to where she was staying in nearby South Bloomfield with an older woman named Dolly.

Now, she acts as if her last-minute cancellation didn't happen. She seems genuinely happy to meet me.

Once we're inside the restaurant, we take seats on opposite sides of a small high-top table in the bar area. We engage in a minute or two of small talk: about how overcast the weather is, about how I've spent my day so far, and about the fact that neither of us has ever been to this restaurant before.

When a server arrives at our table, Rosie orders some kind of non-alcoholic beverage for herself. I order a beer. We settle on the most extravagantly decadent appetizer on the menu: french fries slathered in warm, melted cheese. Comfort food.

I know a little about Rosie but not much. She says she's the daughter of film director Roman Polanski and the late actress, Sharon Tate. Not only that, she insists she was cut from Tate's stomach on the night of her murder more than 30 years ago. Only recently has Rosie decided to make her existence—and the startling sequence of events that she says made it possible—known to the world at large.

Anyone with even a modicum of knowledge about the Manson murder case knows that in August of 1969, Tate was eight-and-a-half months pregnant when she was slaughtered inside her home on Cielo Drive, high in the Hollywood Hills.

I know what readers will think: the baby in Tate's stomach at the time of her death was a *boy*—and the baby died along with his mother. Prosecutor Vincent Bugliosi said as much in his closing statement at the Manson defendants' trial. A recently published book, based primarily on a journal kept by the jury foreman during that trial, includes an explicit reference to the unborn "son" who died when Tate died. According to the official version of the story, the child is buried in a grave next to his mother's, beneath a small stone on which are engraved the words, "Paul Richard Polanski, Their Baby."

End of story, right?

Wrong, says Rosie, fake news. According to her, the official narrative was and is an elaborate lie, part of a carefully orchestrated cover-up that was known to only a small cadre of people, including Hollywood A-listers like Frank Sinatra and Steve McQueen.

As you might suppose, there's a backstory—and what a backstory it is!

My desire to hear the backstory in person is the main reason why I'm here in Lancaster. Plus, I'm eager for the opportunity to take the measure of this woman who claims to have survived one of the most notorious mass killings in modern American history, the same one that Joan Didion designated as the event that brought the '60s to a sudden, screeching halt.

Uncertain how to go about trying to win Rosie's favor and confidence, I decide to start slowly, with an expression of trust.

"So, Rosie," I say, "I've been looking forward to meeting you. Amazing that you're here in Ohio, not just Ohio but Lancaster! I couldn't believe it when I read who your parents are!"

Rosie smiles at me from across the table, peering directly

into my eyes.

"Jeff," she says, "c'mon, man! Just look at me! Look at my *face!*"

She says this as if she's pointing to something so obvious, only a fool would fail to see it.

"Tell me I'm not the spitting image of my mother!" she exclaims.

During Sharon Tate's lifetime, Tate was said to be among the world's most beautiful women. Rosie won't soon be mistaken for one of those.

I'm flustered, briefly. It takes me several moments to size up the situation and regain my composure. In one fleeting moment, I settle on a strategy for handling something that I should have anticipated but didn't. Meanwhile, Rosie is staring straight at me, awaiting my appraisal.

Hoping I can avoid making things any more awkward than they are already, I conduct a lightning-quick survey of Rosie's facial features. I scan her eyes, her nose, her mouth, and her chin. Slowly then, I tilt my head to one side, then the other, scrutinizing her face from multiple vantage points. When I'm done doing that, I shift my gaze upward and hold it there, like I'm pondering the implications of her hair and the way she has it styled.

I squint and fashion my face into an expression that says I'm at least open to the possibility that what Rosie's just said is something other than bullshit of the highest order.

"Wait!" I say, like I'm on the verge of an epiphany. "I can see it now! Definitely!"

In an instant, Rosie's smile gets broader and a whole lot brighter.

And I'm saying to myself, *Nice save.*

• • •

Until two months ago, I'd never even heard the name Rosie Tate-Polanski. On August 21, I happened upon a startling column in my local newspaper, written by reporter Steve Stephens. The column's title? "Conspiracy buffs have a way to go to top this one on Sharon Tate."

Sharon Tate?

Those two words were all I needed to see; instantly, I was hooked. Almost 30 years ago, when I was a junior in college, I began my obsessive personal inquiry into the notorious murder case involving Charles Manson and his band of disciples. I didn't even need to read Stephens' column to know it would be Manson-related. Not many people were still talking about *Eye of the Devil, The Wrecking Crew*, and *Valley of the Dolls*, Sharon Tate's best-known films. Nor were they still talking about Tate's guest appearances on television shows like *Mister Ed* and *The Beverly Hillbillies*. For better or worse, in the years since 1969 Sharon Tate and Charles Manson had become inextricably linked in the popular imagination, two central players in the mythology that had grown up around the Manson murder case.

So I started reading.

Then thought, *Wait, what?*

Stephens reminded his readers that on the morning after Sharon Tate and four other people were murdered on a secluded property off Benedict Canyon Road, high above Beverly Hills and Bel Air, the police thought William ("Bill") Garretson, a teenager originally from a small town in Ohio, was probably the one responsible for the massacre.

At the time of the murders, Garretson was employed as a "caretaker" by property owner Rudi Altobelli, and he was present on the Cielo Drive property when the killings took place. He lived in a small guest cottage, located on the other side of an in-ground swimming pool, a short distance from the rental house that Tate and Roman Polanski had moved into earlier that year. Garretson would later insist that his stereo was on and he knew nothing about anyone being killed on the property that night.

When the police showed up the morning after the murders and discovered the five victims, they arrested Garretson and identified him as their primary suspect. Although he was never formally charged, he was questioned, then given a polygraph examination that came back "inconclusive." After three days, the police finally let him go. He returned home to Ohio but later appeared as a witness at the trial of Manson and his three female codefendants (one of whom was Susan Atkins).

The year before the appearance of Stephens' column, Garretson, who had always shied away from publicity, agreed to be interviewed for a special on *E! Television* that was timed to coincide with the 30-year anniversary of the Manson murders.

Not long after the program aired, Garretson answered the telephone at the house he shared with his mother in tiny Carroll, Ohio, population about 600. Before even identifying herself, the female caller asked the question that was foremost in her mind: "Are you William Garretson, the former caretaker to the Polanski estate at 10050 Cielo Drive?"

As it turned out, Rosie had been watching when the interview featuring Garretson aired on *E! Television*. Now, she wanted assurances that the person on the other end of the phone was *the* William Garretson. Later, she would cite this first phone call as the crucial event that paved the way for their "reunion." It wasn't long before Rosie had made the journey to Ohio and appeared on Bill's doorstep. In a matter of months, the two were engaged to be married.

It seems Rosie had persuaded Bill that a small group of celebrities with close connections to Roman Polanski and Sharon Tate had conspired to keep members of the public from learning the truth, which was that Tate's baby—not a boy but a girl—had survived the Cielo Drive massacre. And Rosie was that baby girl! All grown up now!

For three decades, Garretson had been struggling to come to terms with what exactly happened—and what he himself experienced—before the police led him away in handcuffs the morning after the murders. Rosie was eager to fill in some of the gaps in his memory. She would later say that she and Bill bonded almost instantly over their recognition that they were the "only two survivors" of the nocturnal attack that left five people dead.

Stephens, the *Columbus Dispatch* columnist, apparently knew little, if any, of this background information when he and two Ohio University journalism students accepted invitations to attend a memorial service that Rosie was planning to host at a Best Western motel in Lancaster, not far from Carroll, ostensibly as a way of honoring the memories of the Cielo Drive victims.

In his column, Stephens described the scene he encountered when he showed up for the service, slated to take place in the motel's banquet room.

He wrote that the room was "adorned with photos of the Manson victims, candles, confetti, and Sharon Tate memorabilia." Although the room was designed to accommodate up to 50 people, he, the two journalism students, Bill, Rosie, Rosie's former husband Leslie (her "deepest confidant"), and a woman named Margaret, whom Rosie identified as her closest friend, were the only people present. Well, not quite. There was also four-year-old Sharon Tate, Jr., Rosie's "cute-as-a-button" daughter from her marriage to Leslie.

The small group waited a while to see if any other guests would arrive. None did. Eventually, the group began "its lengthy mélange of prayers, tributes, balloon drops, and music."

Due to "lack of personnel," Stephens himself was recruited to play an active role in the ceremony. Specifically, he was assigned responsibility for lighting a candle to honor the memory of Leno LaBianca, the grocer who, along with his wife, Rosemary, was butchered by members of the Manson Family on the night immediately following the night of the Cielo Drive murders.

With the candle-lighting part of the ceremony behind them, the organizers of the event bestowed posthumous awards upon a number of the decedents. Sharon Tate was named the recipient of a "Lifetime Achievement Award." Hairdresser-to-the-stars Jay Sebring, a former boyfriend of Tate's and another of the Cielo Drive victims, was awarded a "Medal of Honor." The "Humanitarian Award" went to coffee heiress and social activist Abigail Folger, another of the victims.

According to Stephens' firsthand account, at one point during the ceremony Elton John's *Someone Saved My Life Tonight* could be heard playing in the background, on someone's portable stereo. Troubled by the thought that Sebring hadn't been recognized sufficiently for the heroism he displayed by extracting Rosie from her mother's belly (more on that later), Rosie attached an "honorary eagle pin" to his Medal of Honor.

Rosie explained to Stephens that as she saw it, her primary role was to bear public witness to the truth of what really happened on the night of the Cielo Drive murders. "Had I not been the surviving child, I probably never would have believed it either," she said.

But believe it she did (or so she said)—and she'd made a believer out of Garretson, too. She informed Stephens that she and Bill were hoping Roman Polanski would agree to DNA testing. If only they could secure his consent, she knew for certain that the results would establish once and for all that she was, in fact, his and Sharon Tate's biological child.

At the time of the memorial service—which, according to what four-year-old Sharon Jr. told Stephens, wasn't even the first one of its kind—Rosie and Bill hadn't yet set a date for their wedding. Rosie explained to Stephens that not everything had been smooth sailing since their reunion some six months prior. They'd weathered their share of "ups and downs." "But," she added, they'd "survived the same murder(s)"—and no one else could possibly appreciate the shared trauma they'd experienced as a result.

Bill hadn't been all that eager to participate in the memorial service. Rosie told Stephens, "It was very difficult for [Bill] to be here today, but his love for me superseded his fear."

Stephens found Bill a lot less voluble than Rosie. Bill admitted that he himself wasn't entirely sure *what* he remembered from the night of the murders. Rosie, he said, was helping him with that. "It didn't all come back to me all at once," he explained. "It was gradual. And I really started remembering things after I met Rosie. But the truth has a way of coming out."

And that was it: pretty much everything I learned as a result of reading Stephens' column.

I remember thinking, *I don't know how, but one way or an-*

other I need to find a pathway into this story. So I did.

• • •

The same day Stephens' column appeared in the paper, I phoned him and left a message, asking if he'd be willing to provide me with Rosie's contact information. He called back and said sure.

Using the information he provided, I placed a phone call to Rosie. When she picked up, I introduced myself as a forensic psychologist from Columbus and explained that I'd learned about her and her background from reading Stephens' column. I emphasized that even though my work was nearly all forensic in nature, I'd become a close student of the Manson case more than a decade before the idea of becoming a forensic psychologist ever even occurred to me.

She was cordial—but that was about it. There was an undercurrent of wariness in the way she talked to me. After about five minutes of stilted conversation, most of it about the origins of my interest in the Manson case, I told her of my desire to hear more about the story she shared with Stephens. She expressed a willingness to meet with me in person. I proposed that the meeting take place at my office in Columbus. She agreed—but as I've said, she pulled out of the meeting before it could take place.

When she informed me—through a message left on my office answering machine—that she didn't feel comfortable driving up to Columbus to meet with me, I phoned her back, hoping that she'd agree to an alternative plan. What if, instead of her coming to Columbus, I came to her? She thought that sounded like an excellent idea. During the next week, we faxed a few friendly notes back and forth. At her suggestion, we settled on the Lone Star steakhouse in Lancaster as the venue for our meeting.

Meanwhile, she offered to share with me a 15-page, typewritten account of what she was claiming really happened back in 1969, not only in the days and weeks leading up to the carnage on Cielo Drive but on the actual night of the murders.

I assured her of my interest. When she sent the account, she included a brief handwritten note: "If you have any questions feel free to call me. Best regards, Rosie Tate-Polanski."

In truth, I found it hard to believe that Rosie possessed much, if any, information beyond what I already knew. After all, I'd gobbled up pretty much every Manson-related book and article I could get my hands on during a period that spanned almost 25 years.

But still. Who was I to assume I knew what was true and what wasn't about a case that had long since been taken over by the myth-making machinery of American popular culture? In *Helter Skelter*, far and away the best-known account of the case, prosecutor Vincent Bugliosi was highly critical of some of the law enforcement officers who processed the Cielo Drive crime scene. (One of them, blood specialist Joe Granado, ended up joining the FBI and working alongside my dad at the FBI's field office in Buffalo.)

Later, lots of people with firsthand knowledge leveled criticism at Bugliosi. Some of them insisted that he'd misled the public about many important aspects of the case. In fact, I read somewhere that he'd been named as the defendant in multiple civil lawsuits because of things he wrote about people in *Helter Skelter*.

The bottom line: when it came to the Manson murder case, it wasn't always obvious who knew the truth and who didn't—and who was telling it and who wasn't.

At the very least, I was willing to entertain the possibility that some of the case's best-known chroniclers were wrong about certain things. Perhaps, I thought, they were wrong because they themselves had been the victims of a disinformation campaign, spearheaded by powerful people who had something to gain—for example a cluster of very high-profile, career-enhancing convictions—from promoting a false or misleading narrative about what really happened and why that night on Cielo Drive, and about what transpired in the days, weeks, and months that preceded the murders.

Many years later, in a memoir published in 2017, songwriter Jimmy Webb would quote his former close friend Cass

Elliott as having told him that she was actually present at the Cielo Drive site on the night of the murders, after the killers had already left the scene. *That* was never part of the official narrative.

In a 2017 post on the *Manson Family Blog*, which was still seeing an enormous amount of traffic almost 50 years after the murders, someone would write, "One supposes that the true story of what happened at the house on Cielo Drive … will come out sooner or later."

And in 2019, veteran journalist Tom O'Neill would publish a much-discussed book titled *Chaos: Charles Manson, the CIA, and the Secret History of the Sixties* that referenced "the Manson story as we knew it" and pointed to a veritable mountain of new information that called into question nearly every dimension of the official narrative.

Point being, in 2000 there were still plenty of questions about the case that hadn't yet been answered to everyone's satisfaction. As I prepared to read Rosie's account, I paused to reflect on the fact that Bill Garretson—who was actually *there* the night of the murders—was now insisting that her version was his version, too.

I was at least open to listening.

●●●

I hunkered down with Rosie's document, unsure what to expect.

Here, in greatly condensed form, is the truth according to Rosie. (To capture the flavor of Rosie's often melodramatic writing style, I've included any number of unedited quotations, drawn directly from the text of her narrative.)

By the summer of 1969, in the months that immediately preceded the murders, the Tate/Polanski marriage was in serious trouble. So, too, was the relationship between the temporary house guests on Cielo Drive, Voytek Frykowski and Abigail Folger.

Like Sharon Tate's close friend, Jay Sebring, Frykowski and Folger had become involved in the murky world of drugs and drug-dealing. Sebring and Folger had also been dabbling in Satanism. That brought them into contact with members of an organization called The Process Church of the Final Judgment (hereafter referred to as "The Process Church").

Somewhere along the line, all three—Sebring, Frykowski, and Folger—had crossed paths with a lifelong hustler named Charlie.

According to Rosie's account, Sharon Tate was wrestling with the fear that she'd become pregnant "for the wrong reasons," chief among them her desire "to control Roman's skirt-chasing." She was confused and upset, preoccupied with "questions that haunted painfully in her heart." When Tate returned home from Europe that summer, Polanski remained abroad, working on a movie project in England.

Upon Sharon's return to the States, she encountered a scene at the Cielo Drive house that was a far cry from the tranquil scene she'd been hoping for as she prepared to deliver her baby in August. It was a scene of "drug-infested exploitation and mayhem," with Voytek Frykowski presiding.

In July, things took a dark, downward turn. Frykowski sold a bad batch of MDA—a synthetic amphetamine with hallucinogenic properties—to an acquaintance named Gary Hinman, who also happened to know members of the Manson Family. Hinman, in need of fast cash, turned around and sold some of the drugs to members of a biker gang. Subsequently, the gang members became ill.

The bikers set out in search of Manson, convinced that he was somehow at fault for the drug burn (in part because he'd burned them in the past). Manson, alerted to their hostility, tracked down Hinman and Frykowski. He was unhappy about having to take the heat for something he hadn't even done.

During the last week in July, he dispatched several of his followers to Hinman's Topanga Canyon house and instructed them to rob him. As Manson saw it, whatever money they could extract from Hinman would somehow make things even, "level out the karma." When the robbery attempt failed miserably, Hinman wound up dead.

Days later, the police arrested one of Hinman's killers, close Manson Family associate Bobby "Cupid" Beausoleil (who was in possession of Hinman's car at the time of his arrest). Unnerved by Beausoleil's apprehension, Manson sought assistance from The Process Church (through which he'd met Abigail Folger a year or two prior). The Church members surprised him by claiming that there were plenty of people who wanted Frykowski and Folger dead, "due to the drugs and bad dope deals."

Desperate for money to satisfy the debt that the bikers insisted he owed them (because of the bad drugs they'd obtained from Hinman), Manson accepted a deal proposed to him by members of The Process Church. According to the provisions of the deal, the Church would front him the money he needed—if, in return, he would orchestrate the deaths of Folger and Frykowski. To Manson, it apparently sounded like a reasonable quid pro quo.

Through the drug-related grapevine, Sebring and Frykowski got word that Manson had hatched a plan to kill Frykowski and Folger. According to Rosie's account, Frykowski didn't take the rumor seriously. However, Sebring *did*. In fact, Sebring even went so far as to solicit help from some close friends of his, people like Frank Sinatra and Steve McQueen—with the goal of ensuring the safety of Sharon Tate and her unborn baby.

For complicated reasons, Manson came to believe that on the night of August 8-9, Frykowski and Folger would be alone at the Cielo Drive house. The other three people who were there that night, and who ended up dead, were unintended collateral damage.

During the daytime hours before the night of the murders, Bill Garretson spent most of his time at home in the guest cottage. He was nursing a nasty hangover. That evening, he decided to go out to get something to eat. Because he didn't have access to a car, he walked a short distance, then stuck out his thumb and hitched a ride down to Sunset Boulevard.

Subsequently, he got a couple of other lifts. As it turned out, he was picked up not once but twice by members of the

Manson Family. The first time, Manson himself was the driver who picked him up. To Bill, Manson seemed "deranged."

The second time, a small group of young people who Bill later came to believe were members of the Manson Family picked him up and started "acting strangely." Bill noticed that they had some unusual accessories, like rope and a knife. During the relatively brief window of time between these latter two hitchhiking episodes, Bill encountered Manson again. According to Rosie's account, he gave Manson 50 cents.

All these events happened during the evening hours, just prior to the Cielo Drive murders.

The people Garretson thought were "acting strangely" gave him a lift all the way to the gate that provided access to the Cielo Drive property. There, Garretson exited the car. He couldn't figure out why there were electrical wires down on the ground near the gate. Apparently, someone had cut the wires and let them drop. Even more perplexing to Bill was the fact that the people who had driven him to the gate appeared to have an easy familiarity with the location.

Not long after Bill made his way to the guest cottage, he entertained a visitor named Steve Parent. The two had met a few days prior, when Parent provided Bill with a lift. Now, Parent was back, wanting to see if Bill had any interest in purchasing a clock radio. While they were talking, "[a] profound and foreboding feeling was there." The feeling became even more pronounced when Bill asked Parent for a ride to a friend's house, and Parent turned him down.

Parent left by himself. Following his departure, Bill spent the rest of the night alone in the guest cottage. He remembered hearing some unusual sounds, for example loud blasts that he thought might have been either firecrackers or a car backfiring. He convinced himself that the sounds were nothing to worry about. During the summer months, he'd occasionally heard loud sounds, like party noises, coming from the main house. Perhaps there was some sort of social gathering going on tonight, too. In any case, given the history he wasn't easily rattled or alarmed by loud, unexpected noises.

Still, there was a point that night when he had a strong

sense that something different may have been happening. He heard loud screams, including some that sounded like they might have been coming from a woman who believed she was dying.

Fearing for his own safety, he began to compose letters to some close friends and family members. According to Rosie, the letters were his way of saying goodbye. He hoped that if something happened to him that night or, worst case scenario, he ended up dead, the letters would eventually land in the hands of the people for whom they were intended.

Meanwhile, there was a massacre taking place: inside the main house, on the lawn outside the house, and at the foot of the driveway, near the gate. Sharon Tate pleaded with the killers to "let her have her baby," or to "cut the baby out." Ignoring her pleas, one of the killers, Charles "Tex" Watson, plunged a bayonet into her stomach. Another of the killers, Susan Atkins, stuck a knife "into the baby belly."

Jay Sebring, Tate's close friend and former lover, had been shot—but he wasn't yet dead when the killers left the property. According to Rosie's account, he managed to extract the baby from Tate's belly at right around the time when "two of [Sebring's] men" arrived on the scene, ostensibly because they wanted to see whether the rumored hit on Frykowski and Folger had taken place that night. Their thinking was that if Manson's people hadn't carried out the hit, maybe they would.

After Sebring "delivered" Tate's baby, born with the umbilical cord "wrapped around her neck," Sebring cut the cord and "gave what air he could into the child." Not yet dead, Tate asked for reassurance that the baby had "all her fingers and toes." Then, she "died watching her child be put into a blanket."

Sebring's "men," accompanied by the badly wounded Sebring, left the main house and made their way to the guest cottage, where Bill, the sole occupant, came face to face with Sebring at the door. He was "holding a newborn baby." Sebring entered the cottage to "[check] the phone."

Per Rosie, "William noticed the tiny baby wrapped in a blanket had a mark on its head like a third eye. Fascinated, he stared at the child, Sharon's baby. Big blue eyes, straight eyebrows, and this brown birth [mark] or stab wound just above the nose between the eyes."

Sebring handed the baby to Garretson as he and his associates "hovered discussing what to do." Sebring decided to send the baby to "Frank's house." At that point, Bill handed the baby back to one of the "men in suits" and tried to follow the three men as they headed in the direction of the main house. The men threatened him and told him he needed to return to the guest cottage.

"Being carried away was the child of Roman and Sharon Polanski. [Bill and Rosie] wouldn't see one another until 30 years later." The baby wound up at Frank Sinatra's house that night, where the singer's "personal physician" tended to her and made sure she was all right.

Later that same night, Bill, confused but still thinking all the strange voices he'd heard earlier must have been from "another wild party, not murder," felt "drawn to his window." When he looked out, he saw someone who he later realized was Charles Manson, accompanied by a second man. He watched as Manson entered the main house. Then Manson and his companion started "yelling and screaming."

Suddenly, the noise stopped. According to Rosie's account, Sebring was still alive when Manson and the second man arrived at the Cielo Drive property. They bludgeoned Sebring to death after failing to convince him to disclose the whereabouts of Tate's baby. His refusal to comply with their demand "cost him his life."

From his window, Bill observed Manson leave the premises. At this point, Bill still hadn't seen any of the dead bodies (in fact didn't even know a mass murder had taken place). When dawn arrived, he let property owner Rudi Altobelli's dogs go outside "for bathroom calls." Then he laid down on his couch, reflecting, before he fell asleep, on what a strange and confusing night it had been.

Some hours later, the police arrived on the scene. Before long, Bill was "formally booked and arrested [for] the murders of Sharon Tate, Jay Sebring, Abigail Folger, Voytek Frykowski, and Steve Parent." As it turned out, Parent had been shot by the killers just minutes after he left the guest cottage, while he was seated in his car inside the gate at the top of the driveway that led away from the property.

When I was done reading the document Rosie had prepared, I thought, *Is this woman mad?*

Parts of Rosie's account sounded like they might have originated in a hallucinatory fever dream. (Remember, at this point I still hadn't met Rosie—didn't even know what she looked like.)

Just to reiterate, a few highlights from the document Rosie sent me: Bill being given lifts, first from Manson himself and then from a group of Manson Family members—the killers!—in the hours just before the massacre on Cielo Drive; Bill encountering Manson a second time that same evening—and giving him 50 cents; "men in suits" roaming around the crime scene in the middle of the night, shortly after the murders had taken place; an infant with a mark on her head "like a third eye"—Rosie!—being placed into Bill's arms by Sebring and his accomplices; those same accomplices—the "men in suits"—threatening Bill and then whisking Rosie away so that she could be tended to by Frank Sinatra's personal physician.

Not to put too fine a point on it, but those parts of Rosie's account struck me as absolutely bonkers. Even so, I kept reminding myself, *Don't be too quick to judge. Garretson himself is apparently prepared to vouch for the truth of all this.*

Other parts of Rosie's narrative seemed far more plausible. A botched drug deal? Possibly. A revenge "hit" gone wrong? Perhaps. Bill beset with a sense of foreboding just before the murders? Maybe.

Those parts struck me as less far-fetched, especially in light of the fact that well-known commentators on the Manson case had been raising serious questions about the accuracy of many of Vincent Bugliosi's claims almost from the moment *Helter Skelter* hit the bookshelves, way back in 1974.

•••

Next from Rosie came a second typewritten document, this one said to have been authored by "Rosie Tate-Polanski with William Garretson." It included details about what became of Bill in the immediate aftermath of the murders. Also included in the document were additional details about the first chapter of Rosie's life, reportedly based on some things Rosie had been told by other people with firsthand knowledge of the situation.

Conspicuously absent were any details about Rosie's childhood and adolescence—in other words, the long period leading up to the pivotal point when she discovered her true identity. After she found out that she was the daughter of Sharon Tate and Roman Polanski, she embarked on a "ten-year investigation," hoping to build on what little she knew about her own origin story. The investigation culminated with her phone call to Bill Garretson, her appearance on Bill's doorstep, and their decision to get engaged.

According to this second document, Bill was still asleep on the morning of August 9 when Rudi Altobelli's Weimaramer started to bark. The Weimaramer was one of three dogs Bill had been hired to care for that summer. Moments after Bill became aware of the barking, the police entered the guest cottage, their guns drawn. Bill, shoeless and shirtless at the time, asked, "What's wrong?"

The police "pushed him onto the ground" and placed him under arrest. Apparently, they believed they had the person who was responsible for the five dead bodies they'd discovered in the driveway, inside the main house, and on the lawn outside. They instructed Bill to "shut up," then took him down the path that led from the guest cottage to the main house. They planned to observe his reaction when he viewed the mutilated bodies of Abigail Folger and Voytek Frykowski.

Bill kept insisting that he had no knowledge of any murders. Nonetheless, the police placed him in their squad car, transported him to the police station, fingerprinted him, and began questioning him about the events of the night before. Following brief visits from two attorneys, Bill was forced to endure the police officers' "confusion and ... head games" for two entire days. He "couldn't shower, couldn't brush his teeth, or comb his hair." He took a polygraph test that came back "inconclusive."

Meanwhile, "the name-calling, the head games of manipulation, and [the] humiliation" continued unabated. The police wanted to break him … [they] wanted to use him as a scapegoat." They were convinced they "had [their] guy."

Even though Leno and Rosemary LaBianca were murdered the very next night, while Bill was still in police custody, and even though the two crime scenes were eerily similar — e.g., at both sites there were messages left behind in the victims' blood — the police were not convinced of Bill's innocence. As far as they were concerned, the LaBianca murders made sense as the work of a copycat killer.

Finally, three days after Bill's arrest, the police released him. They sent him off with only "a white wrinkled shirt and thongs for his feet." By then, he was "shaken, moody, and tearful. The scars had begun to happen."

It took a while, but the police had finally come around to believing him when he insisted he knew nothing about any murders. Four days after his release from custody, he and his mother, who had flown to California to be with him, returned to Bill's hometown of Carroll, Ohio. First, however, Bill and his attorney, a man named Barry Farlow, "faced the media frenzy together." Farlow answered the reporters' questions; Bill "just [gazed] into the glare of the … camera lights."

• • •

The remainder of the story contained in this second document is told in a voice that clearly belongs to Rosie. Consider: "The burial of my Mother [sic] was on Wednesday, August 13, 1969… My father crumbled many times during and after the service. [Sharon Tate] was laid to rest at Holy Cross Cemetery in Culver City, CA."

Following this glancing reference to Tate's funeral and Polanski's distress, Rosie's account veers wildly away from the "official" narrative: "It had been widely reported that the child Sharon carried had died with her. They also said that the baby was a boy and wrapped in a cloth, placed in a casket at [Sharon's] feet."

Lies, says Rosie; she has "proof."

"Years later," she writes, "it would be revealed to one of the counselors at [the cemetery] that the mortician, Richard Cunningham, never placed a baby there [alongside Sharon Tate's casket]. He admitted only having the one body of Sharon and her papers, not any documents or body of any baby. [The mortician] explained that he prepared Sharon's body for the service and burial. Finally, he [said] there wasn't any baby, just Sharon."

"Later on when he and the coroner were questioned again, they denied all statements and didn't want to be questioned. The counselor from Holy Cross [who] had the information was then fired … They had to get rid of him, he had the knowledge that was so desperately trying to be kept silence [sic]. He had confirmed admission statements from the mortician, and it [sic] had opened Pandora's Box."

If one were inclined to accept Rosie as a reliable informant or even as an informant who *might* be reliable, there would then be some basis for wondering whether the official narrative about the burial of a near-term baby boy named Paul Richard Polanski might have been false from the get-go, part of a deliberate attempt to obscure the truth and mislead the public.

It should perhaps come as no surprise that Rosie's account of "what really happened" features … Rosie!

She writes that after Sharon Tate's funeral, "the decision was rendered" to relocate her [Rosie] from Palm Springs to New York, as far away as possible from the "panic and fear" that was gripping Hollywood in the aftermath of the murders. "The intent was to remove [the baby] completely … [to place her] out of harm's way."

Partly, says Rosie, that was because Manson was so determined to hunt her down and kill her. "Manson was still on the move, and with his wide street network, he was looking for me. Due to the fact he felt humiliated that [one person] had escaped, he vowed to find [me] and put [me] in a shoebox, dressed like a doll. Then he wanted to send the box to my father, to get his point across. For this reason, Frank [Sinatra] only had a selected vast few [sic] have knowledge of my existence … for obvious security reasons."

With Manson fuming over her disappearance, and with the shadowy network of Sinatra-Polanski-Sebring sympathizers intent on keeping her safe, the infant Rosie ended up getting passed around like a hot potato: "It was decided, for my protection, to keep me moving."

Rosie includes a reference to various "agencies" that got involved, the kinds of organizations that specialize in finding help for children considered "high-risk." It "wasn't [quite] like going into Witness Protection, but it was the next best thing," writes Rosie. "Both Frank Sinatra and Jay Sebring had connections with these agencies. So that's where it began, the underground world, the Mafia."

How Rosie might have obtained this information is anyone's guess (if, that is, she didn't just make it all up). I had plans to inquire—but for reasons I'll explain in the following pages, those plans never came to fruition.

"The call went out looking for prospective parents" in the days and weeks following Rosie's birth. Around that time, "a new face … entered the picture, the actress Patty Duke." Duke and Sharon Tate had become friendly when they were filming *Valley of the Dolls* together. Following that movie's release, Tate and Polanski even rented Duke's home for a while.

Jay Sebring and Patty Duke knew many of the same Hollywood scenesters. "It was these friends and favors that were utilized during the first important hours after my birth," writes Rosie. Patty Duke's first cousin, a woman named Noreen McMahon, and Noreen's husband, whose name was Edward Blanchard, "were desperate for a child under any condition [sic]." They hadn't been able to conceive themselves, and their attempts to adopt had so far been unsuccessful. "It seemed like possibly the ideal situation."

Rosie, "the Sebring men" who had removed her from the Cielo Drive property, and Patty Duke all flew to New York on Frank Sinatra's private plane. (At this point, Rosie pauses to remark, "Tina Sinatra [Frank's daughter] makes mention of this flight in general prospective [sic] in her new book, released this month.")

When all was said and done, Rosie ended up with the Blanchard family. Noreen and Edward welcomed her into their lives "with open arms," even though they weren't sure what they were getting into. Before actually seeing Rosie for the first time, they'd assumed she "had Down's syndrome, or was mentally retarded." All they'd been told was that a "high-risk baby" and "high-maintenance child" needed to be placed and placed soon. In part because their "desperation was so high," they agreed to accept Rosie, sight unseen, and to raise her as their own.

There was no formal adoption, then or ever.

"It was obvious from the start, a bonding had occurred." The bond between Rosie and Noreen was especially close. Even so, the two ended up being separated when Manson and his codefendants went on trial. During the trial, Rosie "would be in the home of many, including a convent." The idea was to keep her safe. Rosie's handlers felt certain the Manson Family was still out to get her.

Per Rosie, "Everyone had come this far; they didn't want any mistakes."

There were many "close calls." However, Rosie wouldn't learn of those until years later. Eventually, she would be told that two of Jay Sebring's "associates" took "an oath with regard to [her]," a pledge that they would never tell anyone about her or her whereabouts.

Members of Manson's "underground street network" succeeded in locating the two men. They were both "killed, mysteriously," one in New York, the other in Florida. Their "brutal" murders came about because they refused, "on separate occasions," to disclose Rosie's whereabouts. In the end, they died "protecting [Rosie's] life and true identity."

Following the convictions—and death sentences—of Manson and his three codefendants, "Frank [Sinatra] had to make a crucial decision." It entailed taking steps to keep Rosie's identity secret, not just then but in the coming years.

According to Rosie, he arranged for the creation of a false birth certificate, "with false information." He "also managed to have hospital records [created] and photos of [Rosie] taken, to document that [she] belonged to the Blanchards."

As it turned out, Rosie never did "belong to" them, at least legally. Rosie writes that hers was "considered a black-market adoption, [an] under-the-table type deal"—in other words, no adoption at all. Noreen Blanchard would reportedly say of Rosie in years to come, "She wasn't born with an umbilical cord, she was born with a price tag."

Per Rosie's account, the counterfeit records that Sinatra demanded be produced as a way of "proving" Rosie's fake identity misstated her age to make it appear like she was two years younger than she really was. Rosie: "Since I was quite small and frail for my age, it worked."

Then, "The paper trace [sic] was done, sealed and every piece carefully fitted. The truth had no way to reveal itself then or later. That's what they hoped for, it wasn't meant to stay that way though. I was spared at least until my early twenties."

At that point, Noreen Blanchard finally told her the truth—or at least some of it.

•••

The "truth" might not have set Rosie free—but it did set her in motion. She embarked on a ten-year journey to discover the details of her origin story. According to her own telling of it, what she discovered was a mysterious, multi-layered tale with roots in the Sixties and a colorful cast of gangsters, drug-dealers, amateur Satanists, movie stars, killers, victims ... and a small-town boy named Bill Garretson. Eventually, of course, her path and Bill's converged in Carroll, Ohio.

When Rosie agreed to meet me at the Lone Star steakhouse in Lancaster, she mentioned that maybe Bill would be available to join us there. *Would that be all right with me?* Yes, of course. In truth, I thought meeting Bill Garretson would be a little like coming into possession of the holy grail. After all, he was there on the Cielo Drive property when the murders of Sharon Tate and four others were committed in August of 1969.

On October 14, Rosie faxed me a letter. She said she needed to update me on Bill's situation, which didn't sound good. In a separate letter, she'd already informed me that together, they'd made the decision to call off their engagement. In this most recent note, she told me she had called and left a message on Bill's answering machine, informing him of her plans to meet with me, and telling him he would be welcome to join us. So far, he hadn't responded. She said she was concerned about his mental state. "He is showing signs of severe and deep depression," she wrote. "Part of this is because of our break-up, and second is the fact he feels he will be arrested with regard to the murders."

Arrested with regard to the murders? I hadn't the slightest idea what she was talking about.

She continued, "As I told my father, Roman Polanski, Bill had known the hit was going to happen at our home [those are the words she used, *our home*], and he knew in ample time to warn my Mother [sic]. He chose not to warn anyone in [sic] fear that he would not be believed. In essence, his judgment call could've saved their lives and changed the course of fate."

What she said next made me think Bill was teetering on the edge of madness—or perhaps looking back from somewhere beyond the edge. She reported having gone to his house the day before, ostensibly so that she could collect some of her belongings. When she got there, she noticed that he had "weird signs hanging up in the screened-in porch. One read 'LAPD stay out, not welcome.'"

For reasons not hard to understand, she was alarmed. "All I could do was take in what I had seen," she wrote. She "knew in [her] heart that the repercussions of [the murders] were finally taking their toll on [Bill]." She felt helpless in the face of his deterioration. She added that even though they were no longer planning to get married, she would always have "a special place in [her] heart" for him. She added, "I wish him only the best and some peace for his weary soul."

In light of these developments, I thought it highly unlikely that I would get the chance to meet Garretson. I wasn't prepared to give up, though. I thought the situation might still be fluid.

On October 18, just five days before I was scheduled to meet with Rosie, she faxed me another letter. This one rekindled my hopes. She said she'd spoken to Bill for several hours the day before. He'd informed her that what he wanted most of all was a "private meeting" with me, preferably at his house in Carroll. She explained that due to his work schedule—he was a truck driver who often worked ten-hour days)—he wouldn't be able to join us at the Lone Star steakhouse.

According to her, Bill wanted to talk with me "regarding the murders, the aftermath, and the trauma" he'd experienced. "I can respect his wishes," she wrote. "I hope you understand." I did, or thought I did. I was still doubtful about whether I would actually get to speak with Bill, but Rosie gave me his home phone number and urged me to give him a call.

●●●

Before I have an opportunity to reach out to Bill, I find myself seated opposite Rosie at the steakhouse in Lancaster. Just moments ago, I executed a nifty save after Rosie insisted that I act as a judge in her Sharon Tate look-alike challenge.

Now, I'm facing another challenge. I think I'm ready for it, but I could be wrong.

I'm fully aware that I need to hide my skepticism if I'm to have any hope of accomplishing my goal, which is to coax from Rosie a more detailed account of how she came to believe—if in fact she really *does* believe—that she is who she says she is: a survivor of the Manson-directed mayhem that played out on Cielo Drive more than 30 years ago.

By this time, I've settled on the working hypothesis that Rosie is a kook of some kind, even if I'm not sure what kind.

For obvious reasons, I decide to keep that line of thinking to myself. I'm an experienced interviewer, and I understand the importance of holding my cards close to my chest if I want other people to feel comfortable enough to tell me their stories. When I'm functioning in my role as a forensic psychologist, I spend a lot of time working to establish rapport with some of the least credible people on earth. I'm reasonably confident I can handle Rosie. As it turns out, we get along famously—until we don't.

With Rosie facing me from across the table, I urge her to tell me more about herself and her background. She seems eager to oblige. I'm happy just to let her talk.

For a long time, I say little as she goes back over a lot of information I know as a result of reading the documents she sent for my review. Occasionally, I interject a one- or two-word prompt. Mainly, I want to assure her of my interest in hearing whatever she has to say.

I find it hard to resist the temptation to probe for more detail, and to challenge some of her more implausible claims. But I'm concerned not to come across as skeptical. I tell myself there will be other opportunities down the road, times when I'll be able to request answers to all the follow-up questions I'm filing away in my head.

To hear Rosie tell it, hers was a fairly normal upbringing.

"See, here's the thing, Jeff. Like I told you, I was raised by Patty Duke's cousin and her husband. I didn't ask a lot of questions, and no one provided me with much in the way of background information. That all changed in 1992, when I was in my early-20s. That's when they told me who I was, for the very first time."

She struggled to process the news that she was Sharon Tate's and Roman Polanski's daughter, and she didn't know what, if anything, she should do about it. Eventually, she decided to launch her own "investigation."

She volunteers that as part of that investigation, she traveled cross country, conducted research in and around Los Angeles, and even made her way to the Cielo Drive site before the house there was demolished in 1994.

After seeing the Garretson interview on *E! Television,* she came to the sudden realization that she and Bill were the sole survivors of that horrific night in 1969. She knew then and there that she needed to reach out to him.

Following their introductory phone contact, she traveled west to Ohio, with plans to present herself to Bill in person. In short order, the two became a couple. She said Bill knew she was telling the truth, even if some of his own memories from August 1969 were vague and fragmented. Like her, he believed fate had brought them together.

Although I'm curious about the circumstances surrounding their decision to end their engagement, I choose not to request details, and Rosie chooses not to provide any.

"Can we go back to your own background?" I say. "Did all the information you got come directly from Noreen?"

"Well, she's the one who told me *who I was*. But don't forget, I've been researching everything for almost ten years now."

"Can I ask you a question?" I say.

"Sure, ask me anything you want."

"It should be easy to prove who you are, right? DNA testing and all that?"

"Yeah, and that won't be a problem. The hold-up is that I need my father's permission to go ahead with the testing."

She tells me of contacts she claims to have had with Roman Polanski in the years since she learned the truth about her identity. At the time of our meeting, Polanski remained in exile in France, having fled the United States in 1978 while he was waiting to be sentenced after his plea of guilty to a charge of having unlawful sexual intercourse with a girl who was only 13.

"I have a whole boxful of letters from him," Rosie says. "He acknowledges that I'm his biological daughter, so there's really no doubt about that."

"Any chance of me seeing those letters?"

"Sure," she says with a shrug. "I'll bring 'em with me the next time we get together." (Spoiler alert: There won't *be* a next time.)

"The thing is," she continues, "my father wants to be the one who determines when the testing gets done. It's frustrating, but there's really nothing I can do about it."

At this point, she executes a sharp pivot. She begins to talk about the layout of the Cielo Drive property: where the gate is, where the garage is, where the in-ground swimming pool is, where the guest cottage is, where the bodies of the five victims were found, and so on. She offers to draw me a picture.

I still have it. At the top of the page are the names of the five victims. Noted are each victim's "blood type and subtype." Her sketch includes the driveway leading up to the garage, the garage itself, the guest cottage, and the fence along the periphery of the property, facing "downtown." Names and X's specify the location of each victim's body.

While sketching, she speaks rapidly and with astonishing alacrity. There is nothing even the slightest bit tentative about her presentation of the "facts." She insists she knows exactly what went down that night back in 1969, for example which of the killers did what, in what sequence, to each one of the victims. I listen, trying hard to follow her but contributing very little.

Suddenly, she surprises me with a question that comes out of nowhere.

"Wanna meet Bill?" she says. Just like that. I thought she said he wouldn't be able to join us today.

"Yeah, sure," I say. "I'd *love* to meet Bill. You mean he can come here today? Like, *right now*?"

She smiles coyly, then pulls out her flip-phone. Within seconds, she has someone on the other end of the line. Garretson, I assume.

"I'm here at Lone Star with Dr. Smalldon," she says. "He's cool. Why don't you come and join us for a while?"

I'm not privy to Garretson's side of the conversation, but I hear Rosie say, "Okay, see you soon then." She tells me he'll probably join us in five or ten minutes. I get the feeling that Bill's probably been lurking nearby, awaiting her summons.

I have an image of Garretson in my mind, one based on a well-known photograph that I've seen in any number of books about the Manson case. In the picture, he has no shirt on; his hair is curly; he's rail thin; and he has a look on his face that suggests a combination of confusion and terror. He looks like a kid, which he was. He hadn't yet turned 20 at the time of the murders. Even though I'm well aware that more than 30 years have elapsed since that picture was taken, I suppose I'm still expecting some version of that kid to come walking through the door of the restaurant and into the bar area.

No surprise, then, that I'm a bit taken aback when Bill appears just minutes later. I know it has to be him because Rosie raises her hand in greeting and gestures for him to come join us. Instead of being in his late-teens, he is now in his early-50s. He's stocky and attired in jeans and a sweatshirt. He looks like he might be … an off-duty truck driver from somewhere in the Midwest. Which is exactly what he is.

"Bill, this is Dr. Smalldon," says Rosie. "Dr. Smalldon, Bill." Bill and I shake hands.

"Hi, Bill, good to meet you," I say. "But please, call me Jeff."

"Okay, Jeff," he says in a quiet voice. "Good meeting you, too."

He sits down at our table, to Rosie's immediate left. He glances at the beer I'm drinking, and when our server stops by, he orders a beer for himself. Immediately, I'm struck by how polite, soft-spoken, and reserved he is. He seems nothing at all like Rosie. She's color; he's black and white.

The truth is, I find him unremarkable in every way. He sits with Rosie and me for the better part of two hours, until I need to leave for the drive back to Columbus. But he contributes relatively little to our conversation. For the most part, he seems content to let Rosie act as his spokesperson. She relishes the role.

I get the impression that it's still painful for Bill to have to revisit the events of 1969. He tells me that the Cielo Drive property owner, Rudi Altobelli, hired him to take care of his three dogs, and to help tend to things around the property while Altobelli was away that summer. He seems reluctant to say much about the night of the murders, or to fill me in on what things were like for him during the three days he spent in police custody.

In large part because I assume I'll have the opportunity to meet with him again, I decide not to press him for details beyond those few he volunteers. Foremost in my mind is what Rosie told me about his desire to see me "in private."

That meeting is the one I'm looking forward to the most. I figure I'll probe for more information when only the two of us are present.

At one point, Bill volunteers that much of what he's now remembering about the night of the murders "came back to [him]" after he and Rosie started talking. His own memories had been vague and muddled, made so by the passage of time but also by the many different things he'd read and been told by others. In contrast, Rosie seemed dead certain about the things she was saying.

"I guess I put a lot of it out of my mind," he said, "but now I can remember the men bringing the baby to me in the middle of the night, wrapped up in a blanket." He thinks the men had guns, and he feels pretty certain that they pointed the guns at him—but again, he remarks that many of his memories remain fragmented and indistinct.

"I had no idea what happened to Rosie after they walked away with her," he adds. "And I knew nothing at all about Rosie's life until she filled me in on it." He and Rosie may have ended their engagement, but they still seem friendly and at ease in one another's company.

I notice that whenever Bill stops talking, Rosie starts. Clearly, she's the star of this show. Whenever Bill seems unsure of himself, he turns toward her and pauses long enough for her to clear things up. She obliges each and every time.

Rosie seems to bask in the attention. As far as I can tell, she's eager to claim for herself a starring, if little known, role in one of the most infamous crime sagas in modern American history. Sometimes her rapid-fire chatter continues uninterrupted for long periods of time. I listen intently, keeping my chin propped up with my clasped hands; and Bill either averts his eyes or nods approvingly in response to whatever she's saying.

Rosie predicts that in the days to come, I'll think of many more questions I want to ask her. *No doubt.*

When the time comes for me to head back to Columbus, I settle up with our server, then exchange handshakes with Bill and Rosie. Rosie tells me how much she's enjoyed the evening. "I'll be in touch," I say.

I choose not to mention what Rosie said about Bill wanting to meet with me privately. I figure he and I can make those arrangements later.

The evening ends on a warm, convivial note.

I'll never see them again.

• • •

Two days after that meeting, I mailed Rosie and Bill a letter. I sent it care of Dolly, the older woman with whom Rosie had been staying in South Bloomfield. In my letter, I repeated how much I'd enjoyed our meeting and expressed the hope that we could get together again. I added, "As you predicted, Rosie, I continue to think of questions I would like to [ask] both of you."

I did pose one question. It had to do with timing and the sequence of events.

Recall that according to one of the documents Rosie sent me, Bill noticed telephone wires draped across the ground when the people who he later came to believe were the Manson Family killers dropped him off outside the gate at the top of the driveway leading to the Cielo Drive property. The clear implication was that the killers had cut the wires down earlier that same evening.

Addressing Bill directly, I mentioned that I had gone back and re-read selected excerpts from *Helter Skelter*, including one where he was quoted as having told the police that Steve Parent, his visitor at the guest cottage that night, placed a call using Bill's telephone not long before he left the cottage and ran into the killers at the foot of the driveway, just inside the gate.

"How could he have placed a phone call from your place if the phone wires had already been cut?" I asked.

I also touched on another issue. "Of course," I wrote, "I am totally befuddled by why the killers would have left you unharmed, Bill. According to your own account, they knew full well that you were there—and since you had [driven] to the property with them [not long before] ... they would have assumed you could identify them. Frankly, it doesn't make much sense to me that they would have simply left you alone to bear witness against them later."

As delicately as possible, I reiterated to Rosie my interest in being permitted access to the letters and other materials that she insisted would lend credence to her claim to be Roman Polanski's and Sharon Tate's biological daughter: "Rosie, I wonder if perhaps you'd be willing to review with me ... at least a portion of the documentary evidence you've amassed in support of your alternative account of what really happened (and why) on Cielo Drive. You know I'd be interested. Mainly, I'm referring to all the stuff ... you said you sent for your father [Polanski] to review."

If Rosie was put off by any of my questions, she chose not to make her feelings known. In a handwritten note dated November 25, she wrote, "Happy Holiday Greetings!" She apologized for the "phone tag" we'd been playing, then added some tantalizing remarks that alerted me to the fact that things between her and Bill were rapidly deteriorating.

"Need to meet with you," she wrote. "Bill strikes again—hopefully into prison ... Call me to set something up. Best regards, Rosie."

Months went by. I was busy at work, and I put off calling Rosie. It wasn't until November of the following year, 2001, that I thought I could clear enough space on my calendar for a follow-up meeting with her, or with her and Bill together. I regretted then, and I regret now, that I never got around to arranging a private meeting with Bill.

• • •

I phoned Rosie using the last number I had for her, the one

belonging to Dolly, the older woman from South Bloomfield.

Rosie wasn't at home when I called, but Dolly answered the phone. She and I talked for a while, mostly just idle banter. I don't recall anything even remotely controversial about most of the things either of us said. Mainly, I'd called to wish Rosie happy holidays, to ask her how she was doing, and to sound her out on the possibility of setting up another meeting.

I do remember that during our conversation, Dolly made a passing reference—it seemed vague, deliberately so—to Rosie having had some kind of interaction with a representative from the local child welfare agency. I didn't request any details. When we were done chatting, I asked Dolly to please convey my regards to Rosie, and to tell her that I hoped we could get together again sometime soon.

Not long after that call, Dolly sent me a handwritten note. The tone seemed ominous. "I played back the recording of our conversation [for the record, she never told me the call was being recorded]. Rosie was very upset because I discussed her business. *That you were involved with Children Services and the adoptive mother* [emphasis added]—and that I have betrayed her confidence. I was not warned of any reason I should not speak to you. Rosie and I have broken the confidence barrier and I can no longer represent her in any way."

What?

I had no idea what she was talking about. In no way was I "involved with Children Services," and I was puzzled by her reference to an "adoptive mother." In any case, Rosie apparently felt betrayed by her friend's decision to tell me that Rosie had an interaction—*any* interaction—with a representative from the local child protection services agency.

Later that same evening, I was at home relaxing. The phone rang, and I decided to let the caller leave a message on the answering machine. As soon as I heard Rosie's voice, I could tell she was angry. Not just angry—*furious.* "Stop harassing me!" she yelled. Then she added that any subsequent attempts to contact her should "go through [her] attorney," whose name she provided.

Again, I hadn't the slightest idea what any of this was

about. The last time Rosie reached out to me, nearly a year before, it was to send me "happy holiday greetings," and to urge me to contact her so that we could arrange another meeting. *Now this.*

I spent several days mulling over my options. On December 2, I wrote Dolly a letter. I invited her to share the letter with Rosie if she wanted to. After describing the message that Rosie left on my answering machine, I expressed confusion over why Rosie would have felt the need to tell me not to "harass" her. All I had done was place a call to Dolly's phone number, hoping for the opportunity to wish Rosie happy holidays and inquire about how she was doing.

I explained in my letter that I'd used Dolly's number to try to reach Rosie because it was the only number Rosie had given me (since her breakup with Bill). I said I'd done my best to recall everything we talked about and had so far been unable to come up with anything that would explain Rosie's anger (at least toward me).

I reminded Dolly that while we were talking, she repeated several times her concern about not wanting to betray Rosie's trust, and about not wanting to say anything that Rosie could conceivably regard as an invasion of her privacy.

I said I was befuddled by the references in Dolly's prior note about my alleged involvement "with Children Services and the adoptive mother." I told her I had no idea what those references were about. I stated that I hadn't had any involvement whatsoever with Children Services and emphasized that I knew nothing at all about an "adoptive mother." I added, "I can't imagine why you would have even mentioned ... those subjects."

I repeated that she was welcome to share my letter with Rosie. Toward the end I wrote, "Needless to say, [Rosie] can rest assured that unless the initiative comes from her, she won't need to worry about any further attempts on my part to 'harass' —read 'communicate with' —her."

• • •

That was it. Well, it was and it wasn't. I remained curious about Rosie—and, frankly, uncertain what to make of her. *Was she delusional? Did she actually believe all the things she told me? Did she suffer from what mental health professionals would refer to as a "borderline personality disorder?" Was she just a garden variety attention addict?*

In any event, I heard nothing further from her, Dolly, or Bill. For the time being anyway, their silence came as a relief. But I still hadn't completely given up on the possibility of talking to Bill again, preferably without Rosie present.

Years passed. To be honest, I was too caught up with work to think much about Rosie or what had become of her. Still, at random intervals she crossed my mind. Every time she did, I wondered where her journey had taken her.

I stumbled upon a partial answer to that question in 2012, more than a decade after my interactions with her and Bill. That year, a woman named Alisa Statman, assisted by Sharon Tate's niece, Brie, the daughter of Sharon's sister, Patti, published a meandering but still intriguing book called *Restless Souls*. The book was said to be "the Sharon Tate family's account of stardom, the Manson murders, and a crusade for justice."

One thing about the book immediately caught my attention. Some references to Tate's baby used male pronouns; others used female pronouns. In an early section of the narrative, told in the voice of Tate's father, PJ, there is this: "Sharon's murderer stole something more precious to her than her own life; [he] denied her the breathtaking moment just after birth of seeing her baby, touching his silky skin, or smelling his newborn hair as she kissed the top of his head." *His* silky skin, *his* newborn hair, the top of *his* head. The message seemed clear: Tate's father knew that the baby was a *boy*.

But then, later in the book, there's another section, told in the voice of Sharon's sister, Patti, who was eleven years old when the murders occurred.

Patti recalls accompanying her mother to the airport to greet Sharon upon her return to the United States from Italy, just weeks before the murders. Patti remembers the very pregnant Sharon telling her, "Here, give me your hand, you can feel her moving around … Don't worry, you're not going to hurt her. When we get home, you can lay your head there and hear her heartbeat." *Her* moving around, hurt *her*, hear *her* heartbeat. Again, this was just weeks before Sharon was due to deliver the baby.

I noted the pronoun discrepancy and thought, *Wait, was there actually some factual basis for Rosie's claim that the Tate/Polanski baby was a girl and not a boy?* In any event, I figured it was somewhere in the crack between those his and her references that Rosie discovered the fertilizer necessary to sustain the growth of her improbable story.

In the penultimate chapter of Statman's book, Rosie pops up as an actual character—an unwelcome one—in the lives of Sharon Tate's surviving family members. I was startled to learn that back in the early 1990s, years before she saw Garretson interviewed on television and embarked on her pilgrimage to Ohio, Rosie initiated contact with Tate's parents, claiming to be … *Sharon Tate!* She informed them that she was their daughter, reincarnated. She even began sending Mother's Day greeting cards to Doris Tate, Sharon's mother. One year, on the anniversary of Sharon's death, she appeared on the Tate family's doorstep and greeted PJ, Sharon's father, "Hi, I'm your daughter, Sharon." He slammed the door in her face.

After Sharon's mother's death from brain cancer in 1992, Rosie "turned her attention toward" Patti, the younger sister. According to Patti, she "played along with" Rosie for a while, maintaining contact with her by telephone because of her wish to adhere to her own rule of "always keeping potential enemies close at hand where you can keep an eye on them." She assumed Rosie had to be "delusional." At the same time, she thought she seemed "harmless."

Eventually, after being diagnosed with breast cancer in 1998, Patti decided it was time to bring things to a head with Rosie. She was alarmed that Rosie had turned up at a parole hearing for Susan Atkins, one of the Manson Family killers, despite the fact that Patti had explicitly instructed her to stay away. Patti is quoted in Statman's book: "[My] instincts told me there was something inherently wrong with Rosie."

Still, she "let the charade play out"—until, that is, she finally decided she'd reached her limit. Rosie was not only a loose end, but a fraying one that could rip at any moment.

Intending a confrontation, Patti showed up unannounced at Rosie's two-room apartment in Burbank. When Rosie came to the door, Patti got right to the point: "I don't believe you are Sharon reincarnated." She expected resistance from Rosie, but instead Rosie flashed "a grin that was much too big." She told Patti, "I'm glad you said it, because there's something I've been wanting to tell you, but haven't had the nerve—I'm Sharon's baby … I'm your *niece*! I've been alive all this time!"

Patti tried to nip that story in the bud: "Rosie, stop it. Sharon's baby died with her. It was a boy, and he's buried with her."

Rosie would have none of it: "Well, for once you're wrong, Miss Smarty Pants. Sharon is my mother, and that's all there is to it." When Patti protested, Rosie demanded that she get out. Patti agreed to go—but not before trying to extract from Rosie a commitment not to contact any members of her family, ever again. Rosie went ballistic: "Get out, get out, get out!"

That *still* wasn't the end. A couple months later, Rosie sent Patti a fax, saying that because she was Roman's and Sharon's child, and because a California court had decided in 1969 that Sharon's estate should be transferred from Roman Polanski to Sharon's and Patti's father, Rosie was entitled to a portion of the inheritance.

Patti's summation? "The long story made short is that [Rosie] wanted money."

That may have been true. But if Rosie wanted money, she wanted Bill Garretson, too.

●●●

Rachel Monroe—a writer who would give Rosie more than just a passing nod in her own book, called *Savage Appetites* (2019)—reviewed Statman's book for the *LA Review of Books*. In fact, she began her review with this statement: "Rosie Blanchard began sending Mother's Day cards to Doris Tate in the 1990s, even though the two women had never met."

Monroe summarized Rosie's interactions with members of the Tate family, then pivoted to a discussion of Rosie's truncated engagement to and presumed influence on Bill Garretson, who was now claiming to have lied back in 1969 when he answered questions about what he remembered from the night of the Cielo Drive murders. According to Rosie, Bill had come around to believing her version of what happened, which included him holding her in his arms shortly before she was removed from the crime scene.

Savage Appetites is subtitled *Four True Stories of Women, Crime, and Obsession.* One whole chapter is devoted to Lisa Statman and the complicated, multi-layered saga of "the Manson story."

Monroe repeats some things Statman told her about Rosie, then adds some color of her own. Even after Sharon Tate's father slammed the door in her face, Rosie "kept popping up, buzzing at the margins of the family's life like an unslappable [sic] mosquito."

Rosie persisted in sending holiday greeting cards; she discovered the family's phone number and repeatedly used it to try to establish contact with the family members; and she "threatened" to show up at parole hearings for the imprisoned murderers, ostensibly so that she could demonstrate support for the "family" —the Tate family—that she considered her own.

According to Monroe, by the time Rosie showed up in Ohio and "careened into" Bill Garretson's life, she had "elaborated on her origin story." As Monroe saw it, the Manson murders and their legacy "seemed to have stunted Garretson in some vital, permanent way" that rendered him acutely vulnerable to the influence of someone like Rosie, who'd created for herself an entire identity that depended on the "complicated proposition" of linking herself directly to the victim of a violent, infamous crime. Rosie claimed of Garretson, "[Bill] was the only one who could empathize with my pain."

•••

In 2014, almost a decade and a half after my experiences with Rosie and Bill, I reached out to a woman who knew Rosie during the period when Rosie called central Ohio home, circa 2000-2001. The woman remembered Rosie's story as one of the more fantastic and fascinating she had ever heard. She wrote me that even after the passage of so many years, she still had "no clue" whether Rosie "is who she thinks she is, or whether she is just another schizophrenic personality/conspiracy theorist/psychotic."

•••

Bill "Willy" Garretson passed away on August 16, 2016. The local newspaper printed no formal obituary. The funeral service was private.

Rosie's whereabouts are unknown.

•••

In December of 2019, Roman Polanski sat for an interview with a writer from *Paris Match*.

I undertook an online search, hoping to retrieve a transcript of the interview. The first thing that popped up was this headline: "Roman Polanski: A woman claims to be his [and Sharon Tate's] daughter."

According to what Polanski told the interviewer, a woman had contacted him "a couple of years" prior, claiming that the Manson Family killers spared her on the night of the slaughter on Cielo Drive. She informed him that she was his and his late wife's long-lost daughter. Subsequently, she plied him with "letters, gifts, photos."

To Polanski, it was all just so much "delirium."

10.
The Worst of the Worst

A blunt truth: I chose to become a forensic psychologist because I wanted easier access to killers. There were other reasons—but that was the main one.

In the aftermath of the shattering 1983 double homicide at the hospital where I was then a young administrator, I decided to convert my longstanding interest in murder into something new and more substantial: a career.

By 1990, when my graduate studies were finally in the rearview mirror, I was ready to take the first steps toward getting my private practice up and running. More than anything, I was looking forward to the challenge of having to explain to juries, in plain language, the behavior and motives of killers, especially those killers who prosecutors routinely describe as "the worst of the worst"—those for whom the death penalty is intended. I knew from the start that I wanted capital case consultation to be a primary focus of my practice.

Rightly or wrongly, I felt like I had a leg up on most other psychologists who aspired to doing the same kind of work I wanted to do.

How many of them could say they'd exchanged hundreds of letters with some of the most notorious murderers and would-be murderers in modern American history?

How many could claim to have spent four days with John Wayne Gacy in a private death row visiting room?

And how many knew what it was like to express condolences to a grief-stricken first-time father whose wife had just been brutally murdered—and then to realize, less than three years later, that the same seemingly bereft father had almost certainly played a role in orchestrating the death of his infant daughter's mother, along with the mother's close friend from work?

By any barometer, the defendants who are charged with death penalty-eligible acts of aggravated murder are among the most extreme of all violent offenders. Theirs are crimes that "shock the conscience"—another phrase favored by prosecutors. Journalists often describe their crimes as senseless and motiveless, the idea being that they exist somewhere beyond the reach of rational analysis.

My role as a consultant and expert witness would be to decipher those crimes: situate them in the context of the perpetrators' complicated, often very tragic life stories, and then render them comprehensible to the people who sit on capital case juries. The thinking of most attorneys who do death penalty work is that if they can somehow "humanize" their clients, that is, force jury members to view them as real—if profoundly damaged—human beings rather than simply the terrifying monsters of their worst nightmares, the jury members will be less likely to vote in favor of a death sentence.

Death penalty trials nearly always involve two phases: the first, where the issue is guilt or innocence; and the second, where the issue is life or death. In the second phase, usually referred to as the sentencing or "mitigation" phase, mental health professionals often act as expert witnesses, called upon, usually by the defense, to present findings that relate to the question of how someone who began life as a guileless infant could have developed into an adult whose behavior is judged so egregious that it makes the person a candidate for death at the hands of the state.

I welcomed the challenges implicit in the role of capital case consultant, and I felt confident in my ability to handle them. I had a good memory, so I figured I'd be able to speak directly to juries without having to rely on interview notes and a lot of distracting props; I had little use for technical jargon of the kind that I thought alienated jurors and often made them skeptical about the value of expert testimony; I felt that because of my years studying literature, I had a reasonably good understanding of how to assemble the parts of a compelling narrative; and I was convinced that if I devoted sufficient time and effort to my attempt to unravel the interwoven strands of any defendant's life story, I'd nearly always arrive at a point where I could discern the psychological "meaning" even in the most senseless-seeming acts of violence.

It would never be my role to try to excuse or justify acts of murder. Nor would it be my role to argue in favor of one sentencing option over another. Instead, my role would be to offer testimony that a jury might—*or might not*—regard as a partial basis for recommending a punishment of life in prison instead of death.

In the pages that follow, I won't try to summarize my testimony from any of the numerous death penalty trials where I appeared as an expert witness. There were many times when I testified for hours. In a small subset of cases, my testimony went on for *days*.

Neither will I address in any detail all the legal and diagnostic issues that arose in the context of every capital case consultation I ever performed. (There were close to 300.)

And finally, I won't delve deeply into the multi-faceted role that forensic psychologists play in death penalty cases. Numerous articles and books have been devoted to that complicated subject.

I have a far more modest aim: to offer a short series of revelatory snapshots. Call them field notes: observational, informal. The experiences captured in these snapshots all resulted in some kind of takeaway—an insight, a cautionary reminder, a surrendered assumption, even just a particularly vivid memory—that I could draw on as I sought to improve the quality of my capital case consultations.

•••

For psychologists who aspire to doing death penalty work, there always has to be a first case. For me, that case was *State of Ohio vs. Eddie Vaughn*. I was expecting a baptism by fire.

On June 7, 1990, just six months after I received my license to practice, Eddie Vaughn, an inmate at the maximum-security Southern Ohio Correctional Facility (known to most Ohioans as "Lucasville" because that's the name of the town—population about 1500—where it's located), killed 32-year-old Beverly Taylor inside a staff restroom. At the time of his attack on Taylor, Vaughn, a formidable-looking African-American man who once dreamed of becoming a professional football player, was already serving a life sentence for the 1984 murder of his then-wife's 90-year-old grandmother.

Twelve years before *that*, in 1972, he unlawfully entered a farmhouse west of Columbus, then raped an 18-year-old girl and terrorized her, her brother, and her parents for nine hours straight. While holding the family hostage, he repeatedly threatened to kill them all. A top local law enforcement official who worked that case described Vaughn as "a very vicious, dangerous person" and declared, "[If] there was ever a candidate for the death penalty, [Vaughn would be] at the top of the list."

On that case, Vaughn ended up being convicted of rape, breaking and entering, and four counts of aggravated assault. Paroled from prison in 1979, he successfully completed two years of post-release supervision and stayed out of trouble for about three more years before he killed his wife's grandmother.

Despite his violent history, Vaughn seemed to acclimate well to the structured environment of prison. In fact, he was said to have been a near-model prisoner in the years following his 1984 aggravated murder conviction. He accepted an assignment to serve as Beverly Taylor's aide at the prison school. Taylor liked him—well enough, in fact, to request that he be allowed to continue as her aide when his assignment came up for renewal.

Taylor, who was white and married, lived in Lucasville. Everyone in the small town knew everyone else, and many of the local residents worked at the prison. During the jury selection process that preceded Vaughn's 1992 trial, 50 out of 51 prospective jurors reported familiarity with the case. That came as no surprise to anyone. The case had been the subject of 53 front-page stories in the daily newspaper published in nearby Portsmouth. The only member of the pool of prospective jurors who reported knowing little if anything about the case also reported being unable to read.

Finally convinced that there was no chance Vaughn could get a fair trial in the county where the prison was located, the presiding judge granted a defense motion for a change of venue. He stipulated that the trial would take place in Cincinnati, about 100 miles southwest of Lucasville. It was there that I would have my first experience as an expert witness at the sentencing phase of a death penalty case.

First, however, I needed to get to know Eddie Vaughn, and to find out about his background, including the circumstances of his upbringing. For obvious reasons, officials at the Ohio Department of Rehabilitation and Correction decided that it would not be feasible to keep Vaughn at Lucasville during the two years leading up to his trial.

Members of his defense team informed me that I could interview him at the state prison in Chillicothe, located about 50 miles south of Columbus. I was told that for security-related reasons, Vaughn would not be permitted to leave his cell to meet with me.

When I arrived at the prison, the corrections officer who acted as my escort explained that I could speak to Vaughn through a small opening in his cell door. We wouldn't even be permitted to converse through bars; that was seen as too risky.

Prior to our first meeting, I reviewed a massive set of records pertaining to the murder of Beverly Taylor.

The short version of what I learned: At around 9:30 a.m. on the day of the murder, Vaughn followed Taylor into the staff restroom at the prison school and locked the door behind them. The only security officer who was then on duty at the school couldn't see what was happening from where he was seated. When he heard a muffled scream coming from the direction of the restroom, he summoned emergency backup.

When Vaughn heard the sound of someone trying to gain access to the restroom, he screamed, "If you open that door, I'll cut her throat!" Almost immediately, blood began oozing from underneath the door. As it turned out, Vaughn was armed with a razor and a "shiv" that he'd fashioned from the steel spine of a standard-issue school binder. When prison officials finally managed to force the door open, a "wild-eyed" Vaughn came rushing out, in the words of a school staffer "like a fullback charging a defense line."

I watched a video recording of Vaughn that was made not long after his emergence from the restroom. It left no doubt that he'd been beaten badly by the corrections officers who subdued him.

Later, the local county prosecutor would say that Vaughn's was "a classic death penalty case." Who could argue? Consider the core facts: A hulking African-American man, already serving life for murdering an elderly grandmother, slaughters a young white woman inside a staff restroom at a maximum-security prison—and the victim just happens to be a resident of the small rural town where the prison is located.

Most court watchers viewed the case as a slam dunk for the prosecution. In other words, they saw Vaughn as someone almost sure to get the death penalty.

I met with Eddie three different times. Only the first of those meetings took place at the prison in Chillicothe. Our subsequent meetings took place, respectively, at the Scioto County jail in Portsmouth, where I was given permission to administer a battery of psychological tests; and in an office at the adjoining courthouse. The jail staff reluctantly agreed when I asked them to uncuff Eddie's hands—both so that he could participate in some testing that required him to use his hands, and so that he'd be more comfortable and relaxed during the time that he and I spent talking.

To put it mildly, Eddie's behavior during our meetings didn't square with my expectations. He was soft-spoken, unfailingly polite, and respectful. His deferential manner made him seem almost meek. He never gave me even the slightest bit of trouble.

Justified or not, I concluded that his way of responding to me probably had a lot to do with my way of responding to him. Despite the horrific brutality of the crimes he was accused of committing, I approached him with an attitude of respect and unconditional regard, and I went out of my way never to talk down to him.

He was fully aware that plenty of people wanted to see him die for what he'd done. He was clinging to the slim hope that he'd be permitted to live out the rest of his life in prison. In all likelihood, he saw me as a potential ally, someone whose testimony could perhaps act as a buffer between him and the many people who wanted to see him sentenced to death. For that reason alone, he may have decided it made sense to be on his best behavior while we were together.

To the surprise of no one, the jury at his trial found him guilty of aggravated murder.

The same jury was slated to hear evidence during the trial's sentencing phase. I was to be the defense's star witness. I knew by that time that Eddie was a badly damaged, emotionally very disturbed man. I also knew that his life hung in the balance. The stakes couldn't have been higher.

During my many hours on the witness stand, I testified to the extremely abusive conditions in the home where Eddie grew up. A mitigation specialist who was part of the defense team had conducted interviews with other members of Eddie's family. Their graphic and consistent descriptions of what life had been like in the Vaughn household helped to shape the story I presented for the jury's consideration. So did the massive amount of information I'd gleaned from my review of thousands of pages of background records, documenting nearly every aspect of Eddie's life.

Not directly but by implication, I invited members of the jury to weigh carefully the many reasons why Eddie grew up to become the kind of person he was—that is, the kind of person capable of murdering Beverly Taylor. I never tried to excuse his actions, never tried to make it seem like they were any less horrific than they were. Mainly, I set out to explain the severe emotional consequences of what Eddie experienced as a child, and to link those consequences to his explosion of violence on June 7, 1990.

By the time I was done testifying, I knew the veteran prosecutor had scored some points during his cross-examination. Even so, I felt like I'd accomplished what I set out to accomplish, which was to humanize Eddie Vaughn by telling the story of his life and explaining the devastating impact of his father's abuse. Of course, there was no way of knowing how the jury would respond to my testimony.

When the dust settled on the "mitigation" hearing, the jury voted to spare Eddie's life. No one, not even Eddie's own attorneys, would have predicted that outcome.

Later that same day, a member of the defense team called me at home to tell me the news. At that point, I was still too inexperienced to fully grasp the implications when she excitedly informed me that the jury had returned with a sentencing recommendation of "30 to life."

She tried to impress on me how astonishing that outcome was, especially given the horrific facts of the Vaughn case. In practical terms, what the jury's decision meant was that Eddie would live out the rest of his life in prison. The bottom line, said the attorney who called me, was that Vaughn had "avoided death."

We were about to end our call when the attorney added, "You better get ready, I think your phone's going to start ringing off the hook. As soon as word gets around that Eddie Vaughn got a life sentence and you were the defense expert, you're going to get more death case referrals than you know what to do with."

She was right. Even though I knew she was giving me far more credit than I deserved, from that day forward I was a sought-after capital case expert—in cases that originated in more than 50 different counties throughout Ohio, in cases from neighboring states, and in some federal cases as well.

By the time I retired, 25 years later, I'd worked on nearly

300 capital cases. *State of Ohio vs. Eddie Vaughn* was the first.

•••

My assumption is that for Jerry Hessler, each new day arrives as just the latest chapter of an ongoing nightmare.

Christmas is coming, he's being held without bond at the Franklin County Jail, and the State of Ohio wants him dead.

Just weeks ago, on November 19, 1995, he went on a shooting rampage that left four people dead, two people wounded, and a whole host of others—including five children—profoundly traumatized. Among the dead: an infant girl named Amanda.

I know the broad contours of the backstory, mainly because I've been keeping up with the local news.

Thirty-eight years old at the time of his killing spree, Jerry had been fired from his job at Bank One in October of 1994. Multiple women—including Amanda's mother, also among the dead—had complained to management about Jerry's unwanted advances in the workplace, and about his refusal to pay heed when they told him to leave them alone.

After losing his job at the bank, Jerry became unhinged. *More* unhinged. He threw furniture around his mother's house, he kicked holes in the walls, he barricaded himself in his room, and he terrorized one of his younger brothers by chasing him around with a gun. Frightened half out of her wits, his mother left her house and moved in with Jerry's grandmother.

Finally, in May 1995, his family members and a screener from the local probate court convinced a judge that for his own safety and the safety of others, Jerry needed to be hospitalized on an involuntary basis.

Following two months of inpatient treatment, the hospital released him. After his discharge, Jerry failed to comply with the conditions of his aftercare plan. Some months later, he cried to his mother, "I'm back to doing the same things I did before I went to the hospital."

On November 12, exactly one week before his killing

spree, Jerry ran into an acquaintance of his at a local health club and told her of his intent to settle the score with the people he held responsible for the loss of his job at the bank. He added that for the better part of a year, he'd been ruminating about the need to exact revenge.

Today, I'm thinking back on his rampage, which occurred two weeks ago.

It's now early December, and I'm getting ready to meet Jerry for the first time. His attorneys have hired me to act as their psychological consultant. *What makes this guy tick? What made him do what he did? Is he mentally ill? Should we be pursuing an insanity defense? Is a judge likely to find him competent to stand trial? Is he remorseful? Does it matter to him that he killed a baby? Is there anything about his psychological makeup or background that might convince a jury to spare his life?*

On the drive from my office to the downtown jail, I'm thinking back over some of what I've learned—mainly from the local newspaper—about Jerry's upbringing, and about the trajectory of his young adulthood.

The oldest of three siblings, he has two brothers. His father, who died in the mid-1980s, is recalled as an emotionally abusive alcoholic, prone to episodes of violence. People who knew Jerry when he was a youngster remember that he was a little on the shy side, socially awkward and something of a loner. A long-time friend told a newspaper reporter that he was "a little bit goofy" but still, overall, "a good man."

As a high school student, he developed an interest in Mormonism and soon joined the church. By all available accounts, he was serious about his faith. Eventually, he participated in a two-year mission and drew praise from his superiors. A former friend remembers him as happy and content during that period in his life. For reasons that were never specified at the time, Mormon officials eventually requested that he end his association with the church. Jerry was "devastated." According to the former friend, he "didn't know where to go. He was lost again."

Still aspiring to some higher sense of purpose, he enlisted in the Army. He went on to serve 15 years of active duty in the National Guard, achieving the rank of sergeant first class. His Guard records make no mention of any behavioral problems. In fact, a National Guard spokesperson told a reporter that most of his performance evaluations were "exemplary." Far *less* exemplary was the way he went about handling his relationships, especially with women. In interviews, several of his associates reported that his problems with women began long before the start of his employment at Bank One.

According to recent newspaper stories, all the adults he targeted in his November killing spree were connected in one way or another to his termination at the bank, his history of failed relationships with women, or both.

I'm grappling with the apparent contradictions of Jerry's life as I enter the jail lobby and prepare to sign in as a professional visitor. I'm not sure what to expect of Jerry, but this much seems clear: he's under an incredible amount of stress and has been for some time now.

For starters, he's a multiple murderer, something he wasn't until the third week in November. Not just a multiple murderer but the murderer of an *infant child*. He'll never taste freedom again; surely that reality has settled in by now. And the State wants him dead.

Is he profoundly depressed? Angry and defensive? Remorseful? Desperate to find some way out of his predicament? I'll find out soon enough.

One of his attorneys has agreed to meet me at the jail. "I'll be there to handle the introductions," he told me when we talked on the phone. "Then I'll leave, and you can have Jerry all to yourself."

As I'm being buzzed through security, I try to imagine how it would feel to be in Jerry's shoes. Not so many years ago, he was that shy, retiring youngster remembered by people who knew him back in the day. When he got a bit older, he discovered a renewed sense of purpose through his embrace of the Mormon faith. Then, after the failure of that experiment, he enlisted in the Army and served with distinction in the National Guard, not briefly but for a long time.

In the 14 months that have elapsed since his termination

at Bank One, pretty much everything that could have gone wrong in Jerry's life *has* gone wrong. My thought: *for this missionary-turned-murderer, the inner turmoil and sense of emotional dissonance must seem absolutely overwhelming.*

The deputy who signed me in just moments ago told me I would find Jerry and his attorney in the professional meeting room immediately to my left after I passed through security. Standing outside the door to that room, I announce my presence with a light rap, then enter to see Jerry and the attorney seated on opposite sides of a narrow table. In accordance with jail protocol, the attorney occupies the chair nearest the door.

When I close the door behind me, Jerry pushes his chair back from the table and rises to his feet. He looks exactly like I've imagined he would look. He has short, thinning hair, and glasses. He appears trim and physically fit, even in his jail scrubs.

"Jerry, this is Dr. Smalldon," says his attorney. "He'll be helping us with your case. We need you to cooperate with him, and that includes doing your best to answer all his questions." Jerry smiles, nods in my direction, and greets me with a firm handshake (he's uncuffed).

"Good to meet you," he says, sounding surprisingly upbeat.

"Good to meet you, too," I say.

His attorney gets up from the table, shakes my hand, and says, "Okay. I gotta get to court. Take as much time as you need, but there'll be plenty of other opportunities for the two of you to talk. Jerry, I'll be back to see you tomorrow."

And with that he's gone.

I take my seat at the table and remove a pencil and pad of paper from my briefcase. I've already decided on the approach I intend to take. Before I start asking a lot of questions, I'm going to acknowledge everything Jerry's been through during the past several weeks—and offer him the opportunity to talk with me about all the stress he's been experiencing.

"Well, I know these past weeks have been crazy," I say. "I'm sure you have a lot of complicated feelings about everything that's happened."

"No!" Jerry protests. "Not at all! There's *nothing* complicated about my feelings."

He smiles back at me like he hasn't a care in the world. I'm taken aback by his chipper manner and cheerful tone, though I try not to show it.

"I knew what needed to be done, and I did it," he continues. "It's that simple. I'm just disappointed I wasn't able to finish the job."

The job. I know exactly what he's referring to.

After he killed the four people in Columbus, and injured the two others, he headed north and drove 80 miles to Ashland, where another of his former girlfriends lived with her husband—who Jerry once regarded as a friend—and their four children. An alert police officer who happened to know the family in Ashland phoned to warn them that Jerry might be heading in their direction.

Sure enough, Jerry, outfitted in a bulletproof vest, appeared outside their house and fired three shots at their back door. The husband returned fire and knocked Jerry backward, prompting him to flee the scene. Minutes later, local police spotted Jerry's car and took him into custody.

I'm just disappointed I wasn't able to finish the job.

Less than a year after my first meeting with Jerry, a jury found him guilty of multiple counts of aggravated murder. The same jury recommended that he be sentenced to death. Prior to the start of the sentencing hearing, there was spirited debate—outside the presence of the jury—about whether members of the jury should be made privy to some things Jerry had written on the wall of his holding cell.

In the end, the presiding judge allowed the prosecution to show the jury just one passage from the holding cell graffiti: "Mercilessly plan, relentlessly prepare, violently execute, ruthlessly finish."

Not shown to the jury were some *other* things Jerry had written: "No pity, no regret, no remorse. Am I sorry? Yeah, I'm sorry I didn't get them all. Oh well, better luck next time. A bad day in jail is better than any day dead. Treat me like trash, find out I'm toxic."

I never forgot the brief exchange that occurred at the very front end of the first of my many meetings with Jerry. It was a rookie mistake on my part—one that I tried never to repeat. My error was thinking that I could predict a murderer's thoughts and feelings based on how I imagined I would think and feel if I were in the same predicament. Even at that early juncture in my career, I should have known better.

From his new home on death row, Hessler bombarded me with letters. Invariably, his tone was upbeat and playful, even ebullient.

In a letter dated May 28, 1997, less than a year after his conviction and death sentence, he wrote to tell me of his easy adjustment to life among the condemned. "I am THRIVING!" he wrote. "If I had known I would have this much fun, I'd have come [to death row] a long time ago ... Well, take care! I've got to go now. It's time for our rehearsal (smiley face). We are doing *The Pirates of Penzance*."

In that same letter, he included a passage from a novel he'd read recently, Richard Wright's *The Outsider* ("Great book!"): "He could have waved his hand and blotted them from existence with no more regret of taking human lives than if he had swatted a couple of insects. Why could he never make others realize how dangerous it was for them to make him feel like this?"

At long last, the former missionary had discovered his one true calling.

Hessler died in 2003. Newspaper articles called his death the result of a heart defect.

• • •

Kathy Lundgren is happily married to a convicted mass murderer. Earlier today, July 9, 1996, she visited her husband, Jeffrey Lundgren, at his place of residence: Ohio's death row. It's located about 65 miles north of Columbus, at the Mansfield Correctional Institution (where it will remain until 2011). In a few minutes, she and the Lundgrens' six-year-old daughter, Rasia, will be joining me for a late-afternoon snack at McDonald's.

The Lundgren story dominated national headlines when it broke during the earliest days of 1990. Tipped off by Kathy's then-husband, a man named Keith Johnson, police investigators had discovered a family of five—Dennis Avery, Cheryl Avery, and their daughters, 15-year-old Trina, 13-year-old Becky, and six-year-old Karen—buried together in a shallow grave in a red barn outside the small northeast Ohio town of Kirtland, where, more than a century and a half earlier, Joseph Smith Jr., and some of his disciples built the very first Mormon house of worship. Invariably, news stories referred to the execution of the Avery family as "the Mormon cult killings."

Here's the back story, distilled down to its essential chapters and themes.

Jeffrey Lundgren, a disgruntled former member of the Reorganized Church of Jesus Christ of Latter Day Saints (RLDS), proclaimed that God had anointed him "the last seer," the prophet who would prepare the way for Christ's return to earth and help usher in the new Zion.

In 1984, Lundgren and his first wife, Alice, left their home state of Missouri and moved to Kirtland. They did so because Jeffrey had come to believe that the Kirtland temple was a literal reflection of the mind of God. Following their relocation, Lundgren attracted a group of disciples who shared his contempt for the liberalization of the RLDS and reveled in the special status conferred upon them by Jeffrey's vivid and explicit "revelations" about them as God's chosen people.

In 1987, Dennis Avery, Cheryl Avery, and their three daughters left their Missouri home and moved to Ohio in order to become part of Lundgren's group. Although pleased to accept money from the Averys, Lundgren didn't exactly extend the family a warm welcome. In fact, it wasn't long before he began taking steps calculated to isolate them from the rest of his followers.

He viewed Dennis as weak and overly headstrong, he

thought Cheryl was far too needy, and he complained that the three girls were all bothersome in their way. Despite Jeffrey's barely concealed disdain for the Avery family, Dennis and Cheryl clung to the belief that by joining the Lundgren collective, they were acting in furtherance of a divinely inspired plan for ushering in the End Times.

In the two years that followed their relocation to Ohio, the Avery family's fortunes went from bad to worse. It didn't help that by the summer of 1988, Lundgren was desperate for some new means of asserting his authority and consolidating his power.

Earlier that year, he'd involved his followers in an audacious plan to execute a paramilitary-type takeover of the Temple in Kirtland—complete with the mass slaughter of neighbors and the ritual slayings of the local RLDS stake president and his family—but the plan ended up being thwarted at the eleventh hour when tipsters alerted the authorities to what was about to take place. When Lundgren realized he was under surveillance, he got spooked and called off the raid.

The failure of the takeover plot undermined Lundgren's standing among his followers, at least in the short term. Ultimately, it set the stage for his decision to execute members of the Avery family. He taught his followers that he'd been designated to serve as God's "destroyer," an agent of vengeance whose role was to banish the "wicked" from their ranks so that those who remained could achieve the state of purity that would qualify them to greet the returning Christ when the world as they knew it came to an end.

All the members of Lundgren's group knew that he had no use for the Averys. But now, he'd begun preaching that members of the Avery family were "ripened in iniquity." As Lundgren saw it, God's plan called for their liquidation. By the fall of 1988, Dennis, Cheryl, Trina, Becky, and Karen had less than a year left to live.

The following April, Lundgren killed all five of them. One by one, starting with Dennis, the Averys were tricked into leaving the Lundgren's rented farmhouse and going to the barn outside, where Jeffrey and several of his followers were waiting for them. Almost as soon as they entered the barn, one or two of Jeffrey's accomplices pounced on them, employed duct tape to bind their hands and feet, and tossed them into a pre-dug burial pit. Then, Jeffrey shot them using a .45 pistol.

How were the Avery children lured to their deaths? Trina, the oldest of the three, was told that her mother—who by then was already dead and in the pit—"needed her" out in the barn. Becky, the middle child, perked up at the cheerful-sounding voice of Ron Luff, Jeffrey's second-in-command, when Luff asked her and her younger sister Karen, "Who wants to see the horses out in the barn?" Delighted to be chosen first, Becky eagerly accompanied Luff on the short walk. "What's going on?" she asked when they entered the barn. The adults there assured her they were all just "playing a game." Six-year-old Karen, who'd been told she needed to wait her turn, accepted when Luff offered to give her a piggyback ride so that she, too, could go out to the barn and see the horses.

And Kathy? What role did she play in all this?

In May 1977, after the demise of a short, unhappy first marriage, Kathy married Keith Johnson, an old pal of Jeffrey's from the early 1970s, when the two would hang out together at the RLDS student center at Central Missouri State University in Warrensburg, Missouri. Between 1979 and 1986, Kathy gave birth to four children, all boys.

By all available accounts, she was a force to be reckoned with: smart, athletic, hardworking, a skilled equestrian, a devout Mormon, a licensed insurance agent, the manager of a sizeable farm, and a committed home educator.

In the years following their college-era friendship, Jeffrey and Keith, Kathy's husband, remained in touch. After the Lundgren family's move to Kirtland, in 1984, Jeffrey told Keith of a vision in which Joseph Smith Jr., had appeared and anointed him as his successor. More visions followed, most of them accompanied by divine "revelations" about Jeffrey's exalted status in the eyes of God. Keith wanted to seize the opportunity to be part of something special.

Finally, in March 1989, just one month before the Avery family murders, Keith, Kathy, and their four children moved to Kirtland and joined Jeffrey's group.

The day after the murders, the group left Ohio and set out for the "wilderness" of West Virginia. Mostly, they lived in tents. Several months into their exodus, Lundgren told Kathy she was his "missing rib," sent by God to be his second wife. At first, Kathy wasn't sure what to think. Before long, however, she became convinced that Jeffrey was channeling God's truth when he told her, "You are flesh of my flesh." According to Jeffrey's first wife, Alice, he informed her that Kathy's vagina had appeared to him in a dream. Soon, he told everyone in the group, including his old friend Keith, that Kathy was pregnant with his child.

Finally, after months of increasing disillusionment with Lundgren and his teachings, Keith Johnson went to the authorities and told them that eight months prior, Jeffrey had murdered the five members of the Avery family and buried their bodies in the barn outside the farmhouse he and Alice had been renting at the time. Days later, on January 4, 1990, police dug up the bodies of Dennis, Cheryl, Trina, Becky, and Karen Avery.

On January 7, police arrested Jeffrey on the other side of the country, in San Diego. They arrested Kathy three days later, also in San Diego County. By the time of these arrests, the Lundgren group had all but fallen apart.

Neither Keith nor Kathy Johnson was physically present when the Avery family murders took place. However, Keith admitted to authorities that he'd helped dig the grave where police discovered the bodies of the five victims.

A grand jury indicted Kathy on five counts of complicity to commit aggravated murder. Prosecutors felt certain she had known in advance of Jeffrey's plan to kill the Avery family, including the three children. Eventually, however, she was allowed to plead guilty to a single count of obstructing justice. At her sentencing hearing, she declared herself guilty of one thing and one thing only: "loving Jeffrey Lundgren." She served one year in prison, then relocated to Missouri.

The same jury that found Jeffrey guilty of five counts of kidnapping and five counts of aggravated murder recommended that he be sentenced to death. However, before the jury members began their sentencing-related deliberations, Lundgren delivered an unsworn statement that went on for *five hours.*

As its name implies, an unsworn statement is not given under oath and is not subject to cross-examination. It is, in short, an opportunity for convicted persons to enter their thoughts and feelings into the official court record. It's also their final opportunity to try and persuade members of the jury to view them as salvageable human beings.

In my experience, most defense attorneys who handle death penalty cases discourage their client from making an unsworn statement—unless, that is, they're firmly convinced that their client is capable of offering a sincere expression of remorse.

Jeffrey Lundgren had no intention of taking direction from his attorneys or anyone else. And, he had no interest in expressing remorse because he felt none. He did, however, seem to recognize that members of the jury would probably want to know the basis for his belief that the three Avery children needed to die along with their parents. Several hours into his meandering and often abstruse monologue, he decided it was time to address the elephant in the room.

"Children, a touchy subject," he began. He referenced the prophet Elisha and explained that some children once mocked Elisha because he was bald. How did Elisha respond? Jeffrey: "[He] called a bear out of the woods, as strange as that sounds, and stood there and watched the bear kill all 42 children."

Lundgren then cited a story that he said came from the Book of Joshua. A greedy man surreptitiously took some gold and hid it in his tent. His disobedience and selfishness "brought a plague on the House of Israel." Eventually, the gold-hoarder came forward and confessed his wrongdoing. As punishment, other members of the community "took [him] and his family, wife, children, girls and boys, put them in a pit and … killed them."

As Lundgren saw it, these stories provided a kind of Biblical template for his decision to end the lives of the Avery children. He argued that the children needed to be "hewn" from his group of followers, just like their parents.

The jury decided that Lundgren himself needed to be hewn from the human community: sentenced to death.

Six years later: Lundgren's appellate attorney has asked me to perform an evaluation to help determine whether Lundgren's trial-level attorneys may have erred in deciding not to mount an insanity defense.

(Although discussion of that complicated issue is far beyond the scope of this case-related snapshot, for the record I submitted an affidavit in which I made the case that even though Lundgren was, indisputably, a narcissist and epic manipulator, he was also delusional, thoroughly "convinced … he was acting in accordance with God's will" at the time of the Avery family murders. I offered the opinion that consistent with Ohio law, he should have been viewed as a viable candidate for a defense of Not Guilty by Reason of Insanity.)

In nearly all capital case consultations—whether they're being done at the time of trial or at some point during the appeals process—the psychological evaluation includes collateral interviews, that is, interviews with third parties who possess relevant background information (or at least might).

That's why I've arranged to meet Kathy today. Accompanied by her six-year-old daughter, she's made the trip to Ohio so that she can visit her husband in prison. Kathy and her previous husband, who was offered immunity in exchange for his willingness to assist the authorities with their investigation and prosecution of the Lundgren group, divorced some years back. Their four sons reside with their father. Kathy's loyalty to Jeffrey has cost her dearly.

It was Jeffrey himself who told me of Kathy's plans to be in Ohio this week. He and I had our first meeting just a few days ago. As the meeting was drawing to a close, he gave me Kathy's phone number and urged me to reach out to her so that the two of us could make plans to get together. I called Kathy at her home in Missouri. We agreed to meet at a Flying J travel plaza, located between Mansfield and Columbus.

Right now, I'm in the parking lot, awaiting her arrival. She should be here any minute. From my vantage point near the center of the lot, I'm able to monitor cars as they come and go. Kathy told me what kind of car she'd be driving. I figure I'll have no trouble spotting her when she arrives.

Within minutes, I see a car that I'm certain is hers. I lower my window and identify myself with a slight wave of my hand. Kathy pulls her car alongside mine so that we can converse through our driver's side windows. For the first time, I see a small child on the seat behind her.

"Dr. Smalldon?" says Kathy through her open window.

She's an attractive woman with an appealing smile. Her voice is pleasant, her tone warm and welcoming. I can see that she's casually but fashionably dressed. For a fleeting moment, I pause to consider how she might have come across back in the days when she was selling insurance.

"Hi Kathy," I say. "But please, call me Jeff."

"Okay, Jeff," she says. "This is Rasia. Rasia, can you say hi to Dr. Smalldon?"

The child in the back seat smiles wanly, murmurs "Hi," and then averts her gaze. She's a cute kid.

"Good to meet you, Rasia," I say. "I've been looking forward to seeing you and your mom today."

When we spoke by telephone, Kathy and I agreed that we would have our informal meeting at the McDonald's just across the way, on the other side of I-71. I checked out the location when I drove through here yesterday, on my way to see another inmate at the prison in Mansfield. I was pleased to see that the McDonald's had a large outdoor play area. I figured Rasia would be able to entertain herself while her mom and I were talking. If Kathy and I sat outside, at one of the tables there, we'd have an unobstructed view of her while she was playing.

I tell Kathy, "I'll see you over at the McDonald's."

"Sounds good," she says. "See you there."

As she turns her car around and points it in the direction of the travel plaza exit, I'm afforded my first glimpse of her back bumper. Affixed to it is a sticker bearing the familiar "pro-life" slogan: "It's not a choice. It's a child."

I think, *Wait. This car, with that bumper sticker, is being driven by the wife of a man who confessed to shooting three children and their parents?*

I know there's no way I can pass up the opportunity to ask Kathy about this. *Don't you think it's a little ironic for you to have a "pro-life" bumper sticker on your car when you're married to a man who confessed to killing three children?* Of course I won't raise the issue until I've been able to develop at least a modicum of rapport with Kathy—and besides, I have a number of background questions I want to ask her first: about the composition of the Lundgren group, about her relationship with Jeffrey, about her own upbringing, and so forth.

Inside the McDonald's, we order our snacks, then take them outside to a table that's located alongside the play area. Before we even have a chance to settle in, Rasia's off like a shot. Kathy looks amused as she watches her scramble to the top of the slide.

"Especially with Rasia here, I won't keep you long," I say. "Mainly, I just wanted a chance to introduce myself since I'll be working with Jeff. Maybe we can talk again at some point down the road, when there's more time. By the way, how did you find Jeff today?"

"He's fine," says Kathy. "About as good as can be expected, I guess. He's always happy when he gets to see Rasia. The two of them have a wonderful relationship."

"Am I remembering this correctly? You and your former husband and your children arrived in Kirtland only about a month before all of you left for West Virginia."

"Yeah, that sounds about right," says Kathy. "And maybe you know this, maybe you don't, but before the Averys died, I only met the family one time."

I'm a little surprised by how casually she introduces the subject of the murders that sent her husband to death row. She sounds matter of fact, neither defensive nor apologetic. It's as if she regards the execution of a family of five as no big deal, something that had to happen and did, end of story.

She switches gears and begins talking about the Temple that meant so much to Jeffrey.

"All of us were very focused on the words of Ezekial 43," she explains. "They tell all about the restoration of God's temple. The chapter includes a lot of detail about exactly what the restored temple would look like. In Kirtland, Jeffrey spent a lot of his time studying. He was focused on the pattern of the House there, all its unique architectural characteristics."

She tells me of the strong RLDS emphasis on "God living with us," then adds that she and Jeff have never regarded the *Bible* and the *Doctrine and Covenants* as ancient documents that can be put on the shelf and left to gather dust. She says that for them, and for all the people who looked up to Jeff as a prophet, scriptural teachings informed nearly every aspect of daily life.

"You're looking, you're always looking," she says. She and the other group members were ever alert to signs of the coming "last days." They wanted to be ready when Christ appeared to establish the new Zion.

Of their seven months in the "wilderness," she says, "We wandered, just like in the *Book of Mormon*."

I ask her what things were like during that period, when all the members of their group shared the knowledge that the bodies of the Avery family members were back in Ohio.

"Well, we'd burned our bridges," she says. She and the other group members knew they were now existing on "a different plane." There was no returning to the way things used to be.

She's eager to have me realize that the media's portrayal of Jeffrey as a coercive control freak is a gross distortion of reality. "We were a cohesive group," she says. "Jeff was away a lot. It's not like he was making people do things they didn't want to do."

According to her, when the group finally splintered, and when former members began angling for plea agreements with the authorities, issues of self-interest often trumped the truth. "A lot of people told a lot of lies," she says, "mainly, excuse my language, to save their own butts."

"Jeff's worry all along was what was going to happen to me," she explains. She chuckles softly and concedes that there were times when her gullibility made it difficult for her to see things—and other people—as clearly as Jeffrey did. "I see the good in everybody," she says.

She answers a few questions about her own background and Jeffrey's. I'm a little surprised when she volunteers that she still hasn't met her in-laws.

We've been at it for about 45 minutes when I finally decide that it's time to ask the question I've been longing to ask. I figure that soon, Rasia will arrive at our table to announce that she's done playing.

"Kathy, I don't want to offend you, but there's one other thing I need to ask you about."

"Oh, you're fine!" she says. "Go ahead, you won't offend me."

"Well, I couldn't help noticing that your car has a bumper sticker that says, 'It's not a choice. It's a child.' A lot of people would see that and think it's sort of ironic that the wife of a man who killed three children would choose to display that particular slogan on her car."

"No, no, I totally get it," she says with a light laugh. "I know what you're saying. But to me, there isn't any contradiction. When Jeffrey took the lives of the Avery children, he was acting in accordance with God's will. When he gave his statement in court, he explained the Biblical basis for it. But he and I are adamantly opposed to the killing of innocent children. Abortion is wrong, and we feel very strongly about that."

"But don't you think most people would say that the Avery children were innocent, too?"

"Maybe. A lot of them probably would. But those people haven't studied the scriptures the way Jeffrey has."

"Okay. Well, thanks for letting me ask the question, and for not getting offended."

"Oh, it's no problem!" she says. "I've gotten used to questions like that."

Right on cue, Rasia comes over to our table and grabs a few French fries.

"Did you have fun on the playground" Kathy asks her.

"Yeah, but can we go now?"

"Sure, we were just wrapping up. Works out perfectly."

Kathy and I toss our garbage and leftovers into a nearby trash can. Then the three of us head outside to where our cars are parked. I watch as Kathy helps Rasia get settled in the back seat of her car.

I tell Rasia that I'm happy I got to meet her and her mom. Kathy and I shake hands and agree it was good talking. She gets into her car, and I get into mine.

"Thanks again, Kathy. I appreciate your time," I say through my open driver's side window. "Safe travels, and tell Jeff I'll see him again soon."

I steer my car behind hers as she heads for the parking lot exit.

I see it again, the bumper sticker: "It's not a choice. It's a child."

The words haunt me on my drive back to Columbus.

Now, more than 25 years later, they still haunt me.

• • •

If there were a contest called Build-a-Bogeyman, chances are that the contestant whose entry most closely resembled the man I'm about to meet would be the odds-on favorite to win.

It's May 15, 1997. The man's name is Alva Campbell. Most everyone in Columbus knows who he is.

A few minutes ago, with the noon hour looming, I arrived at Jackson Pike, the south side annex of the main Franklin County Jail, which is located downtown.

My attire is a little more formal today than it is on most days when my agenda calls for a visit to the jail. I've come directly from court, where I spent the morning testifying at a child custody hearing. I'm still wearing my navy-blue blazer, accompanied by a white dress shirt, charcoal grey slacks, and a bright red tie with navy blue diagonal stripes. I think of it as my court uniform: conservative, professional, nothing flashy.

I'm familiar with Jackson Pike. Almost without exception, the check-in here goes off without a hitch. The deputies all know me, which helps to move things along. I provide my name and identification at the front window, produce a copy of the court order that authorizes my access to the inmate I've come to see, and then prepare to be buzzed through the two security doors that lead to the row of professional meeting rooms.

But today isn't just any day. As soon as I say the name Alva Campbell, the deputy at the sign-in desk looks up from the visitors' log, draws a deep breath, and places her pen down on the counter.

"I'll need to call the major," she says. "Have a seat, and he'll be with you shortly."

About ten minutes later, the major, a man I've seen but don't know personally, strides across the lobby to where I'm seated.

Mornin', Doc. You're here to see Campbell?" he says.

"Yes, sir."

He asks to see my court order. When I produce it, he reads it over line by line, then hands it back to me.

"Campbell's up on the second floor," he says, "in one of our high-security cells. We can't bring him down to this level. You ever been upstairs before?"

"No, sir."

"We're not taking any chances with Campbell."

"I understand."

"You're aware that he already served time for a prior murder conviction?"

"Yes."

"And are you aware that in a different case, he shot and wounded a state trooper?"

"Yes, sir. I am."

"And that he was in custody, awaiting trial on a bunch of armed robbery charges, when he caught *this* case?"

"Yes."

"I'm not sure how much you've been told, but he managed to convince everyone here at the jail that he was paralyzed from the waist down because of a gunshot wound he sustained at the time of his arrest. On the day of his arraignment, he jumped up out of his wheelchair, attacked one of my female deputies, stole her gun, and then killed the young man whose car he hijacked outside the courthouse."

"I read the newspaper, Major."

"Anyway, there's a picnic table right outside his cell. You can interview him there. A deputy will have to be in the room with you at all times, but I'll tell him to sit far enough back so that he won't be able to hear what you and Campbell are saying."

"That'll work," I say. "Just so long as he won't be able to hear us. Oh, and one other thing, Major. Can I please have Campbell uncuffed? He'll need to have use of his hands for some of the testing I want to do."

"Will he need *both* hands?"

"Well, some of the tests involve speed and dexterity—so yeah, he'll need both."

The major blows a long, audible stream of air out through his puckered lips.

"I'll talk to the deputy who's on duty up there," he says. Before we leave the lobby, he searches my leather shoulder bag. I've made sure it contains nothing except my notepad, my case file (with the court order), some neon pink Post-it notes, and several disposable pencils. Apparently, it passes muster. The major hands it back to me without saying another word.

Once we're up on the second floor, we arrive at a long, narrow room. In the center of the room is a short row of cells, maybe four or five altogether. A deputy seated just inside the doorway stands up to greet us.

"This is Dr. Smalldon," says the major. "He's here to see Campbell. They can use the picnic table, but you'll need to stay in the room with them at all times. Sit far enough back so that you can't hear what they're talking about."

"No problem," says the deputy.

"And, the doc says he'll need to have Campbell uncuffed for some of his testing."

"Wow," says the deputy, pursing his lips and looking toward the row of cells in the center of the room.

"Yeah," says the major. "So, keep a close eye." Then he leaves.

The deputy motions for me to sit down on the side of the picnic table closest to where we're standing. Then he unlocks the door leading to a cell that's located just to my left. After opening the door and informing Campbell of my presence ("A shrink's here to see you"), he begins the pat-down.

First, the deputy instructs Campbell to open his mouth. *Wider.* Next, he orders him to face the wall and lean forward, with his arms stretched high above his head and his palms resting against the wall's surface. He uses the fingers of his hands to search for contraband in the areas around Campbell's chest, back, and underarms. Satisfied that there's no contraband there, he then runs his hands briskly up and down Campbell's pant legs and feels the area around his groin. Finally, he inspects the bottoms of Campbell's bare feet, one at a time. He has to bend down for this part of the process because Campbell's wearing leg irons that make it impossible for him to lift his feet more than a few inches off the ground.

When the deputy has completed his pat-down, he instructs Campbell to extend his arms out in front of him, hands close together. Then he takes the pair of handcuffs attached to his wide utility belt and clicks them tightly around Campbell's wrists.

Campbell shuffles out of his cell, eyes me warily, and pauses alongside the picnic table. His skin has a sallow look, he's hollow-cheeked, and his dark hair is slicked straight back, tight against his head. We shake hands and I introduce myself as the psychologist his attorneys have hired to assist them. He says he's been expecting me. I invite him to take a seat on the other side of the table.

"Let me know when you get to the testing part, Doc," says the deputy. "I'm going to leave his cuffs on for the time being."

"Okay, I'll let you know."

The deputy walks away and sits down in a chair that's located about 15 yards from where Campbell and I are seated. I place my shoulder bag on the ground next to the picnic table, remove from it a pencil and a pad of lined yellow paper, and begin the interview process by asking Campbell to state his complete name and date of birth.

Just as I'm about to take up the important topics of privilege and confidentiality, I hear the deputy's voice, coming from behind me.

"Hey, Doc," he says, speaking loudly enough so I'm able to hear him. "Can I have a quick word with you?"

Taking my pencil and notepad with me, I get up from the picnic table and head in his direction. He gestures with his open palm, urging me to move slightly to the side so I'm not obstructing his view of Campbell.

"I've seen you here plenty of times before," he whispers, "so I know you've been around the block. Don't take this the wrong way, but can I tell you something?"

"Sure, what's that?"

Still whispering, and still with his eyes trained on Campbell, he says, his lips hardly moving, "If Campbell thought he could use your necktie to strangle you and somehow escape from here, he'd do it in a hot second. He wouldn't miss a beat. So just be careful—and don't let your guard down."

"Okay, I appreciate your concern."

He's right, and I know it.

Back at the picnic table, Campbell looks across at me with a thin, bemused smile. I'm guessing he was able to intuit the nature of the private confab, even without knowing the particulars.

The next ten minutes drag on like 30. I can't stop thinking about my tie. While Campbell and I are talking, mostly about matters pertaining to confidentiality and privilege, I maintain steady eye contact with him, taking an occasional note but never looking downward for more than a second or two at a time.

I have a plan in mind. I'm hoping I can execute it as a kind of stealth operation. I hunch my shoulders just a little, then crane my neck to the left and to the right. Still holding Campbell's gaze, I reach up with my right hand, the one holding the pencil, and tug gently at the knot of my tie.

When I'm convinced I've managed the set-up about as well as I can, I use the fingers of my other hand to pull apart the knot, slowly draw the tie out from under my collar, and unbutton the top button of my shirt. I drape the tie across my lap and fold it twice before placing it inside my shoulder bag, which is still on the floor, resting against a leg of my chair.

"Better," I say.

Then Campbell looks across at me with that same thin smile. "Ya gonna be alright now?"

Afterword

This isn't quite the book I originally had in mind writing. When I began work on it, I planned to view my life experiences through a wider-range lens than the one I ended up using.

I thought I'd recount stories not just about my many encounters with killers but about my adventures among snake-handling fundamentalists in the southwestern corner of West Virginia; about the time I spent on Inishere, the smallest of the Aran islands, back in 1978; about my pilgrimage to meet the English polymath Colin Wilson, whose famous first book, *The Outsider* (1956), published when Wilson was just 24, has never gone out of print; about my enduring fascination with the complicated dynamics characterizing the relationship between sideshow freaks and the people who flocked to see them; about my long friendship with Jack Kerouac's muse, Beat Generation legend Carolyn Cassady; about a famous kidnapping case that touched my family and altered the way I thought about my dad and his work as an FBI agent; and about a handful of mind-bending celebrity encounters that changed my approach to drawing the outermost boundaries of the world I dared to consider my own.

Back in those days when I was first compiling the stories I intended to use in my book, I toyed with titles like *Boundary Rider, Odd Man In, We'll Meet on Edges,* and *Plucking the Wild Goat's Beard.*

I liked that last title best of all. It's a slight paraphrase of a

Virginia Woolf quote: "If we didn't live venturously, plucking the wild goat by the beard, and trembling over precipices, we should never be depressed, I've no doubt; and already should be faded, fatalistic, and aged." In other words, even if there's a price to be paid for choices that involve uncertainty, a degree of risk, and even a dollop of danger, it's probably a price that's worth paying.

From an early age, I decided that I wanted to live venturously, even if I didn't have a clear strategy for accomplishing that goal. Perhaps it should come as no surprise that I ended up a forensic psychologist. Be that as it may, it's an outcome I never would have predicted when I was 26 years old, just back from a year abroad, clueless about what to do with the rest of my life, and wide open to suggestions about what path I should take.

Despite all the twists and turns and false starts that marked the first 30 years of my life, I stayed true to my early determination to live venturously. As a result, I managed to accumulate as many uncommon experiences as just about anyone I know. So many, in fact, that I realized early on that there was no way I could write about all of them in a single book. For that reason, I chose to narrow my focus so that the stories compiled here would all center around my five decades of encounters with killers.

As I see them, the stories in my book raise provocative questions about such matters as identity, the parameters of what we mean when we use the word "normal," the kinds of cues we use when we make decisions about when it's safe to let down our guard around other people, the categories we use when we try to divide up the human pie, and the complicated transactions that occur at the always-being-renegotiated boundary that separates "them"—all those quirky people, all those strange agents—from the rest of us.

These murder stories are salutary in the sense that they can arouse us from our everyday torpor and remind us of the importance of paying attention—close attention—to all the people around us, including those with whom we share our neighborhoods and even our homes.

My daughter Lacey is 31 now. I'm pretty sure she knows I'm not a serial killer. But if the tiniest sliver of a doubt remains, perhaps that's as it should be.

Recall the words of Hilton Als: "[The] bogeyman may be your father, and hope is a flimsy defense against dread."

And the words of Ted Bundy: "Take care."

Acknowledgements

Now, finally, I get the chance to say thank you to the friends, family members, role models, and technical support people who provided the inspiration, encouragement, and know-how that made it possible for this first-time author to convert his long-time dream into the reality of a published book.

It's been my good fortune to know many brilliant writers. They inspired me by their example; they helped me to believe in my own potential; and they taught me to see resilience as perhaps the most important tool in a writer's toolbox.

Some of the writers I've known and looked to for inspiration are no longer with us. Still, I want to use this opportunity to acknowledge their kindness and generosity of spirit.

I'm thinking especially of Beat Generation icon Carolyn Cassady, who encouraged me to believe I had the talent to turn some of my vivid and uncommon life experiences into a book that others would want to read, and who, back in 1990, mailed me a first English edition of her landmark memoir, *Off the Road: Twenty Years with Cassady, Kerouac, and Ginsberg*, inscribed with these uplifting words, "With so much gratitude for your warm friendship and encouragement in the intellectual arena"; the maverick English polymath, Colin Wilson, who wrote me in 1991 to express his appreciation for the essay I'd written about him and his work, called *Human Nature Stained: Colin Wilson and the Existential Study of Modern Murder*, who later hosted my wife and me at his home in Cornwall, and who urged me to write about the experiences I'd had with some of the most notorious murderers of our time; and Elisabeth Young-Bruehl, acclaimed biographer of Hannah Arendt and Anna Freud, who took me under her wing during my year-long pre-doctoral internship in Connecticut and told me, repeatedly, that I, too, could write a book—if I committed myself to the process and refused to be deterred, even in the face of the inevitable bouts of disappointment.

Fortunately, many of my other writer friends and acquaintances are still very much alive. They include: Joyce Carol Oates, Gerald Clark, Donald Ray Pollock, James B. Stewart, Stephen Michaud, Karen Kukil, Gail Crowther, James Neff, Geoff Dutton, Andrew Welsh-Huggins, John Futty, Lauren Pond, Joe Oestreich, Carolyn Buffington, Linda Kass, Alec Wightman, Dan McAdams, Michael Glenday, Steven Epstein, and Robin Yocum. I'm indebted to all of you for your encouragement and support—and for helping make it possible for me to inhabit the role of "writer" in my mind.

I need to single out two of these friends whose kindness and generosity have been, as they say, next level.

I first met Don Pollock not long after he'd published *Knockemstiff*, the celebrated collection of short stories that launched his career, and that shares its name with the holler where Don grew up. During the 15 years that have elapsed since our initial meeting, Don has served for me as an enormously important sounding board and mentor. "Remember," he's told me more times than I can count, "just keep going. And above all else, *be patient*." Don, I'm deeply grateful to you for your friendship and wise counsel.

I haven't known Andrew Welsh-Huggins as long as I've known Don Pollock. But in the years since our first meeting, Andrew's been an extraordinarily helpful and unselfish guide as I've struggled to make my way in the world of publishing, which to me has often felt like a foreign territory. When, over lunch one day, I described to him a particularly difficult experience, one that had left me feeling deflated and discouraged, he listened with evident empathy, then said, when I finally stopped talking, "You should have called me. If anything like that ever happens again, call me!" That's Andrew. Thank you, my friend.

In all likelihood, I would have had a much different kind of career had it not been for the faith of two old friends, Jane Core Thomas and Linda Pudvan Richter. Jane and Linda were mitigation specialists at the Office of the Ohio Public Defender when I opened my practice in 1990 and, through indirect means, made it known to them that I was interested in performing death penalty case consultations. They recommended me to their colleagues, and they saw to it that I was afforded just the kinds of opportunities I was looking for. I'm fortunate to still count them among my friends, all these years later. Thank you, Jane and Linda.

This book wouldn't exist without Alina Hart—and I mean that literally. Not only did Alina assist me with many of the more technical aspects of manuscript preparation and formatting, she acted as an informal grammar coach, she shared many of the lessons she's learned from her years of work in the publishing industry—and, perhaps most important of all, she worked hard to revive my spirits at times when she could sense I was struggling. Thank you, Alina. You're a gem, and I was lucky to find you when I did.

Alina's son, Walden, assisted too, by lending his technical expertise to help me solve some knotty computer-related problems that arose along the way. I also owe thanks to Pat Tuure and Hector Morales of Out There Web Designs; Paige Weber and Cath Quiambao of Shine Thru Branding and Marketing; Hailey Gonya of Hailey Lauren Photography; freelance photographer Mason Miller; and graphic designer par excellence, Erika Hinkle.

I want to say thank you to my agent, Linda Langton, of Langton's International Agency, and to Linda's friendly and able assistant, Lindsay; as well as to Kerry McQuisten at Black Lyon Publishing—who offered me the opportunity to reach an audience of readers prepared to gamble on a true crime book that's different from most other books in the true crime genre.

I owe a debt of gratitude to the late William Whalen, who bent over backward in order to accommodate my request for an interview with his client, serial killer Donald Harvey, then serving multiple life sentences at the Warren Correctional Institution in Lebanon, Ohio.

There are many family members, close friends, and long-time acquaintances who supported me as I traveled the winding and uneven road that finally led to the publication of *That Beast Was Not Me*. My older sister, June, has always been there for me, and always had my back. My niece, Beth, who has both an MFA in Creative Writing and a PhD in comparative literature, has been a valuable source of information and practical advice whenever I've asked her to act as a sounding board. My incomparable father-in-law, Bob LaGrow, who I love dearly, has been my tireless cheerleader, ever since he learned that I'd begun dating his daughter—more than 40 years ago.

Others who've helped and lent me their support along the way include my old high school buddy Tom Zuch, Valerie Grotheer, Bill Graston, John Spear (my freshman year college roommate—a mere 53 years ago), Dick Davis, Dr. David Tennenbaum, Brenda Hennick, Jim Crates, Mike Miller, Harry Trombitas, Steve Nolder, and Larry Ankrom, the retired FBI Supervisory Special Agent who authored the profile of the unknown suspect who turned out to be one of Ohio's most infamous killers, serial sniper Thomas Lee Dillon.

A well-deserved shout-out to my buddy Rick Topper, a retired attorney, tireless activist, and estimable writer. He never turned me away when I sought him out for a few beers, or when I needed him to help lift my spirits with his zest for life and trademark optimism. Thank you, Topper.

Sadly, neither of my parents lived long enough to see this book—which had a long gestational period—make its way into print. My dad, Jack Smalldon, was an old-school G-man who never withdrew his support for me, even when he was forced to watch me go wandering down certain paths in life that he himself would never have dreamed of wandering down.

He stuck with me even during that epically weird summer of 1975, when the likes of Charles Manson, Squeaky Fromme, and Sandy Good were sending me letters addressed to the house he shared with my mom in North Tonawanda, New York.

Ruth Smalldon, my mother, wasn't always quite able to fathom my interests and inclinations—but she remained one of my staunchest and most faithful supporters, right up until the time of her death, in 2019. Thanks, Mom and Dad.

A huge thank you to my adult children, Lucas and Lacey, and to their respective spouses, Anoosha and Abed. Their love and support helped to sustain me through the long process that culminated in the publication of this book. Lucas and Lacey are both excellent writers themselves. Whenever I approached them for feedback, advice, or even just a dose of encouragement, they always obliged. You guys are the best. I love you beyond words.

And as for my grandchildren: Maya, Kareem, Yasiin, and Harrison. You inspire me each and every day—when I'm with you and when I'm not. You can't yet appreciate a parent's profound love for his children's children—but someday you will.

It almost feels like I have another very special family—the Leahy family—across the ocean in Ireland. Maura, you were far and away my closest friend during the year I spent studying at Trinity College (1978-79). Is it possible that 45 years have elapsed since then? What an enormous thrill it was for me to get to spend time with you, Colm, Kate, Anne, Fergus, and so many of your friends and relatives during my trip to Ireland last September. The decades seemed to melt away. Thanks to all of you for your love, encouragement, and support.

And finally: How can I adequately express my thanks and appreciation to my beautiful, kind, generous, and long-suffering wife, Betsy, who's been by my side and often out in front of me for more than 40 years now? I can't.

But I can at least conjure the indelible memory of that evening in 1984 when you invited me to dance with you at the Valley Dale Ballroom and my entire life, which had seemed monochrome, turned to Technicolor in an instant. I knew before the evening was over that I'd met the woman of my dreams. *From the bottom of my heart, thank you Betsy—for everything.*

Photo Gallery

Photo courtesy of Jeffrey L. Smalldon
The author's father, practicing his marksmanship at the FBI's training facility in Quantico, Virginia.

Photo courtesy of Jeffrey L. Smalldon
The author's father, Hoover-era G-man Jack R. Smalldon, in the mid-1950s.

Photo courtesy of Jeffrey L. Smalldon

The author's family and paternal grandmother posed with J. Edgar Hoover during Jeffrey's third grade year, when Jack Smalldon was assigned to FBI headquarters in Washington.

Photo courtesy of Jeffrey L. Smalldon

The view over the gate and up the driveway leading to 10050 Cielo Drive in the Hollywood Hills, where actress Sharon Tate and four others were murdered by members of the Manson Family on August 9, 1969.

Photo courtesy of Jeffrey L. Smalldon

The house on Waverly Drive in the Los Feliz section of Los Angeles where Leno and Rosemary LaBianca were murdered by members of the Manson Family on August 10, 1969.

Photo courtesy of Jeffrey L. Smalldon

In a fit of rage, Manson sent the author an airmail letter from San Quentin during the summer of 1975.

Photo courtesy of Jeffrey L. Smalldon

Manson sent the author this doctored photograph in 1975. The message? "I'm being forced to carry the weight of your entire world on my back."

When Manson started slashing on the page, there was no mistaking his rage.

Photo courtesy of Jeffrey L. Smalldon

The envelope that contained Lynette "Squeaky" Fromme's first letter to the author, sent during the early part of 1975. Note the floral accents.

Photo courtesy of Jeffrey L. Smalldon

Sandy Good sent the author this picture of herself — ostensibly "planting seeds for peace."

March 17, 1975

Hello

We received your letter yesterday, Sandra & I.

I can't quite muster up a commendation for Bugliosi & Sanders but I see that you are coming from no opinion & that is say I'm glad you wrote.

The companionship you speak of between us at the ranch was based on an understanding of truth and a thought to raise ourselves by loving

Photo courtesy of Jeffrey L. Smalldon

The first page of Squeaky Fromme's first letter to the author.

June 30,

Dear Jeff,

Good to hear from you and that your
moving for clean up - not just talking about
it :) Who is killing deer & what department
is justifying it. Call TV station & get info & send to
us. Fish & Game Dept might know

Jeff - in your meanest most vicious
voice — call up the responsible parties
most preferably at their homes & tell
them to "stop killing those animals
or Manson will put YOUR blood on
the wall. Try to speak to the wife or wives. If
they say Who? tell them MANSON
remember Sharon Tate? Tell the earth &
air & water killers to use all their
money to clean air etc — or Manson
will send for their heads. Tell

**Squeaky's roommate and best friend, fellow Manson Family member
Sandy Good, wrote the author a lengthy letter full of violent, rageful
rhetoric approximately two months before Squeaky attempted to assassinate President Gerald Ford.**

Photo courtesy of Jeffrey L. Smalldon
After Squeaky Fromme attempted to assassinate President Ford in September 1975, the FBI found a cache of the author's letters in the attic apartment Fromme shared with Sandy Good and one other woman.

Photo courtesy of Jeffrey L. Smalldon
Susan Atkins sent the author this photo of herself, taken in prison.

a direct promise! If you are really
for real in this – I've no reason to believe
you aren't – simply, sincerely ask Jesus
to reveal himself to you. To allow
you to see clearly, & ask Him to
come into your heart & be your personal
Savior & Lord. He said He would &
He doesn't lie. Romans 10:9-10 says
" If thou shalt ~~believe~~ confess with thy
mouth the Lord Jesus, and shall believe
in thine heart that God raised Him
from the dead, thou ~~shalt~~ be saved.
For with the heart man believeth
unto righteousness and with the mouth
confession is made unto Salvation."
    It's really that simple Jeff.
    Since your interested in where I've been
+ where I am now here's a small ☺
diagram of my life to date, just for fun!

Birth —SIN—3YRS—SIN—14YRS.—SIN-SODOM-GOMORA—PRISION—26½ YRS—Christ in me
                                                              FOREVER
    Now is daily walking with   FREE FROM SIN
Jesus, learning more about Him
by prayer & reading God's Word. Truly
in here I've much time to devote to
my relationship.
    Thank you for writing. I hope I've
helped you some! Thank you truly for
being a non-entity. I'll try an answer
any more questions you may have.
I'll pray for your revelation!

                    Truly in Christian
                    FAITH   HOPE
                         LOVE

                    Susan Atkins

In her first letter to the author, written in early-1976, notorious Manson Family member Susan "Sadie" Atkins included a timeline representing her life. The 14 years of "Sodom and Gomorrah" includes her time with Manson. In prison, she claimed to have traded her devotion to Manson for a devotion to Christ.

Photo courtesy of Jeffrey L. Smalldon

Ted Bundy's holiday greeting.

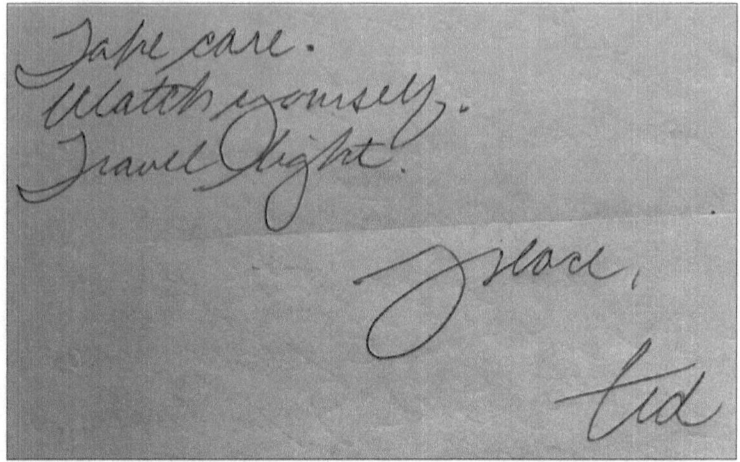

Photo courtesy of Jeffrey L. Smalldon
Ted Bundy's gamey, vaguely menacing sign-off, December 1985.

Photo courtesy of Jeffrey L. Smalldon
John Wayne Gacy, photographed with the author on death row at the Menard Correctional Facility in 1986.

Photo courtesy of Jeffrey L. Smalldon

Painting by John Wayne Gacy of the Seven Dwarfs from *Snow White*. Note the shovel in the bottom left corner. The crawlspace under Gacy's suburban home was crammed full of the corpses of Gacy's victims.

Photo courtesy of Jeffrey L. Smalldon

With the author in mind, Gacy painted this knock-off of Picasso's famous drawing of Don Quixote. He placed the author's initials on the shield, explaining, "I see you as someone in search of the truth."

Photo courtesy of Jeffrey L. Smalldon
Handpainted Christmas card that Gacy sent the author in 1988.

Photo courtesy of Jeffrey L. Smalldon
Gacy pencil drawing of the crucified Christ. Gacy strongly identified with the martyr theme.

Photo courtesy of Jeffrey L. Smalldon

Former site of Nissan's Pharmacy in Des Plaines, Illinois. It's where Gacy kidnapped teenager Rob Piest, his last victim, while Piest's mother moved back and forth between the pharmacy and the parking lot. Ironically, a combined daycare/preschool center now occupies the site.

Photo courtesy of Jeffrey L. Smalldon

This upscale house now occupies the site at 8213 W. Summerdale Ave., where Gacy lived and buried most of his victims in the 1970s.

Photo courtesy of Jeffrey L. Smalldon

In the rural community of Magnolia, Ohio, Thomas Lee Dillon lived in this house with his wife and young son during his killing years, 1989-1992.

Photo courtesy of Jeffrey L. Smalldon

Jerry Hessler's killing spree began at this house in Columbus. After forcing his way through the front door, he killed three people, including an infant, and injured a fourth.

Photo courtesy of Jeffrey L. Smalldon

Hessler gunned down the father of a woman he once dated in the doorway of this house located just north of Columbus.

Photo courtesy of Jeffrey L. Smalldon

Hessler's killing spree ended at this house located in Ashland, Ohio, located about a hundred miles north of Columbus. He was met at the back door by gunfire from the husband of a former love interest. The police arrested him minutes later.

Photo courtesy of Jeffrey L. Smalldon

The Mormon Temple in Kirtland, Ohio, designed by Joseph Smith and built by his early followers. For a time, Jeffrey Lundgren—who went on to execute a family of five, including three children—served as a Temple tour guide.

Photo courtesy of Jeffrey L. Smalldon

Outside these loading docks beneath the county courthouse in Columbus, Ohio, Alva Campbell, who was feigning "hysterical paralysis," attacked the deputy who was assigned to him and later murdered a young man whose vehicle he carjacked.

Public Domain Photos

Susan Atkins' mugshot from 1969 compared to her prison photo in 2001.

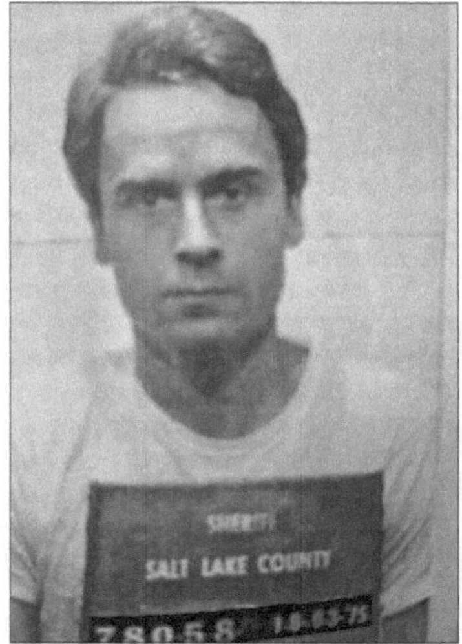
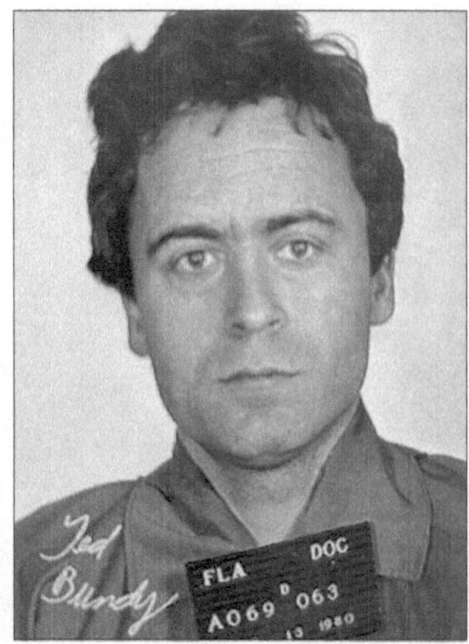

Public Domain Photos
Ted Bundy's 1975 and 1980 mugshots.

Public Domain Photo
Mugshot of Kathy Lundgren.

Public Domain Photo
Mugshot of Jeffrey Lundgren.

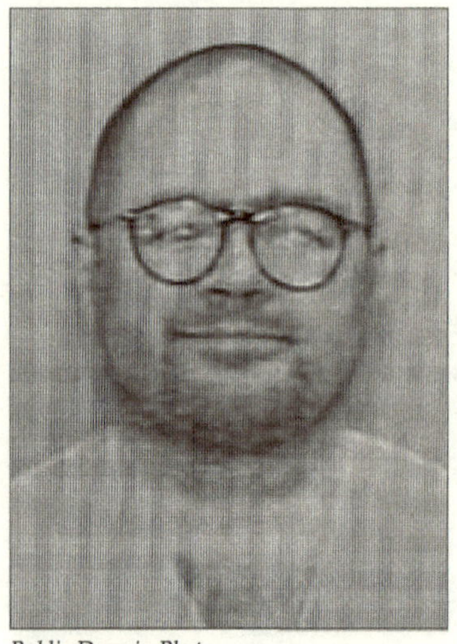

Public Domain Photo
Mugshot of spree killer Jerry Hessler.

Public Domain Photo
Mugshot of serial sniper-killer Thomas Lee Dillon.

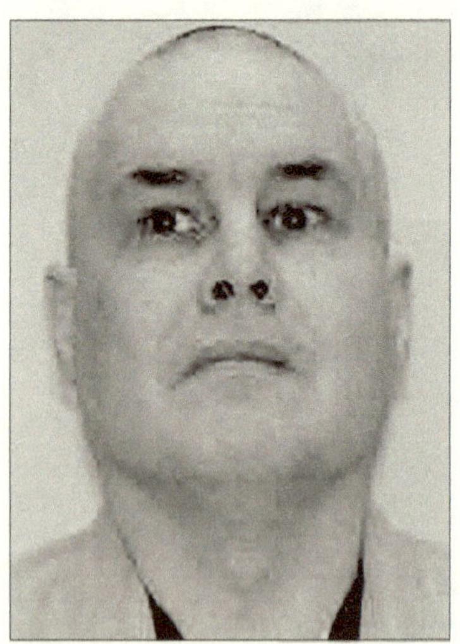

Public Domain Photo
Mugshot of Thomas Dillon.

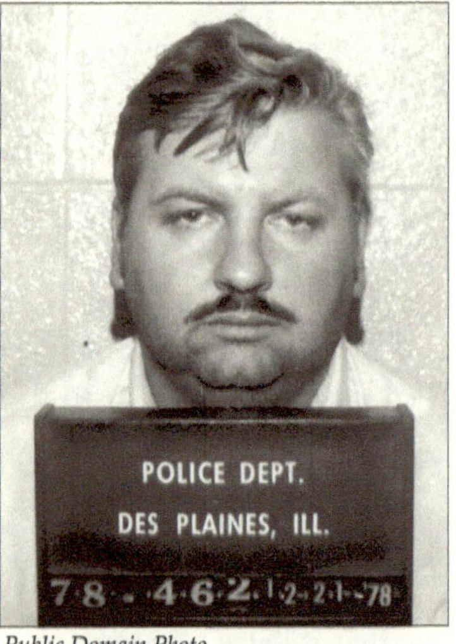

Public Domain Photo
Mugshot of John Wayne Gacy.

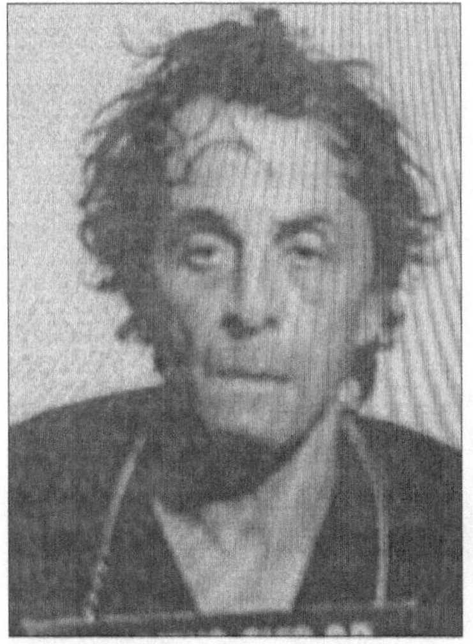

Public Domain Photo
Mugshot of Alva Campbell.

Public Domain Photo
Mugshot of Donald Harvey.

Public Domain Photos
Infamous mugshots and prison photos of Charles Manson.